Understanding the Income and Efficiency Gap in Latin America and the Caribbean

DIRECTIONS IN DEVELOPMENT
Countries and Regions

Understanding the Income and Efficiency Gap in Latin America and the Caribbean

Jorge Thompson Araujo, Ekaterina Vostroknutova, Konstantin M. Wacker, and Mateo Clavijo, Editors

WORLD BANK GROUP

Contents

Boxes

Figures

Tables

Acknowledgments

This book was written as part of a World Bank project coordinated by Jorge Thompson Araujo, Ekaterina Vostroknutova, Konstantin M. Wacker, and Mateo Clavijo (editors) under guidance from John Panzer (Director, GMFDR), Humberto Lopez (Country Director, LCC2C), Rodrigo A. Chaves (Country Director, EACIF), Auguste Tano Kouame (Practice Manager, GMFDR), and Pablo Saavedra (Practice Manager, GMFDR).

Chapter 1 was written by Jorge Thompson Araujo (LCRVP, World Bank), Ekaterina Vostroknutova (GMFDR, World Bank), Konstantin M. Wacker (Johannes Gutenberg-Universität Mainz), and Mateo Clavijo (Universitat Pompeu Fabra). Chapter 2 was written by Francesco Caselli (London School of Economics, BREAD, CEP, CEPR, and NBER). Chapter 3 was prepared by Maya Eden (DECMG, World Bank) and Ha Nguyen (DECMG, World Bank). Marc Schiffbauer (DECWD, World Bank), Hania Sahnoun (DECWD, World Bank), and Jorge Thompson Araujo (LCRVP, World Bank) coauthored chapter 4. Chapter 5 was a result of collaboration by J. David Brown (U.S. Census and IZA), Gustavo A. Crespi (Competitiveness and Innovation, IADB), Leonardo Iacovone (GTCDR, World Bank), and Luca Marcolin (KU Leuven). Chapter 6 was written by Ha Nguyen (DECMG, World Bank) and Patricio A. Jaramillo (DECMG, World Bank). Chapter 7 was authored by Konstantin M. Wacker (Johannes Gutenberg-Universität Mainz).

Valuable input and comments were received from Daniel Lederman (Lead Economist, LCRCE, World Bank), Norman V. Loayza (Lead Economist, DECMG, World Bank), and Antonio Nucifora (Lead Economist, GMFDR, World Bank). The peer reviewers were Pedro Cavalcanti Ferreira (Professor, Fundação Getulio Vargas, Rio de Janeiro, Brazil), Zafer Mustafaoglu (Lead Economist and Program Leader, LCC7C, World Bank), and Margaret McMillan (Professor, Tufts University, and IFPRI).

The team is especially grateful to Silvia Gulino, Giselle Velasquez, and Patricia Chacon Holt (all of GMFDR, World Bank), and Eric Palladini (LCROS, World Bank) for their administrative and editorial assistance during the preparation of this publication.

About the Contributors

Editors

Jorge Thompson Araujo, a Brazilian national, is an economic adviser in the Office of the Vice President, Latin America and the Caribbean. Mr. Araujo joined the World Bank in 1996 as an economist. He has since held various positions in the Middle East and North Africa, Sub-Saharan Africa, and Latin America and the Caribbean Regions, as well as corporate assignments in the organization. Prior to joining the Bank, he was an associate professor of economics at the University of Brasilia, Brazil. Mr. Araujo has published widely in the areas of economic growth, functional distribution of income, and public finance. He coauthored the recent World Bank regional report, *Beyond Commodities: The Growth Challenge in Latin America and the Caribbean* (forthcoming in the Latin America Development Forum series). He holds a PhD in economics from the University of Cambridge and an MSc in economics from the University of Brasilia.

Ekaterina (Katia) Vostroknutova is a lead economist in the World Bank's Europe and Central Asia Region. Ms. Vostroknutova joined the World Bank in 2003 through the Bank's Young Professionals Program in the core team for the World Development Report, and has since held various positions in the East Asia and Pacific and Latin America and the Caribbean Regions. She holds a PhD in economics from the European University Institute, in addition to a degree in applied mathematics from Moscow State University and a master's degree in economics from the European University at St. Petersburg. Ms. Vostroknutova's fields of interest include microeconomic foundations of economic growth and fiscal and monetary policy.

Konstantin M. Wacker is an assistant professor at the Gutenberg University of Mainz, Germany. He holds a PhD in economics and applied statistics from the University of Göttingen and has also studied in Vienna, Alicante, and Beijing. He previously worked for the World Bank, ECB, IMF, UNU-WIDER, and the Lower Austrian Chamber of Labor.

Mateo Clavijo Munoz, a Colombian national, is a financial analyst in the World Bank's Finance and Markets Global Practice for the Latin America and the

Caribbean Region. Mr. Clavijo joined the World Bank in 2012 as a junior professional associate in the Macroeconomics and Fiscal Management Unit, where he worked on growth and country risk assessments in Latin America. He has also worked as a consultant for the International Finance Corporation and in the private sector in Colombia. His research has focused on cross-country income differences and the effects of financial system imbalances on economic cycles. He holds a master's (MSc) degree in economics and finance from Universitat Pompeu Fabra and master's (MA) and bachelor's (BA) degrees in economics from the Universidad de los Andes.

Authors

J. David Brown is a senior economist in the Center for Economic Studies at the U.S. Census Bureau and a research fellow at the Institute for the Study of Labor (IZA). He was previously a reader in finance at Heriot-Watt University (2001–09) and an assistant professor at the Stockholm Institute of Transition Economics and the Stockholm School of Economics (1996–2001). He is the author of several articles on enterprise restructuring and privatization, published in such journals as the *Journal of Political Economy, American Political Science Review, Economic Journal, Journal of Regional Science, Economic Development and Cultural Change,* and *Journal of Comparative Economics.*

Francesco Caselli is the Norman Sosnow Professor of Economics at the London School of Economics. He earned his undergraduate degree at the University of Bologna in 1992 and a PhD at Harvard University in 1997. Previous appointments include assistant professor of economics at the University of Chicago Graduate School of Business, and Paul Sack Associate Professor of Economics at Harvard University. His research interests include macroeconomics, economic development, and political economy, on which he has published extensively in the major professional journals. He is an elected fellow of the British Academy, the director of the Macroeconomics and Growth Programme at the Centre for Economic Policy Research, and an editor of *Economica.* Previously, he served as managing editor of the *Review of Economic Studies,* coeditor of the *Journal of Economic Development,* member of the governing council of the European Economic Association, member of the London School of Economics Growth Commission, and director of the macroeconomics programs at the Centre for Economic Performance and the International Growth Centre.

Gustavo Crespi is a principal science and technology specialist at the Inter-American Development Bank. He holds a PhD from the University of Sussex (SPRU), an MA from the University of Chile, and a bachelor's degree from the National University of Cordoba, Argentina. He was a senior program officer of IDRC, Canada. He has published many articles in journals such as *World Development, Research Policy, Journal of Technology Transfer, Oxford Review of Economic Policy, Technovation,* and *Small Business Economics.* He is a member of the editorial board of *Research Policy* and the *International Journal of Technology Learning, Innovation and Development*.

Maya Eden is an economist in the Macroeconomics and Growth Team of the Development Economics Research Group at the World Bank. She joined the group in 2011, after completing a PhD in economics at the Massachusetts Institute of Technology. She also holds a BSc in mathematics and economics from the Hebrew University of Jerusalem, Israel. Her research interests include international finance and macroeconomics. In addition to her work at the World Bank, she holds a visiting position at the Office of Financial Research of the United States Treasury.

Ha Minh Nguyen is an economist in the Macroeconomics and Growth Team of the Development Research Group. He joined the Bank in 2009 in the Young Professionals Program, after earning a PhD in economics from the University of Maryland, College Park. He also holds MA and BA degrees in economics from The University of Adelaide, Australia. His research interests include international finance and economic growth. His current research is on the financial crisis and the real exchange rate.

Leonardo Iacovone is a senior economist with the World Bank's Trade and Competitiveness Global Practice where he is engaged in analytical, operational, and impact evaluation work in areas dealing with microeconomic determinants of growth related to innovation and entrepreneurship. Before joining the World Bank as a Young Professional, he served as an economic advisor for the Government of Mozambique and as a consultant for several international organizations. He was trained at Bocconi University (Milan, Italy) and the University Torquato di Tella (Buenos Aires, Argentina). He received a PhD in Economics from the University of Sussex. His research has been widely published. In 2009 he won a Young Economists' Essay Award from the European Association for Research in Industrial Economics; his paper also won the 2009 Paul Geroski Prize for the most significant policy contribution. More recently, his "Tomorrow's Jobs" project was awarded an Innovation Challenge Grant to develop a new pilot aiming at analyzing the potential for job creation and global expansion of new business ideas.

Luca Marcolin is an economist in the Science, Technology and Industry Directorate of the Organisation for Economic Co-operation and Development (OECD), where he is mainly involved in the analysis of the link between global value chains and economic performance (especially productivity), and in the improvement of the measurement agenda for intangible capital. Before joining the OECD, he consulted with the World Bank (Trade and Competitiveness Global Practice) and the European Bank for Reconstruction and Development (Office of the Chief Economist), and interned at the Bureau of the Policy Advisers of the European Commission, and the United Nations Conference on

Trade and Development, Division of Investment and Enterprise, in research projects exploring issues related to international trade, productivity, and innovation outcomes. He studied economics at the University of Bologna, the Paris School of Economics, and the Ecole Normale Supérieure de Paris. He received a PhD in economics at the Catholic University of Leuven (KUL, Belgium), focusing on wage and productivity dynamics.

Patricio Jaramillo is head of modeling at the Superintendency of Banks and Financial Institutions of Chile and has been consultant to the World Bank Group since 2013. Before that he worked at the research department of the Central Bank of Chile for five years. He has published papers on empirical macroeconomics and financial economics in such journals as *Review of World Economics, Applied Economics Journal, Emerging Markets Finance and Trade*, and *El Trimestre Económico*. He holds a BA in economics and an MS in financial economics from the University of Santiago of Chile, and an MA in economics from Georgetown University.

Hania Sahnoun is an economist primarily working on macroeconomic issues as a consultant with the World Bank Group. She has contributed to reports on issues related to economic growth, firm dynamics, and competition. She also collaborated with the team preparing the 2016 *World Development Report* on digital dividends. She has worked with the World Bank Group as a consultant since 2004. Ms. Sahnoun holds a diploma of advanced studies in economics and a master's degree from the University of Paris I Pantheon-Sorbonne (Paris School of Economics).

Marc Schiffbauer is a senior country economist working on the Andean countries with a focus on Peru. He joined the World Bank in 2009, working in the Poverty Reduction and Economic Management unit within the Eastern Europe and Central Asia as well as the Middle East and North Africa Regions. In the past year, he was part of the team preparing the 2016 *World Development Report* on digital dividends, leading the first chapter on information and communications technology and growth. Before joining the World Bank, Mr. Schiffbauer worked for the Economic and Social Research Institute in Dublin, and as a consultant for the European Central Bank and the International Monetary Fund on issues related to economic growth, firm productivity, and competition. He has a PhD in economics from the University of Bonn in Germany and was a one-year visiting scholar at Universidad Pompeu Fabra and University of British Columbia.

Executive Summary

Even nearly 10 years of solid growth cannot guarantee long-term income convergence. The countries of the Latin America and the Caribbean Region (LAC), like other emerging economies, have benefited from a decade of remarkable growth and some income per capita convergence toward the United States and other high-income countries. Yet, despite this recent progress, LAC still faces a significant per capita income gap with the developed world. The studies in this volume contribute to the ongoing debate on the reasons for this persistent income gap and the potential drivers of convergence, and propose some broad avenues for reform.

Differences in total factor productivity, or efficiency in using the production factors, such as physical and human capital, explain a large part of LAC's persistent income gap. A development accounting exercise conducted for this volume indicates that if the average LAC country closed its efficiency gap relative to the United States, its income per worker could double from its current level, without any additional accumulation of capital.

To narrow this income gap, it is critical that the region reduce its efficiency gap. To that end, the studies in this volume seek to identify the main candidates to explain the differences in efficiency between LAC and the United States, as well as to look for factors that drive convergence at all levels of the economy. Theory suggests two main channels through which the efficiency gap can be affected: technology adoption or innovation and resource allocation.

Macro-level evidence on the efficiency gap between LAC and the United States suggests that resource misallocation is more important than the speed of technology adoption. At this higher level of aggregation, the analysis in this volume shows that technology adoption explains about one-fifth of the efficiency gap, leaving the rest to be explained by misallocation of resources.

The macro-level diagnostic is broadly confirmed at the sector level. At the sector level, distortions and inefficient allocation of resources also hamper labor productivity growth and convergence. In particular, low services sector productivity has reduced the contribution of the structural change process to growth. In addition, although the manufacturing sector has displayed unconditional convergence at the global level, this effect is subdued in LAC, as manufacturing productivity growth has been slower in the region.

Furthermore, firm-level evidence for Colombia and Mexico also puts the spotlight on resource misallocation. When looking at the drivers of firm-level productivity convergence in these two countries, technology adoption and innovation emerge as the main drivers of productivity convergence in the manufacturing sector. Improvements within the firm, not resource reallocation between firms, are largely behind the growth in firms' productivity in the past decade. This is in line with the sector-level finding that improvements in resource allocation contributed less than they could have to the growth of firms.

Resource misallocation can also translate into "pockets of inefficiency" associated with relatively high poverty levels and exacerbated by macroeconomic volatility. Confronted with poverty and a dearth of opportunities, poorer workers may not be able to move into high-productivity sectors. They have no other choice than to perform basic activities, usually in the informal sector, such as working in basic retail trade, becoming street vendors, or working in other informal services. Since these insulated sectors are "pockets of inefficiency," the lack of access to finance and poor entrepreneurship prevent innovation and improved productivity. This phenomenon is magnified by macroeconomic volatility.

At the same time, there is significant room for improvement when it comes to technology adoption and innovation more broadly. The quality of the available technology in LAC is low, and there is very little innovation. Although firms can use innovation to reach productivity at the global productivity frontier, weak institutions reduce incentives to innovate. Only a few firms catch up to the technological frontier, and even then, convergence seems mostly limited to the *domestic* frontier, not the global one.

Understanding the reasons behind LAC's income gap is a necessary step toward designing appropriate growth strategies, particularly in the context of the current growth slowdown. Drawing on the findings of the studies in this volume, several broad policy directions emerge: (i) increasing focus on closing the efficiency gap—beyond mere factor accumulation—is critical to reduce the income gap and improve LAC's convergence prospects; (ii) eliminating distortions that cause misallocation of resources will also improve the incentives to innovate; and (iii) reducing macroeconomic volatility will alleviate the negative impact of the poverty gap on growth.

In practice, some of the key structural and macroeconomic approaches that are needed to speed up LAC's income convergence can be outlined. On the structural side, the main priorities for improving resource allocation and the incentives to innovate include (i) enhancing market competition in key network industries (transport, financial, telecommunications, logistics, communications, and distribution services); (ii) increasing labor market flexibility (e.g., addressing skill mismatches and social barriers); (iii) removing informational frictions (including complex tax regimes and credit rationing); (iv) strengthening property rights; and (v) improving the rule of law. From a macroeconomic standpoint, policies aimed at addressing macroeconomic volatility would also have positive longer-run supply response effects.

Abbreviations

AAEN	Akcigit, Alp, Eden, and Nguyen
AMS	Annual Manufacturing Survey (United States)
BLS	Bureau of Labor Statistics (United States)
CCKW	Crespo-Cuaresma, Klasen, and Wacker
CHAT	Cross-Country Historical Adoption of Technology
DANE	Departamento Administrativo Nacional de Estadística (Colombia)
EAM	Manufacturing Survey (Colombia)
EAP	East Asia and Pacific
ECA	Europe and Central Asia
EIA	Annual Industrial Survey (Mexico)
FE	fixed effects
GDP	gross domestic product
GNI	gross national income
I2D2	International Income Distribution Data Set
ICT	information and communications technology
IDB	Inter-American Development Bank
IMF	International Monetary Fund
INEGI	Mexican National Institute of Statistics
ISIC	International Standard Industrial Classification
IV	instrumental variable
LAC	Latin America and the Caribbean
LMICs	lower-middle-income countries
MNEs	multinational enterprises
MRI	magnetic resonance imaging
NAICS	North American Industry Classification System
OECD	Organisation for Economic Co-operation and Development
OLS	ordinary least squares
PC	personal computer
PIM	perpetuay inventory method
PISA	Program for International Student Assessment
PPP	purchasing power parity

PRP	property rights protection
PWT	Penn World Table
R&D	research and development
RCAs	revealed comparative advantages
SCIAN	Système de classification des industries de l'Amérique du Nord
SITC	Standard International Trade Classification
TFP	total factor productivity
WDI	World Development Indicators
WGI	Worldwide Governance Indicators

CHAPTER 1

Overview

Jorge Thompson Araujo, Ekaterina Vostroknutova, Konstantin M. Wacker, and Mateo Clavijo

Introduction

Beginning in the late 1990s, low- and middle-income economies, including those in the Latin America and the Caribbean (LAC) Region, have benefited from remarkable economic growth. The impact of such growth on the welfare of millions of the citizens of these countries has been impressive. The accelerated growth of the economies in LAC was underpinned by structural reforms and macroeconomic stabilization, and propelled by a favorable external environment. Since the early 2000s, growth rates in LAC have been considerably above those in earlier decades.

Despite higher growth rates and improved overall well-being, the LAC Region has not been able to close its historical income gap with the United States. LAC's average per capita gross domestic product (GDP) has hovered around 30 percent of U.S. per capita GDP for more than a century (World Bank 2011a). This stands in stark contrast to the performance—during the past century—of Japan, the East Asia and Pacific (EAP) "Tigers," and, more recently, China and EAP's middle-income countries, all of which went through a process of catching up with the U.S. economy during the second half of the 20th century (figure 1.1). In addition, income growth has been systematically higher in EAP than in LAC at similar per capita income levels (figure 1.2).

This volume looks into the reasons for LAC's failure to reduce its income gap with the United States (and high-income countries more generally). The starting point for the analysis is a development accounting exercise,[1] in which the income gap is decomposed into an *efficiency gap* (differences in the efficiency of use of inputs) and a *capital gap* (differences in physical and human capital).[2] Recognizing the macroeconomic data's varied quality and limited ability to shed light on the micro foundations of convergence in per capita incomes, we include other levels of analysis. However, working at the macro, sector, and micro levels requires the use of different, but complementary, empirical strategies.

The chapters in this volume provide a multidimensional view of the possible causes of slow productivity growth and speed of convergence in the region.

Figure 1.1 LAC Has Been Overtaken by EAP in Income per Capita Convergence in LAC and EAP

average GDP per capita relative to the United States

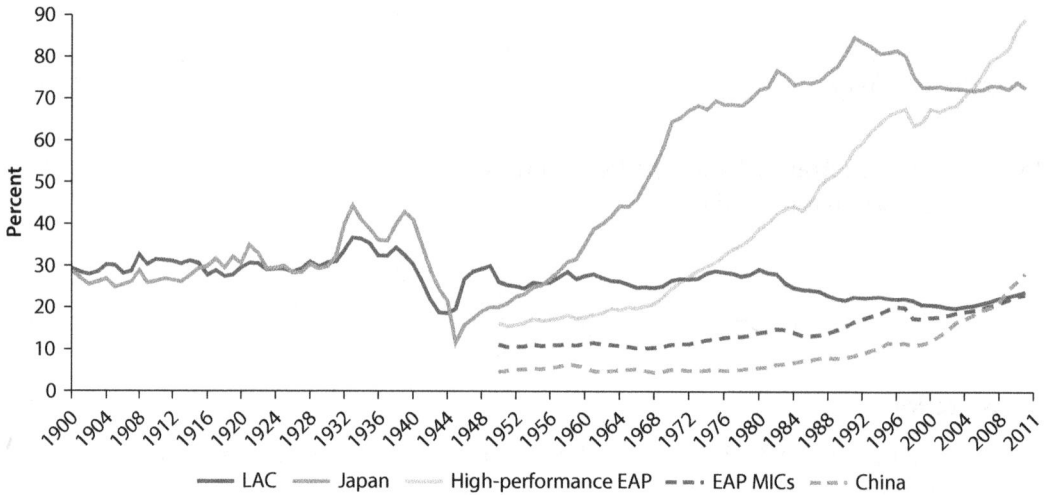

Source: Reproduced from World Bank 2011a.
Note: Values are average GDP per capita relative to the United States. The figure suggests that LAC has gone through "one hundred years of growth solitude," with the absence of a systematic process of convergence. The high-performance EAP economies include Hong Kong SAR, China; the Republic of Korea; Singapore; and Taiwan, China. The EAP middle-income countries (EAP MICs) include Indonesia, Malaysia, the Philippines, and Thailand. LAC includes Argentina, Bolivia, Brazil, Chile, Colombia, Costa Rica, Dominican Republic, Ecuador, El Salvador, Guatemala, Haiti, Honduras, Jamaica, Mexico, Nicaragua, Panama, Paraguay, Peru, Uruguay, and República Bolivariana de Venezuela. EAP = East Asia and Pacific; GDP = gross domestic product; LAC = Latin America and the Caribbean; MICs = middle-income countries.

Figure 1.2 Income Growth in Countries in EAP Has Been Higher Than in Countries in LAC with Similar per Capita Income Levels

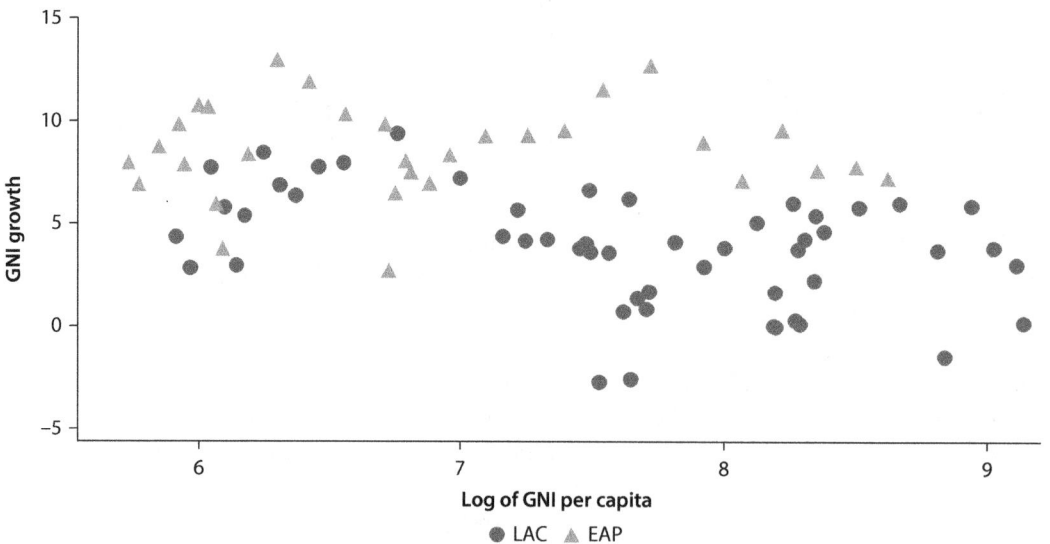

Source: Calculations based on World Development Indicators.
Note: Values are GNI growth vs. log GNI per capita, by country, 1983–2013. GNI is measured using the Atlas method (in current US$). EAP = East Asia and Pacific; GNI = gross national income; LAC = Latin America and the Caribbean.

The chapters focus on how efficiency, including technology adoption, innovation, and allocation of production factors between firms and sectors, can influence productivity. Based on the questions asked and the availability of data, each chapter adopts a different empirical approach, sample size, time horizon, and comparator countries or regions.

Chapter 2, by Francesco Caselli, explains differences in income using a development accounting framework to measure the relative importance of gaps in terms of efficiency, or total factor productivity (TFP), and the accumulation of the quantity and quality of the basic factors used to produce goods and services. Chapter 3, by Maya Eden and Ha Nguyen, analyzes the relationship between the timing of technological innovations in the United States and the timing of these innovations in LAC. The authors use aggregate and sector-level time-series data to identify the significance of these lags in technology adoption. Chapter 4, by Marc Schiffbauer, Hania Sahnoun, and Jorge Thompson Araujo, looks into structural change issues and considers whether resources were increasingly allocated toward sectors, products, and technologies with lower productivity, and how this could explain the region's slow productivity growth. Chapter 5, by J. David Brown, Gustavo A. Crespi, Leonardo Iacovone, and Luca Marcolin, focuses on Colombia and Mexico, and analyzes the process and drivers of firm-level convergence toward the domestic and global productivity frontiers.[3] Chapter 6, by Ha Nguyen and Patricio A. Jaramillo, measures returns to innovation among Latin American firms and compares the returns in LAC countries with those in the Europe and Central Asia (ECA) Region. Finally, chapter 7, by Konstantin M. Wacker, examines the implications of poverty gaps (and their interaction with macroeconomic volatility) for income convergence.

Closing the Efficiency Gap Is Fundamental for Income Convergence

Differences in efficiency or accumulation of physical and human capital explain the gap in income per worker between LAC and the United States. Output per worker can be thought of as a product of human capital per worker, physical capital per worker (quality-adjusted labor), and TFP or efficiency (see box 1.1). Growth in output per worker can therefore be attributed to changes in the accumulation of factors of production or changes in efficiency.

Differences in efficiency—or TFP—explain a large part of the income gap and variation across countries. Previous work, often relying on growth accounting, already stressed the role of TFP to explain a large part of growth variation across countries, as well as the differences in the speed of convergence. Based on the aggregate production function, low efficiency means low income per capita. But low efficiency also reduces incentives to invest in equipment, infrastructure, and schooling. It reduces the potential returns on these investments and, as a result, prevents faster capital accumulation and perpetuates existing income gaps. By contrast, higher efficiency can reduce the income gap by improving returns on existing investments and motivating increased investments in factors of production.[4]

Understanding the Income and Efficiency Gap in Latin America and the Caribbean
http://dx.doi.org/10.1596/978-1-4648-0450-2

Box 1.1 Total Factor Productivity

The analytical tool at the core of development accounting is the aggregate production function, which maps the amount of physical and human capital (the aggregate input quantities) to the amount produced (the output quantities). Assuming that increasing the amount of inputs leads to an equivalent increase in outputs (constant returns to scale), the aggregate production function can be written in per-worker terms. Thus, using the augmented Cobb-Douglas aggregate production function, output per worker is a product of human capital per worker (adjusted for quality), physical capital per worker, and a term called total factor productivity (TFP) or efficiency.

However, TFP is a subject of much controversy. Practitioners refer to it as technology, a measure of our ignorance, or the Solow residual. In this volume, we refer to TFP as efficiency. Annex 1B provides a literature review on this topic.

Source: Caselli, chapter 2, this volume.

If the average country in LAC closed its *efficiency* gap relative to the United States, LAC's average income per worker could double from its current level, without any additional accumulation of capital. The LAC Region generally suffers from an efficiency gap and a capital gap, although there is considerable heterogeneity within the region. Average factor accumulation per worker in LAC is about 40 percent of that in the United States.[5] LAC workers produce on average about one-fifth the output of U.S. workers (figure 1.3).[6] The efficiency of LAC workers is about half that of U.S. workers. In addition, the stocks of physical and human capital in LAC are far lower than in the United States. But part of this capital gap itself is likely to be explained by the efficiency gap and diminished incentives to invest.

Slow technology adoption and misallocation of resources are the main candidates to explain the efficiency gap between LAC and the United States. Annex 1B summarizes the empirical literature on the determinants of TFP, or economywide efficiency. Based on this review, the reasons for the efficiency gap include (i) delayed adoption and diffusion of technology and lack of innovation, (ii) poor allocation of resources between firms or sectors, and (iii) organizational inefficiency (within firms).

The remainder of this chapter looks at technology adoption and allocation of resources in countries in LAC at the economywide (macro), sector, and firm levels. We review the lag in technology adoption at the macro and micro levels between LAC and the United States, and the role it plays in income convergence.[7] We also consider structural changes operating through the technology and resource allocation channels that contribute to low efficiency.[8] We consider firm-level productivity and factor allocation between firms and sectors as drivers of overall economywide productivity.[9] Because we find that innovation is the main driver of firm-level productivity convergence, we look at factors outside the

Figure 1.3 Capital and Efficiency Gaps
income per worker relative to the United States

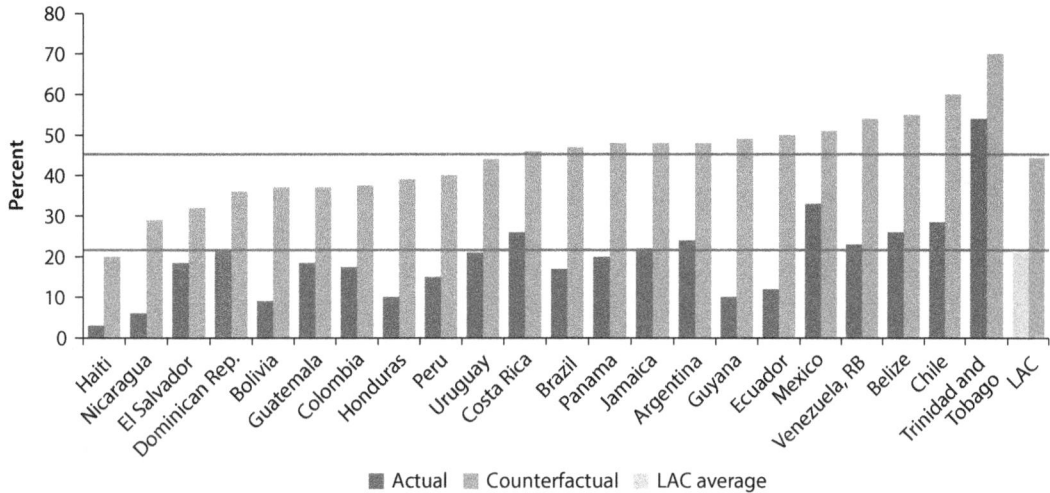

Source: Caselli, chapter 2, this volume.
Note: Values are income per worker in countries in LAC relative to the United States. Actual = with current efficiency; counterfactual = with the same TFP as in the United States. Baseline calibration for the broad sample is used. Horizontal lines show sample means. LAC = Latin America and the Caribbean; TFP = total factor productivity.

firm—such as institutions—that affect incentives to innovate.[10] Finally, the chapter looks at other factors—such as initial poverty rates—that can have an impact on convergence.[11]

Quality of Technological Makeup is Low and There Is Very Little Innovation

LAC's relative technological backwardness is reflected in lower overall productivity, idiosyncratic production structures in manufacturing, and lower innovation effort. The 40 percent efficiency gap is a manifestation of LAC's technological backwardness. This means that the technologies used in LAC are less productive and more obsolete compared with those in the United States. Other factors—such as efficient allocation of resources—are also at play, suggesting that the technologies used in LAC are less productive compared with those in the United States. The level and quality of frontier or adaptation-based innovation are also good indicators of the ability of an economy to invent or absorb technology.

Firms in LAC do very little innovation compared with other regions. Defining innovation as the introduction of new or improved products, only 22 percent of firms in LAC innovate, compared with 62 percent of firms in ECA. LAC firms have not kept pace with industries in the EAP Region and other middle-income economies.[12] This means that less than a fifth of the firms in LAC have introduced a new or significantly improved product to the market in the past three years (see figure 1.4).

Figure 1.4 LAC Economies and Frontier Innovation Outcomes

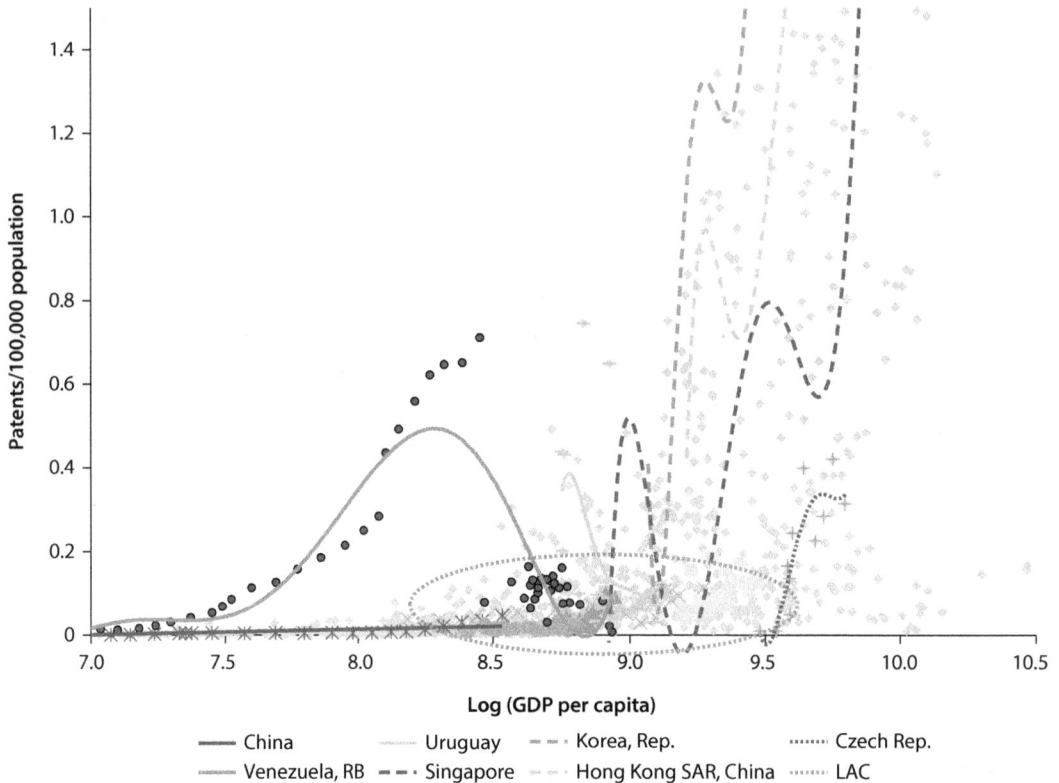

Source: World Bank calculations based on Brahmbhatt and Hu 2010.
Note: Only a fragment of the distribution is shown.

Moreover, the quality of innovation and technological makeup in LAC tends to be low.[13] In addition, the ability of LAC firms to produce complex goods or perform the tasks needed for production is lower than in similar countries in East Asia. The difference is in terms of knowledge applicability. Some knowledge (such as technology or processes) can be more readily adapted to make new products in other sectors, while other knowledge is limited in its scope of application. Compared with EAP, LAC's history of developing such abilities has been relatively erratic and inconsistent (figure 1.5).

Despite the substantial progress achieved over the past 30 years, countries in LAC have tended toward lower export diversification than their peers in EAP. Overall, Latin America succeeded in developing a relatively diversified manufacturing base over the past 30 years. The region's prospects for further diversification into new and potentially higher technology products are greater than those in the Middle East and North Africa or Sub-Saharan Africa. However, in

Figure 1.5 Capability to Produce Complex Products in LAC
index

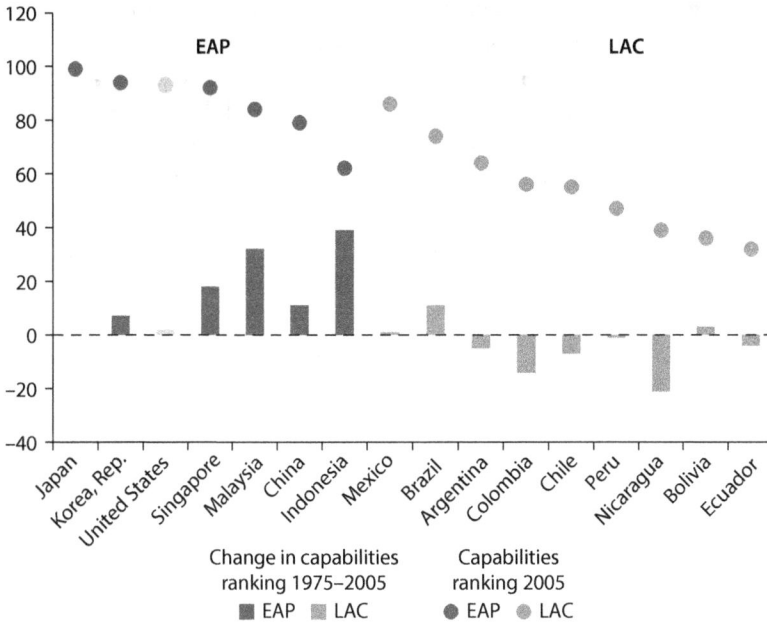

Change in capabilities
ranking 1975–2005
■ EAP ▦ LAC

Capabilities
ranking 2005
● EAP ● LAC

Source: World Bank calculations based on Hidalgo 2012.
Note: Capabilities refer to the level of sophistication of companies in a country to perform more tasks so as to produce a greater variety of products. The original indicator was normalized so that a higher number reflects more capabilities.

diversification and the formation of clusters, countries in LAC have consistently lagged behind economies in EAP with similar levels of income.[14]

The prevalence of idiosyncratic production structures limits the capacity of LAC firms to absorb or imitate more productive foreign technologies. Economies that initially specialize in exporting goods that embody broadly applicable knowledge subsequently grow faster. However, the LAC Region appears to have specialized in technologies that are idiosyncratic, or not well connected. An idiosyncratic export means that there are fewer capabilities to create products from other product groups. Consequently, most countries in LAC have low and slow-growing knowledge applicability, except for Chile.

As a result, manufacturing in LAC is less productive than the worldwide average. The regional average growth of manufacturing labor productivity (net of year-industry specific effects) has only been 1.2 percent, compared with the average 4.2 percent across all 104 countries with available data. There are also substantial growth differences across the region. This calls for a more detailed analysis of manufacturing productivity developments on a micro level, which we discuss throughout this volume.

Innovation Drives Firm-Level Productivity Catch-Up

Aggregate productivity growth depends on the productivity growth of individual firms and the allocation of factors between firms.[15] A country's productivity rises because the productivity of firms has risen (within-firm aspect). However, it could also be that the more productive firms in the country acquire more production factors and thus expand their production, while less productive firms decline in importance or go out of business (between-firms aspect). This section looks at what drives manufacturing firms' convergence to the productivity frontier by comparing manufacturing firm-level data for Colombia, Mexico, and the United States.[16] In these countries, after 2000, the main driver of manufacturing productivity was productivity growth *within* firms and not reallocation of factors or resources *between* firms.[17]

In Colombia and Mexico, only a few firms are productive at the global level.[18] Figure 1.6 shows the number and percent of Mexican firms that have achieved the global productivity frontier. Figure 1.7 compares the within-firm productivity of the two countries and the domestic frontier. It appears that the domestic productivity frontiers of Colombia and Mexico are not converging toward the international productivity frontier, because the manufacturing productivity frontier in the United States is growing much faster than that of nearby countries.

In these economies, innovation is the most important determinant of firm-level productivity growth, with little contribution from the resource reallocation channel.[19] This is true even among more capital-intensive firms, which seem to enjoy higher productivity growth. The degree of engagement in international trade does not seem to influence productivity growth positively, except in the

Figure 1.6 Mexican Firms and the Global Productivity Frontier

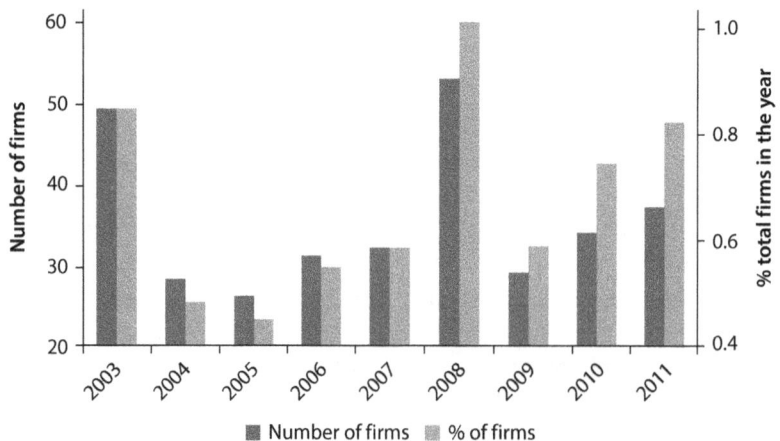

Source: Brown et al., chapter 5, this volume.

Figure 1.7 Within-Firm Productivity and Convergence to the Domestic Frontier

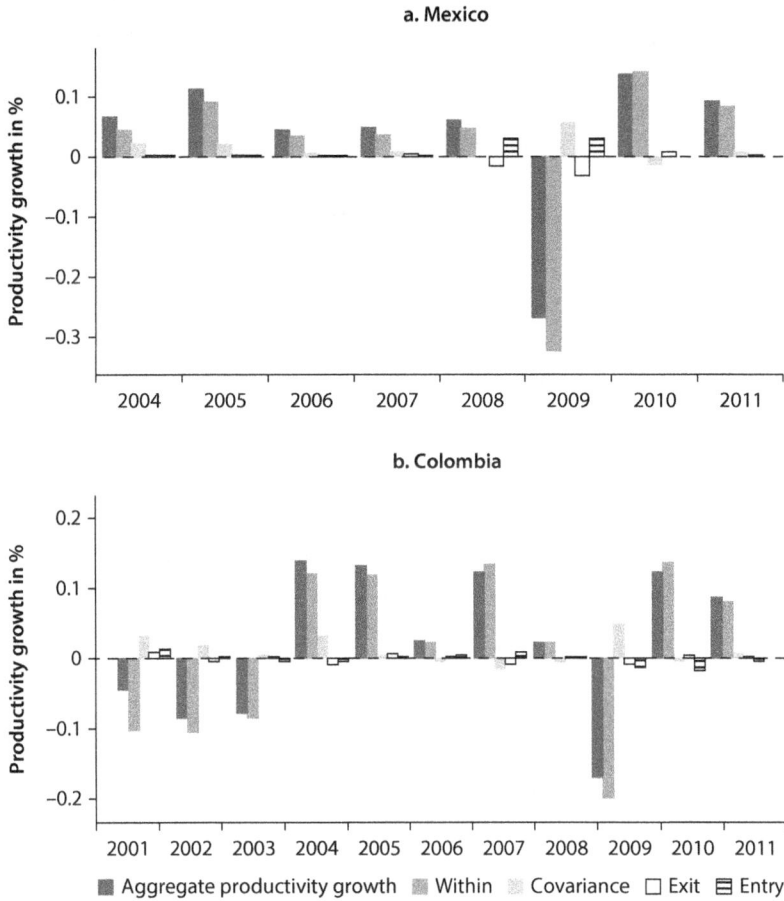

a. Mexico

b. Colombia

■ Aggregate productivity growth ▨ Within ▧ Covariance ☐ Exit ▤ Entry

Source: Brown et al., chapter 5, this volume.
Note: The covariance component describes the joint distribution of firms' productivity and market share. The extent of resource misallocation can be inferred by the covariance term, with a larger positive value indicating that more productive firms use higher industry input shares. Increases in the covariance term would therefore imply improvements in the allocation of productive inputs (workers) across firms (within the industry).

case of the United States. On average, within-firm productivity growth (that is driven by technological adoption or innovation) accounts for more than two-thirds of overall productivity growth in the manufacturing sector. In Mexico, on average, changes in the allocation of factors between firms accounted for 22 percent of overall productivity growth; in the United States, these changes accounted for 8 percent. Reallocation made almost no contribution to productivity growth in Colombia. This finding also means that, in the 2000s, Colombia and Mexico have done relatively better on technology adoption than on reducing resource misallocation.

Incentives to Innovate are Inhibited by Weak Institutions

In Brazil, Ecuador, Guatemala, Honduras, and Nicaragua, returns to innovation are low, creating little incentive for firms to innovate.[20] Overall, it is found that, after a firm innovates, its sales per worker increase by 18 percent.[21] In contrast, in the Latin American countries for which this analysis was conducted—namely, Brazil, Ecuador, Guatemala, Honduras, and Nicaragua—the difference in sales and sales per worker between firms that do and do not innovate is not statistically different from zero.[22] This finding indicates that returns to innovation in Latin America are very small.

Institutional factors, such as weak property rights protection and rule of law, explain such low returns. Returns to innovation increase in LAC—disproportionately more than in ECA—with better property rights protection (7.4 percent vs. 0.8 percent) and better institutions (12.6 percent vs. 1.9 percent). Regulations and other institutional arrangements can prevent firms from absorbing existing technologies or innovating, even after correcting for the economic structure and level of development. These weak institutions constrain technology adoption and reduce firm-level incentives to innovate. The innovation shortfall caused by these distortions seems to be particularly pronounced in Argentina, Ecuador, Mexico, Panama, Peru, and República Bolivariana de Venezuela (figure 1.8). This is one example of the distortions that inhibit productivity growth, which are discussed in the following sections.

Distortions Leading to Misallocation of Factors Explain Most of the Efficiency Gap

Technology adoption explains about one-fifth of the efficiency gap between countries, leaving the rest to be explained by misallocation of factors. The role of technology in the region's efficiency gap with the United States is a function of the speed of technology adoption. The adoption lag of technology is the length of time between the invention of the technology and its eventual adoption. Estimated at the macro level, the rate at which an economy adopts new technology indicates the degree to which technology improves efficiency. Slow adoption indicates that technology backwardness is indeed a major problem. Fast adoption means that other factors, such as institutions and misallocation of resources, are more important. Any shock to TFP growth in the United States that affects the adopting countries with a lag is a technology shock.

Based on TFP time-series data, we find that, on average, technologies in the United States are fully or nearly-fully adopted by firms in LAC after 8 to 10 years (figure 1.9). Assuming that the technology frontier in the United States grows about 1 percent per year, an eight-year lag translates into an 8 percentage point widening of the productivity gap. This leaves 80 percent of the efficiency gap to be explained by distortions leading to the misallocation of factors of production.

This result is consistent with the fact that technology adoption and innovation drove convergence to domestic productivity frontiers in Colombia and Mexico. It is important to distinguish between what explains the efficiency gap

Figure 1.8 Barriers to Knowledge Absorption and Productivity in LAC

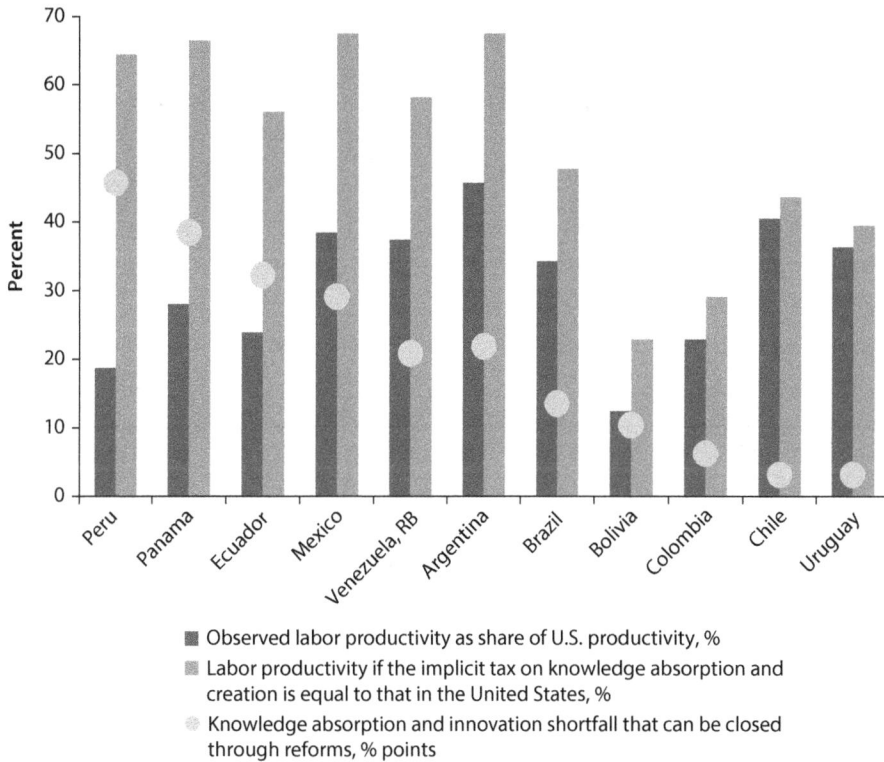

Observed labor productivity as share of U.S. productivity, %

Labor productivity if the implicit tax on knowledge absorption and creation is equal to that in the United States, %

Knowledge absorption and innovation shortfall that can be closed through reforms, % points

Source: World Bank calculations based on Maloney and Rodriguez-Clare 2007.

between countries and the drivers of the observed convergence to domestic productivity frontiers. Although technology adoption only explains 20 percent of the existing efficiency gap, based on macro-level evidence of shocks to TFP, this does not mean that *changes* in the speed of technology adoption, or in conditions that determine this speed—such as the incentive structure for innovation, institutions, etc.—account for the same share in the observed firm-level productivity increases. Indeed, we find that innovation has been driving firm-level productivity, which in turn drove productivity convergence to the *domestic* frontier in Colombia and Mexico. The lack of improvements in between-firms factor allocations has prevented convergence to the global productivity frontier. There has therefore been very little reallocation of factors toward more productive firms: factors that experience little change also contribute little to the dynamics of convergence.

There is some heterogeneity in the speed of technology adoption among LAC countries, sectors of the economies, and specific technologies. Studies using data on specific technologies have estimated longer lags (about 20 years), potentially explaining about half of the efficiency gap. However, we find that the various

Understanding the Income and Efficiency Gap in Latin America and the Caribbean
http://dx.doi.org/10.1596/978-1-4648-0450-2

Figure 1.9 Adoption of Frontier Technology in LAC

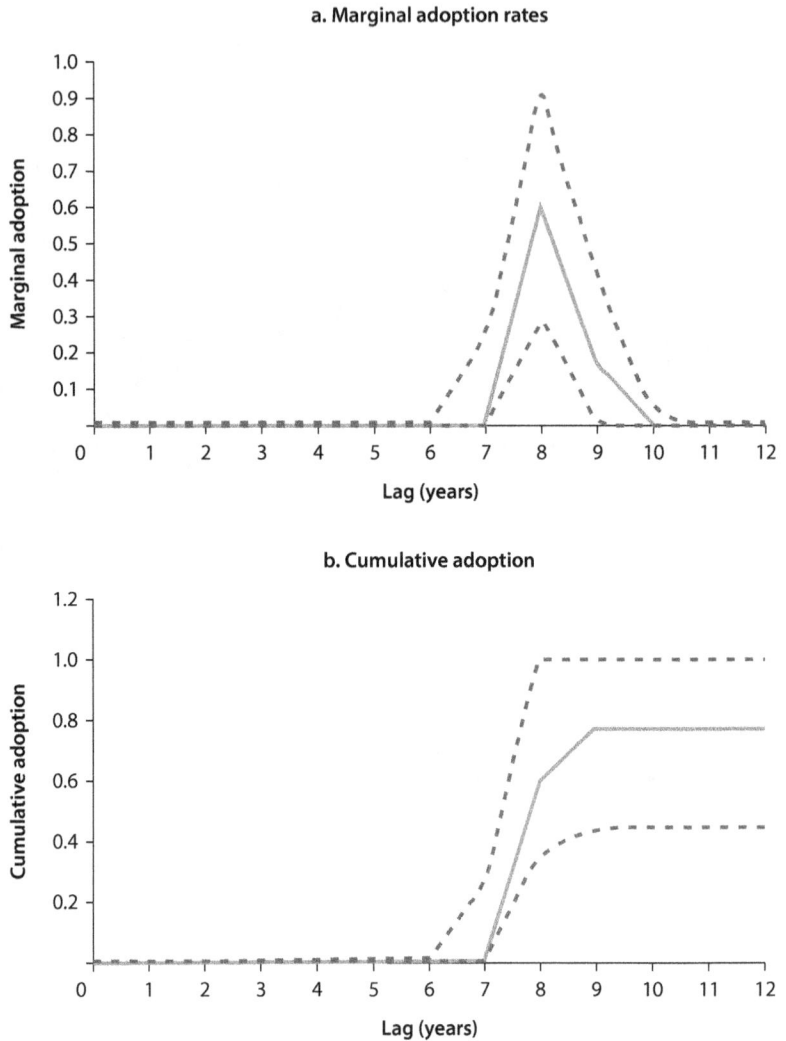

a. Marginal adoption rates

b. Cumulative adoption

Source: Eden and Nguyen, chapter 3, this volume.
Note: The figure depicts the marginal rate and cumulative adoption of frontier technology in LAC, based on a baseline estimation from Akcigit et al. (2014). Measured TFP growth is constructed as the growth of a Solow residual, at an annual frequency. The United States is the frontier country and the adopting country is a GDP-weighted average of LAC countries. The dotted lines represent the 90 percent confidence intervals. GDP = gross domestic product; LAC = Latin America and the Caribbean; TFP = total factor productivity.

results can be reconciled, taking into account the differences between macro and micro data estimations (see box 1.2).

Misallocation can affect efficiency directly and through the optimal technology adoption decisions by firms. Weak institutions can reduce firm-level incentives to innovate, and thus become a binding constraint to innovation and technology adoption. Moreover, weak institutions can result in misallocation of factors and affect efficiency through the optimal technology adoption decision of agents.

Box 1.2 Reconciling the Different Technology Adoption Lags at the Macro and Micro Levels

Comin and Hobijn (2010) use microeconomic evidence on specific technologies and find the technology adoption gap to be around 20 years on average. At least on the surface, this gap is inconsistent with the result found in this volume and in Akcigit et al. (2014), which shows an eight-year lag for Latin America and the Caribbean. Eden and Nguyen (chapter 3 in this volume) discuss this result in detail. They show that because of different definitions of the lag in technology adoption measured at the macro and micro levels, these results are broadly in line.

Eden and Nguyen reconcile the two findings with two insights. First, technologies tend to be adopted first in more productive firms. Because the first adopting firms tend to be more productive, the productivity gains from the first technology adopters are relatively larger than the productivity gains from later adopters. The macro-level adoption lag accounts for this, by weighting technology adoptions by their respective productivity gains. The micro-level adoption lag, in contrast, assigns equal weights to all adopters; thus, it is likely to be relatively longer than the macro-level lag.

Second, more effective technologies are likely to be adopted faster. Technologies that improve productivity are more likely to be adopted faster, as the return to adoption is higher. This implies shorter lags associated with technologies that are more productivity enhancing. The macro-level adoption lag focuses on aggregate productivity gains from technology adoption, which are likely driven disproportionately by more productive technologies. In contrast, the micro-level adoption lag weighs technologies equally, and is thus likely to be longer. Since the relative importance of adopting firms and productivity improvements matters for aggregate productivity, the macro approach is more important in explaining the latter.

Distortions and Factors outside the Firm Hamper Productivity Growth in Manufacturing

LAC's efficiency gap is not all about sector resource allocation, but also about inefficient resource use *within* key sectors. Structural change has contributed less to growth in the region not only because of the movement of labor from manufacturing to lower-productivity activities, but also because of slower manufacturing productivity growth. Unconditional convergence in manufacturing labor productivity across countries has emerged as an empirically robust stylized fact (Rodrik 2013a). That is, manufacturing labor productivity in poorer countries is catching up (on average) with manufacturing labor productivity in high-income countries unconditional on low- and middle-income countries' policies, quality of institutions, education, or other growth determinants. In one interpretation, this phenomenon can be attributed to the tradable nature of manufacturing as well as to its cross-border technological transferability (Rodrik 2013b).

Firm-level productivity is also affected by factors and distortions outside the firm, including through spillover effects. One example is the reduction in returns to innovation caused by weak institutions. For example, when an industry improves overall productivity, the firms in the same sector of the same country also improve their productivity. However, the variation in productivity among firms within an industry can also hinder an individual firm's ability to catch up. That is, the spillover effect of improved productivity dissipates with the distance from the frontier. The farther away a firm is from the productivity frontier, the less it benefits from the improvements. Similarly, there was no evidence of spillovers from the global frontier (which is generally more distant).

High labor costs and wage inequality also hinder convergence. In Colombia and Mexico, high wages reduce the catch-up speed toward the domestic frontier. In Colombia, the wage differential between skilled and unskilled workers negatively affected productivity convergence. In contrast, the opposite was true for U.S. firms. These findings reflect the fact that convergence is more difficult in an environment where high skills are scarce and the costs of labor mobility are high (Artuç, Lederman, and Porto 2013), as in Colombia, and where skilled workers earn a considerable wage premium.

Low Labor Productivity in "Insulated" Sectors Reduces Overall Value Added per Worker

Movement of labor to sectors with lower value added per worker is correlated with overall slow growth in value added in LAC (McMillan and Rodrik 2011). This aspect of structural transformation appears to have been the pattern across the region in recent decades. In seven of a sample of nine countries in LAC between 1990 and 2005, structural change was associated with lower value added per worker.[23] The cases of Argentina and Costa Rica illustrate the issue of labor productivity. In Argentina, several large services sectors experienced the highest increases in employment. Although these "insulated" economic activities provide many jobs, they also tend to generate lower value added per worker. The result was an overall decline in value added per worker in the entire economy. By contrast, in Costa Rica, although structural change also shifted labor to services, the workers' productivity was higher, thus resulting in an overall increase in value added per worker in the economy. Figure 1.10 illustrates the cases of Argentina and Costa Rica.

The role of the services sector in explaining the contribution of structural change to average value added per worker varies across the region. In cases where the tertiary sector remains relatively less productive than the manufacturing sector, which seems the more common pattern in the region, employment reallocation from the latter to the former would reduce economywide growth in value added per worker. In contrast, higher services sector productivity helps explain why countries such as Costa Rica and Mexico have seen structural change contributing to aggregate productivity growth.

High Poverty Rates Weaken Income Convergence through Sector Misallocation

Countries with deep initial poverty converge more slowly in income per capita. Although there are additional forces influencing poverty and convergence, the initial poverty and associated lack of opportunity *do* play a role in income

Figure 1.10 Structural Change and Value Added per Worker: Two Contrasting Cases

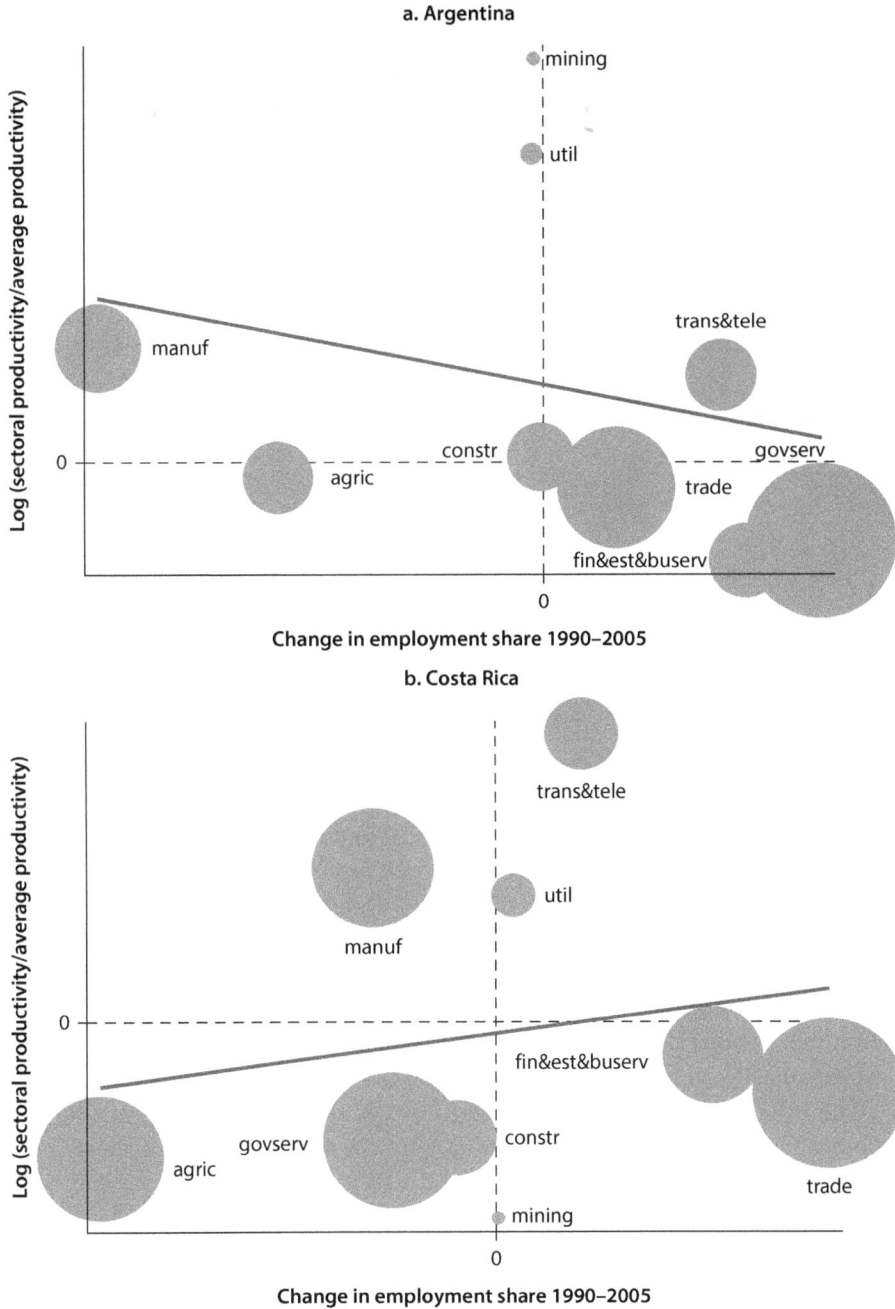

a. Argentina

Change in employment share 1990–2005

b. Costa Rica

Change in employment share 1990–2005

Source: Schiffbauer, Sahnoun, and Araujo, in this volume.
Note: The figures plot the logarithm of sectoral value added per worker (relative to the average across all sectors) and the change in the employment share for nine sectors of an economy between 1990 and 2005. The size of the circle reflects the employment share in 2005. On the vertical axis, sectors above zero are relatively more productive compared with an average sector in the economy. On the x-axis, sectors to the right from zero have had increases in their employment shares. agric = agricultural sector; constr = construction sector; fin&est&buserv = financial, real estate and business services; govserv = government services; manuf = manufacturing sector; trans&tele = transport and telecommunications.

Figure 1.11 Convergence Speed and the Initial Poverty Level

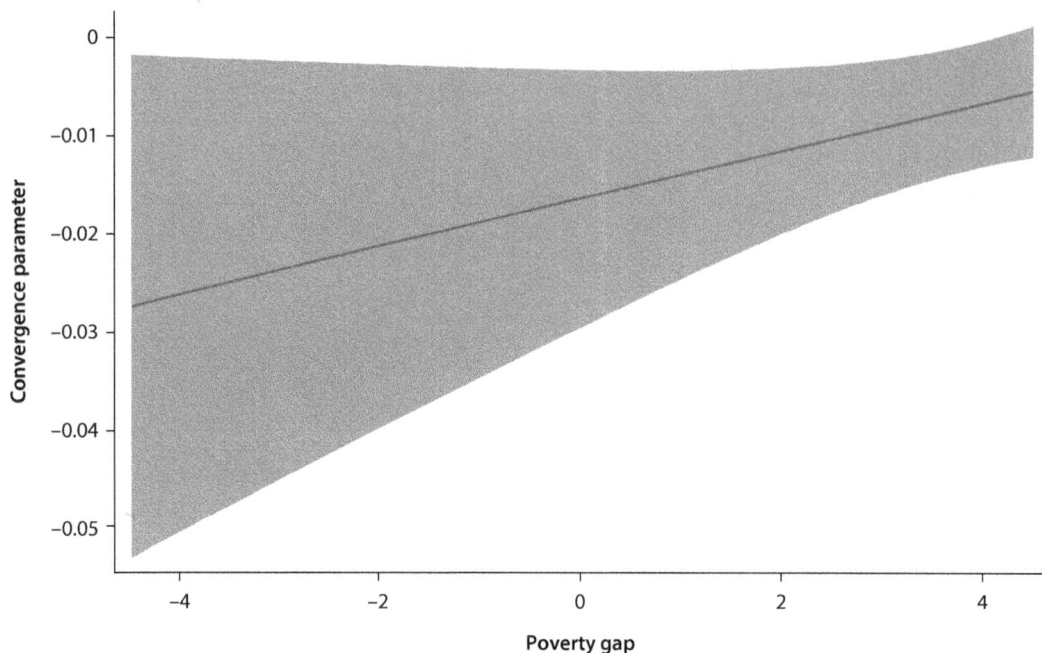

Source: World Bank calculations based on World Development Indicators data.

convergence. Figure 1.11 shows how the speed of convergence of income per capita depends on the initial poverty level. Lower poverty gaps are associated with faster convergence speed, while convergence speed slows down as poverty rises. Interestingly, controlling for poverty is sufficient to observe convergence in a sample of 102 low- and middle-income countries that do not converge unconditionally.

Poverty and slow convergence reduce opportunities for low-skill workers and favor the development of inefficient insulated sectors. Workers facing poverty and lacking opportunity may not be able to move into high-productivity sectors, for various reasons.[24] The workers have no other choice than to perform basic activities, usually in the informal sector, such as basic retail trade, street vending, or other informal services. Many of these services are essentially nontradable and do not operate in a competitive environment. In addition, because these insulated sectors are "pockets of inefficiency," the lack of access to finance and poor entrepreneurship prevent innovation and improved productivity.

The LAC Region's relatively high poverty rates, given the levels of income, have hindered convergence. Countries in LAC stand out for their higher than expected poverty gaps, given their income levels. In addition, the region's history of informality, limited access to finance, and skill mismatches have counteracted the "advantages of backwardness" that should otherwise have helped these countries to converge toward higher income levels.

This effect is magnified by macroeconomic volatility, potentially creating a vicious cycle. The negative effect of poverty on growth further increases with

Figure 1.12 Volatility and Impact of Poverty on Growth

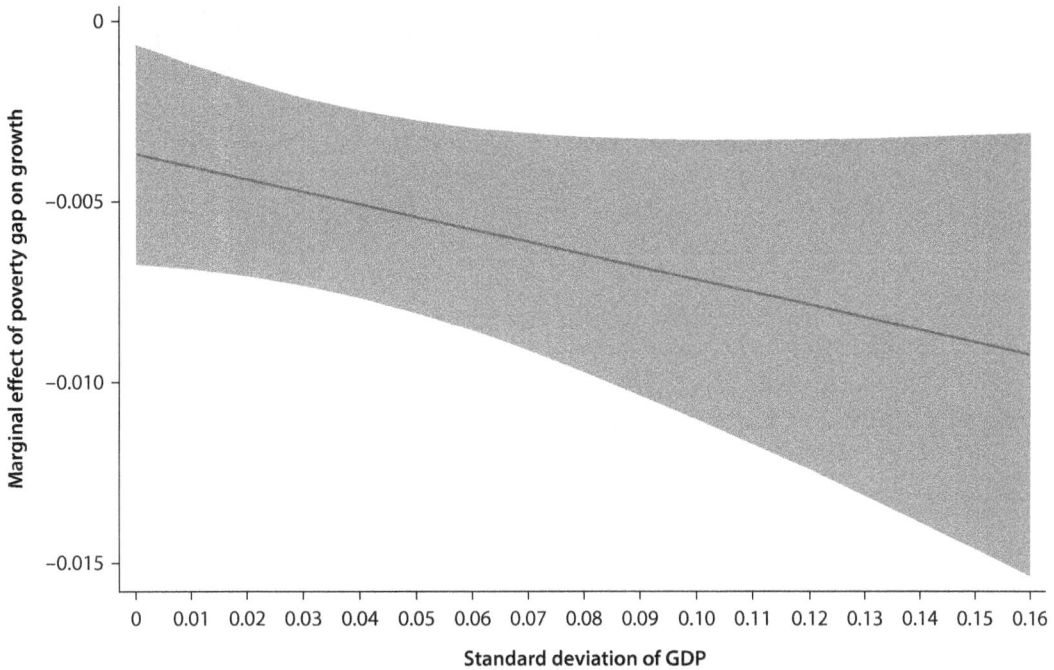

Source: World Bank calculations based on World Development Indicators data.

macroeconomic volatility and uncertainty, because the poor will refrain from investing.[25] Volatility prevents poorer workers from moving to sectors that are more profitable and productive. This missing reallocation gives rise to ex post allocation inefficiency, which could further adversely impact growth and poverty reduction.[26] Figure 1.12 shows the impact of poverty on growth at different levels of volatility (measured by the standard deviation of GDP). The adverse effect of poverty on growth becomes more pronounced as GDP volatility increases.

What These Findings Mean for Growth Policies

Understanding the reasons behind LAC's income gap is a necessary step toward designing appropriate growth strategies. To inform the ongoing debate on growth strategies for LAC, the findings of the chapters in this volume point to some broad policy directions:

• Prioritizing policies to reduce the efficiency gap is an effective way to address the income gap.
• Implementing policies aimed at reducing distortions and misallocation of factors can improve efficiency and the speed of technology adoption.
• Reducing macroeconomic volatility will improve income convergence by alleviating the negative impact of the poverty gap on growth.[27]

Understanding the Income and Efficiency Gap in Latin America and the Caribbean
http://dx.doi.org/10.1596/978-1-4648-0450-2

To Reduce the Income Gap, Close the Efficiency Gap

Closing the efficiency gap will lead to significant growth and welfare gains. If LAC had closed its efficiency gap relative to the United States, the region's income per worker would have been twice as high as its current level. This result would not have required a massive savings or investment effort to close the capital gap. In addition, efficiency improvements would themselves have provided the incentive for investments, thereby reducing the capital gap.[28]

However, the supply-side angle—the determinant of TFP—is critical if LAC is to achieve higher and sustained rates of noninflationary growth. Since many of the economies in LAC are already operating close to their full capacity, it is not enough to seek alternative (domestic) sources of demand. The region's economies also need to remove or relieve constraints to productivity growth. Otherwise, policies that focus exclusively on stimulating aggregate demand run the risk of further straining countries' productive capacity and leading to inflationary pressures.

To Increase Productivity, Reduce Distortions That Lead to Resource Misallocation and Weak Incentives to Innovate

Building more efficient economic institutions will improve the allocation of factors. Misallocation plays a major role in explaining the LAC Region's overall efficiency gap.[29] Barriers for the flow of labor and capital to the most productive entities reduce aggregate productivity. Where there is a great variety of efficiency levels within an industry, convergence is slow and the benefits of knowledge spillovers are reduced. In addition, firms that are farther away from the frontier find innovation efforts too costly and ineffective and cannot benefit from advances in technology. Therefore, improving the allocation of resources toward more productive firms will boost aggregate productivity and expand production.

Countries need to identify and address country-specific distortions that prevent resources from moving to the most productive activities (sector or firm level). In a well-functioning policy and market environment, capital and labor should move from firms and sectors with low productivity to firms with high (marginal) productivity and allow the latter to grow and the former to shrink (or exit the market). However, myriad policy and market failures can affect the efficient allocation of capital and labor across firms. These failures reduce productivity because they give an inordinate market share to less productive firms, while restricting the growth of the more productive firms. The policy inadequacies that discourage the ability of productive firms to survive and grow, and the closure of unproductive firms, include the following: (i) limited market competition in key network industries (transport, financial, telecommunications, logistics, communications, and distribution services), (ii) limited labor market flexibility (including skill mismatches and social barriers), and (iii) informational frictions (including complex tax regimes and credit rationing).

Therefore, the goal should be to lift productivity levels in lagging sectors that are receiving labor and upgrade human capital across the board. These policies will help to enable newly unemployed workers to find jobs in more productive sectors that could potentially absorb labor.[30] At the sector level, the following considerations emerge from the analysis in this volume:

- Natural resource wealth, if appropriately managed, can generate economy-wide benefits. Although Chile's economy is missing an industrialized manufacturing core, its economic performance has been impressive.
- High-productivity services are not unlike manufacturing in some respects and could also potentially display unconditional convergence.[31] Given the relatively low levels of service exports in LAC, a key policy goal for the region would be to make the services sector more productive and tradable.[32]
- Insulated economic activities—particularly in the tertiary sector—are less productive, but provide a large number of jobs. Enhancing product and labor market competition can remove the implicit protection that such insulated sectors receive and thus reduce resource misallocation.[33]

Innovation effort is the main driver of firm-level convergence, but certain factors prevent firms from absorbing the technology that is readily available. The firm-level study of convergence to the domestic frontier (innovation largely contributes to observed productivity convergence), and the discussion on the technology space (the importance of knowledge applicability as a growth engine) highlight the importance of innovation in the convergence process. It takes about eight years for frontier technologies to have an impact on efficiency in LAC. Moreover, macro-level factors, such as institutional quality and slow technology absorption, reduce firms' incentives to innovate and have a disproportionately larger negative effect in LAC than elsewhere.

Removing distortions will also speed up technology adoption. Similar distortions adversely affect *both* resource allocation and incentives to innovate, suggesting that certain horizontal policies can operate through resource allocation and technology adoption. To increase their capabilities to innovate or absorb new technology, LAC countries need to invest more in human capital and work toward removing distortions.[34] Furthermore, a weak or adverse institutional environment discourages firms from investing in new products. These distortions also affect the ability of resources to move toward their most productive use, thereby contributing to resource misallocation. Therefore, certain horizontal policies—focused on institutional strengthening, human capital accumulation, and infrastructure upgrading—can help raise efficiency through both channels examined in this volume.[35]

To Alleviate the Negative Impact of the Poverty Gap on Growth, Reduce Macroeconomic Volatility

Containing macroeconomic volatility helps reduce the negative impact of the poverty gap on growth. Policies that reduce macroeconomic volatility will also weaken the negative link between initial poverty and income convergence. As a result, the potential vicious cycle between relatively high poverty and aggregate growth can be addressed. This conclusion also supports the notion that growth strategies need to take into account equity and volatility. As a corollary, policies aimed at addressing macroeconomic volatility would also have positive longer-run *supply response* effects.[36]

Issues for Future Research

As this volume narrows the search for the determinants of LAC's income gap, it also raises new issues for future research. The volume emphasizes the relevance of closing the efficiency gap and the fact that technology adoption only plays a limited role in this process. Issues of structural change, innovation, and equity deserve more attention. Despite these insights, this volume is only one contribution in an ongoing debate. There is a need to focus in more detail on certain aspects.

For example, why do we see domestic convergence of firms' productivity despite the fact that more productive firms are adopting new technologies faster than the less productive firms? Is this because of the low importance of technology adoption for productivity or because domestic convergence is a phenomenon of just the past decade (or of only Colombia and Mexico)? Has LAC's progress in equity during the past decade contributed to this pattern? And what is the causal relationship between poverty, volatility, and convergence more generally? Under which conditions does productivity-increasing structural change (between and within sectors) occur? We hope that this volume provides a basis for addressing these and other research questions.

Annex 1A Understanding LAC's Income Gap: A Summary

		Motivation: Despite a decade of convergence, LAC still faces a significant per capita income gap vis-à-vis the United States	
Working hypotheses	*Level of analysis*	*Key findings*	*Policy implications*
• Low total factor productivity may be the main explanation for LAC's long-term performance in income convergence.	Macro	The region suffers from an *efficiency gap* as much as it suffers from a *capital gap*. However, much of the capital gap itself is likely due to diminished incentives to invest in equipment, infrastructure, and schooling, because of the efficiency gap (Caselli, chapter 2).	If LAC closed its efficiency gap relative to the United States, its income per worker would have been twice as high as its current level, without requiring a massive savings/investment effort to close the capital gap, which would probably be inconsistent with the social compact observed across the region and the maintenance of the recent gains in reducing inequality.
• The efficiency gap between LAC and the United States could be driven by slow technology adoption or resource misallocation.	Macro/sectoral	Macro-based evidence indicates that the technology adoption lag between LAC and the United States (eight years) is shorter than the current micro-based evidence suggests, and explains only a small part of the observed productivity gap (Eden and Nguyen, chapter 3).	Given the relatively limited contribution of adoption lags to the income gap, attention should also be paid to policies aimed at improving domestic institutions and correcting misallocation of resources.

annex continues next page

Working hypotheses	Level of analysis	Key findings	Policy implications
• Structural change, operating through the technology and resource allocation channels, may have contributed negatively to productivity growth in LAC.	Sectoral	(i) Structural change has resulted in decreased economywide value added per worker in most LAC countries in the sample; (ii) LAC's manufacturing productivity growth has been below the world average; and (iii) There is a prevalence of idiosyncratic production structures, which hurt technology adoption prospects (Schiffbauer, Sahnoun, and Araujo, chapter 4).	Searching for an optimal economic structure is futile. The conditions under which *any* sector would contribute to productivity growth are more important than the sectoral composition of output per se. Insulated economic activities, particularly in the tertiary sector, display lower productivity and have become a recipient of labor in many countries in LAC. Enhancing product and labor market competition can remove the implicit protection that such insulated sectors receive and thus lead to more productive resource allocation.
• Firm-level growth ("within" component) and market reallocation ("between" component) may be important in explaining productivity growth and convergence at the firm level.	Micro (Colombia and Mexico)	(i) On average, the "within" component (firm-level growth) accounts for more than two-thirds of overall productivity growth in the manufacturing sector; (ii) Convergence toward the global frontier is much weaker than convergence to the domestic one; and (iii) Firms' innovation effort is the most important determinant of firm-level productivity growth, and therefore of convergence to the domestic productivity frontier (Brown et al. chapter 5).	Since the contribution of the "between" component (market reallocation) is weak, there is a degree of misallocation that has not been addressed. At the same time, *when it occurs*, innovation effort, operating through the "within" component, is a key driver of convergence, at least to the domestic frontier.
• Although innovation effort is key for firm-level growth, incentives to innovate might be inadequate in LAC.	Micro (Brazil, Ecuador, Guatemala, Honduras, and Nicaragua)	Looking at ECA and LAC, after a firm innovates, its sales per worker increase by 18 percent. When only looking at firms in LAC, the difference in sales and sales per worker between firms that do and do not innovate is not statistically different from zero. Returns to innovation are influenced by institutional factors, such as property rights protection and the rule of law. Existing regulations and institutional arrangements can prevent firms from absorbing existing technologies or innovating (Nguyen and Jaramillo, chapter 6).	Weak institutions reduce firm-level incentives to innovate, and thus become a constraint to innovation and technology adoption.

annex continues next page

Understanding the Income and Efficiency Gap in Latin America and the Caribbean
http://dx.doi.org/10.1596/978-1-4648-0450-2

Working hypotheses	Level of analysis	Key findings	Policy implications
• Convergence may be slowed even further by high initial poverty.	Macro/micro	The negative impact of the poverty gap on growth is exacerbated by macroeconomic volatility (Wacker, chapter 7).	Equity and volatility need to be taken into account in the formulation of growth strategies, providing an empirical basis for the Birdsall, de la Torre, and Caicedo (2010) notion of an incomplete agenda for growth in LAC in the past and suggesting that shared prosperity is also supportive of income convergence.

Note: ECA = Europe and Central Asia; LAC = Latin America and the Caribbean.

Annex 1B Survey of the Literature on the Determinants of Total Factor Productivity[37]

Recent advances in development accounting confirm that the large income differences across countries cannot be explained by differences in the accumulation of physical or human capital. Instead, variations in total factor productivity (TFP) have been found to account for at least 50 percent of cross-country income differences directly (among others, Caselli 2005; Caselli and Coleman 2006; Caselli and Feyrer 2007). Furthermore, variations in TFP indirectly affect income differences through their impact on physical and human capital accumulation (Hsieh and Klenow 2010). It follows that a successful theory of economic growth and convergence needs to explain why some countries experience high TFP growth while others lag behind. The subsequent literature explaining TFP differences can be broadly classified into three approaches.

I. Technology Diffusion and Adoption

A first strand of the literature extends endogenous growth theories to show differences in international technology diffusion and adoption rates across countries (for example, Barro and Sala-i-Martin 1997; Howitt 2000). Among others, Keller (2004) summarizes the empirical evidence on international technology diffusion documenting the importance of geographic, economic, or cultural distances between countries. He finds that 90 percent of technology diffusion occurs through indirect technology spillovers rather than through the acquisition of technology licenses. Comin and Hobjin (2010) use data on the diffusion of 15 technologies in 166 countries over the past two centuries and reveal significant lags in adoption (on average, countries have adopted technologies 45 years after their invention). But why are firms in some countries more successful or eager to adopt new technologies than firms in other countries?

Differences in the speed of diffusion have been associated with several economic factors influencing the incentives of firms in low- and middle-income countries to adopt new (foreign) technologies. Most of these contributions are based on theoretical models, in some cases paired with some suggestive cross-country or case study evidence. Several studies highlight the role of cross-country differences in (the quality of) human capital (Benhabib and Spiegel 1994, 2005; Hanushek and Kimko 2000; Hanushek and Woessmann 2012). However, while all of these studies imply higher social relative to private returns to schooling, several studies reject different returns empirically (for example, Krueger and Lindahl 2001), suggesting that there might be a nontrivial mapping from (quality) measures of schooling to the quality of the labor force.

Other explanations focus on transmission channels for the diffusion of technologies that differ across countries, such as trade (Caselli and Wilson 2004; Eaton and Kortum 2002; Grossman and Helpman 1995; Keller 2002) and foreign direct investment (Antras and Helpman 2004; Javorcik 2004; Keller and Yeaple 2009; Larrain, Lopez-Calva, and Rodriguez-Clare 2000; Rodriguez-Clare 1996; Xu 2000). Other factors that have been shown to affect (distort) the incentives of firms to adopt superior foreign technologies include macroeconomic volatility (Acemoglu and Zilibotti 1997; Aghion et al. 2010), financial development (Benhabib and Spiegel 2000; Levine, Loayza, and Beck 2000), product market competition (Aghion et al. 2001; Aghion et al. 2005; Aghion et al. 2009); industrial or innovation policy (Grossman and Helpman 1995; Hausmann and Rodrik 2003); and institutional barriers to technology adoption (Acemoglu, Johnson, and Robinson 2002, 2005; Bloom et al. 2013; Faccio 2006; Fisman 2001; Parente and Prescott 1999).

II. Efficiency in Resource Allocation
A parallel strand in the literature focuses on cross-country differences in resource allocation within or across industries to explain differences in TFP. These contributions document that resources in low- and middle-income countries are over-proportionally allocated toward sectors with lower productivity. McMillan and Rodrik (2011) and Rodrik (2013a) show that such misallocations of labor across sectors, in particular a decline in the manufacturing sector, lead to productivity differences across countries. Similarly, Arnold et al. (2012) reveal strategic links between subsectors in the economy that matter for firm productivity growth. Bartelsman, Haltiwanger, and Scarpetta (2013); Hsieh and Klenow (2012); and Restuccia and Rogerson (2008) show the extent to which the allocation of resources across heterogeneous firms induces aggregate cross-country TFP differences. Hsieh and Klenow (2012) reveal substantial differences in productivity growth over the life cycle of firms in India, Mexico, and the United States.

Although the empirical significance and theoretical underpinnings of cross-country differences in resource allocation are by now well established, most approaches fall short in mapping these distortions to specific policies. The fundamental question arises: Are policy distortions leading to resource misallocation across firms any different from policies affecting firms' incentives to adopt new technologies?

Understanding the Income and Efficiency Gap in Latin America and the Caribbean
http://dx.doi.org/10.1596/978-1-4648-0450-2

III. Managerial Quality

Finally, other approaches argue that differences in the organizational efficiency of firms across countries lead to cross-country TFP differences. In particular, Bloom and Van Reenen (2007) and Bloom et al. (2013) attempt to measure cross-country differences in managerial efficiency based on surveys of management practices and find that managerial efficiency varies significantly across firms in different countries.

Notes

1. See Caselli (2008): "Level accounting (more recently known as development accounting) consists of a set of calculations whose purpose is to find the relative contributions of differences in inputs and differences in efficiency with which inputs are used to cross-country differences in GDP. It is therefore the cross-country analogue of growth accounting" (p. 1, online version).

2. See Caselli, chapter 2 in this volume.

3. The domestic productivity frontier is defined as the average productivity of the top decile of firms, in sales per worker, in an economy or sector. The same indicator for the United States is the proxy for the international frontier.

4. See a review of the literature in annex 1B. See also Cole et al. (2005), Daude and Fernandez-Arias (2010), Ferreira, Pessoa, and Veloso (2012), and Loayza, Fajnzylber, and Calderon (2004).

5. Caselli, chapter 2 in this volume, considers several calibrations to arrive at the estimates of relative capital and relative efficiency for LAC countries. The capital and efficiency gaps vary depending on the sample (defined by data availability) and whether quality of human capital measures is taken into account. Relative efficiency estimates for LAC vary between 0.44 (broad sample, baseline calibration) and 0.6 (narrow sample, aggressive calibration). Broad sample estimates are used throughout the overview.

6. For each country, this exercise calculates the actual income per worker (based on actual factor accumulation and efficiency) relative to the United States and the counterfactual income per worker (based on actual factor accumulation) relative to the United States for 2005. The counterfactual income level is a hypothetical income level for LAC economies, assuming that they used their physical and human capital as efficiently as the United States. The actual income per worker in LAC amounts on average to one-fifth of the U.S. level; the difference compared with the counterfactual income level can be used to determine the size of the efficiency gap.

7. See Akcigit et al. (2014) and Comin and Hobijn (2010).

8. See McMillan and Rodrik (2011) and Rodrik (2013b).

9. See Hsieh and Klenow (2009), Iacovone and Crespi (2010), and IDB (2010).

10. The innovation-related hypotheses come from a large literature on returns to innovation, including, more recently, Elmslie and Tebaldi (2014).

11. The hypothesis that poverty is an impediment to convergence builds on the findings of Crespo-Cuaresma, Klasen, and Wacker (2013) and Ravallion (2012), and the literature on poverty traps.

12. See Nguyen and Jaramillo, chapter 6 in this volume (based on a sample of 1,229 firms in LAC and 2,526 firms in ECA, from the World Bank Enterprise Survey).

13. By technological makeup, we mean the level of the available technology and the ability to use it effectively. We also mean whether the technology is up to date.

14. See Schiffbauer, Sahnoun, and Araujo, chapter 4 in this volume, for detailed evidence.

15. Following Hsieh and Klenow (2009).

16. The productivity frontier is defined as the mean of the top quartile of the firm-level distribution of value added per employee. The U.S. frontier is taken as a proxy for the international productivity frontier.

17. See Brown et al., chapter 5 in this volume. We chose Colombia and Mexico because the appropriate data were available at the time of the study.

18. Although their share is quite different across industries.

19. Innovation was defined as firm-level expenditure shares in innovation and investments in capital equipment.

20. Innovation is an introduction of a line or a product that is new to a firm, but does not necessarily represent innovation at the technological frontier.

21. This result is for a pulled sample of the ECA and LAC (including only Brazil, Ecuador, Guatemala, Honduras, and Nicaragua) regions. See Nguyen and Jaramillo, chapter 6 in this volume.

22. In a spin-off of the model in Akcigit et al. (2014) and Eden and Nguyen, chapter 3 in this volume. Akcigit et al. (2014) show that technology adoption incentives decrease with the level of distortions in the economy, which they call "static wedges" and proxy by misallocation and competitiveness. They also show that the distance to the world knowledge frontier is positively affected by static wedges.

23. The exceptions were Costa Rica and Mexico. High productivity in the services sectors explains why structural change contributed to aggregate productivity growth in these economies.

24. For example, workers may not have the necessary education or skills, or they may not be able to move to another part of the country, or they may not be aware of opportunities.

25. Wacker, chapter 7 in this volume, and Crespo-Cuaresma, Klasen, and Wacker (2013).

26. Dixit and Rob (1994). Most countries in the region had relatively liberalized capital accounts—which gave rise to boom and bust cycles (aside from Dutch-disease type effects on economic structure)—while being less open to trade in goods and services, which could help mitigate the adverse effect of volatility on growth (see Kose, Prasad, and Terrones 2006). Notably, the situation in East Asia was quite the reverse.

27. In several ways, these results complement the findings and conclusions of the 2010 IDB flagship *The Age of Productivity* (IDB 2010). Although the present volume finds that addressing resource allocation issues would play a significant role in addressing the efficiency gap, in line with the IDB flagship, it also shows the criticality (and the costs) of innovation for firm-level convergence as well as the importance of reducing macroeconomic volatility for the simultaneous pursuit of growth and equity.

28. Furthermore, as shown by other research, TFP can be interpreted as a measure of aggregate welfare, and TFP comparisons across countries and time would proxy for welfare comparisons along the same dimensions. See Basu et al. (2012).

29. As noted by Jones (2015): "Development accounting tells us that poor countries have low levels of inputs, but they are also remarkably inefficient in how they use those inputs. Misallocation provides the theoretical connection between the myriad of

distortions in poor economies and the TFP differences that we observe in development accounting" (p. 55).

30. For a similar approach applied to the case of Brazil, see World Bank (2014b).

31. Rodrik (2013a, p. 53): "(...) some service industries may be acquiring manufacturing-like properties (...) If such service activities are also subject to absolute productivity convergence, as seems plausible, they could act as the escalator industries of the future." See also Ghani and O'Connell (2014).

32. See World Bank (2013): "At any rate, rather than completely discarding it as an undesired Dutch Disease by-product, proactive development policies should embrace sophisticated services as crucial to the Latin American path to sustainable development" (p. 45).

33. Silva and Ferreira (2013) argue that low growth in the tertiary sector explains much of the divergence between LAC and the United States after 1980.

34. Examples of distortions include credit market failures that prevent firms from investing in "lumpy" and risky innovations and labor market rigidities that act as barriers to new technology adoption. See Maloney and Rodriguez-Clare (2007).

35. This does not mean that vertical policies cannot be effective in some contexts. However, the appropriateness of vertical approaches is not addressed in this volume.

36. Therefore, by incorporating equity and volatility concerns, development policy design needs to go beyond the incomplete agenda of the Washington Consensus for growth in LAC. See Birdsall, de la Torre, and Caicedo (2010).

37. Prepared by Marc Schiffbauer.

Bibliography

Acemoglu, D. 2008. "Growth and Institutions." In *Economic Growth. The New Palgrave Economics Collection*, edited by S. N. Durlauf and L. E. Blume. New York: Palgrave MacMillan.

Acemoglu, D., S. Johnson, and J. Robinson. 2002. "Reversal of Fortune: Geography and Institutions in the Making of the Modern World Income Distribution." *Quarterly Journal of Economics* 107: 1231–94.

———. 2005. "Institutions as a Fundamental Cause of Long-Run Growth." In *Handbook of Economic Growth 1*, edited by P. Aghion and S. Durlauf 385–472. San Diego, CA: Elsevier.

Acemoglu, D., and F. Zilibotti. 1997. "Was Prometheus Unbound by Chance? Risk, Diversification, and Growth." *Journal of Political Economy* 105: 709–51.

———. 2001. "Productivity Differences." *Quarterly Journal of Economics* 116: 563–606.

Aghion, P. 2008. "Schumpeterian Growth and Growth Policy Design." In *The New Palgrave Dictionary of Economics*. Online version. http://www.dictionaryofeconomics.com/dictionary.

Aghion, P., G.-M. Angeletos, A. Banerjee, and K. Manova. 2010. "Volatility and Growth: Financial Development and the Cyclical Composition of Investment." *Journal of Monetary Economics* 57 (3): 246–65.

Aghion, P., N. Bloom, R. Blundell, R. Griffith, and P. Howitt. 2005. "Competition and Innovation: An Inverted-U Relationship." *Quarterly Journal of Economics* 120 (2): 701–28.

Aghion, P., R. Blundell, R. Griffith, P. Howitt, and S. Prantl. 2009. "The Effects of Entry on Incumbent Innovation and Productivity." *Review of Economics and Statistics* 91 (1): 20–32.

Aghion, P., and S. Durlauf, eds. 2005. *Handbook of Economic Growth*, Volumes 1 and 2. San Diego, CA: Elsevier.

Aghion, P., and P. Howitt. 1992. "A Model of Growth through Creative Destruction." *Econometrica* 60 (March): 323–406.

Aghion, P., C. Harris, P. Howitt, and J. Vickers. 2001. "Competition, Imitation and Growth with Step-by-Step Innovation." *Review of Economic Studies* 68 (3) 467–92.

Akcigit, Ufuk, Harun Alp, Maya Eden, and Ha Nguyen. 2014. "Identifying Technology Adoption Lags from Macro Data." Development Economics Department, World Bank, Washington, DC.

Antras, P., and E. Helpman. 2004. "Global Sourcing." *Journal of Political Economy* 112: 552–80.

Arnold, J. M., B. Javorcik, M. Lipscomb, and A. Mattoo. 2012. "Services Reform and Manufacturing Performance: Evidence from India." Policy Research Working Paper 5948, World Bank, Washington, DC.

Artuç, E., D. Lederman, and G. Porto. 2013. "A Mapping of Labor Mobility Costs in Developing Countries." Policy Research Working Paper 6556, World Bank, Washington, DC.

Ball, Laurence. 2014. "Long-Term Damage from the Great Recession in OECD Countries." NBER Working Paper 20185, National Bureau of Economic Research, Cambridge, MA.

Barro, R., and J. W. Lee. 2010. "A New Data Set of Educational Attainment in the World, 1950–2010." NBER Working Paper 15902, National Bureau of Economic Research, Cambridge, MA.

Barro, R., and X. Sala-i-Martin. 1997. "Technology Diffusion, Convergence, and Growth." *Journal of Economic Growth* 2: 1–27.

Bartelsman, E., J. Haltiwanger, and S. Scarpetta. 2013. "Cross-Country Differences in Productivity: The Role of Allocation and Selection." *American Economic Review* 103 (1): 305–34.

Basu, S., L. Pascali, F. Schiantarelli, and L. Serven. 2012. "Productivity and the Welfare of Nations." NBER Working Paper 17971, National Bureau of Economic Research, Cambridge, MA.

Bénassy-Quéré, A., B. Coueré, P. Jacquet, and J. Pisani-Ferry. 2010. *Economic Policy: Theory and Practice*. Oxford: Oxford University Press.

Benhabib, J., and M. Spiegel. 1994. "The Role of Human Capital in Economic Development: Evidence from Aggregate Cross-Country Data." *Journal of Monetary Economics* 34: 143–73.

———. 2000. "The Role of Financial Development in Growth and Investment." *Journal of Economic Growth* 58 (5): 341–60.

———. 2005. "Human Capital and Technology Diffusion." In *Handbook of Economic Growth*, edited by P. Aghion and S. Durlauf. San Diego, CA: Elsevier.

Bernard, A., and C. Jones. 1996. "Comparing Apples and Oranges: Productivity Convergence and Measurement across Industries and Countries." *American Economic Review* 86 (5): 1216–38.

Birdsall, N., A. de la Torre, and F. V. Caicedo. 2010. "The Washington Consensus: Assessing a Damaged Brand." Policy Research Working Paper 5316, World Bank, Washington, DC.

Bloom, N., B. Eifert, A. Mahajan, D. McKenzie, and J. Roberts. 2013. "Does Management Matter? Evidence from India." *Quarterly Journal of Economics* 128 (1): 1–51.

Bloom, N., and J. Van Reenen. 2007. "Measuring and Explaining Management Practices across Firms and Countries." *Quarterly Journal of Economics* 122 (4): 1351–408.

Bloom, N., B. Eiffert, A. Mahajan, D. McKenzie, and J. Roberts. 2013. "Does Management Matter? Evidence from India." *Quarterly Journal of Economics* 128 (1): 1–51.

Bosworth, B., and S. Collins. 2003. "The Empirics of Growth: An Update." *Brookings Papers on Economic Activity* 34 (2): 113–206.

Brahmbhatt, Milan, and Albert Hu. 2010. "Ideas and Innovation in East Asia." *The World Bank Research Observer* 25 (2): 177–207.

Busse, M., and C. Spielmann. 2006. "Gender Inequality and Trade." *Review of International Economics* 14: 362–79.

Busso, M., L. Madrigal, and C. Pages. 2012. "Productivity and Resource Misallocation in Latin America." IDB-WP-306, Inter-American Development Bank, Washington, DC.

Cardenas, M., and S. M. Helfland. 2011. "Latin American Economic Development." In *The New Palgrave Dictionary of Economics Online*, edited by Steven N. Durlauf and Lawrence E. Blume. London: Palgrave Macmillan.

Caselli, F. 2005. "The Missing Input: Accounting for Cross-Country Income." In *Handbook of Economic Growth*, edited by P. Aghion and S. Durlauf. San Diego, CA: Elsevier.

———. 2008. "Level Accounting." In *New Palgrave Dictionary of Economics*. Online version. http://www.dictionaryofeconomics.com/dictionary.

Caselli, F., and J. Coleman. 2006. "The World Technology Frontier." *American Economic Review* 96: 499–522.

Caselli, F., and J. Feyrer. 2007. "The Marginal Product of Capital." *Quarterly Journal of Economics* 122 (2): 535–68.

Caselli, F., and D. Wilson. 2004. "Importing Technologies." *Journal of Monetary Economics* 51 (1): 1–32.

Cole, H. L., L. E. Ohanian, A. Riascos, and J. A. Schmitz, Jr. 2005. "Latin America in the Rearview Mirror." *Journal of Monetary Economics* 52 (1): 69–107.

Comin, D., and B. Hobijn. 2010. "An Exploration of Technology Diffusion." *American Economic Review* 100: 2031–59.

Crespo-Cuaresma, J., S. Klasen, and K. M. Wacker. 2013. "Why We Don't See Poverty Convergence: The Role of Macroeconomic Volatility." Courant Research Centre: Poverty, Equity, and Growth Discussion Paper 153, Georg-August University of Göttingen, Germany.

Daude, C., and E. Fernandez-Arias. 2010. "On the Role of Productivity and Factor Accumulation in Economic Development and the Caribbean." IDB Working Paper Series 155, Inter-American Development Bank, Washington, DC.

de Vries, K., M. P. Timmer, and G. J. de Vries. 2013. "Structural Transformation in Africa: Static Gains, Dynamic Losses." GGDC Research Memorandum GD-136, Groningen Growth and Development Centre, University of Groningen, Groningen, Netherlands.

Dixit, A., and R. Rob. 1994. "Switching Costs and Sectoral Adjustments in General Equilibrium with Uninsured Risk." *Journal of Economic Theory* 62 (1): 48–69.

Durlauf, S. N., and L. E. Blume, eds. 2006. *Economic Growth: The New Palgrave Economics Collection*. New York: Palgrave MacMillan.

———. 2011. *The New Palgrave Dictionary of Economics Online*. London: Palgrave Macmillan. http://www.dictionaryofeconomics.com/dictionary.

Eaton, J., and S. Kortum. 2002. "Technology, Geography, and Trade." *Econometrica* 70: 1741–79.

Elmslie, B., and E. Tebaldi. 2014. "Does Institutional Quality Impact Innovation? Evidence from Cross-Country Patent Grant Data." *Applied Economics* 45 (7): 887–900.

Faccio, M. 2006. "Politically Connected Firms." *American Economic Review* 96 (1): 369–86.

Feenstra, R. C., R. Inklaar, and M. Timmer. 2013. "The Next Generation of the Penn World Table." NBER Working Paper 19255, National Bureau of Economic Research, Cambridge, MA.

Ferreira, P.C., S.A. Pessoa, and F. Veloso. 2012. "On the Evolution of Total Factor Productivity in Latin America." *Economic Inquiry* 51 (1): 16–30.

Fisman, R. 2001. "Estimating the Value of Political Connections." *American Economic Review* 91: 1095–102.

Gaddis, I., and S. Klasen. 2014. "Economic Development, Structural Change, and Women's Labor Force Participation." *Journal of Population Economics* 27 (3): 639–81.

Ghani, E., and S. O'Connell. 2014. "Can Service Be a Growth Escalator in Low-Income Countries?" Policy Research Working Paper 6971, World Bank, Washington, DC.

Grossman, G., and E. Helpman. 1995. "Technology and Trade." In *Handbook of International Economics*, Volume 3, edited by Gene Grossman and Kenneth Rogoff. Amsterdam: North-Holland Publishers.

Harrison, A., and A. Rodriguez-Clare. 2010. "From Hard to Soft Industrial Policies in Developing Countries." Vox Research-based policy analysis and commentary from leading economists (online), June 27.

Hanushek, E., and D. Kimko. 2000. "Schooling, Labor-Force Quality, and the Growth of Nations." *American Economic Review* 90: 1184–208.

Hanushek, E., and L. Woessmann. 2012. "Schooling, Educational Achievement, and the Latin American Growth Puzzle." *Journal of Development Economics* 99: 497–512.

Hausmann, R., J. Hwang, and D. Rodrik. 2005. "What You Export Matters." NBER Working Paper 11905, National Bureau of Economic Research, Cambridge, MA.

Hausmann, R., and D. Rodrik. 2003. "Economic Development as Self-Discovery." *Journal of Development Economics* 72 (2): 603–33.

Heston, A., R. Summers, and B. Aten. 2012. "Penn World Table Version 7.1." Center for International Comparisons of Production, Income and Prices at the University of Pennsylvania, Philadelphia, PA.

Hidalgo, C. 2012. "The Dynamics of Economic Complexity and the Product Space over a 42 Year Period." CID Working Paper 189, Harvard.

Howitt, P. 2000. "Endogenous Growth and Cross-Country Income Differences." *American Economic Review* 90: 829–46.

Hsieh, C.-T., and P. J. Klenow. 2009. "Misallocation and Manufacturing TFP in China and India." *Quarterly Journal of Economics* 124 (4): 1403–48.

———. 2010. "Development Accounting." *Quarterly Journal of Economics* 124 (4): 1403–48.

———. 2012. "The Life Cycle of Plants in India and Mexico." *Quarterly Journal of Economics*. doi:10.1093/qje/qju014.

Iacovone, L., and G. Crespi. 2010. "Catching Up with the Technological Frontier: Micro-Level Evidence on Growth and Convergence." *Industrial and Corporate Change* 19 (6): 2073–96.

IDB (Inter-American Development Bank). 2010. *The Age of Productivity*. IDB Flagship Report. Washington, DC: Inter-American Development Bank.

Jankowska, A., A. Nagengast, and J. R. Perea. 2012. "The Product Space and the Middle-Income Trap: Comparing Asian and Latin American Experiences." OECD Development Centre Working Paper 311, Issy Les Moulineaux, France.

Javorcik, B. 2004. "Does Foreign Direct Investment Increase the Productivity of Domestic Firms? In Search of Spillovers through Backward Linkages." *American Economic Review* 94 (3): 605–27.

Jones, C. I. 2015. "The Facts of Economic Growth." Preliminary and incomplete manuscript, Stanford University, Stanford, CA.

Keller, W. 2002. "Geographic Localization of International Technology Diffusion." *American Economic Review* 92: 120–42.

———. 2004. "International Technology Diffusion." *Journal of Economic Literature* 52: 752–82.

Keller, W., and S. Yeaple. 2009. "Multinational Enterprises, International Trade, and Productivity Growth: Firm-Level Evidence from the United States." *Review of Economics and Statistics* 91 (4): 821–31.

Klasen, S. 2002. "Low Schooling for Girls, Slower Growth for All? Cross-Country Evidence on the Effect of Gender Inequality in Education on Economic Development." *World Bank Economic Review* 16 (3): 345–73.

Klasen, S., and F. Lamanna. 2009. "The Impact of Gender Inequality in Education and Employment on Economic Growth: New Evidence for a Panel of Countries." *Feminist Economics* 15 (3): 91–132.

Kose, A. M., E. S. Prasad, and M. E. Terrones. 2006. "How Do Trade and Financial Integration Affect the Relationship between Growth and Volatility?" *Journal of International Economics* 69 (1): 176–202.

Krueger, A., and M. Lindahl. 2001. "Education for Growth: Why and for Whom?" *Journal of Economic Literature* 39: 1101–36.

Larrain, B., L.-F. Lopez-Calva, and A. Rodriguez-Clare. 2000. "Intel: A Case Study of Foreign Direct Investment in Central America." Working Paper 58, Center for International Development, Harvard University, Cambridge, MA.

Lederman, D., and W. Maloney. 2012. *Does What You Export Matter? In Search of Empirical Guidance for Industrial Policies*. Washington, DC: World Bank.

Levine, R., N. Loayza, and T. Beck. 2000. "Finance and the Sources of Growth." *Journal of Financial Economics* 58: 261–300.

Lin, J. Y., and V. Treichel. 2012. "Learning from China's Rise to Escape the Middle-Income Trap: A New Structural Economics Approach to Latin America." Policy Research Working Paper 6165, World Bank, Washington, DC.

Loayza, N., P. Fajnzylber, and C. Calderon. 2004. "Economic Growth in Latin America and the Caribbean: Stylized Facts, Explanations, and Forecasts." Central Bank of Chile Working Papers 265, Santiago, Chile.

Lora, E., and C. Pages. 2011. "Face-to-Face with Productivity." *Finance and Development* 48 (1).

Lucas, R. 1988. "On the Mechanics of Economic Development." *Journal of Monetary Economics* 22: 3–42.

Maloney, W. 2002. "Missed Opportunities: Innovation and Resource-Based Growth in Latin America." Policy Research Working Paper 2935, World Bank, Washington, DC.

Maloney, W., and A. Rodriguez-Clare. 2007. "Innovation Shortfalls." *Review of Developing Economics* 11 (4): 665–84.

McMillan, M., and D. Rodrik. 2011. "Globalization, Structural Change, and Productivity Growth." NBER Working Paper 17143, National Bureau of Economic Research, Cambridge, MA.

Melo, A., and A. Rodriguez-Clare. 2006. "Productive Development Policies and Institutions in Latin America and the Caribbean." Working Paper C-106, Research Department Competitiveness Studies Series, Inter-American Development Bank, Washington, DC.

Nelson, R., and E. Phelps. 1966. "Investment in Humans, Technological Diffusion, and Economic Growth." *American Economic Review* 61: 69–75.

Parente, S., and E. Prescott. 1999. "Monopoly Rights: A Barrier to Riches." *American Economic Review* 89: 1216–33.

Ramey, Garey, and Valerie A. Ramey. 1995. "Cross-Country Evidence on the Link between Volatility and Growth." *American Economic Review* 85 (5): 1138–51.

Ravallion, M. 2012. "Why Don't We See Poverty Convergence?" *American Economic Review* 102: 504–23.

Restuccia, D., and R. Rogerson. 2008. "Policy Distortions and Aggregate Productivity with Heterogeneous Plants." *Review of Economic Dynamics* 11: 707–20.

Rodriguez-Clare, A. 1996. "Multinationals, Linkages, and Economic Development." *American Economic Review* (86): 852–73.

Rodrik, D. 2011. "Unconditional Convergence." NBER Working Paper 17546, National Bureau of Economic Research, Cambridge, MA.

———. 2013a. "The Past, Present, and Future of Economic Growth." Working Paper No. 1, Global Citizen Foundation.

———. 2013b. "Unconditional Convergence in Manufacturing." *Quarterly Journal of Economics* 128 (1): 165–204.

Romer, P. 1990. "Endogenous Technological Change." *Journal of Political Economy* 98: S71–S102.

Silva, L. F., and P.C. Ferreira. 2013. "Structural Transformation and Productivity in Latin America." Mimeo, Fundação Getúlio Vargas, Rio de Janeiro, Brazil.

Timmer, M. P., and G. J. de Vries. 2009. "Structural Change and Growth Accelerations in Asia and Latin America: A New Sectoral Data Set." *Cliometrica* 3 (2): 165–90.

World Bank. 2000. *Beyond Economic Growth: Meeting the Challenges of Economic Development*. Washington, DC: World Bank.

———. 2011a. *Latin America and the Caribbean's Long-Term Growth: Made in China?* Washington, DC: World Bank.

———. 2011b. *On the Edge of Uncertainty: Poverty Reduction in Latin America and the Caribbean during the Great Recession and Beyond*. Washington, DC: World Bank.

———. 2011c. *World Development Report 2012: Gender Equality and Development*. Washington, DC: World Bank.

———. 2013. *Latin America and the Caribbean as Tailwinds Recede: In Search of Higher Growth*. Washington, DC: World Bank.

———. 2014a. *Diversified Development: Making the Most of Natural Resources in Eurasia*. Washington, DC: World Bank.

———. 2014b. *Implications of a Changing China to Brazil: A New Window of Opportunity?* Washington, DC: World Bank.

Wright, G., and J. Czelusta. 2006. "Resource-Based Growth Past and Present." In *Natural Resources: Neither Curse nor Destiny*, edited by D. Lederman and W. Maloney. Palo Alto, CA: Stanford University Press.

Xu, B. 2000. "Multinational Enterprises, Technology Diffusion, and Host Country Productivity Growth." *Journal of Development Economics* 62: 477–93.

CHAPTER 2

The Latin American Efficiency Gap

Francesco Caselli

Introduction

The average Latin American country produces about one-fifth of the output per worker of the United States. What are the sources of these enormous *income gaps*? This chapter reports development accounting results for Latin America. Development accounting compares differences in income per worker between low- and middle-income countries and high-income countries with counterfactual differences attributable to observable components of physical and human capital. Such calculations can serve a useful preliminary diagnostic role before engaging in deeper and more detailed explorations of the fundamental determinants of differences in income per worker. If differences in physical and human capital—or *capital gaps*—are sufficient to explain most of the difference in incomes, then researchers and policy makers need to focus on factors holding back investment (in machines and people). Instead, if differences in capital are insufficient to account for most of the variation in income, it must be concluded that low- and middle-income countries are also hampered by relatively low efficiency at using their inputs—*efficiency gaps*. The research and policy agenda would then have to focus on technology, allocative efficiency, competition, and other determinants of the efficient use of capital.[1]

This chapter presents development accounting results for 2005 for three samples of Latin American countries: a broad sample of 22 countries, a narrow sample of nine countries, and an intermediate sample of 15 countries.

The three samples differ in the data available to measure human capital. In the broad sample, human capital is measured in the context of a Mincerian framework, where the key inputs are schooling (years of education) and health (as proxied by the adult survival rate). In the narrow and intermediate samples, I augment the Mincerian framework with measures of cognitive skills, to account for additional factors such as schooling quality, parental inputs, and other influences on human capital not captured by years of schooling and health. The measures of cognitive skills are based on tests administered to school-age children. In the narrow sample, the test is a science test whose results are directly comparable between Latin America and the benchmark high-income country.

In the intermediate sample, the tests were only administered in Latin America and can be compared with the benchmark country only on the basis of some ad hoc assumptions.

In all three samples, I measure physical capital as an aggregate of reproducible and natural capital. Reproducible capital includes equipment and structures, while natural capital primarily includes subsoil resources, arable land, and timber.

Given measures of physical capital gaps, as well as gaps in the components of human capital, development accounting uses a calibration to map these gaps into counterfactual income gaps, or the income gaps that would be observed based on differences in human and capital endowments only. Because these counterfactual incomes are bundles of physical and human capital, I refer to the ratio of Latin American counterfactual incomes to the U.S. counterfactual income as *relative capital.*

For each of the three samples, I present results from two alternative calibrations, a baseline calibration and an aggressive calibration. The baseline calibration makes use of the existing body of microeconomic estimates of the Mincerian framework in the way that most closely fits the theoretical framework of development accounting. As it turns out, this leads to coefficients for the components of human capital that are substantially lower than in much existing work in development accounting, leading to relatively smaller estimated capital gaps and, correspondingly, larger efficiency gaps. The aggressive calibration thus uses more conventional figures as a robustness check.

When I use my benchmark calibration, irrespective of sample/cognitive skill correction, I find that relative capital and relative efficiencies are almost identical. For example, in the broad sample, average relative capital and average relative efficiency are both 44 percent—or roughly double actual average relative incomes. Hence, capital gaps and efficiency gaps are very large: the average Latin American country has less than half the capital (human and physical) per worker of the United States, and uses it less than half as efficiently.

Using the aggressive calibration, capital gaps are naturally larger, and efficiency gaps correspondingly smaller. Nevertheless, even under this best-case scenario for the view that capital gaps are the key source of income gaps, average Latin American efficiency is at most 60 percent of the U.S. level, still implying a vast efficiency gap.

In assessing this evidence, it is essential to bear in mind that efficiency gaps contribute to income disparity directly—as they mean that Latin America gets less out of its capital—and indirectly—since much of the capital gap itself is likely caused by diminished incentives to invest in equipment, structures, schooling, and health, because of low efficiency. The consequences of closing the efficiency gap would correspondingly be far reaching.

Explaining the Latin American efficiency gap is therefore a high priority for scholars and policy makers. It is likely that this task will require firm-level evidence. Firm-level evidence would also be invaluable in checking the robustness of the development accounting results, which are subject to severe data quality limitations.

Conceptual Framework

The analytical tool at the core of development accounting is the aggregate production function. The aggregate production function maps aggregate input quantities into output. The main inputs considered are physical capital and human capital. The empirical literature so far has failed to uncover compelling evidence that aggregate input quantities deliver large external economies, so it is usually deemed safe to assume constant returns to scale.[2] Given this assumption, the production function can be expressed in intensive form, that is, by specifying all input and output quantities in per worker terms.

To construct counterfactual incomes, a functional form is needed. Existing evidence suggests that the share of capital in income does not vary systematically with the level of development, or with factor endowments (Gollin 2002). Hence, most practitioners of development accounting opt for a Cobb-Douglas specification. In sum, the production function for country i is

$$y_i = A_i k_i^\alpha h_i^{1-\alpha}, \tag{2.1}$$

where y is output per worker, k is physical capital per worker, h is human capital per worker (quality-adjusted labor), and A captures unmeasured/unobservable factors that contribute to differences in output per worker.

The variable A is subject to much speculation and controversy. Practitioners refer to it as total factor productivity, technology, a measure of our ignorance, etc. Here I will refer to it as efficiency. Countries with a larger A are countries that, for whatever reasons, are more efficient users of their physical and human capital.

The goal of development accounting is to assess the relative importance of efficiency differences and physical and human capital differences in producing the differences in income per worker we observe in the data. To this end, counterfactual incomes, or capital bundles, are constructed as

$$\tilde{y}_i = k_i^\alpha h_i^{1-\alpha}, \tag{2.2}$$

which are based exclusively on the observable inputs. Differences in these capital bundles are then compared with income differences. If counterfactual and actual income differences are similar, then observable factors are able to account for the bulk of the variation in income. If they are quite different, then differences in efficiency are important. Establishing how significant efficiency differences are has important repercussions for research and policy.

To construct the counterfactual $\tilde{y}$ values, we need to construct measures of k_i and h_i, as well as calibrate the capital share parameter α. Standard practice sets the latter to 0.33, and we stick to this practice throughout. Annex 2A presents robustness checks using a larger capital share, that is, 0.40. This higher share implies somewhat larger capital gaps and somewhat smaller efficiency gaps, although the main message of the paper is unchanged.[3]

The rest of this section focuses on the measurement of physical and human capital.

Understanding the Income and Efficiency Gap in Latin America and the Caribbean
http://dx.doi.org/10.1596/978-1-4648-0450-2

Existing development accounting calculations measure k exclusively on the basis of *reproducible* capital (equipment and structures). But in most low- and middle-income countries, where agricultural and mining activities still represent large shares of gross domestic product (GDP), natural capital (land, timber, ore, etc.) is also very important. Caselli and Feyrer (2007) show that omitting natural capital can lead to very significant understatements of total capital in low- and middle-income countries relative to high-income countries. Hence, this study will measure k as the sum of the value of all reproducible and natural capital.

Human capital per worker can vary across countries as a result of differences in knowledge, skills, health, etc. The literature identifies three variables that vary across countries and that may capture significant differences in these dimensions: years of schooling (Hall and Jones 1999; Klenow and Rodriguez-Clare 1997), health (Weil 2007), and cognitive skills (Hanushek and Woessmann 2012b). To bring these together, the following model is postulated for human capital:

$$h_i = \exp(\beta_s s_i + \beta_r r_i + \beta_t t_i). \tag{2.3}$$

In this equation, s_i measures average years of schooling in the working-age population, r_i is a measure of health in the population, and t_i is a measure of cognitive skills. The coefficients β_s, β_r, and β_t map differences in the corresponding variables into differences in human capital.[4]

The model in equation 2.3 is attractive because it offers a strategy for calibration of the parameters β_s, β_r, and β_t. In particular, combining equations 2.1, 2.3, and an assumption that wages are proportional to the marginal productivity of labor, we obtain the Mincerian formulation

$$\log(w_{ij}) = \alpha_i + \beta_s s_{ij} + \beta_r r_{ij} + \beta_t t_{ij}, \tag{2.4}$$

where w_{ij} (s_{ij}, etc.) is the wage (years of schooling, etc.) of worker j in country i, and α_i is a country-specific term.[5] This suggests that by using within-country variation in wages, schooling, health, and cognitive skills, one might in principle identify the coefficients β. In practice, there are severe limitations in following this strategy, which will be discussed after introducing the data.

Data

There are three samples: broad, narrow, and intermediate. The broad data set contains all Latin American countries for which data are available for y, k, s, and r, all observed in 2005. There are 22 such countries (excluded are Barbados, Cuba, and Paraguay, for which there are no capital data). The other two samples add alternative measures of t. The trade-off is that one measure offers a more credible comparison with the benchmark high-income country, but is only available for nine Latin American economies. The more dubious but more plentiful measure is available for 15 countries. All but one of the countries in the narrow sample are also in the intermediate sample (Trinidad and Tobago is the exception).

The data set also includes data from the United States, which is used as the benchmark high-income country.

Per-worker income y_i is variable *rgdpwok* from version 7.1 of the Penn World Tables. Figure 2.1 shows per-worker income in each country in the broad sample relative to the United States, or y_i/y_{US}. Countries that are also included in the narrow sample are in green, and countries that are in the intermediate but not the narrow sample are in orange. With the exception of Trinidad and Tobago, all Latin American countries have per-worker incomes well below 40 percent of the U.S. level, sometimes much below. The horizontal lines in the figure show the three (unweighted) sample averages, indicating that the average country is only one-fifth as productive as the United States.[6]

World Bank (2012) presents cross-section estimates of the *total* capital stock, k, as well as its components, for various years. The total capital stock includes reproducible capital, but also land, timber, mineral deposits, and other items that are not included in standard national accounts–based data sets. The basic strategy of the World Bank team that constructed these data begins with estimates of the rental flows accruing from different types of natural capital, which are then capitalized using fixed discount rates. I construct the total capital measure by adding the variables *producedplusurban* and *natcap*.

Measuring the total capital stock as the sum of natural and reproducible capital amounts to an assumption of perfect substitutability between the two

Figure 2.1 Income per Worker Relative to the United States

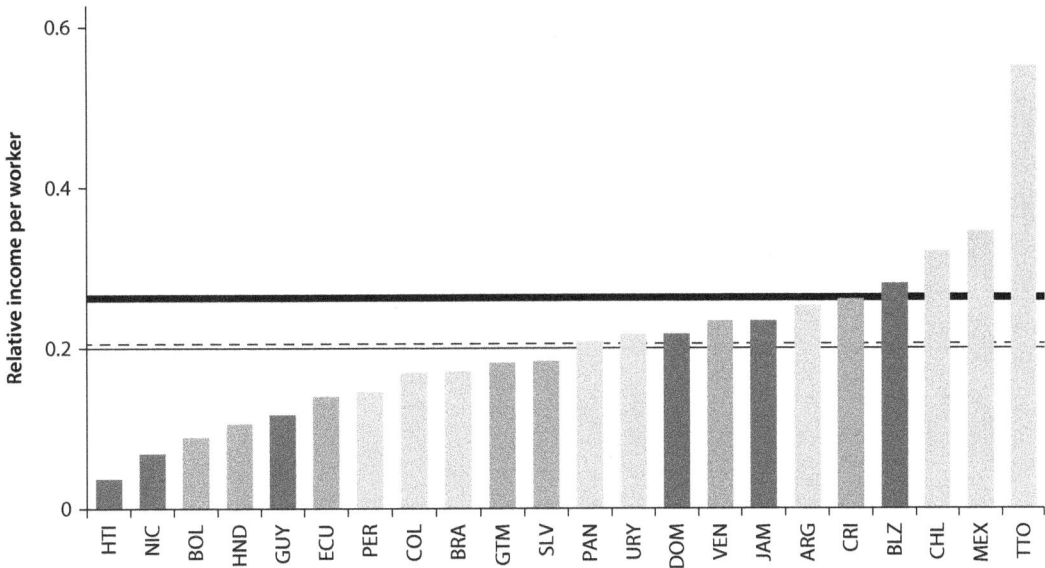

Source: Penn World Tables version 7.1.
Note: Blue bars: only broad sample. Orange bars: only broad and intermediate samples. Green bars: all samples (except Trinidad and Tobago not in intermediate). Dashed line: broad sample mean. Light solid line: intermediate sample mean. Heavy solid line: narrow sample mean.
ARG = Argentina; BLZ = Belize; BOL = Bolivia; BRA = Brazil; CHL = Chile; COL = Colombia; CRI = Costa Rica; DOM = Dominican Republic; ECU = Ecuador; GTM = Guatemala; GUY = Guyana; HND = Honduras; HTI = Haiti; JAM = Jamaica; MEX = Mexico; NIC = Nicaragua; PAN = Panama; PER = Peru; SLV = El Salvador; TTO = Trinidad and Tobago; URY = Uruguay; VEN = República Bolivariana de Venezuela.

Understanding the Income and Efficiency Gap in Latin America and the Caribbean
http://dx.doi.org/10.1596/978-1-4648-0450-2

capital types. To evaluate this assumption, it is useful to conceive of GDP as the sum of the added values of the primary sector (essentially agriculture and mining), where natural capital is heavily used, and of the secondary and tertiary sectors (essentially manufacturing and services), where natural capital plays virtually no role. Then, perfect substitutability is most defensible if the primary sector uses little or no reproducible capital, or if the primary sector is a relatively small share of the economy. Admittedly, the former assumption is not particularly credible, while the latter clearly does not apply to the typical Latin American country. Intuitively, though, this should result in an overestimate of the capital gap, and consequently an underestimate of the efficiency gap. If the primary sector is large and reproducible capital plays a significant role in the primary sector, reproducible capital and natural capital should boost each other's productivity, resulting in a larger capital bundle than in the case when they are perfect substitutes. In other words, by assuming perfect substitutability, the analysis underestimates the total contribution of capital more in poorer Latin American countries than in the richer benchmark country.

Figure 2.2 shows total (reproducible plus natural) capital per worker estimates for Latin American countries relative to the United States, k_i/k_{US}. The average Latin American worker is endowed with approximately one-fifth of the physical capital of the average U.S. worker.

Figure 2.2 Physical Capital per Worker Relative to the United States

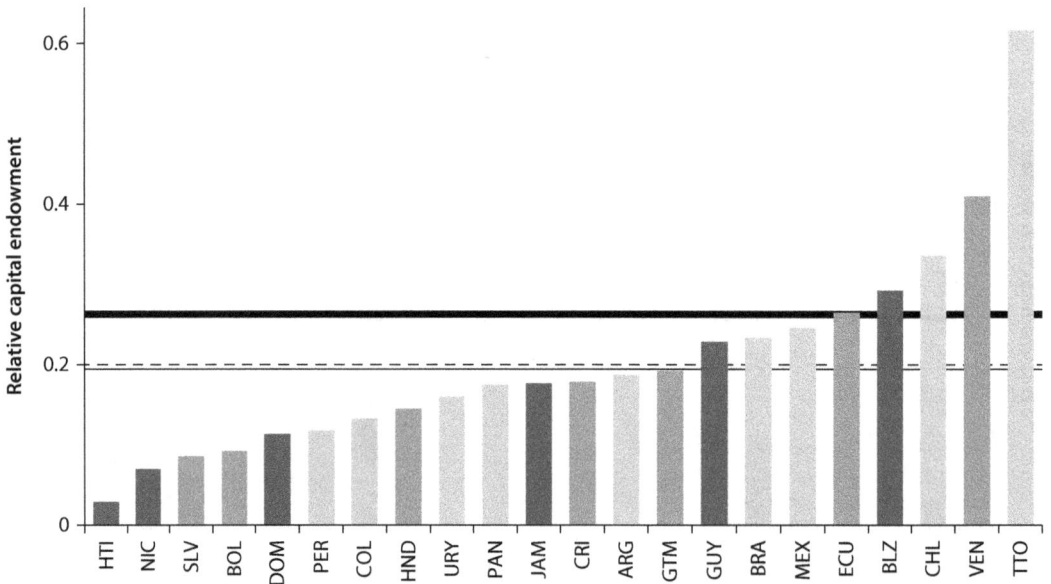

Source: World Bank 2012.
Note: Blue bars: only broad sample. Orange bars: only broad and intermediate samples. Green bars: all samples (except Trinidad and Tobago not in intermediate). Dashed line: broad sample mean. Light solid line: intermediate sample mean. Heavy solid line: narrow sample mean.
ARG = Argentina; BLZ = Belize; BOL = Bolivia; BRA = Brazil; CHL = Chile; COL = Colombia; CRI = Costa Rica; DOM = Dominican Republic;
ECU = Ecuador; GTM = Guatemala; GUY = Guyana; HND = Honduras; HTI = Haiti; JAM = Jamaica; MEX = Mexico; NIC = Nicaragua; PAN = Panama;
PER = Peru; SLV = El Salvador; TTO = Trinidad and Tobago; URY = Uruguay; VEN = República Bolivariana de Venezuela.

Figure 2.3 Differences in Years of Schooling Compared with the United States

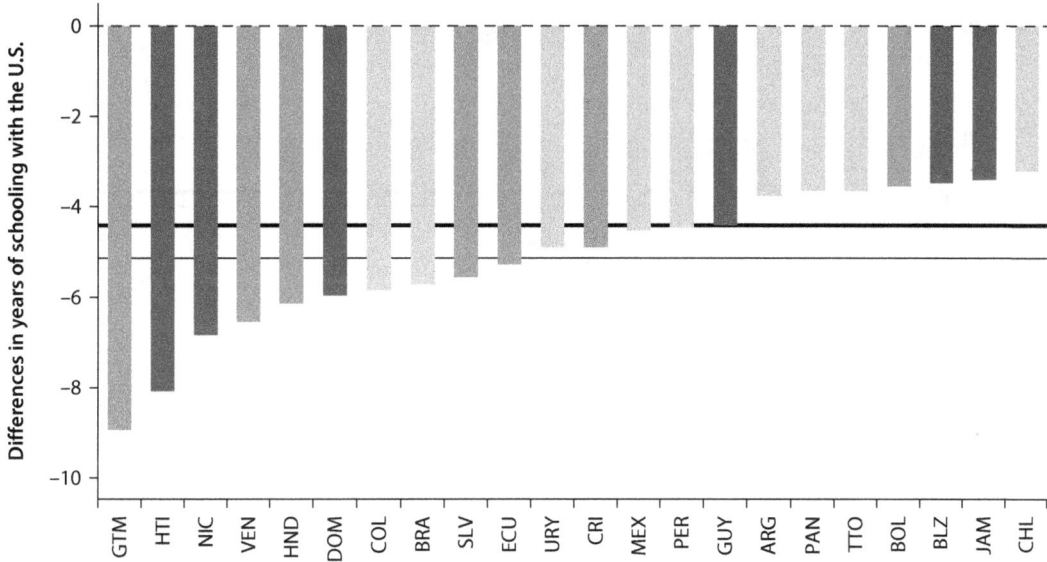

Source: Barro and Lee 2013.
Note: Blue bars: only broad sample. Orange bars: only broad and intermediate samples. Green bars: all samples (except Trinidad and Tobago not in intermediate). Dashed line: broad sample mean. Light solid line: intermediate sample mean. Heavy solid line: narrow sample mean.
ARG = Argentina; BLZ = Belize; BOL = Bolivia; BRA = Brazil; CHL = Chile; COL = Colombia; CRI = Costa Rica; DOM = Dominican Republic; ECU = Ecuador; GTM = Guatemala; GUY = Guyana; HND = Honduras; HTI = Haiti; JAM = Jamaica; MEX = Mexico; NIC = Nicaragua; PAN = Panama; PER = Peru; SLV = El Salvador; TTO = Trinidad and Tobago; URY = Uruguay; VEN = República Bolivariana de Venezuela.

For average years of schooling in the working-age population (which is defined as between 15 and 99 years of age), I rely on Barro and Lee (2013). From equation 2.3, for the purposes of constructing *relative* human capital h_i/h_{US} what is relevant is the *difference* in years of schooling s_i–s_{US}. The same will be true for r and t. Accordingly, Figure 2.3 plots schooling-year differences compared with the United States in 2005. Latin American workers always have at least three year less schooling than American workers, and five years less on average.

As a proxy for the health status of the population, r, Weil (2007) proposes using the *adult survival rate*. The adult survival rate is a statistic computed from age-specific mortality rates at a point in time. It can be interpreted as the probability of reaching the age of 60 years, conditional on having reached the age of 15 years, *at current rates of age-specific mortality*. Since most mortality before age 60 is caused by illness, the adult survival rate is a reasonably good proxy for the overall health status of the population at a given point in time. Relative to more direct measures of health, the advantage of the adult survival rate is that it is available for a large cross-section of countries. I construct the adult survival rate from the World Bank's World Development Indicators. Specifically, this is the weighted average of male and female survival rates, weighted by the male and female shares in the population.

Figure 2.4 shows differences in the adult survival rate compared with the United States. Survival rate probabilities are lower in Latin America than in

Figure 2.4 Differences in Survival Rate Compared with the United States

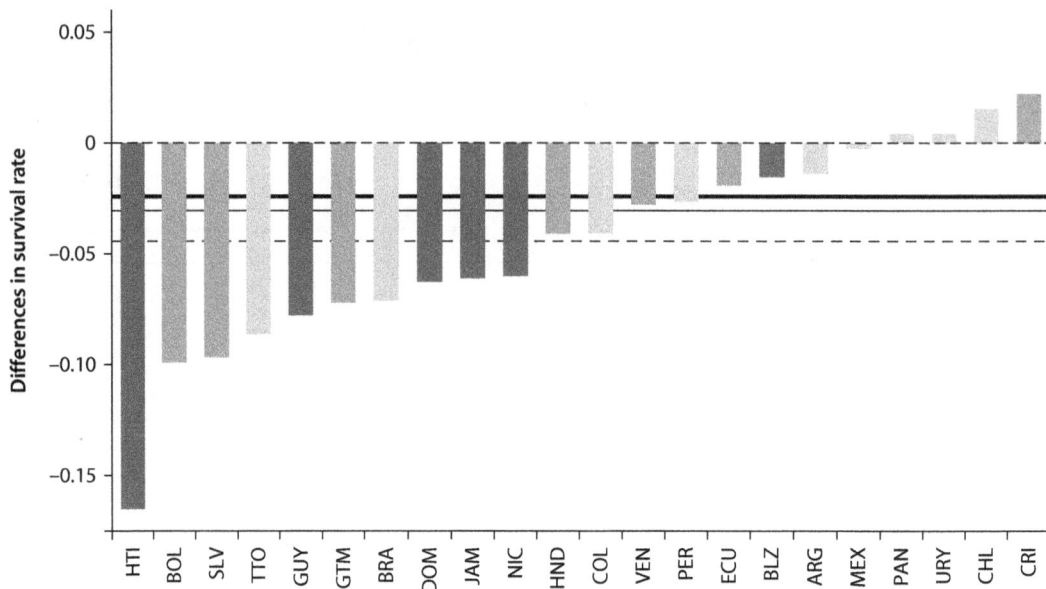

Source: World Development Indicators.
Note: Blue bars: only broad sample. Orange bars: only broad and intermediate samples. Green bars: all samples (except Trinidad and Tobago not in intermediate). Dashed line: broad sample mean. Light solid line: intermediate sample mean. Heavy solid line: narrow sample mean.
ARG = Argentina; BLZ = Belize; BOL = Bolivia; BRA = Brazil; CHL = Chile; COL = Colombia; CRI = Costa Rica; DOM = Dominican Republic;
ECU = Ecuador; GTM = Guatemala; GUY = Guyana; HND = Honduras; HTI = Haiti; JAM = Jamaica; MEX = Mexico; NIC = Nicaragua; PAN = Panama;
PER = Peru; SLV = El Salvador; TTO = Trinidad and Tobago; URY = Uruguay; VEN = República Bolivariana de Venezuela.

the United States, but perhaps not vastly so. On average, Latin American 15-year-olds are only 4 percentage points less likely to reach the age of 60 than U.S. 15-year-olds.[7]

Following work by Gundlach, Rudman, and Woessmann (2002); Hanushek and Woessmann (particularly 2012b); Jones and Schneider (2010); and Woessmann (2003), the analysis also accounts for differences in cognitive skills not already accounted for by years of schooling and health. The ideal measure would be a test of average cognitive ability in the working population. Hanushek and Zhang (2009) report estimates of one such test for a dozen countries, the International Adult Literacy Survey, but only one of the countries is in Latin America (Chile).

As a fallback, I rely on scores on internationally comparable tests taken by school-age children. In the narrow sample, I use scores from a science test administered in 2009 to 15-year-olds by the Program for International Student Assessment (PISA). There are in principle several other internationally comparable tests (by subject matter, year of testing, and organization testing) that could be used as an alternative to or in combination with the 2009 PISA science test. However, there would be virtually no gain in country coverage by using them or combining them with other years (the PISA tests of 2009 are the ones with the greatest participation, and virtually no Latin American country participated in other worldwide tests and not in the 2009 PISA tests).[8] Focusing only on one test bypasses the potentially thorny issues of aggregation across years, subjects, and methods of administration. Cross-country correlations in test results are very high anyway, and very stable over time.[9] Data on PISA test score results are from the World Bank's Education Statistics.

Aside from the worldwide tests of cognitive skills used in the narrow sample, there are also two regional tests of cognitive skills that have been administered to a group of Latin American countries. The first was in 1997 by the Laboratorio Latinoamericano de Evaluación de la Calidad de la Educación, covering reading and math in the third and fourth grades. The second was in 2006 by the Latin American bureau of the United Nations Educational, Scientific, and Cultural Organization, covering the same subjects in third and sixth grades. These tests are described in greater detail in Hanushek and Woessmann (2012b), who also argue that these tests may better reflect *within–Latin America* differences in cognitive skills.

From the perspective of this study, the main attraction of these alternative measures of cognitive skills is that they cover a significantly larger sample. The biggest problem, of course, is that they exclude the United States (or any high-income country) and so, on the face of it, they are unusable for constructing counterfactual relative incomes. However, Hanushek and Woessmann (2012b) propose a methodology to splice the regional scores into their worldwide sample. Although this splicing involves a large number of assumptions that are difficult to evaluate, it is worthwhile to assess the robustness of my results to these data.[10]

Measuring t by the above-described test scores is clearly very unsatisfactory, as in most cases the tests reflect the cognitive skills of individuals who have not joined the labor force as of 2005, much less those of the average worker. The average Latin American worker in 2005 was 36 years old, so to capture their cognitive skills, test scores from 1984 would be needed.[11] Implicitly, then, test score gaps in current children are interpreted as proxies for test score gaps in current workers. If Latin America and the United States have experienced different trends in cognitive skills of children since 1984, this assumption is problematic.

The 2009 PISA science tests are reported on a scale from 0 to 1,000, and they are normalized so that the average score *among OECD countries* (that is, among all pupils taking the test in this set of countries) is (approximately) 500 and the standard deviation is (approximately) 100.[12] The regional scores are put on the PISA scale by Hanushek and Woessmann's splicing, so they can be directly compared.

Figure 2.5 shows test score differences $(t_i - t_{US})$ for the narrow and intermediate samples. Differences in PISA scores are very significant: the average Latin American student in 2009 shows cognitive skills that are below those of his U.S. counterpart by about one standard deviation of the OECD distribution of cognitive skills. Only Chile is a partial standout, with a cognitive gap closer to one-half of one standard deviation. Differences in Hanushek and Woessmann's spliced regional tests are even more significant, with the average gap exceeding 1.5 standard deviations. The PISA scores are directly comparable between countries in

Understanding the Income and Efficiency Gap in Latin America and the Caribbean
http://dx.doi.org/10.1596/978-1-4648-0450-2

Figure 2.5 Differences in Test Scores Compared with the United States

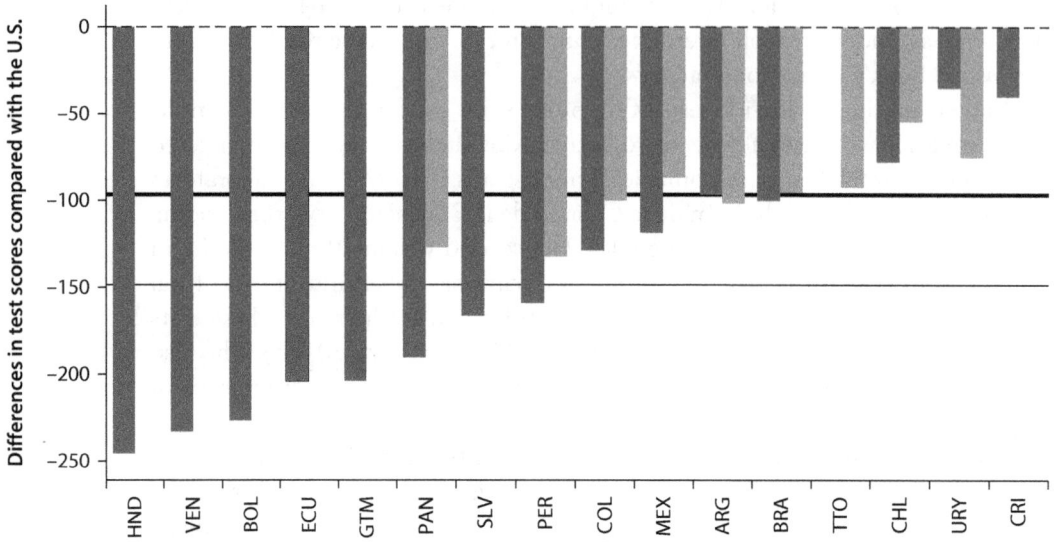

Sources: World Bank Education Statistics; Hanushek and Woessmann 2012a, 2012b.
Note: Blue bars: regional test/intermediate sample. Orange bars: PISA test/narrow sample. Light solid line: regional-test mean. Heavy solid line: PISA-test mean. PISA = Program for International Student Assessment; ARG = Argentina; BOL = Bolivia; BRA = Brazil; CHL = Chile; COL = Colombia; CRI = Costa Rica; ECU = Ecuador; GTM = Guatemala; HND = Honduras; MEX = Mexico; PAN = Panama; PER = Peru; SLV = El Salvador; TTO = Trinidad and Tobago; URY = Uruguay; VEN = República Bolivariana de Venezuela.

Latin America and the United States, while the spliced regional tests—while arguably giving a more accurate sense of within-Latin America differences—are less suitable for poor country–rich country comparisons. Hence, the discrepancy in cognitive skill gaps between the PISA and regional scores implies that the latter should be treated with caution.

Calibration

The last, and most difficult, step in producing counterfactual income gaps between the United States and Latin America is to calibrate the coefficients β_s, β_r, and β_t. As discussed, equation 2.4 indicates that, using *within-country* data on w, s, r, and t, in principle these coefficients could be identified by running an extended Mincerian regression for log-wages. In implementing this plan, we are confronted with (at least) two important problems.

The first problem is that one of the explanatory variables, the adult survival rate r, by definition does not vary within countries. Estimating β_r directly is therefore a logical impossibility. To solve this problem, Weil (2007) notices that, in the time series (for a sample of 10 countries for which the necessary data are available), there is a fairly tight relationship between the adult survival rate and average height. In other words, he postulates $c_i = \alpha_c + \gamma_c r_i$, where c_i is average height and the coefficient γ_c is estimated from the above-mentioned time-series relation (he obtains a coefficient of 19.2 in his preferred specification). Since height does vary within countries as well as between countries, this opens the way to identifying β_r by means of the Mincerian regression

$$\log(w_{ij}) = \alpha_i + \beta_s s_{ij} + \beta_c c_{ij} + \beta_t t_{ij},$$

where $\beta_r = \beta_c \gamma_c$.[13]

The second problem is that measures of t are not consistent at the macro and micro levels. In particular, although we have micro data sets reporting results from tests of cognitive skills and wages, the test in question is simply *a different test* from the tests we have available at the level of the cross-section of countries. Call the alternative test available at the micro level d. Once again the solution is to *assume* a linear relationship $d_i = \gamma_d t_i$. The difference with the case of the height–survival rate is that, as far as I know, there is no way to check the empirical plausibility of this assumption. Given the assumed linear relationship, γ_d can be backed out as the ratio of the *within-country* standard deviation of d_{ij} and t_{ij}. With γ_d at hand, β_t can be backed out from the modified Mincerian regression

$$\log(w_{ij}) = \alpha_i + \beta_s s_{ij} + \beta_c c_{ij} + \beta_d d_{ij}, \qquad (2.5)$$

using $\beta_t = \beta_d \gamma_d$.

In choosing values for β_s, β_c, and β_d from the literature, it is highly desirable to focus on microeconomic estimates of equation 2.5 that include all three right-hand variables. This is because s, c, and d are well-known to be highly positively correlated.[14] Hence, any ordinary least squares (OLS) estimate of one of the coefficients from a regression that omits one or two of the other two variables will be biased upward.[15]

A search of the literature yielded one and only one study reporting all three coefficients from equation 2.5. Vogl (2014) uses the two waves (2002 and 2005) of the nationally representative Mexican Family Life Survey to estimate equation 2.5 on a subsample of men ages 25–65 years. In his study, w is measured as hourly earnings, s as years of schooling, c is in centimeters, and d is the respondent's score on a cognitive skill test administered at the time of the survey.[16] The cognitive skill measure is scaled, so its standard deviation in the Mexican population is 1.[17]

The coefficients reported by Vogl are as follows (see his table 4, column 7). The return to schooling β_s is 0.072, which can be plugged directly into equation 2.3. The return to height β_c is 0.013. Hence, the coefficient associated with the adult survival rate in equation 2.3 is $0.013 \times 19.2 = 0.25$, where I have used Weil's mapping between height and the adult survival rate. Finally, the reported return to cognitive skills β_d is 0.011. Since the standard deviation of d is one by construction, and the standard deviation of the 2009 Science PISA test in Mexico is 77, the implied coefficient on the PISA test for the purpose of constructing h is $0.011/77 = 0.00014$.[18]

The coefficients in my baseline calibration are considerably lower than those used in other development accounting exercises. For schooling, applications usually gravitate toward the modal Mincerian coefficient of 0.10. For the adult survival rate, Weil (2007) uses 0.65, on the basis of considerably higher estimates of the returns to height than those reported by Vogl. For the return to cognitive skills, Hanushek and Woessmann (2012b) advocate 0.002, which is more than one order of magnitude larger than the value I derive from the Vogl estimates.[19]

The fact that the parameters calibrated on the Vogl estimates are smaller than those commonly used is consistent with the discussion in this chapter. In particular, the alternative estimates are often based on regressions that omit one or two of the variables in equation 2.5, and are therefore upward biased. Another consideration is that there is considerable cross-country heterogeneity in the estimates, and researchers often focus on estimates from the United States, which are often larger.[20,21]

However, Vogl's regressions are admittedly estimated via OLS, and there is a real concern with attenuation bias from measurement error. To gauge the sensitivity of my results to possibly excessively low values of the calibration parameters because of attenuation bias, I also present results based on an aggressive calibration, which uses a Mincerian return of 0.10, Weil's 0.65 value for the mapping of the adult survival rate to human capital, and Hanushek and Woessmann's 0.002 coefficient on the PISA test.[22]

Figure 2.6 Human Capital per Worker Relative to the United States: Baseline Calibration

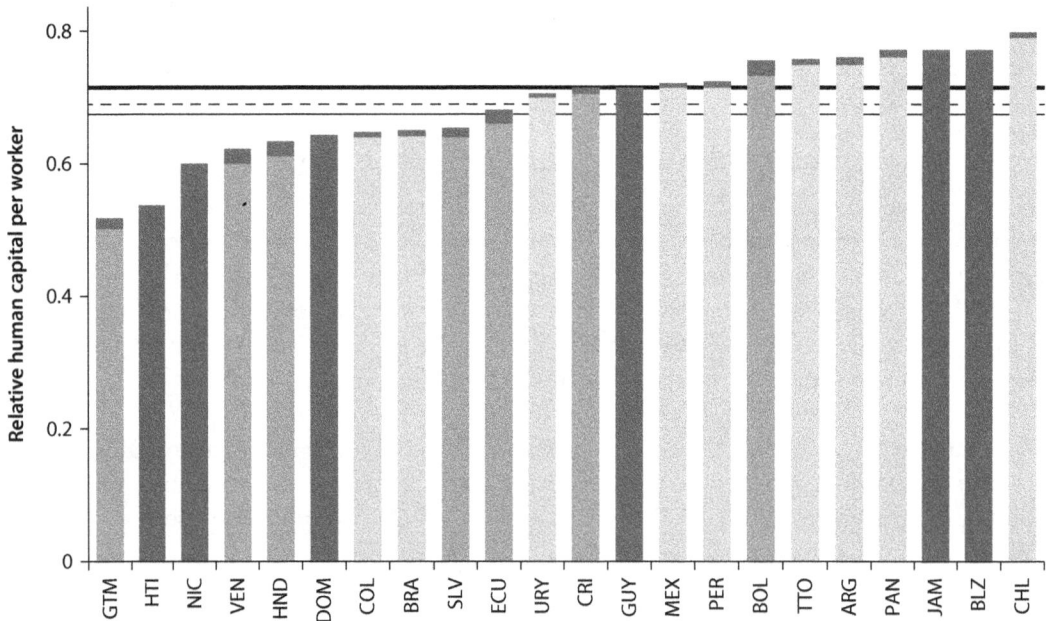

Source: World Bank calculations.
Note: Overall height: relative human capital per worker without cognitive-skill correction. Orange (green) bars: relative human capital per worker with cognitive-skill correction based on regional (PISA) tests. Dashed line: average with no cognitive-skill correction. Light (heavy) solid line: average with regional (PISA) test correction. PISA = Program for International Student Assessment; ARG = Argentina; BLZ = Belize; BOL = Bolivia; BRA = Brazil; CHL = Chile; COL = Colombia; CRI = Costa Rica; DOM = Dominican Republic; ECU = Ecuador; GTM = Guatemala; GUY = Guyana; HND = Honduras; HTI = Haiti; JAM = Jamaica; MEX = Mexico; NIC = Nicaragua; PAN = Panama; PER = Peru; SLV = El Salvador; TTO = Trinidad and Tobago; URY = Uruguay; VEN = República Bolivariana de Venezuela.

Figure 2.7 Human Capital per Worker Relative to the United States: Aggressive Calibration

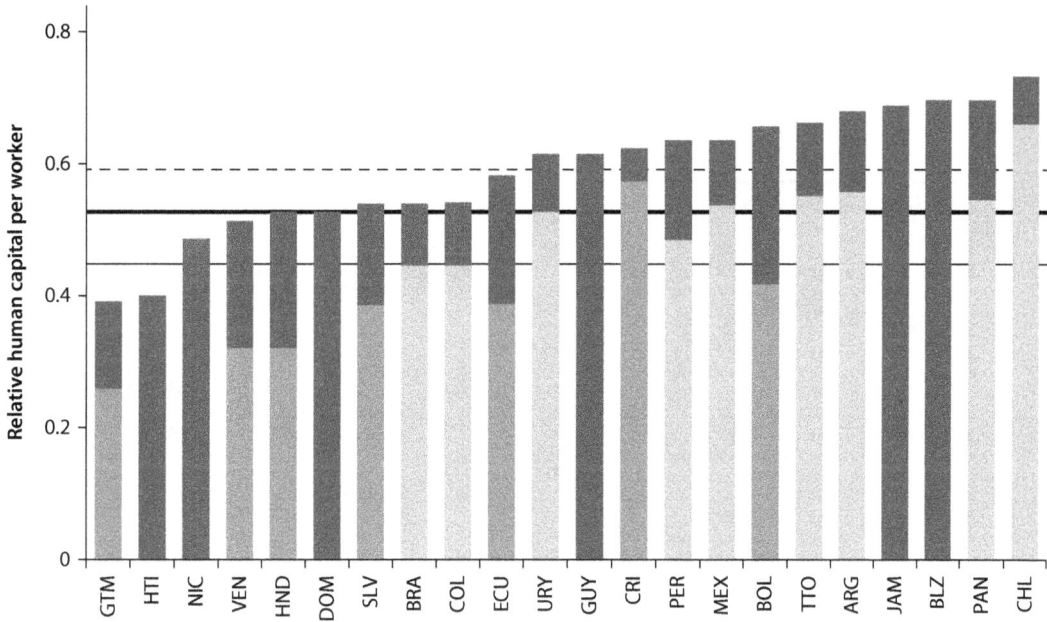

Source: World Bank calculations.

Note: Overall height: relative human capital per worker without cognitive-skill correction. Orange (green) bars: relative human capital per worker with cognitive-skill correction based on regional (PISA) tests. Dashed line: average with no cognitive-skill correction. Light (heavy) solid line: average with regional (PISA) test correction. PISA = Program for International Student Assessment; ARG = Argentina; BLZ = Belize; BOL = Bolivia; BRA = Brazil; CHL = Chile; COL = Colombia; CRI = Costa Rica; DOM = Dominican Republic; ECU = Ecuador; GTM = Guatemala; GUY = Guyana; HND = Honduras; HTI = Haiti; JAM = Jamaica; MEX = Mexico; NIC = Nicaragua; PAN = Panama; PER = Peru; SLV = El Salvador; TTO = Trinidad and Tobago; URY = Uruguay; VEN = República Bolivariana de Venezuela.

Figure 2.6 shows estimates of human capital per worker for Latin American countries relative to the United States, h_i/h_{US}, under my baseline calibration. The full height of the bar shows the value of h_i/h_{US} when excluding cognitive skills, and is thus fully comparable across all countries in the figure. The green/orange bars are the values when including cognitive skills. Irrespective of sample and cognitive-skill correction, the average Latin American worker is endowed with approximately 70 percent of the human capital of the average U.S. worker.

Figure 2.7 is analogous to figure 2.6, but shows the aggressive calibration instead. Not surprisingly, using the aggressive calibration results in significantly lower relative human capital for Latin America, since the impact of differentials in schooling, health, and cognitive skills is magnified. Human capital gaps become particularly large when including the cognitive skill corrections.

Results

Baseline Calibration

In the broad sample, there is no cognitive skill information for more than half of the countries, so I set $\beta_t = 0$. Figure 2.8 shows each country's counterfactual income relative to the United States (relative capital) in 2005, $\tilde{y}_i/\tilde{y}_{US}$, as well as

Figure 2.8 Relative Capital, Baseline Calibration, No Cognitive-Skill Correction

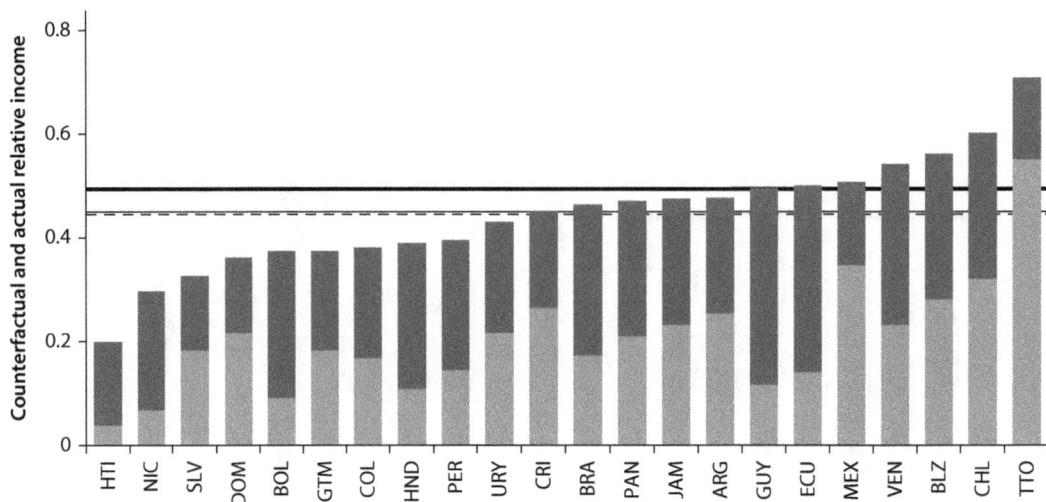

Source: World Bank calculations.
Note: Overall height: relative capital per worker. Orange bars: relative income per worker. Dashed line: broad sample mean. Light solid line: intermediate sample mean. Heavy solid line: narrow sample mean. ARG = Argentina; BLZ = Belize; BOL = Bolivia; BRA = Brazil; CHL = Chile; COL = Colombia; CRI = Costa Rica; DOM = Dominican Republic; ECU = Ecuador; GTM = Guatemala; GUY = Guyana; HND = Honduras; HTI = Haiti; JAM = Jamaica; MEX = Mexico; NIC = Nicaragua; PAN = Panama; PER = Peru; SLV = El Salvador; TTO = Trinidad and Tobago; URY = Uruguay; VEN = República Bolivariana de Venezuela.

the relative incomes y_i/y_{US} already shown in figure 2.1. For each country, the overall height of the bar is relative capital, and the height of the orange bar is relative income.

As is apparent, there is a lot of variation in relative capital, ranging from 20 percent to almost 70 percent. This reflects considerable heterogeneity in rates of physical and human capital accumulation among Latin American countries. Sample means are between 44 percent (broad and intermediate samples) and 49 percent (narrow sample). This means that observed distributions of physical and human capital are consistent with Latin American workers being between 44 and 49 percent as productive as U.S. workers. This measure can be interpreted as a measure of the *capital gap* between Latin America and the United States.

Figure 2.9 extends the calculations to include information on cognitive skills based on worldwide PISA test scores. The sample size correspondingly drops to nine countries. The effect of including cognitive skills under the baseline calibration is virtually nil: the mean remains unchanged at 0.49. This result is expected given the very small calibrated loading on cognitive skills implied by Vogl's estimates. Very similar patterns emerge when using the regional scores/intermediate sample, as seen in figure 2.10.

"Aggressive" Calibration

My baseline calibration uses coefficients for mapping years of schooling, health, and cognitive skills into human capital that, taken individually, are lower than those presented in other contributions. In this section, I explore the robustness

Figure 2.9 Relative Capital, Baseline Calibration, PISA Cognitive Skills

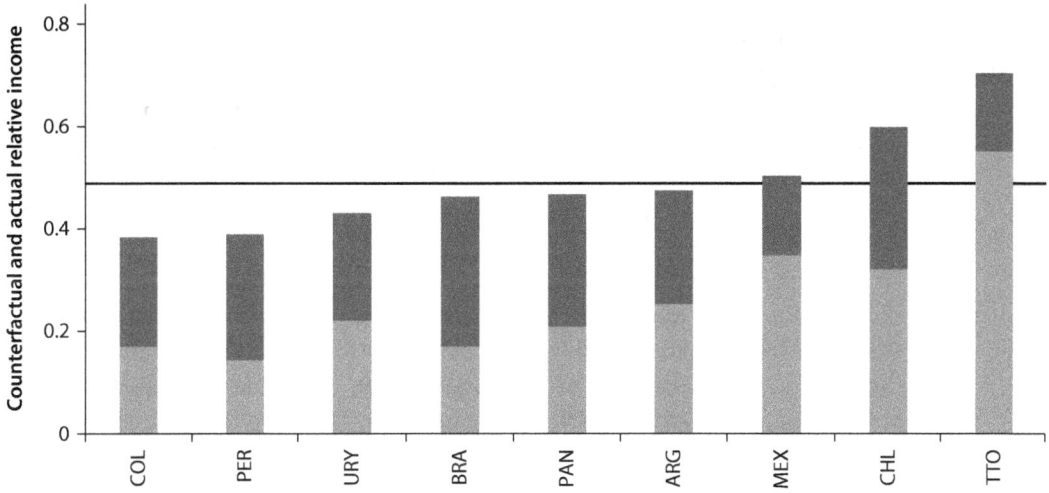

Source: World Bank calculations.
Note: Overall height: relative capital per worker. Orange bars: relative income per worker. Solid line: mean. PISA = Program for International Student Assessment; ARG = Argentina; BRA = Brazil; CHL = Chile; COL = Colombia; MEX = Mexico; PAN = Panama; PER = Peru; T.TO = Trinidad and Tobago; URY = Uruguay.

Figure 2.10 Relative Capital, Baseline Calibration, Regional Test Cognitive Skills

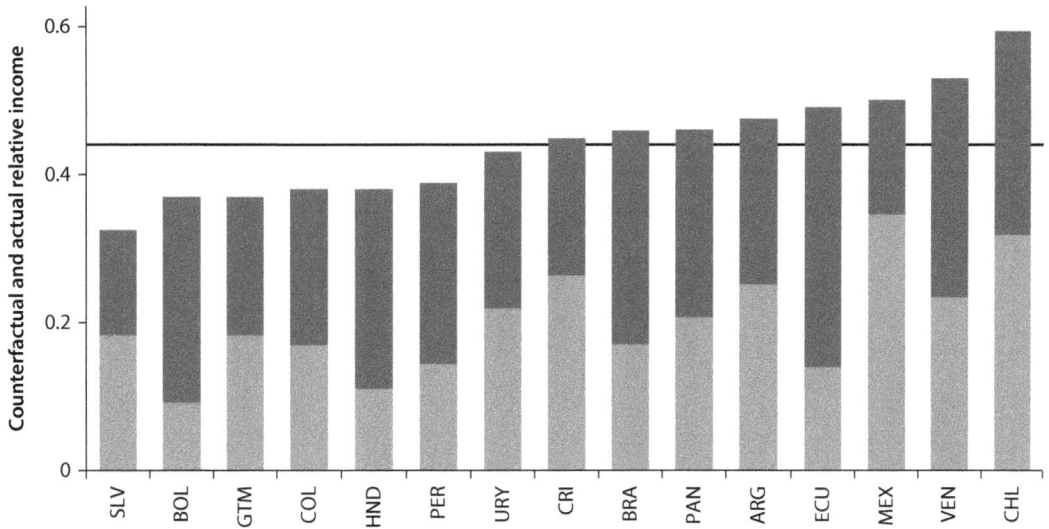

Source: World Bank calculations.
Note: Overall height: relative capital per worker. Orange bars: relative income per worker. Solid line: mean. ARG = Argentina; BOL = Bolivia; BRA = Brazil; CHL = Chile; COL = Colombia; CRI = Costa Rica; ECU = Ecuador; GTM = Guatemala; HND = Honduras; MEX = Mexico; PAN = Panama; PER = Peru; SLV = El Salvador; URY = Uruguay; VEN = República Bolivariana de Venezuela.

Understanding the Income and Efficiency Gap in Latin America and the Caribbean
http://dx.doi.org/10.1596/978-1-4648-0450-2

of my results to more commonly used values. Hence, I set $\beta_s = 0.10$, $\beta_r = 0.65$, and $\beta_t = 0.002$.

The results for the large sample with the aggressive calibration are shown in figure 2.11. Given the larger coefficients, the counterfactual incomes are necessarily smaller than under the baseline calibration. Yet quantitatively the difference is not very large. Average relative capital drops to 40 percent, which is still roughly double relative income.

Figure 2.12 shows the results for the aggressive calibration with the PISA test scores. Including cognitive skills in the calculation of relative capital has a much larger impact than under the baseline, because the coefficient on cognitive skills is an order of magnitude larger. The average counterfactual relative income falls to 40 percent, compared with 49 percent in the baseline calibration (within the same narrow sample). This is a large gain in the explanatory power of the observables. For many countries, the gap between relative income and relative capital shrinks considerably.

Finally, figure 2.13 reports the results for the aggressive calibration with the regional test scores. These tests tend to show even larger cognitive gaps compared with the United States. Correspondingly, using these tests in combination with the aggressive calibration leads to an even better alignment between relative capital and relative income.

Figure 2.11 Relative Capital, Aggressive Calibration, No Cognitive-Skill Correction

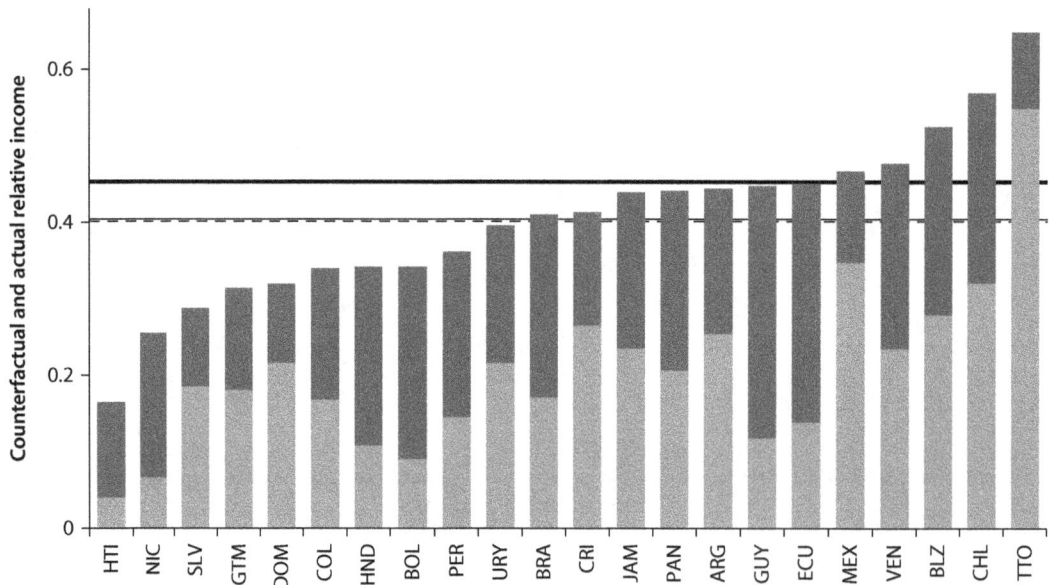

Source: World Bank calculations.
Note: Overall height: relative capital per worker. Orange bars: relative income per worker. Dashed line: broad sample mean. Light solid line: intermediate sample mean. Heavy solid line: narrow sample mean. ARG = Argentina; BLZ = Belize; BOL = Bolivia; BRA = Brazil; CHL = Chile; COL = Colombia; CRI = Costa Rica; DOM = Dominican Republic; ECU = Ecuador; GTM = Guatemala; GUY = Guyana; HND = Honduras; HTI = Haiti; JAM = Jamaica; MEX = Mexico; NIC = Nicaragua; PAN = Panama; PER = Peru; SLV = El Salvador; TTO = Trinidad and Tobago; URY = Uruguay; VEN = República Bolivariana de Venezuela.

Figure 2.12 Relative Capital, Aggressive Calibration, PISA Cognitive Skills

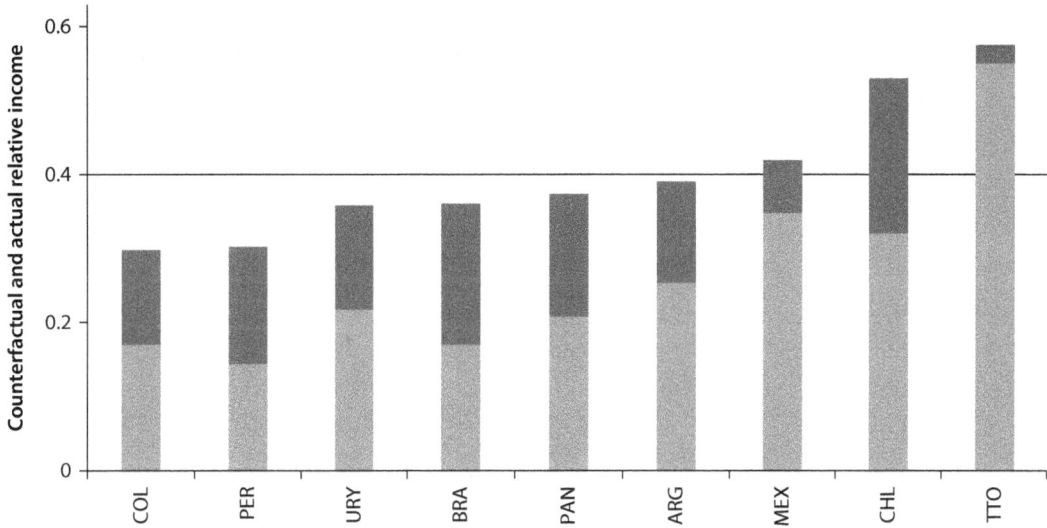

Source: World Bank calculations.
Note: Overall height: relative capital per worker. Orange bars: relative income per worker. Solid line: mean. PISA = Program for International Student Assessment; ARG = Argentina; BRA = Brazil; CHL = Chile; COL = Colombia; MEX = Mexico; PAN = Panama; PER = Peru; TTO = Trinidad and Tobago; URY = Uruguay.

Figure 2.13 Relative Capital, Aggressive Calibration, Regional Test Cognitive Skills

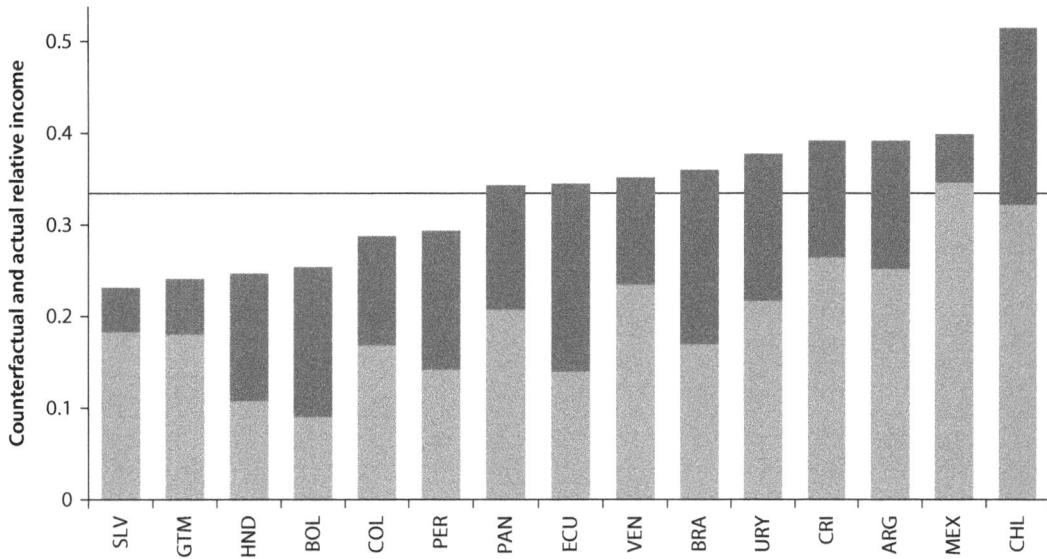

Source: World Bank calculations.
Note: Overall height: relative capital per worker. Orange bars: relative income per worker. Solid line: mean. ARG = Argentina; BOL = Bolivia; BRA = Brazil; CHL = Chile; COL = Colombia; CRI = Costa Rica; ECU = Ecuador; GTM = Guatemala; HND = Honduras; MEX = Mexico; PAN = Panama; PER = Peru; SLV = El Salvador; URY = Uruguay; VEN = República Bolivariana de Venezuela.

Implications for Efficiency Gaps

The analysis has shown that, depending on cognitive skill correction, counterfactual income ratios (relative capital) in Latin America tend to be much larger than actual income ratios. This discrepancy implies that Latin America suffers from an *efficiency gap* as much as it suffers from a capital gap.

The efficiency gaps can be quantified by noting, from equations 2.1 and 2.2, that

$$\frac{A_i}{A_{US}} = \frac{y_i/y_{US}}{\tilde{y}_i/\tilde{y}_{US}}.$$

Hence, Latin American efficiency gaps can be directly gleaned from figures 2.8 to 2.13 by dividing the height of the orange bars by the overall height of the bars.

Table 2.1 reports the sample averages of the implied efficiency gaps, for the various cognitive skill correction–calibration combinations. For completeness, the table also reports the corresponding averages for relative income and relative capital, as well as labor force weighted means.

Using the baseline calibration, average relative capital and average relative efficiency are almost identical, irrespective of the sample, cognitive skill correction, or weighting. One way to put this is that capital gaps and efficiency gaps contribute equally to Latin American income gaps. When the aggressive calibration is used, the relative importance of capital gaps increases, particularly when the cognitive-skill corrections are added. Still, even under the most aggressive scenario, average Latin American relative efficiency is only 60 percent of U.S. efficiency.[23]

To appreciate the importance of these efficiency gaps, it is crucial to note that, under almost any imaginable set of circumstances, physical (specifically, reproducible) and human capital accumulation respond to a country's level of efficiency. The higher the value of A, the higher is the marginal productivity of capital, leading to enhanced incentives to invest in equipment and structures,

Table 2.1 Summary of Results

| | | Calibration | | | |
| | | Baseline | | Aggressive | |
Sample/Cognitive skill measure	Relative GDP	Relative capital	Relative efficiency	Relative capital	Relative efficiency
Broad/None	**0.21**	**0.44**	**0.44**	**0.40**	**0.49**
	0.21	0.46	0.45	0.41	0.50
Narrow/PISA	**0.26**	**0.49**	**0.52**	**0.40**	**0.64**
	0.22	0.46	0.47	0.37	0.59
Intermediate/"Regional"	**0.20**	**0.44**	**0.45**	**0.33**	**0.60**
	0.22	0.46	0.46	0.36	0.60

Source: World Bank calculations.

Note: Bold entries are unweighted sample means. Plain entries are labor-force weighted sample means. GDP = gross domestic product; PISA = Program for International Student Assessment.

schooling, etc. Although quantifying this effect is difficult, most theoretical frame-works would lead one to expect it to be large. Hence, it is legitimate to conjecture that a significant fraction of the capital gap may be caused by the efficiency gap.[24]

Implications and Conclusions

There is a large gap in income per worker between Latin America and the United States: Latin American workers are only about one-fifth as productive as workers in the United States. A development accounting calculation reveals that capital gaps and efficiency gaps contribute to this overall productivity gap. In particular, a Cobb-Douglas aggregate of observable physical and human capital per worker is roughly on the order of 45 percent of the corresponding U.S. level (capital gap). This finding implies that the efficiency with which inputs are used in Latin America is also on the order of 45 percent of U.S. levels (efficiency gap). Reducing this efficiency gap would reduce the overall productivity gap directly, by allowing Latin America to reap greater benefits from its physical and human capital, and indirectly, since much of the capital gap is likely caused by the efficiency gap itself. Closing the efficiency gap would stimulate investment at rates potentially capable of closing the capital gap as well.

These conclusions are contingent on the quality of the underlying macroeconomic data. There is growing concern about the quality and reliability of the purchasing power parity national accounts figures in the Penn World Tables and similar data sets (such as Johnson et al. 2013). Similar concerns apply, no doubt, to the proxies for human capital as well (particularly in the context of cognitive skills). It is true that such concerns are most often voiced in the context of implied comparisons of changes, especially over short time spans: cross-country comparisons of *levels* reveal such gigantic differences that they seem unlikely to be entirely dominated by noise. Still, exclusive reliance on these macro data is highly inadvisable.

Fortunately, the exclusive reliance on macro data is also increasingly unnecessary. The increasing availability of *firm-level* data sets, particularly when matched with employee-level information (for example, about schooling), provides an opportunity to supplement the macro picture with microeconomic productivity estimates that are comparable across countries.

The benefit of producing such micro productivity estimates is by no means limited to permitting a check of the robustness of conclusions concerning average capital and efficiency gaps, although this benefit alone is sufficient to make such exercises worthwhile. An additional benefit is to uncover information on the within-country *distribution* of physical capital, human capital, and efficiency. A relatively concentrated distribution would suggest that efficiency gaps are mostly caused by aggregate, macroeconomic factors that affect all firms fairly equally (for example, impediment to technology diffusion from other countries). A very dispersed distribution, with some firms close to the world technology frontier, would be more consistent with allocative frictions that prevent capital and labor from flowing to more efficient and talented managers.

Understanding the Income and Efficiency Gap in Latin America and the Caribbean
http://dx.doi.org/10.1596/978-1-4648-0450-2

More generally, firm-level data are likely to prove essential in the quest for the determinants of the large efficiency gaps revealed by the development accounting calculation. After all, (in)efficiency is, by definition, a firm-level phenomenon. Most of the most plausible possible explanations for the efficiency gap are microeconomic in nature—whether the explanation is about firms unable to adapt technologies developed in more technologically advanced countries, failures in the market for managers or capital, frictions in the matching process for workers, etc. It seems implausible that evidence for or against these mechanisms can be found in the macro data. Yet understanding the sources of the Latin American efficiency gap is unquestionably the most urgent task for those who want to design policies aimed at closing the Latin American income gap.

Annex 2A Alternative Capital Share

Expanding on previous work by Gollin (2002), Bernanke and Gurkaynak (2001) present estimates of the labor share in income for a cross-section of countries. Using the method that yields the largest number of observations, they produce estimates for 13 countries in Latin America and the Caribbean. In this group of 13, the average labor share is 0.62, implying a capital share of 0.38, which is larger than the standard development accounting benchmark. An alternative method, which Bernanke and Gurkaynak consider more accurate, yields estimates for nine Latin American and Caribbean countries, averaging 0.61.

These estimates prompt me to explore the robustness of the results to an alternative choice of α, namely 0.4. Before doing so, it is important to note that the estimate of the U.S. capital share implied by the figures in Bernanke and Gurkaynak is actually 0.29. Hence, while using 0.4 may more accurately reflect the relative contributions of physical and human capital in Latin America, it greatly distorts their relative contributions in the benchmark country. Unfortunately, as discussed in footnote 4, I do not know of a method for development accounting that allows country-specific capital shares and preserves the unit invariance of the results to the measurement of capital. Perhaps 0.33 is a reasonable compromise after all.

Another reason to be wary of the 0.4 figure is that deviations from perfect competition, in the labor and product markets, are likely to weigh more heavily in Latin American countries than in the United States. Monopsonistic labor markets and monopolistic product markets are likely to result in a labor share in income that is less than the elasticity of output to labor, that is, the technological parameter $1-\alpha$. Of course some of the difference compared with the United States may be caused by true underlying technological differences, or to differences in the sector composition of the economy. But the presence of deviations from perfect competition should imply that 0.4 is too high an estimate of α even for Latin American countries.

With these caveats, table 2A.1 presents the results for relative capital and relative efficiency when using $\alpha = 0.4$ in the calibration. Compared with the case

Table 2A.1 Summary of Results with $\alpha = 0.4$

Sample/Cognitive skill measure	Relative GDP	Calibration				
		Baseline		Aggressive	
		Relative capital	Relative efficiency	Relative capital	Relative efficiency
Broad/None	0.21	0.41	0.49	0.37	0.53
	0.21	0.42	0.49	0.38	0.54
Narrow/PISA	0.26	0.45	0.56	0.38	0.68
	0.22	0.43	0.51	0.35	0.63
Intermediate/"Regional"	0.20	0.40	0.50	0.31	0.64
	0.22	0.42	0.50	0.34	0.63

Source: World Bank calculations.
Note: Bold entries are unweighted sample means. Plain entries are labor-force weighted sample means.
GDP = gross domestic product; PISA = Program for International Student Assessment.

where $\alpha = 0.33$, the capital gaps increase (relative capital falls) and efficiency gaps correspondingly shrink (the relative efficiency of Latin America goes up). The reason for this is that the gap in physical capital between Latin America and the United States is larger than the gap in human capital. Hence, when more weight is given to physical capital, the overall capital stock of Latin America drops, decreasing the role of efficiency gaps in accounting for income differences. Even so, relative efficiency only increases by 4 or 5 percentage points, depending on the calibration and the sample. The big picture of large efficiency gaps remains unchanged.

Notes

1. For a detailed exposition of development accounting, see, among others, Caselli (2005). For previous applications with a focus on Latin America, see Cole et al. (2005) and Hanushek and Woessman (2012b). Cole et al. in particular stress the importance of total factor productivity (TFP) gaps, consistent with my findings.

2. See, for example, Iranzo and Peri (2009) for a recent review and some new evidence on the quantitative significance of schooling externalities.

3. There may well be significant heterogeneity among Latin American countries and, more importantly, between Latin America and the benchmark high-income country, in the value of α. However, it is not known how to perform development accounting with country-specific capital shares. This is because measures of the capital stock are indices, so that a requirement for the exercise to make sense is that the results should be invariant to the units in which k is measured. Now $(K_i/K_j)^\alpha$ is unit-invariant, but $(k_i^{\alpha_i}/k_j^{\alpha_j})$ is not.

4. Some caveats as to the validity of the functional form assumption in equation 2.3 are in order. There is considerable micro and macro evidence against the assumption that workers with different years of schooling are perfect substitutes (Caselli and Coleman 2006). In this chapter, I abstract from the issue of imperfect substitutability. Caselli and Ciccone (2013) argue that consideration of imperfect substitution is unlikely to reduce the estimated importance of efficiency gaps.

Understanding the Income and Efficiency Gap in Latin America and the Caribbean
http://dx.doi.org/10.1596/978-1-4648-0450-2

5. Note that this approach to the measurement of human capital is robust to a broad range of deviations from perfect competition. In particular, the wage does not need to equal the marginal productivity of labor, but just be proportional to it. Many models of monopsony in labor markets and monopolistic competition have this property.

6. In the narrow sample, the average is higher because of the disproportionate weight of Trinidad and Tobago. Labor force weighted averages are reported in table 2.1.

7. The population-weighted mean survival rate in the broad sample is 0.85.

8. The only exception is Belize, which participated in some of the reading tests administered by the Progress in International Reading Literacy Study.

9. Repeating all my calculations with the PISA math scores yielded results that were virtually indistinguishable from those with the science test.

10. Hanushek and Woessman (2012b) splice the regional scores into worldwide scores that are themselves aggregates of multiple waves and multiple subject areas, obtained with the methodology described in Hanushek and Woessman (2012a).

11. The method for estimating the average age of workers is described in Caselli (2005, footnote 25).

12. I say approximately in parentheses because the normalization was applied to the 2006 wave of the test. The 2009 test was graded to be comparable to the 2006 test. Hence, it is likely that the 2009 mean (standard deviation) will have drifted somewhat away from 500 (100), although probably not by much. The PISA math and reading tests were normalized in 2000 and 2003, respectively, so their mean and standard deviation are more likely to have drifted away from the initial benchmark. This is one reason why I use the science test for my baseline calculations.

13. If we had cross-country data on average height, there would be no need to use the survival rate.

14. See, for example, the literature review in Vogl (2014).

15. An alternative would be to use instrumental variables estimates of the βs, but instruments for the variables on the right-hand side of equation 2.5 are often somewhat controversial, especially for height and cognitive skills.

16. The test is the short-form Raven's Progressive Matrices Test.

17. There are aspects of Vogl's treatment that imply the regressions he runs are not a perfect fit for the conceptual framework of the chapter. It may have been preferable for the purposes of this chapter to include men and women. Vogl also controls for ethnicity, age, and age squared, which do not feature in my framework. Finally, he notes that the Raven's score is a coarse measure of cognitive skills, giving rise to concerns about attenuation bias.

18. Hanushek and Woessmann's splicing procedure implies that the same coefficient can be used for the regional tests used in the intermediate sample. In particular, the relevant standard error is the average of the standard deviations of the PISA science and math tests in Mexico, which is 80. Then we have 0.011/80 = 0.00014.

19. This is based on Hanushek and Zhang (2009), who use the International Adult Literacy Survey to estimate the return to cognitive skills in a set of 13 countries. The value of 0.002 is the one for the United States.

20. For example, in Hanushek and Zhang (2009), the estimated market return to cognitive skills varies (from minimum to maximum) by a factor of 10. The estimate for the United States that is used in Hanushek and Woessman (2012b) is the *maximum* of this distribution.

21. This is actually an issue with the capital share α as well. However, the issue is less severe, as observed capital shares do not vary systematically with y, so it should be possible to ascribe the observed variation to measurement error. In other words, the patterns of variation in α do not necessarily raise the issue of model misspecification.

22. As described above, the Hanushek and Zhang (2009) estimate for the United States comes from a test d different from t. To go from their coefficient β_d to the coefficient of interest β_t, we need to multiply the former by the ratio of the standard deviation of $d_{US,i}$ to the standard deviation of $t_{US,i}$. Since Hanushek and Zhang standardize the variable d, we just have to multiply by the inverse of the standard deviation of $t_{US,i}$. But in the test we are using this is just 0.98, so the correction would be immaterial using the same value in the narrow and intermediate samples.

23. In the narrow sample, it is probably best to focus on the labor force weighted results, as the unweighted results give disproportionate weight to Trinidad and Tobago.

24. In principle, it could be argued that there is a reverse direction of causation, with larger physical and human capital stocks leading to higher efficiency. In particular, this would be true if the model was misspecified, and there were large externalities. But the empirical literature has not to date uncovered significant evidence of externalities in physical and human capital.

Bibliography

Barro, Robert J., and Jong-Wha Lee. 2013. "A New Data Set of Educational Attainment in the World, 1950-2010." *Journal of Development Economics* 104: 184–198.

Bernanke, B., and R. S. Gurkaynak. 2001. "Is Growth Exogenous? Taking Mankiw, Romer, and Weil Seriously." In *NBER Macroeconomics Annual 2001*, Volume 16, edited by B. Bernanke and K. S. Rogoff, 11–57. Cambridge, MA: MIT Press.

Caselli, Francesco. 2005. "Accounting for Cross-Country Income Differences." In *Handbook of Economic Growth*, volume 1A, edited by Philippe Aghion and Stephen Durlauf, 679–741. San Diego, CA: Elsevier.

Caselli, Francesco, and Antonio Ciccone. 2013. "The Contribution of Schooling in Development Accounting: Results from a Nonparametric Upper Bound." *Journal of Development Economics* 104: 199–211.

Caselli, Francesco, and Wilbur John Coleman. 2006. "The World Technology Frontier." *American Economic Review* 96: 499–522.

Caselli, Francesco, and James Feyrer. 2007. "The Marginal Product of Capital." *Quarterly Journal of Economics* 122: 535–68.

Cole, Harold L., Lee E. Ohanian, Alvaro Riascos, and James A. Schmitz, Jr. 2005. "Latin America in the Rearview Mirror." *Journal of Monetary Economics* 52: 69–107.

Gollin, Douglas. 2002. "Getting Income Shares Right." *Journal of Political Economy* 110: 458–74.

Gundlach, E., D. Rudman, and L. Woessmann. 2002. "Second Thoughts on Development Accounting." *Applied Economics* 34 (11): 1359–69.

Hall, Robert, and Charles Jones. 1999. "Why Do Some Countries Produce So Much More Output Per Worker Than Others?" *Quarterly Journal of Economics* 114: 83–116.

Hanushek, Eric, and Ludger Woessmann. 2012a. "Do Better Schools Lead to More Growth? Cognitive Skills, Economic Outcomes, and Causation." *Journal of Economic Growth.* 17 (4): 267–321.

———. 2012b. "Schooling, Educational Achievement, and the Latin American Growth Puzzle." *Journal of Development Economics* 99 (2): 497–512.

Hanushek, Eric, and Lei Zhang. 2009. "Quality-Consistent Estimates of International Schooling and Skill Gradients." *Journal of Human Capital* 3 (2): 107–43.

Iranzo, Susana, and Giovanni Peri. 2009. "Schooling Externalities, Technology, and Productivity: Theory and Evidence from US States." *Review of Economics and Statistics* 91: 420–31.

Johnson, Simon, William Larson, Chris Papageorgiou, and Arvind Subramanian. 2013. "Is Newer Better? Penn World Table Revisions and Their Impact on Growth Estimates." *Journal of Monetary Economics* 60 (2): 255–74.

Jones, Garett, and W. Joel Schneider. 2010. "IQ in the Production Function: Evidence from Immigrant Earnings." *Economic Inquiry* 48 (3): 743–55.

Klenow, Peter, and Andres Rodriguez-Clare. 1997. "The Neoclassical Revival in Growth Economics: Has It Gone Too Far?" In *NBER Macroeconomic Annual*, volume 12, MIT Press.

Vogl, Tom S. 2014. "Height, Skills, and Labor Market Outcomes in Mexico." *Journal of Development Economics* 107: 84–96.

Weil, David. 2007. "Accounting for the Effect of Health on Economic Growth." *Quarterly Journal of Economics* 122: 1265–1306.

Woessmann, Ludger. 2003. "Specifying Human Capital." *Journal of Economic Surveys* 17 (3): 239–70.

World Bank. 2012. *The Changing Wealth of Nations*. Washington, DC: World Bank.

CHAPTER 3

Reconciling Micro- and Macro-Based Estimates of Technology Adoption Lags in a Model of Endogenous Technology Adoption

Maya Eden and Ha Nguyen

Introduction

There is a large and persistent income gap between countries in Latin America and the Caribbean (LAC) and the United States. In 2000, average income in LAC was only 23 percent of the average income in the United States. Total factor productivity (TFP) is among the leading factors of the observed income gap. TFP in LAC, measured as the Solow residual after carefully accounting for inputs, is about half of that in the United States (Caselli, chapter 2, this volume).

LAC's technology backwardness is being debated as one of the key factors that explain this large TFP gap. To explain the extent to which technology backwardness matters, it is important to estimate precisely the technology adoption lags between LAC and the United States—the technology frontier. A slow adoption lag would indicate that technology backwardness is indeed the problem. However, a faster adoption lag would point to other factors, such as institutions and misallocation of resources, along the lines of analysis by Hsieh and Klenow (2009). The two sets of issues have fundamentally different policy implications. If technology adoption is key, the policy focus should be on removing barriers to technology adoption (such as increasing international integration or improving human capital). If institutions are more important, policies should aim to improve domestic institutions and correct the misallocation of resources.

The literature currently offers conflicting views about the speed of technology adoption in LAC. An adoption lag at the technology level is defined as the length of time between the invention and eventual adoption of the technology. Micro-based evidence drawn from Comin and Hobijn (2010) suggests that adoption lags at the technology level between LAC and the United States are long, 20 years on average. By contrast, macro-based evidence from Akcigit, Alp, Eden, and Nguyen (2014) (henceforth AAEN) suggests a much shorter lag. Based on the TFP time-series data and the assumption that any shock to TFP growth in the United States that affects the adopting countries (LAC) with a lag is a technology shock, they find that the lag is only about eight years. Which number is correct affects the debate about the role of technology adoption in LAC's convergence.

This chapter argues that the two findings might be consistent and, for the purpose of explaining the TFP gap, the macro-based number is more relevant. We reconcile the two findings with two insights. First, technologies tend to be adopted first by more productive firms. Since the first adopting firms tend to be more productive, the productivity gains from the first technology adopters are relatively larger than the productivity gains from later adopters. The macro-level adoption lag accounts for this, by weighting technology adoptions by their respective productivity gains. The micro-level adoption lag, by contrast, assigns equal weights to all adopters; thus, it is likely to be relatively longer than the macro-level lag.

The second insight is that more effective technologies are likely to be adopted faster. Technologies that improve productivity by more are likely to be adopted faster, as the returns to adoption are higher. This situation implies that shorter lags are associated with technologies that are more productivity enhancing. The macro-level adoption lag focuses on aggregate productivity gains from technology adoption, which is likely driven disproportionately by more productive technologies. By contrast, the micro-level adoption lag weights technologies equally, and is thus likely to be longer. We discuss this disparity in a model with endogenous technology adoption, in which (i) the most productivity-enhancing technologies are adopted first, and (ii) production units that have the largest productivity gains from adopting new technologies are the first to adopt. We illustrate that reasonable parameters can generate the observed differences between the micro- and macro-based estimates of technology adoption lags.

The model suggests that the macro-based estimate by AAEN can be consistent with the micro-based estimate by Comin and Hobijn (2010). However, when it comes to explaining the TFP gap, the macro estimate is more appropriate, because it works directly on TFP. AAEN's result therefore is relevant to argue that technology adoption lags at the TFP level are short—about eight years. AAEN's result implies that other factors, such as institutions, remain the sticking points for lack of convergence in income between LAC and the United States.

The next section revisits in detail the micro- and macro-based evidence. The following section lays out a model to reconcile the two estimates. The chapter then provides a numerical illustration of the model.

Micro- and Macro-Based Technology Adoption Lags in LAC

This section discusses the details of the micro- and macro-based evidence for the technology adoption lags in LAC. The section analyzes the Cross-Country Historical Adoption of Technology (CHAT) data set constructed by Comin and

Hobjin (2009) for the micro-based evidence, and goes into detail about the results obtained by AAEN for the macro-based evidence.

Micro-Based Evidence from the CHAT Data Set

Comin and Hobijn (2010) estimate the diffusion of 15 technologies in 166 countries over the past two centuries. Their analysis shows that, in general, countries take a long time to adopt new technologies: on average, countries have adopted technologies 45 years after their invention. However, there is substantial variation across technologies. Recent technologies are adopted faster than old ones. Figure 3.1 is borrowed from Comin and Hobijn (2010) to illustrate this fact.

We replicate Comin and Hobijn's (2010) adoption lags for LAC and the United States. Table 3.1 shows the average adoption lags—the length of time between the invention and the eventual adoption of the technologies—for LAC and the United States. On average, the United States takes about 19.8 years to adopt a new technology, while LAC takes about 40 years. This difference means that LAC is about 21 years behind the United States in adopting new technologies.

Figure 3.1 Technology Adoption Lags Decrease for Later Inventions

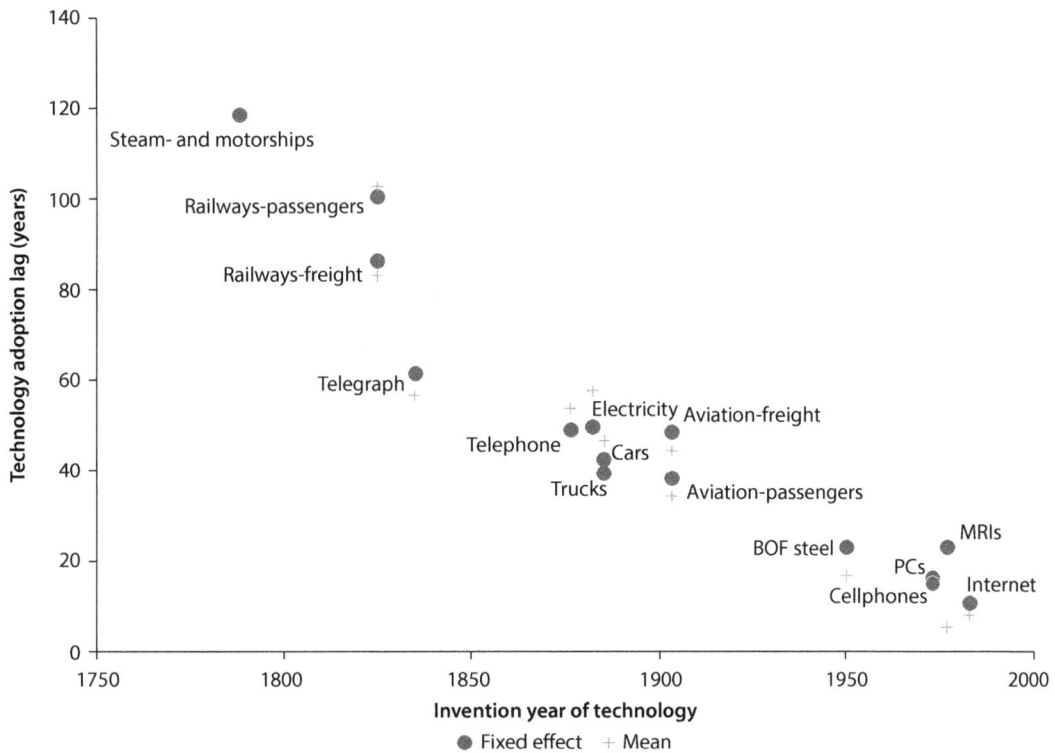

Source: Comin and Hobijn 2010.
Note: BOF = basic oxygen furnace; MRI = magnetic resonance imaging; PC = personal computer.

Table 3.1 Adoption Lags for LAC and the United States
years

Technology name	U.S.	Latin America	All countries
Aviation freight	24.39	32.62	43.48
Aviation passengers	26.16	28.94	33.89
Blast oxygen steel	8.83	17.09	16.31
Cars	14.23	37.67	43.68
Cellphones	9.80	16.78	14.61
Electricity	19.40	51.67	56.36
Internet	4.40	8.68	7.79
MRI	2.92		5.30
PCs	7.66	15.53	13.96
Railway freight	43.93	85.23	79.59
Railway passengers	55.81	98.36	97.32
Ships	29.71	111.07	120.45
Telegraph	31.85	53.27	45.61
Telephone	−0.31	40.35	51.45
Trucks	18.34	29.81	39.13
TOTAL	19.81	42.08	45.48

Sources: Comin and Hobijn 2010; World Bank calculations.
Note: LAC = Latin America and the Caribbean; MRI = magnetic resonance imaging; PCs = personal computers.

For older technologies, LAC lags quite far behind the United States in adoption. For example, for cars and electricity, LAC is 23 and 31 years behind the United States, respectively. However, for more recent technologies, such as personal computers or the Internet, the adoption lag gaps are much smaller. LAC is 7.8 and 4.3 years behind the United States for the two technologies, respectively.

How do adoption lags vary between countries in LAC? Annex table 3A.1 shows the adoption lags for individual countries in LAC and for individual technologies. Within each technology, the adoption lags vary across countries. It is expected that there is a negative association between adoption lags and countries' levels of development. The association can go both ways. Richer countries might have fewer obstacles and higher incentives that encourage technology adoption, and hence have shorter adoption lags for them. Faster technology adoption enables the countries to grow faster and reach a higher level of development. We pick the two arguably most influential technologies—electricity and personal computers—to check if there are significant relationships between the level of development and adoption lags. Indeed, this is the case (see figure 3.2).

Macro-Based Evidence from AAEN

AAEN develop a methodology to estimate the adoption lags between a technology frontier and subsequent technology adopters, based on aggregate macro data such as TFP and output. An advantage of this approach is that it can be

Figure 3.2 GDP per Capita and Adoption Lags for PCs and Electricity

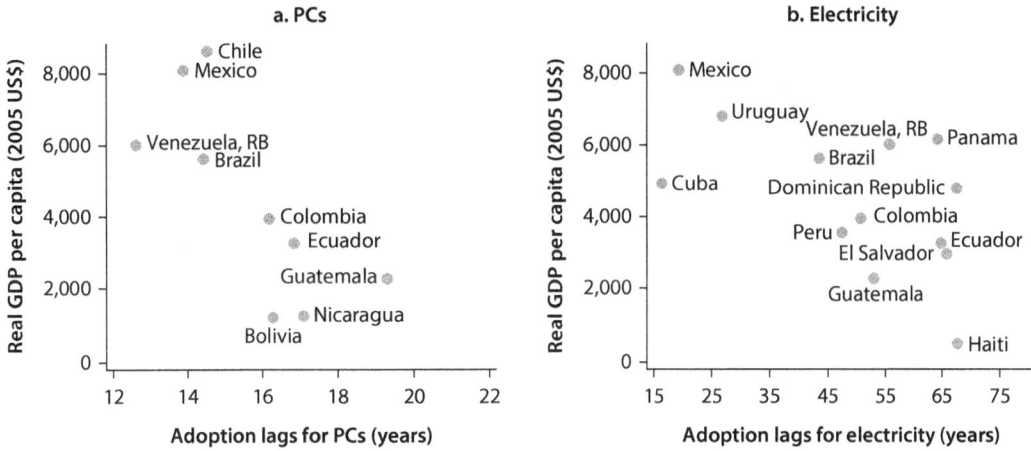

Source: World Bank calculations.
Note: GDP = gross domestic product; PCs = personal computers.

agnostic about which technologies are important. Unlike the approach based on micro data that necessarily has to assume a mapping between the prevalence of specific technologies and aggregate productivity, the macro approach does not have to take a stance about which technology should be the focus. AAEN find that LAC's technology adoption is about eight years behind that of the United States.

The identifying assumption is that any shock to productivity growth in the frontier country (the United States) that affects the adopting countries (LAC) with a lag is a technology shock. The technological component is then used to study the effects of a technology shock on TFP growth in LAC, in terms of timing and magnitude. In other words, although nontechnology shocks (for example, demand shocks) may be contemporaneously correlated across countries, technology shocks are likely to have a lagged effect on TFP growth in the adopting countries.

In particular, the framework used in AAEN (2014) is as follows. Denote $A_{i,t}$ as a country's TFP at time t. $A_{i,t}$ consists of a technology component $X_{i,t}$ and a non-technology component $Z_{i,t}$:

$$A_{i,t} = X_{i,t} Z_{i,t}$$

The nontechnology component, $Z_{i,t}$, is a catch-all phrase that includes all aspects of the economy that affect measured TFP, excluding technology. For example, $Z_{i,t}$ includes misallocation, competition, as well as policies that may distort the efficient use of factors. In log form, TFP is written as follows:

$$a_{i,t} = x_{i,t} + z_{i,t}$$

Understanding the Income and Efficiency Gap in Latin America and the Caribbean
http://dx.doi.org/10.1596/978-1-4648-0450-2

There is one country that is identified as the frontier, and the rest of the countries are identified as adopters. We denote the frontier economy *us* and the adopting countries *lac*. Technology growth in the frontier represents the growth of the frontier technology. In adopting countries, a technological innovation may affect TFP growth with some lag, reflecting the possibility of learning and adoption frictions. Thus, current technology growth in adopting countries is a function of current and lagged values of the technological progress in the frontier (for example, growth in LAC today may reflect technological innovation in the United States several years ago, as the technology is adopted with some delay). AAEN assume that this function takes the following linear form:

$$x_{lac,t} = \sum_{j=0}^{\infty} \lambda_j x_{us,t-j}$$

The sum $\sum_{j=0}^{\infty} \lambda_j$ is interpreted as the long-run adoption rate: an innovation in the technological frontier today will have a contemporaneous effect of λ_0, an effect of λ_1 in the next period, and so on. AAEN (2014) provide further details about the estimation. Here we will show the results only.

Figure 3.3, panel a, represents the estimated marginal adoption rates (λj), and figure 3.3, panel b, represents the estimated cumulative adoption rates ($\sum_{j=0}^{\infty} \lambda_j$). The estimation suggests that the bulk of technology adoption happens at an eight-year lag. The point estimate suggests that technological innovations in the frontier have a somewhat smaller effect on productivity in LAC: the point estimate of the infinite sum $\sum_{j=0}^{\infty} \lambda_j$ is about 0.8, suggesting that a 1 percent improvement in technology in the United States increases long-run productivity in LAC by only 0.8 percent. However, it is important to note that the 90 percent confidence interval cannot reject full adoption in the long run (and in fact, after eight years). In this case, technological innovations in the United States have the same effect on TFP in LAC, with an eight-year lag.

AAEN also conduct the analysis by (i) including each country in LAC as a separate adopting country, and (ii) estimating the marginal adoption rates by industry. These extensions allow for the sequence of marginal adoption rates to differ across countries and across industries. However, although there is some variation in the results, they broadly confirm the findings at the aggregate level.

The results are presented in figure 3.4. The results are highly consistent with those obtained with the LAC aggregate. For most countries in LAC (12 of 19), the point estimates suggest full adoption of technologies after eight years at most. Although there are some variations across countries, the variation is not statistically significant in the sense that full adoption after eight years is within the 90 percent confidence interval for all countries in our sample.

At the industry level, AAEN proxy measured productivity growth with growth in value added per worker by industry, using the value added in constant

Figure 3.3 Estimated Marginal and Cumulative Adoption Rates: LAC Aggregate

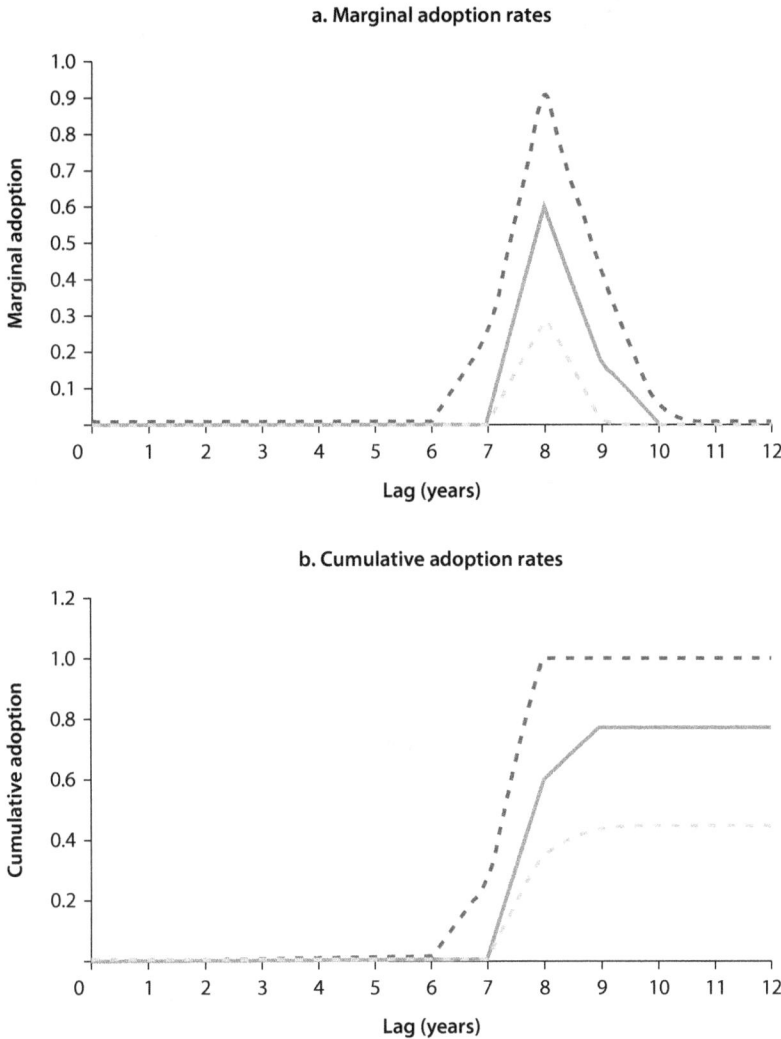

a. Marginal adoption rates

b. Cumulative adoption rates

Source: World Bank calculations.
Note: Dotted lines represent the bounds of the 90 percent confidence intervals. LAC = Latin America and the Caribbean.

prices from the Groningen Growth and Development Centre 10-sector database for countries in LAC and the United States. For countries in LAC, only nine sectors are available. Data are available from 1950 to 2005. AAEN carry out the estimation for each industry separately, using a LAC weighted average in which weights are given by real value added in each industry. The results are presented in figure 3.5. Broadly, the results at the aggregate level are consistent with the industry-level results, in the sense that full adoption within 12 years (as well as 0.8 long-run adoption) fall within the confidence intervals of each of the industry-level results.

Understanding the Income and Efficiency Gap in Latin America and the Caribbean
http://dx.doi.org/10.1596/978-1-4648-0450-2

Figure 3.4 Estimated Cumulative Adoption Rates: Individual Countries in LAC

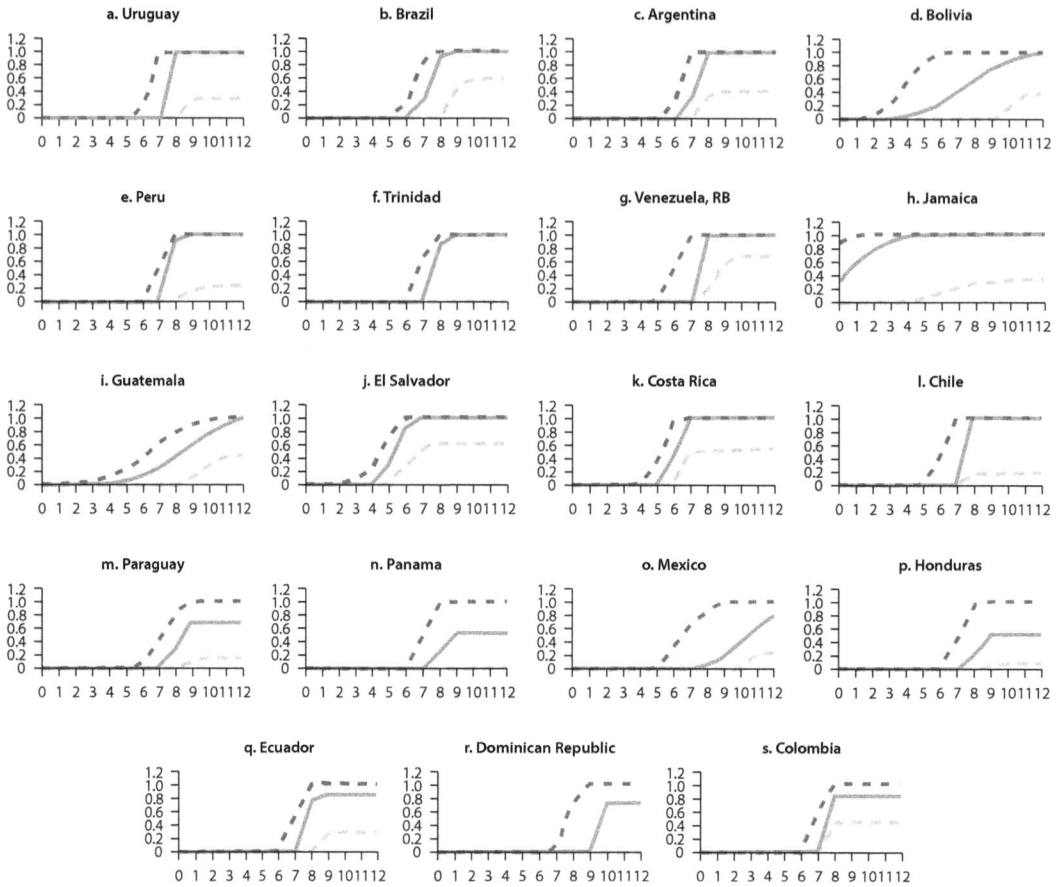

Source: World Bank calculations.
Note: Dashed lines represent the bounds of the 90 percent confidence intervals. LAC = Latin America and the Caribbean.

However, there is some interesting variation across industries in the point estimates and the confidence intervals. For example, manufacturing—a sector that is widely viewed as a fast adopter—delivers point estimates suggesting full adoption after eight years, with a relatively tight confidence interval. Mining, a sector with significant foreign presence, seems to exhibit faster adoption, with the bulk of adoption occurring at a one-year lag (however, the magnitude of long-run adoption is rather imprecisely estimated, although statistically significant). By contrast, agriculture sees longer adoption lags.

The differences between the micro evidence and the macro evidence are quite clear. The micro evidence suggests an average lag of 21 years between LAC and the United States in technology adoption, while the macro evidence is quite consistent at eight years. There is strong variation across countries in

Figure 3.5 Estimated Cumulative Adoption Rates: Individual Industries

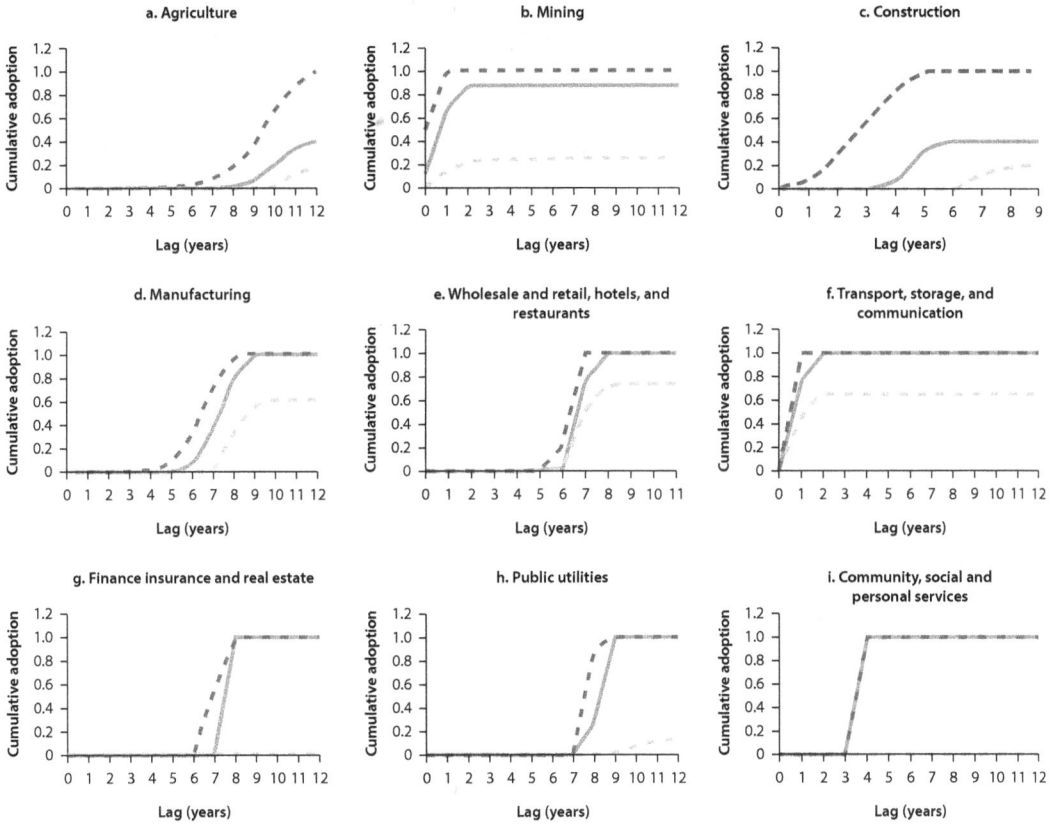

LAC in the micro evidence, but it is not as clear in the macro evidence. However, the macro and micro evidence point to some adoption heterogeneities across sectors and technologies.

Model

This section presents a model to reconcile the two findings. We consider a simplified model in which capital is the only input in production. The economy is endowed with a unit measure of production units, each with a single unit of capital; for simplicity, we abstract away from capital accumulation.

Production units are heterogeneous with respect to the extent that they can benefit from technology. Denoting the stock of technology in production unit x by T_x, the output of production unit x is given by:

$$y_x(T_x, k_x) = x \min\{T_x, k_x\}$$

By assumption, $k_x = 1$ for all x. Technology and capital are strongly complementary; thus, the amount of technology demanded by the firm is bounded by the amount of its capital. In this formulation, production units with higher levels of x benefit more from technology.

Technology adoption is costly. For simplicity, it will be useful to think of this cost as a "user fee" (that may include, for example, royalties for the inventor of the technology). The cost of adopting a unit of technology is p. The firm's profits are therefore given by:

$$\pi_x = y_x(T_x, k_x) - pT_x$$

The production unit's optimization problem is:

$$\max_{T_x} \pi_x$$

The solution to the production unit's problem is trivial: if $p > x$, it is optimal to choose $T_x = 0$. If $p < x$, it is optimal to choose $T_x = 1$.

The distribution of production units is given by a pdf $f(x)$, with support in $[0,\infty]$ (in other words, it is assumed that all production units weakly benefit from technology).

The distribution $f(x)$ is a joint characteristic of production units and the technology. It captures the extent to which a specific technology improves productivity in a specific firm. Thus, different technologies will typically be associated with different distributions of x.

Dynamics

Time evolves continuously and is indexed t. There are two countries: a frontier country (f) and an adopting country (a). At $t = 0$, there are two technological innovations, indexed 1 and 2, associated with distributions f_1 and f_2, respectively. It is useful to assume that technology 1 is more effective than technology 2, in the sense that the distribution f_1 stochastically dominates the distribution f_2. In other words, the productivity gains from adopting technology 1 are greater, on average, than the productivity gains from adopting technology 2. We assume for simplicity that the adoption costs p are the same across technologies.

In the frontier country, it is costless to adopt technologies, and $p_{f,t} = 0$ for all t; thus, all production units adopt the technology instantaneously. In the adopting country, the price of adoption, p, falls over time according to:

$$p_{a,t} = p_t = \exp(-\lambda t)$$

for some $\lambda > 0$. In the frontier country, the price of adoption is always 0; thus, all production units in the frontier country immediately adopt the technology. To abstract away from strategic delays in adoption (due to the anticipation of a falling price), it is convenient to assume that the adoption cost p must be paid in each period that the technology is used.

Equilibrium

At any time t, all production units with $x > p_t$ purchase the technology. Aggregate output is therefore given by:

$$Y_t = \int_0^\infty f_1(x) y_x(T_x, k_x) dx + \int_0^\infty f_2(x) y_x(T_x, k_x) = \int_{pt}^\infty (f_1(x) + f_2(x)) x dx$$

Micro and Macro Adoption Lags

In this framework, technologies are never fully adopted in finite time, since there are always some production units (with x close to 0) for which adoption is too costly. It is therefore useful to define adoption lags with respect to almost-full adoption rather than full adoption. Specifically, we consider some small $\varepsilon > 0$ and define adoption lags as follows. The technology-specific micro-level adoption lag, l^{micro}, is defined as the time elapsed until the difference between the technology stock in the adopting country and the technology stock in the frontier country (which is always 1) is less than ε. The technology-specific micro adoption lag is then:

$$x_\varepsilon = pl^{micro} = \exp(-\lambda l^{micro}) \Rightarrow l^{micro} = -\frac{\ln(x_\varepsilon)}{\lambda}$$

Let l_1^{micro} and l_2^{micro} be the technology-specific micro-adoption lags associated with technologies 1 and 2, respectively. The (aggregate) micro-level adoption lag, L^{micro}, is then defined as the simple average of the technology-specific micro adoption lags:

$$L^{micro} = \frac{1}{2}\left(l_1^{micro} + l_2^{micro} \right)$$

In this framework, aggregate output is the same as aggregate productivity, since capital is the only input of production and is in fixed supply. Thus, the macro-level adoption lag is defined as the elapsed time necessary for the output difference between the adopting country and the frontier country to be less than ε. Formally, define $\hat{x}_\varepsilon$ as:

$$\int_{\hat{x}_\varepsilon}^\infty (f_1(x) + f_2(x)) x dx = (1-\varepsilon) \int_0^\infty (f_1(x) + f_2(x)) x dx$$

The macro adoption lag is the time elapsed until a production unit with $x = \hat{x}_\varepsilon$ finds it optimal to adopt the technology:

$$\hat{x}_\varepsilon = pL = \exp(-\lambda L^{macro}) \Rightarrow L^{macro} = -\frac{\ln(\hat{x}_\varepsilon)}{\lambda}$$

Understanding the Income and Efficiency Gap in Latin America and the Caribbean
http://dx.doi.org/10.1596/978-1-4648-0450-2

The micro-level adoption lag and the macro-level adoption lag may be very different, depending on the distribution of firms. Specifically, the macro lag is typically shorter than the micro lag, for two reasons:

1. Technologies are adopted first in production units in which they are relatively more effective. Thus, the productivity gains from the first technology adoptions are larger relative to the productivity gains from later adoptions. The macro-level adoption lag accounts for this, by weighting technology adoptions by their respective productivity gains. The micro-level adoption lag, by contrast, assigns equal weights to all adoptions; thus, the micro-level lag is likely to be relatively longer than the macro-level lag.
2. More effective technologies are likely to be adopted faster. Technologies that improve productivity by more are likely to be adopted faster, as production units are more willing to pay the adoption costs. This implies shorter lags associated with technologies that are more productivity enhancing. The macro-level adoption lag focuses on aggregate productivity gains from technology adoption, which is likely driven disproportionately by more productive technologies. By contrast, the micro-level adoption lag weights technologies equally, and is thus likely to be longer.

This framework illustrates that, when technology adoption is costly and the decision to adopt technology is related to its effectiveness, macro-level adoption lags will tend to be shorter than micro-level adoption lags. The next section offers a simple numerical illustration of this principle, with parameters chosen to match key features of micro- and macro-level adoption lags in LAC.

Numerical Illustration

This section proposes a simple numerical illustration of the model, with the following features, which are roughly consistent with the patterns of technology adoption in LAC:

1. A 20-year (aggregate) micro-level adoption lag
2. Some technologies adopted within approximately 10 years (for example, Internet) and some technologies adopted within approximately 30 years (for example, electricity)
3. An eight-year macro-level adoption lag
4. No adoption within the first eight years, and almost-full adoption after eight years

Consider an economy with two technologies, 1 and 2, and the following distributions of technology effectiveness. There are two types of production units. A measure δ_i of production units has a value of $\bar{x}_i$, and the remaining measure $1 - \delta_i$ has a value of $x_i < \bar{x}_i$.

The adoption patterns do not uniquely pin down δ_i and x_i. In what follows, we present two examples: one in which the difference between micro- and macro-adoption lags is driven entirely by differences in technology effectiveness across technologies, and one in which the difference is driven entirely by differences in technology effectiveness across production units.

Example 1: Differences across Technologies

As a first example, consider an environment in which there is no heterogeneity across production units. For technology i to be adopted after t_i years, it must be the case that:

$$\bar{x}_i = \exp(-\lambda t_i)$$

Thus, to match the micro adoption lags, we need to match

$$\bar{x}_1 = \exp(-10\lambda)$$
$$\bar{x}_2 = \exp(-30\lambda)$$

Note that the micro-level adoption lag is the average of 10 and 30, which is 20. For the macro-level adoption lag to be 10, it must be the case that the productivity gains from technology 2 are negligible:

$$\bar{x}_1 \geq (1-\varepsilon)(\bar{x}_1 + \bar{x}_2) \Rightarrow \frac{\varepsilon}{1-\varepsilon}\bar{x}_1 \geq \bar{x}_2$$

Choosing $\varepsilon = 0.001$, the above holds, for example, for $x_1 = 0.5x_2$:

$$\bar{x}_1 = \exp(-10\lambda)$$
$$0.5\bar{x}_1 = \exp(-30\lambda)$$

Solving for λ:

$$0.5\exp(-10\lambda) = \exp(-30\lambda) \Rightarrow \exp(-20\lambda) = 0.5 \Rightarrow \lambda = -\frac{\ln(0.5)}{20} \approx 0.035$$

Substituting in yields $x_1 = 0.7$ and $x_2 = 0.35$.

We have thus constructed an example in which heterogeneity across technologies in terms of the productivity gains that they generate resulted in a difference between micro and macro adoption lags that is consistent with the experience of LAC.

Understanding the Income and Efficiency Gap in Latin America and the Caribbean
http://dx.doi.org/10.1596/978-1-4648-0450-2

Example 2: Differences across Production Units

In this second example, we focus on the role of heterogeneity across production units in generating a difference between the micro and macro technology adoption lags. For this purpose, we abstract away from differences across technologies and simplify by assuming a single technology that has a micro adoption lag of $L^{micro} = 20$ and a macro adoption lag of $L^{macro} = 10$.

To construct this example, the following conditions must hold:

$$(1-\delta) > \varepsilon$$
$$\delta\bar{x} \geq (1-\varepsilon)\left(\delta\bar{x} + (1-\delta)\underline{x}\right)$$
$$\bar{x} = \exp(-10\lambda)$$
$$\underline{x} = \exp(-20\lambda)$$

The first equation states that the micro adoption lag is given by the time elapsed until all production units adopt the technology. The second equation states that the macro adoption lag is given by the time elapsed until the first δ production units adopt the technology; thus, the macro adoption lag is driven by the most productive uses of the technology, while the micro adoption lag is driven by the least productive uses of the technology. The third and fourth equations state that the adoption lags of the first δ adopters and the last $1 - \delta$ adopters should be 10 and 20 years, respectively, consistent with the pre-specified micro- and macro-level adoption lags.

Given $\varepsilon = 0.001$, these equations have four unknowns: δ, λ, $\bar{x}$, and $\underline{x}$. Thus, since the first two equations are inequality constraints, there may be infinite solutions. We focus on one possible solution. We assume that the first inequality constraint holds with equality, and thus $\delta = 1 - \varepsilon = 0.999$. Further, we assume that $\underline{x} = 0.5\bar{x}$, and verify that the second constraint holds:

$$0.999\bar{x} \geq 0.999\left(0.999\bar{x} + 0.001.0.5\bar{x}\right) \Leftrightarrow 0.999 \geq 0.999\left(0.999 + 0.0005\right)$$

The inequality on the right-hand side holds, because $0.999 + 0.0005 < 1$ (it is easy to see that this inequality would hold for any $\underline{x} < \bar{x}$). Thus, we can proceed in solving for λ by imposing:

$$0.5\exp(-10\lambda) = \exp(-20\lambda) \Rightarrow 0.5 = \exp(-10\lambda) \Rightarrow \lambda = -\frac{\ln(0.5)}{10} \approx 0.07$$

Yielding $\lambda = 0.07$, $\bar{x} = 0.5$, and $\underline{x} = 0.25$.

These examples illustrate that the observed differences between micro- and macro-level adoption lags can be generated with reasonable heterogeneity across technologies or production units in technology effectiveness, and that it is actually quite easy to reconcile the two estimates. However, absent further data on the prices of technology adoption (that pin down λ) or the distribution of technology effectiveness (that governs f), the parameters of the model are not uniquely pinned down, and therefore the quantitative relevance of the model remains an open question.

Table 3A.1 Adoption Lags for Individual Countries in Latin America and the Caribbean

	Aviation passengers	Cars	Cellphones	Electricity	Internet	PCs	Ships	Telegraph	Telephone	Trucks	Blast oxygen steel	Rail passengers
Argentina	31.72		15.60		8.79	14.21	64.28	27.53			10.32	101.23
Belize												
Bolivia		41.63	17.59			16.28						116.67
Brazil	28.74	37.56	16.88	43.41	7.69	14.42	75.99	36.29	24.05	31.86	17.28	90.62
Chile	27.03		15.45		8.59	14.52	62.58			6.84	23.14	96.21
Colombia	24.46	28.03		50.67	7.73	16.17	140.89	68.46	30.11	16.86	16.56	
Costa Rica		29.80	17.49		8.94				27.93	28.24		
Cuba			15.93	16.47			134.07					111.37
Dominican Republic		55.51	16.06	67.52					65.88	48.97		
Ecuador	39.56	47.38	19.41	64.77	8.04	16.85	177.48		54.29	46.14		
El Salvador		27.25		65.80						31.03		
Guatemala		20.52	16.48	52.92		19.30	96.80	53.18	19.61	5.93		
Mexico	25.47	29.63	14.69	19.35	7.56	13.88			23.18	26.24	18.13	92.47
Nicaragua		24.28	19.28			17.09	155.85			26.99		
Panama		50.80		64.20	10.73		91.17	58.51	67.54	41.38		
Peru			16.31	47.42	10.77							81.94
Puerto Rico		58.89	18.16	66.52					56.65	41.83		
Uruguay			18.12	26.84				52.41				96.40
Venezuela, RB	25.65	38.49	14.32	55.66	8.04	12.61	111.58	76.55	34.20	35.22		

Source: World Bank calculations.

Conclusion

This chapter proposed that endogenous technology adoption may account for the difference between micro-level adoption lags—defined as the cross-country differences in technology prevalence rates—and macro-level adoption lags—defined as the productivity gap attributed to differences in technology. When technology adoption is endogenous, the most effective technologies are adopted first, and by their most effective users. Thus, differences in technology prevalence rates tend to overstate the differences in TFP.

We illustrated numerically that, in a model with endogenous technology adoption, it is easy to generate the observed disparity between the micro-level adoption lags estimated by Comin and Hobijn (2010) and Comin and Mestieri (2014), and the macro-level technology adoption lags estimated by AAEN. This finding suggests that the two estimations are not inconsistent with one another. However, assessing the consistency of the two estimates requires a better understanding of (i) the rate at which technology adoption costs diminish over time and (ii) the distribution of technology effectiveness across production units. We hope to pursue this question further in future work.

References

Akcigit, Ufuk, Harun Alp, Maya Eden, and Ha Nguyen. 2014. "Identifying Technology Adoption Lags from Macro Data." Development Economics Vice Presidency, World Bank, Washington, DC.

Comin, Diego, and Bart Hobijn. 2009. "The CHAT Dataset." NBER Working Paper 15319, National Bureau of Economic Research, Cambridge, MA.

———. 2010. "An Exploration of Technology Diffusion." *American Economic Review* 100 (5): 2031–59.

Comin, Diego, and Martí Mestieri. 2014. "Technology Diffusion: Measurement, Causes, and Consequences." In *Handbook of Economic Growth*, volume 2, edited by Philippe Aghion and Steven N. Durlauf, 565–622. San Diego, CA: Elsevier.

Hsieh, Chang-Tai, and Peter J. Klenow. 2009. "Misallocation and Manufacturing TFP in China and India." *Quarterly Journal of Economics* 124 (4): 1403–48.

CHAPTER 4

Structural Change in Latin America: Does the Allocation of Resources across Sectors, Products, and Technologies Explain the Region's Slow Productivity Growth?

Marc Schiffbauer, Hania Sahnoun, and Jorge Thompson Araujo

Introduction

The objective of this chapter is to assess the role of structural change in explaining the persistent productivity gap between countries in Latin America and high-income countries. Recent contributions by Pages (2010) and McMillan and Rodrik (2011) find that labor flows between sectors reduced aggregate labor productivity growth in several Latin American countries between 1990 and 2005. This chapter documents the evolution of employment, productivity, and technologies across sectors in Latin America and several benchmark countries between 1960 and 2005, and uses newly available data to analyze the robustness of the findings.

Theories of structural change show that the reallocation of activity across sectors accompanying generalized balanced growth can originate from income effects generated by nonhomothetic preferences for different consumption goods (Kongsamut, Rebelo, and Xie 2002; Pasinetti 1981), changes in relative prices caused by technological progress that differs across sectors (Baumol 1967; Ngai and Pissarides 2007), or changes in relative prices caused by differences in capital intensities or elasticities of substitution in production across sectors (Herrendorf, Rogerson, and Valentinyi 2013b).

In the following, we take the source of structural change as given and analyze the extent to which the sectoral reallocation associated with structural change has affected aggregate labor productivity growth in Latin America. We note that structural change does not affect aggregate labor productivity growth in a neo-classical closed economy framework, assuming perfect competition in output and factor markets. In this framework, wages and labor flows between sectors fully adjust (for example, after a sector-specific technology shock), equating marginal labor productivities across sectors.

In the presence of market failures, distortions, and rigidities (such as those caused by product or labor market regulations), wages and labor flows do not fully adjust, which drives a wedge between marginal productivities across sectors. Although the impact of these distortions is difficult to measure, it is likely that they are more severe in low- and middle-income countries. For instance, Herrendorf and Valentinyi (2012) find large sectoral total factor productivity (TFP) differences relative to the United States in agriculture, manufacturing, and services. Moreover, the sectoral TFP gaps relative to the United States are larger in agriculture and services than in manufacturing. The latter finding is consistent with Rodrik (2013), who finds unconditional convergence in labor productivity in manufacturing despite the absence of aggregate convergence. These findings imply that aggregate labor productivity is affected by the sectoral composition of the economy (Duarte and Restuccia 2010; Herrendorf, Rogerson, and Valentinyi 2013a).

Duarte and Restuccia (2010) and Echevarria (1997) show that sectoral reallocation associated with structural change can explain most of the cross-country differences in aggregate productivity growth if countries are at different stages of the process of structural change. In particular, Duarte and Restuccia (2010) reveal that during the process of structural change, the reallocation of labor from agriculture to manufacturing leads to catching up in aggregate productivity relative to the United States, and the reallocation from manufacturing to services leads to falling behind. The results are based on a three-sector model that does not distinguish between the large potential differences in productivity and tradability across different service subsectors. In the following, we account for differences in labor productivity levels across different service sectors using the Groningen 10-sector database.

Our findings show that the contribution of sectoral reallocation associated with structural change to aggregate labor productivity growth in Latin America has been relatively small and even negative in some countries. In contrast, for some countries, within-sector labor productivity growth has been as high as in East Asian countries. We also find substantial heterogeneity in both effects across Latin American countries.

The results suggest that it is important to account for differences in labor flows and productivity across different service subsectors. For instance, we find that the employment-intensive retail and wholesale trade sector has expanded in all Latin American countries. However, the performance of the sector, that is, its relative level of productivity in the economy, has differed widely across countries. As a result, the reallocation of labor has tended to increase aggregate productivity growth in countries with good sector performance (relative to other sectors in the economy) and to reduce growth in countries with relatively low levels of retail and wholesale trade productivity.

Moreover, we find that employment shares in manufacturing have declined in most Latin American countries. This trend potentially slows down the region's speed of convergence, as it counterweights the aggregate impact of unconditional convergence of labor productivity in manufacturing with the rest of the world (Duarte and Restuccia 2010; Rodrik 2013). This finding warrants a more detailed analysis of the evolution of manufacturing production structures across countries in Latin America.

We use the product space approach to compare the patterns of specialization in manufacturing in Latin America and the Caribbean with other regions, especially East Asia. Despite the limitations of the analysis,[1] it remains a relevant analytical approach to capture differences in the evolution of manufacturing across regions over the past 30 years. We find a lack of formation of production clusters among related manufacturing products or industries relative to other regions.

Finally, we analyze whether manufacturing firms in countries in Latin America tend to be specialized in resource-intensive, idiosyncratic production technologies that are unrelated to processes or technologies applied in large employment or technology-intensive manufacturing clusters. Therefore, we apply the recently developed "knowledge applicability" measure (Cai and Li 2013), which captures the scope for technology spillovers embodied in the technological specialization of firms in a given country. In contrast to East Asian economies, we find that manufacturing firms in Latin America tend to be specialized in idiosyncratic instead of general purpose technologies, limiting the scope for the adoption of foreign technologies and integration into global value chains.

Labor Productivity and Structural Change in Latin America

Are There Large Productivity Differences across Sectors within Latin American Countries?

Productivity growth in Latin America has differed significantly between sectors of the economy. Figure 4.1, panel a, shows that productivity growth in the service sectors has lagged behind agriculture and manufacturing. Since 1970, labor productivity in agriculture, public utilities, and mining has grown faster than in other sectors of the economy. After the period of import substitution policies and the debt crisis, labor productivity in 1990–2005 grew in the manufacturing sector by about 2 percent annually. However, regional labor productivity in services stagnated during the same period and even declined in several countries.

Figure 4.1, panel b, illustrates that among the large sectors in terms of employment,[2] the highest labor productivity growth was observed in agriculture, manufacturing, and transportation. However, labor moved from agriculture and manufacturing to the service sectors with the lowest productivity growth, such as retail and wholesale trade, government services, and finance, real estate, and business services.

Figure 4.1 Labor Productivity Growth and Change in Employment Share
percent

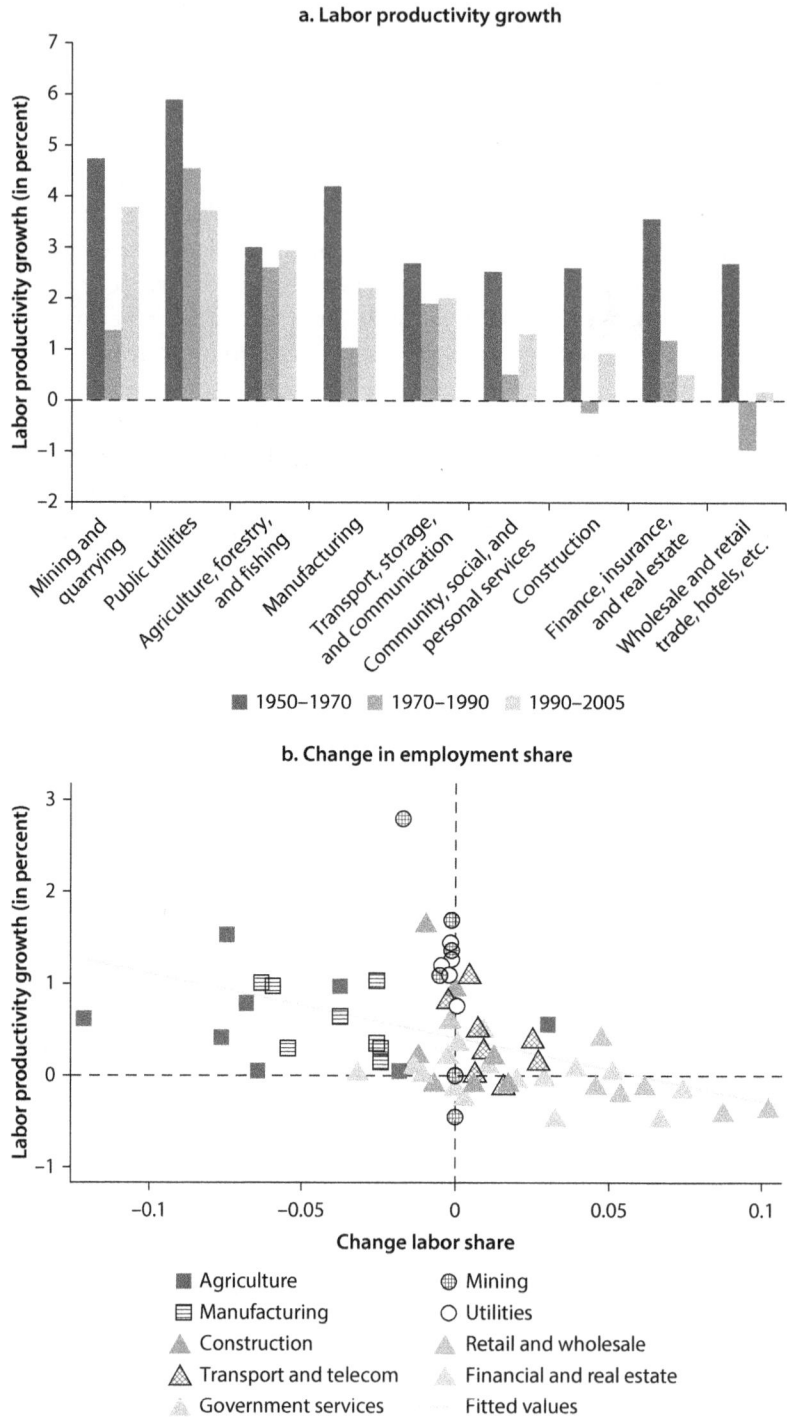

a. Labor productivity growth

1950–1970   1970–1990   1990–2005

b. Change in employment share

Agriculture   Mining

Manufacturing   Utilities

Construction   Retail and wholesale

Transport and telecom   Financial and real estate

Government services   Fitted values

Source: World Bank calculations based on Timmer and de Vries 2009.

The distribution of productivity growth across sectors does not appear to reflect a process of convergence in productivity levels between sectors. Among others, Herrendorf and Valentinyi (2012) and McMillan and Rodrik (2011) find stark differences in productivity levels across sectors in low- and middle-income countries, while differences in productivity levels across sectors in high-income countries are typically minor, reflecting the outcome of past structural change. That is, the latter has been interpreted to signify an equilibrium balanced growth path in high-income countries whereby initial productivity differences across sectors have been marginalized over time as labor moved to the sectors with the highest marginal productivity, equalizing productivity levels.[3] Thus, market forces in low- and middle-income countries should reallocate resources to the sectors with the highest marginal productivity. Instead, the distribution of productivity growth across sectors in figure 4.1 suggests that the forces of labor reallocation across sectors are imperfect in the region, implying the prevalence of market failures and distortions. Retail trade, construction, and government services, which are typically relatively low-productivity sectors in low- and middle-income countries, had the lowest productivity growth rates since 1970 but increased their employment shares significantly in most countries. This situation is counterbalanced, however, by strong productivity growth and declining labor shares in agriculture, which is often the sector with the lowest labor productivity level. In line with Herrendorf and Valentinyi (2012), Pages (2010), and others, the evidence indicates that there exist substantial differences in labor productivity levels and growth across sectors in Latin American countries.[4]

The increase in the employment shares of lower productivity sectors can potentially explain Latin America's low aggregate productivity growth. Structural change is defined as the reallocation of input factors between sectors with different productivity.[5] In practice, the analysis is reduced to the reallocation of labor, since time-series data on capital stocks at the more detailed sector level are typically not available for low- and middle-income countries.[6] Given the relatively large differences in productivity levels across sectors in countries in the region, the increase in employment shares in lower-productivity sectors can help explain low aggregate productivity growth and hence the lack of income convergence despite the successful technological catch-up of individual firms or industries in Latin America.[7]

Therefore, we aim to extend the work of McMillan and Rodrik (2011), documenting in detail the evolution of employment and productivity across sectors in nine Latin American countries and several benchmark countries between 1960 and 2005. In particular, we decompose labor productivity into a *within* component, measuring changes in sector-level productivity, and a *structural change* component, measuring changes arising from a reallocation of labor between sectors, as follows:

$$\Delta Y_t = \sum_{i=n} s_{i,t-k} \Delta y_{it} + \sum_{i=n} y_{i,t} \Delta s_{it} \qquad (4.1)$$

Understanding the Income and Efficiency Gap in Latin America and the Caribbean
http://dx.doi.org/10.1596/978-1-4648-0450-2

In equation 4.1, ΔY_t is the change in aggregate labor productivity between t and $t-k$, s_{it} is the employment share in sector i at time t, and y_{it} is the productivity level in sector i at time t. The first term is the "within" component and the second term is the "structural change" component.

Data limitations in the analysis require a number of assumptions. Previous studies using the same data sources have been criticized for several empirical shortcomings. First, aggregate productivity must not always lead to higher aggregate welfare (at least in a static setting abstracting from dynamic productivity or technology spillovers a la Aghion and Howitt [1992] or Romer [1990]). For example, productivity may be higher in sectors with monopoly power. Reallocation of labor to these sectors would contribute positively to structural change, but would not necessarily enhance welfare. Moreover, differences in the coverage of the informal sector (in terms of GDP and employment) across countries can bias the results.

Most important, however, previous studies such as McMillan and Rodrik (2011) and Pages (2010) measure differences in the average instead of the marginal rates of labor productivity across sectors. Under perfect competition in input and output markets, however, labor should move to the sector with the highest marginal productivity (wage), equalizing marginal rates across sectors over time. Under a Cobb-Douglas production function specification, the marginal productivity of labor is the average productivity multiplied by the share of labor in GDP. Thus, large differences in labor shares, that is, in capital intensities across sectors, drive a wedge between marginal and average labor productivity levels.

For instance, public utilities and mining are likely to have higher capital intensities, potentially overstating their measured marginal productivities when approximated with averages. McMillan and Rodrik (2011) argue, however, that in the case of the other sectors, which employ the most labor, it is not clear that there is a significant bias.[8] Thus, we assume in the following that large gaps in average productivity across sectors within a country are positively correlated with the underlying unobservable gaps in marginal productivities across sectors.[9] Moreover, we provide a robustness test by approximating the marginal productivity of labor with the estimated labor share of income in annex 4A. Using World Bank International Income Distribution Data Set (I2D2) data, we calculate the income share of labor using wage data for Peru and Chile.[10] We find that gaps in marginal productivities measured by average wages across sectors are smaller than gaps measured by value added per worker, but sectoral differences remain significant.[11]

Do Changes in the Allocation of Labor across Sectors Explain the Region's Laggard Aggregate Productivity Growth?

Aggregate productivity growth in Latin American countries between 1960 and 2005 was well below that of the region's East Asian peers during the same period. Figure 4.2 illustrates that average annual aggregate productivity growth ranged between 2.5 and 4.5 percent in India; Indonesia; Malaysia; Taiwan, China;

Figure 4.2 Decomposition of Labor Productivity Growth (Unweighted Averages), 1960–2005

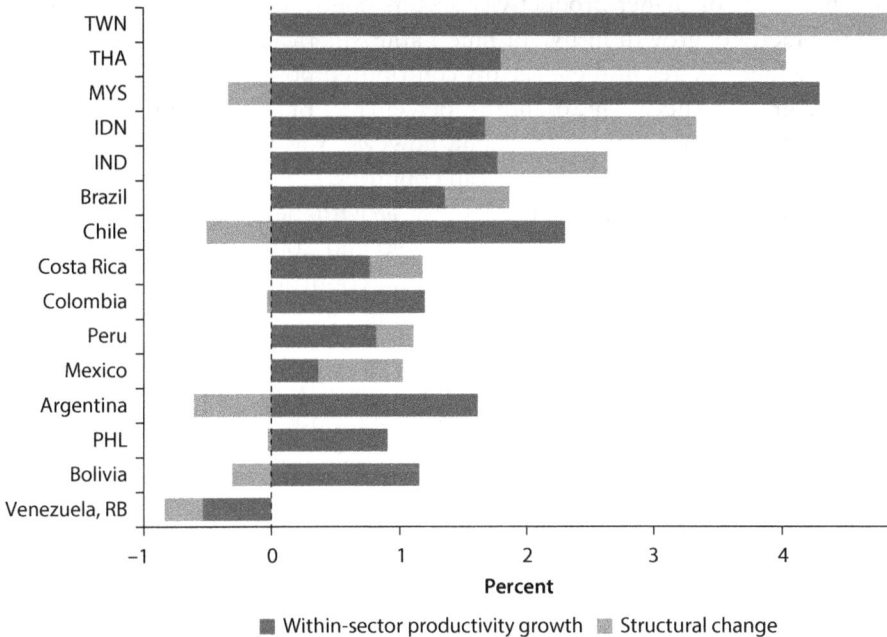

Source: World Bank calculations.
Note: IDN = Indonesia; IND = India; MYS = Malaysia; PHL = Philippines; THA = Thailand; TWN = Taiwan, China.

and Thailand. In contrast, average annual productivity growth was about 1.8 percent between 1960 and 2005 in Brazil and Chile, and around 1 percent for all other Latin American countries, apart from the República Bolivariana de Venezuela, where it was negative. The only East Asian country with available data and similar productivity growth around 1 percent is the Philippines.

Within-sector productivity growth in Argentina and Chile between 1960 and 2005 was comparable or higher than in East Asian countries, but the labor shares of higher productivity sectors declined in both countries, reducing aggregate productivity growth. Within-sector productivity growth in Argentina was as high as in India or Indonesia; however, the relative decline in employment in higher productivity sectors reduced aggregate productivity growth in Argentina from 1.6 to 1 percent annually, while increasing labor shares in these sectors raised aggregate productivity growth in India and Indonesia to 2.6 and 3.3 percent, respectively. Likewise, within-sector growth in Chile was 0.5 percent higher than in Thailand, but the declining labor shares in higher productivity sectors reduced annual aggregate growth to 1.8 percent in Chile while increasing labor shares in these sectors raised it to 4 percent in Thailand between 1960 and 2005.

Thus, while structural change accounted for −61 and −28 percent of aggregate productivity growth in Argentina and Chile, respectively, it accounted for

55 and 50 percent in Indonesia and Thailand, respectively. Overall, a decline in the labor share of higher productivity sectors contributed negatively to aggregate productivity growth in five of nine Latin American countries. In contrast, increasing labor shares in these sectors contributed positively to aggregate productivity growth (between 26 and 64 percent) in Brazil, Costa Rica, Mexico, and Peru; the within-sector component, however, was relatively weak (around 1 percent) in these four Latin American countries.

The changes in aggregate productivity growth between 1990 and 2005 mirror these long-term trends. Between 1990 and 2005, aggregate productivity growth stagnated in most Latin American countries apart from Chile and Peru, and to some extent Argentina, where it was comparable to East Asian countries except China. Aggregate productivity in China grew by 8.8 percent annually from 1990 to 2005, outperforming the second highest growth country (India) by 4.6 percent annually. Aggregate productivity also grew strongly in Chile and Peru and at comparable rates to Indonesia, Thailand, and Turkey during that period.

The labor shares of higher productivity sectors declined in seven of nine Latin American countries from 1990 to 2005, but slightly increased in Costa Rica and Mexico. Within-sector growth was about 4 percent in Bolivia, Chile, and Peru, second only to China. However, declining labor shares in higher productivity sectors reduced aggregate productivity by 0.4, 0.9, and 3 percent in Peru, Chile, and Bolivia, respectively, while the relative increase in employment in these sectors raised aggregate productivity growth in the East Asian peer countries. Overall, the structural change component was strongest in China, India, Indonesia, Thailand, and Turkey, where it contributed between 1 and 2 percent to aggregate annual productivity growth.

Overall, these findings show that reallocation of labor across sectors was pivotal in many Latin American countries to explain their inferior aggregate productivity growth performance during the past 50 years relative to their East Asian peers. This trend was even more pronounced in the more recent subperiod between 1990 and 2005, as shown in figure 4.3. What are the major trends in sector employment shares causing this slow structural change in Latin American countries? To answer this question, we analyze the changes in employment shares by sector in Latin American countries between 1990 and 2005 in more detail in figures 4.4 and 4.5.

In most Latin American economies, labor shares in manufacturing and agriculture declined between 1990 and 2005, while labor moved to various service sectors. Where these service sectors were more productive, labor reallocation associated with structural change made a positive contribution to overall productivity growth (figures 4.4 and 4.5). For example, in Costa Rica, labor reallocation increased aggregate productivity growth, showing movement of labor from agriculture to transport and telecommunications, finance, real estate and business services, and wholesale and retail trade. Notably, wholesale and retail trade in Costa Rica has relatively high average labor productivity, which contrasts with all other Latin American countries

Figure 4.3 Decomposition of Labor Productivity Growth (Unweighted Averages), 1990–2005

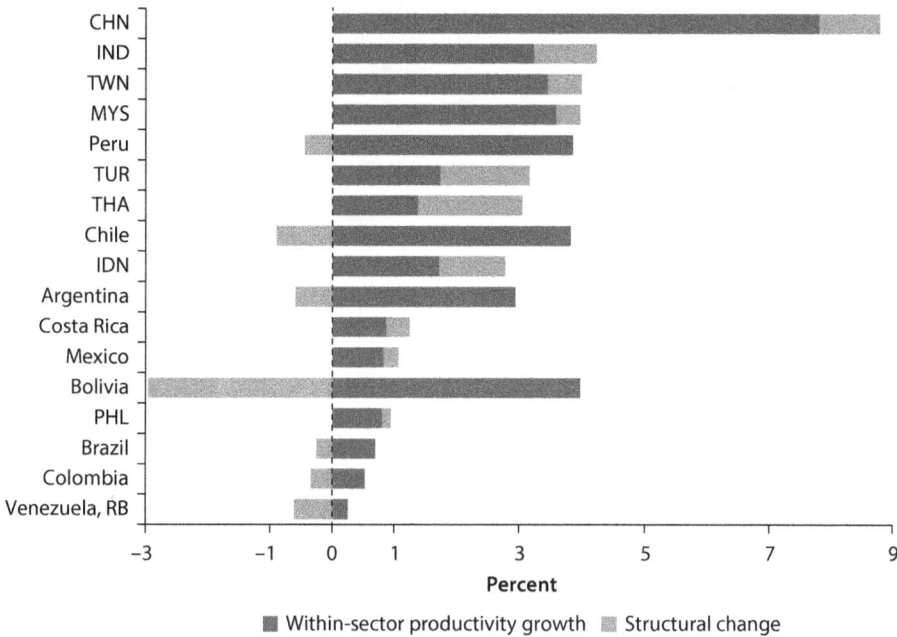

Source: World Bank calculations.
Note: CHN = China; IDN = Indonesia; IND = India; MYS = Malaysia; PHL = Philippines; THA = Thailand; TUR = Turkey; TWN = Taiwan, China.

in the sample except Mexico. Apart from this overall finding, five additional observations are salient.

First, the productivity level of the wholesale and retail trade sector is pivotal to explain the contribution of structural change to aggregate productivity growth among Latin American countries. Figures 4.4 and 4.5 demonstrate that a significant share of the labor force is working in wholesale and retail trade; the sector's employment shares increased in all countries in Latin America (apart from Peru) between 1990 and 2005. The sector had relatively high productivity levels in Costa Rica and Mexico, contributing to aggregate productivity growth in these countries. In contrast, the productivity levels in wholesale and retail trade were low in all other Latin American countries, reducing aggregate growth; notably, the sector's relative productivity level was the lowest among all sectors in Brazil, Chile, and Colombia. The latter suggests that in many Latin American countries redundant labor from other sectors often ends up working in unproductive small-scale activities (for example, street vendors) in the retail trade sector, which typically hosts a large share of informal labor. In contrast, the relatively high productivity levels in Costa Rica and Mexico might indicate a higher degree of formalization in the sector, possibly due to the past entry of a large number of foreign (U.S.) wholesale and retail trade franchises in both countries.

Understanding the Income and Efficiency Gap in Latin America and the Caribbean
http://dx.doi.org/10.1596/978-1-4648-0450-2

Figure 4.4 Structural Change in Argentina, Bolivia, Brazil, and Chile, 1990–2005

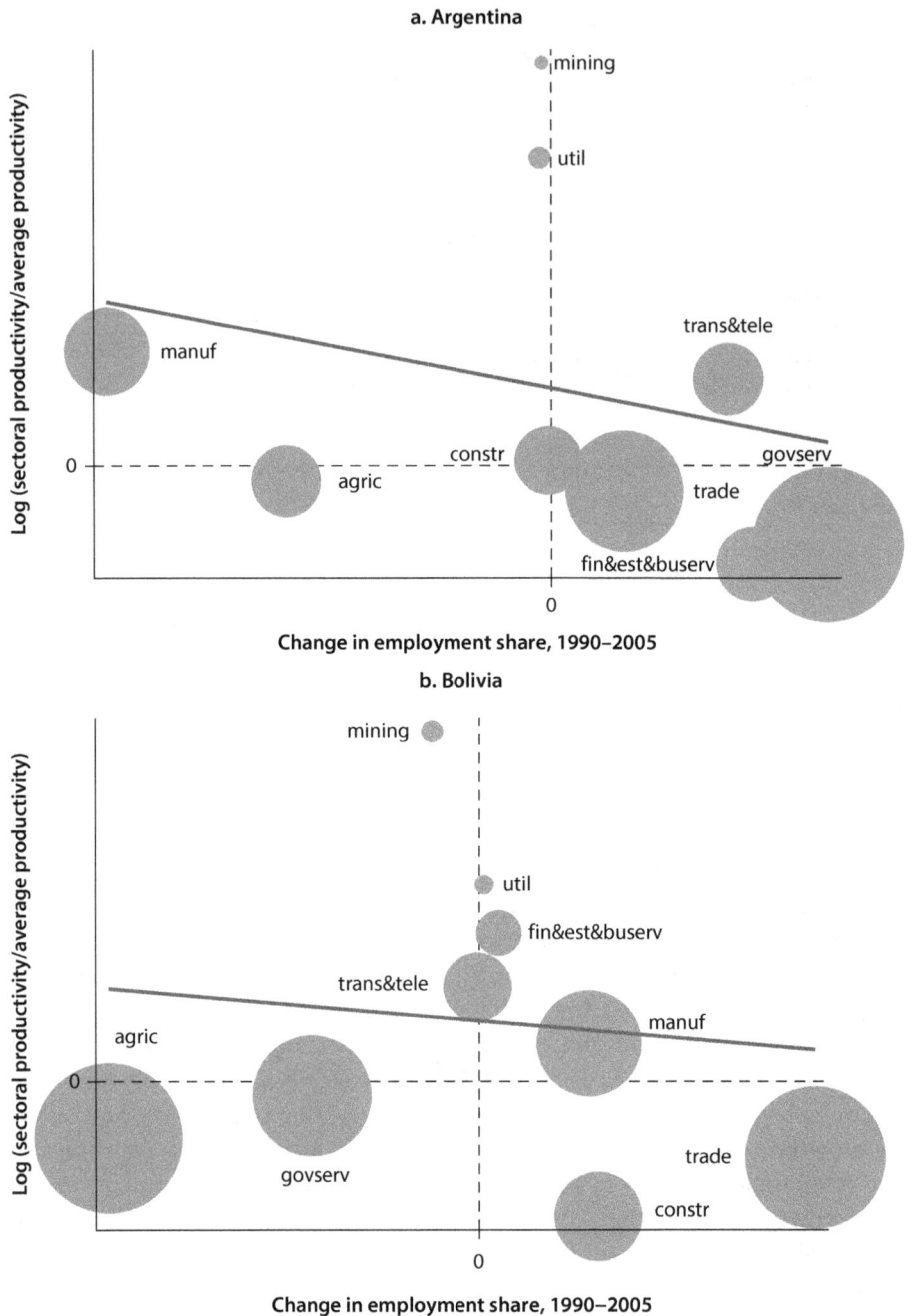

a. Argentina

b. Bolivia

figure continues next page

Figure 4.4 Structural Change in Argentina, Bolivia, Brazil, and Chile, 1990–2005 *(continued)*

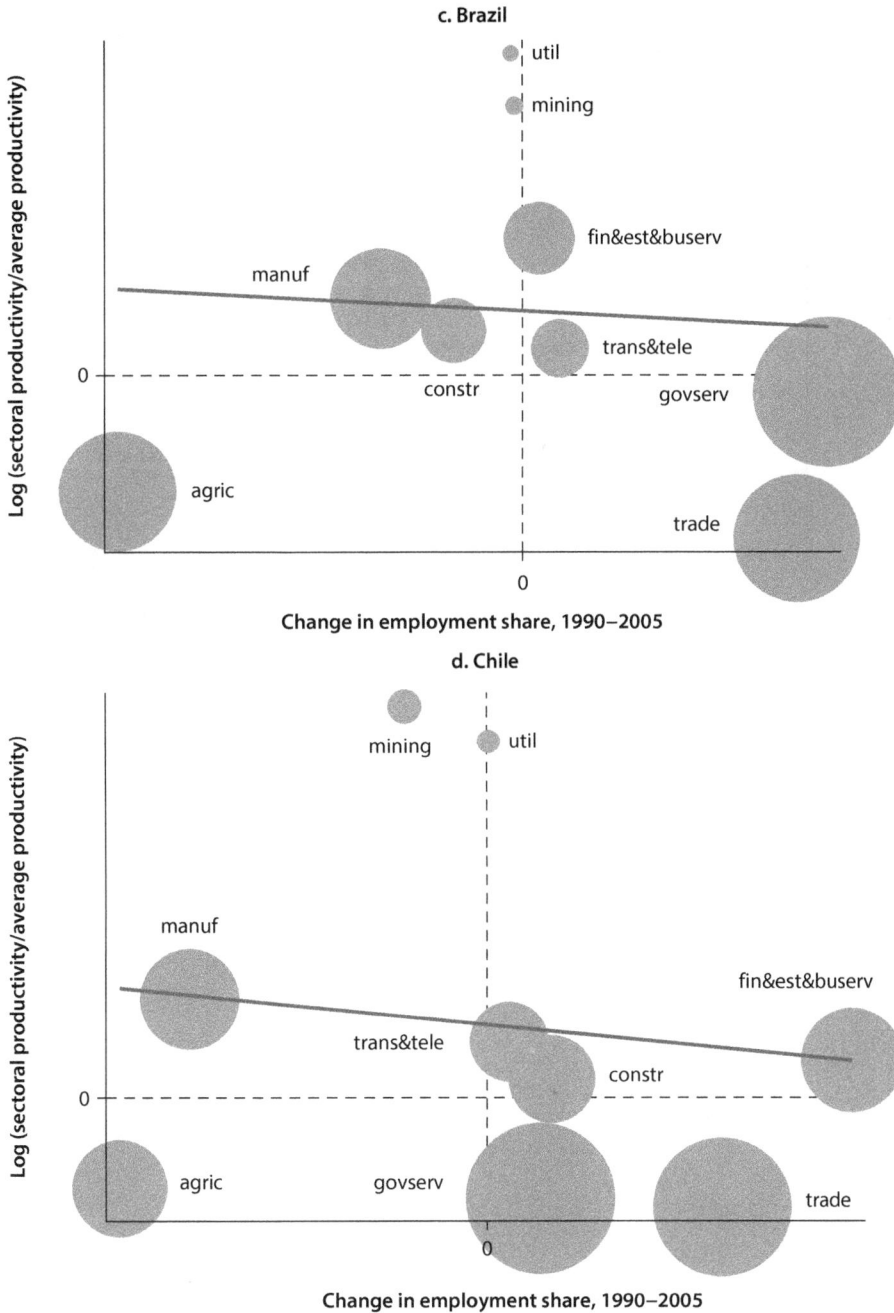

c. Brazil

Change in employment share, 1990–2005

d. Chile

Change in employment share, 1990–2005

Sources: McMillan and Rodrik 2011; Timmer and de Vries 2009; World Bank calculations.
Note: The figure plots the logarithm of sectoral value added per worker (relative to the average across all sectors) and the change in the employment share for nine sectors of the economy between 1990 and 2005. The size of the circles reflects the employment share in 2005. On the vertical axis, sectors above zero are relatively more productive compared with an average sector in the economy. On the x-axis, sectors to the right from zero have had increases in employment shares. agric = agricultural sector; constr = construction sector; fin&est&buserv = financial, real estate and business services; govserv = government services; manuf = manufacturing sector; trans&tele = transport and telecommunications.

Understanding the Income and Efficiency Gap in Latin America and the Caribbean
http://dx.doi.org/10.1596/978-1-4648-0450-2

Figure 4.5 Structural Change in Colombia, Costa Rica, Mexico, and Peru, 1990–2005

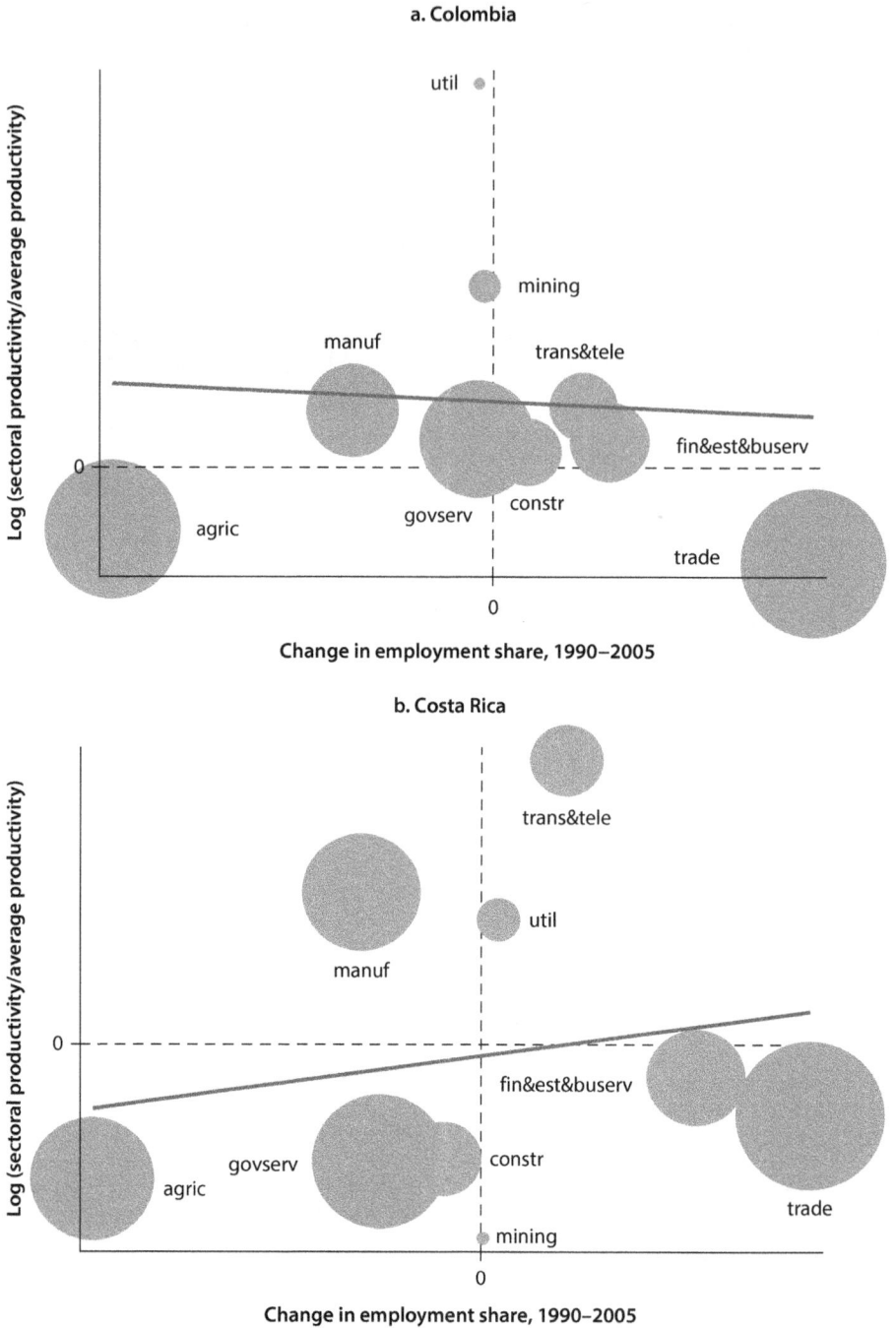

a. Colombia

Change in employment share, 1990–2005

b. Costa Rica

Change in employment share, 1990–2005

figure continues next page

Understanding the Income and Efficiency Gap in Latin America and the Caribbean
http://dx.doi.org/10.1596/978-1-4648-0450-2

Figure 4.5 Structural Change in Colombia, Costa Rica, Mexico, and Peru, 1990–2005 *(continued)*

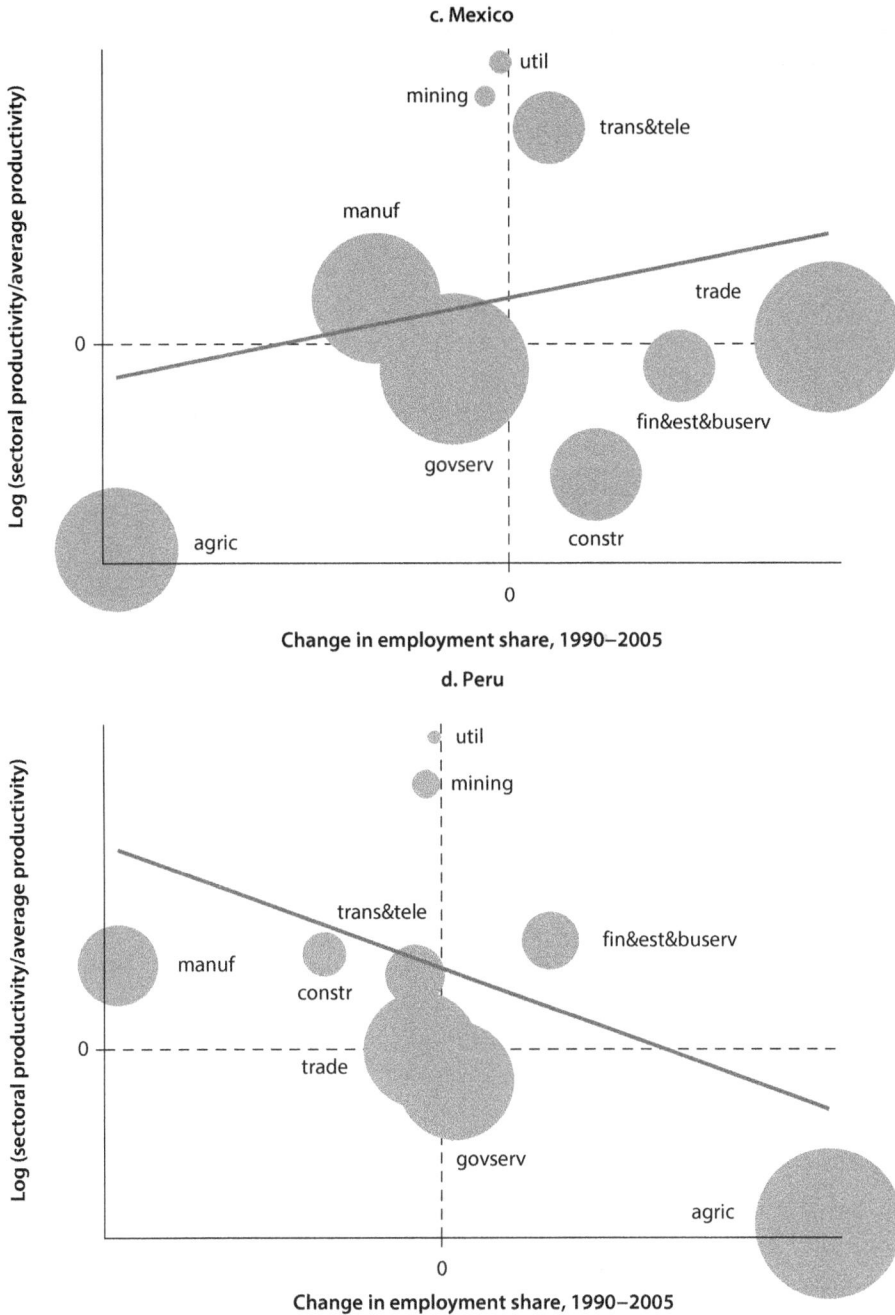

c. Mexico

Change in employment share, 1990–2005

d. Peru

Change in employment share, 1990–2005

Sources: McMillan and Rodrik 2011; Timmer and de Vries 2009; World Bank calculations.
Note: The figure plots the logarithm of sectoral value added per worker (relative to the average across all sectors) and the change in the employment share for nine sectors of the economy between 1990 and 2005. The size of the circles reflects the employment share in 2005. On the vertical axis, sectors above zero are relatively more productive compared with an average sector in the economy. On the x-axis, sectors to the right from zero have had increases in employment shares. agric = agricultural sector; constr = construction sector; fin&est&buserv = financial, real estate and business services; govserv = government services; manuf = manufacturing sector; trans&tele = transport and telecommunications..

This finding implies that case studies analyzing differences in the performance of specific service sectors across different Latin American countries can help explain the underlying causes of cross-country differences in aggregate productivity growth. For instance, the World Bank database on service trade restrictions provides comparable information across 103 countries for five key service sectors (Borchert, Gootiiz, and Mattoo 2012). The indicators focus on policies and regulations discriminating against the entry of foreign service providers. The data show significant variations in services trade restrictions across Latin American countries.

Second, the share of labor working in manufacturing sectors declined in all Latin American countries except Bolivia. The manufacturing sector is among the most productive sectors in all countries. In Argentina and Peru, it was the sector with the strongest labor share decline (stronger than agriculture). This trend slowed down aggregate productivity growth. In particular, aggregate productivity growth would have been higher if a larger share of new labor market entrants or redundant labor from agriculture and the government sector would have been absorbed by manufacturing instead of the lower productivity (partially informal) retail and wholesale trade sector. The decline in the size of the manufacturing sector was particularly notable in Argentina, Brazil, Chile, Peru, and República Bolivariana de Venezuela. Our findings are consistent with those of Duarte and Restuccia (2010).

Third, the employment share in the relatively low-productivity agriculture sector typically declined, contributing positively to aggregate productivity growth. The contribution was especially high in Brazil, Costa Rica, Colombia, and Mexico, because of the strong decline in the relatively high initial employment shares in agriculture in these countries. The only Latin American country in the sample where the labor share in agriculture increased is Peru.

Fourth, increases in the public sector employment share between 1990 and 2005 slowed down aggregate productivity growth in Argentina and to some degree also in Brazil. The government service sector is the largest employer in Argentina, Brazil, Chile, and Mexico. For instance, in Argentina and Brazil, labor moved primarily from agriculture and manufacturing to lower-productivity wholesale and retail trade as well as government services.

Fifth, increases in the labor shares of the finance, real estate, and business services sectors contributed positively to aggregate productivity growth in Chile, Colombia, Costa Rica, and Mexico. These relatively high-productivity sectors employ only a relatively small share of labor in some Latin American countries, such as Bolivia, Peru, and República Bolivariana de Venezuela. In contrast, the sectors are relatively large employers and fast-expanding in Chile, Colombia, Costa Rica, and Mexico. The measured productivity levels of the sectors vary noticeably across countries: while productivity is above average in most countries, it is particularly low in Argentina and Peru. The sectors include finance as well as professional services, which often have major restrictions to foreign entry in Latin America. Borchert, Gootiiz, and Mattoo (2012) show that both sectors have low restrictions on service trade in Colombia and Costa Rica, and both countries are labeled as virtually open to foreign entry.

These findings suggest several promising directions to deepen the analysis to help explain the slow aggregate productivity growth in Latin American countries. One striking feature is certainly the decline in the size of the manufacturing sector in almost all the countries. Given that manufacturing productivity appears to be substantially higher relative to most other sectors, its decline contributed to lower aggregate productivity growth in the region. Moreover, it has been argued that manufacturing activities, which are usually freely tradable and more internationally mobile, embody aggregate growth externalities. That is, their exposure to trade and the integration of global value chains potentially facilitate international knowledge transfers or lead to more competitive market structures.

Is Manufacturing Labor Productivity in Latin America Catching Up with High-Income Countries? Is the Convergence Rate in the Region Different from Other Developing Regions?

Recent academic findings suggest that the declining share of labor working in Latin America's manufacturing sector might have particular consequences for the region's (speed of) convergence. Rodrik (2013) reveals the empirically robust stylized fact of *unconditional convergence* in manufacturing labor productivity across countries. That is, manufacturing labor productivity in poorer countries is catching up (on average) with manufacturing labor productivity in high-income countries independent of the policies, qualities of institutions, education, or other growth determinants of low- and middle-income countries. Arguably, his findings are also valid for tradable service sectors, but data limitations limit the scope of the analysis to manufacturing.

Rodrik (2013) uses recently constructed United Nations data (INDSTAT) that allow for robust empirical analysis covering a large sample consisting of 23 manufacturing subsectors from most countries in the world over several decades. The manufacturing labor shares are often very low (5–10 percent), as the data mostly cover formal employment. Rodrik (2013) also shows that convergence in manufacturing productivity does not imply aggregate convergence because of the low and often declining manufacturing labor shares in low- and middle-income countries. Although the article includes a battery of empirical robustness checks across different time periods and levels of sector aggregation, it does not report testing for potential differences in the convergence rate in manufacturing labor productivity across specific developing regions.

In this chapter, we test whether the finding of *unconditional convergence* in manufacturing productivity also holds among Latin American countries, and whether convergence rates differ across the region. In other words, we test whether there are specific factors in Latin America holding back manufacturing productivity that are fundamentally different from the rest of the world. If this is the case, the declining size of manufacturing sectors in Latin America is a potential concern for policy makers. In other words, policy makers should focus

on removing product and labor market constraints that are (i) preventing manufacturing firms from expanding (potential entrepreneurs from entering) and/or
(ii) holding back employment and labor productivity growth in tradable service
sectors.

Over the period studied, manufacturing productivity growth in Latin
America was significantly lower than the worldwide average; however, there
were substantial growth differences across Latin American countries. Figure 4.6
illustrates the (compound) average annual labor productivity growth rate across
23 manufacturing sectors for the latest decade with available data (post 1990).
The growth rate is measured net of year-industry specific effects and the sample
corresponds to Rodrik's baseline post-1990 specification. Accordingly, manufacturing labor productivity growth (net of year-industry specific effects)
amounted to 4.2 percent across all 104 countries with available data. By contrast, average growth among Latin American countries is only 1.2 percent. The
difference in growth rates is statistically significant (at the 5 percent level as
indicated by the asterisk).

The average growth rate is even lower among large Latin American countries,
including Argentina, Brazil, Chile, Colombia, Mexico, and Peru. However, the
average conceals a substantial degree of heterogeneity among these countries.
Manufacturing productivity growth in Argentina, Chile, Costa Rica, and Mexico
was not statistically significantly different from the world average. By contrast,
growth in Brazil, Peru, and República Bolivariana de Venezuela was negative and
statistically significantly different from the world average (at the 1 percent level).

Figure 4.6 Manufacturing Labor Productivity Growth Rates

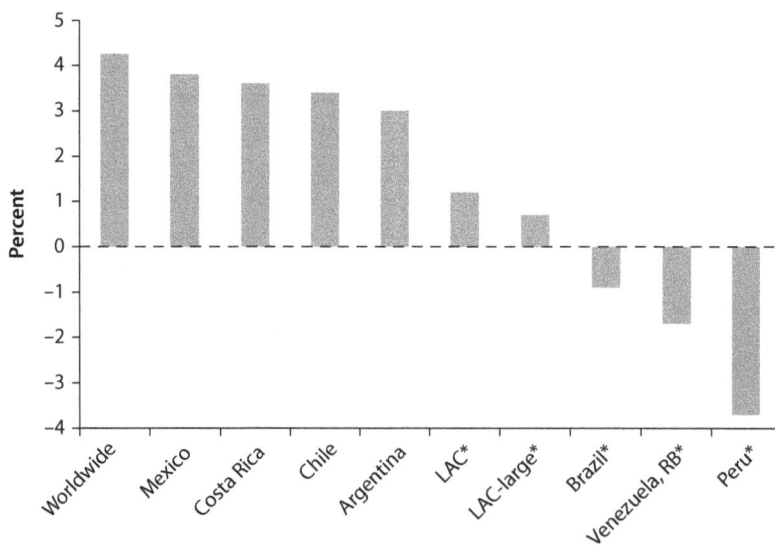

Source: World Bank calculations.
Note: LAC = Latin America and the Caribbean; LAC-large = Argentina, Brazil, Chile, Colombia, Mexico, and Peru.
* Growth rate in the region or country was statistically significantly different from the worldwide
manufacturing labor productivity growth rate (that is, 4.2 percent).

In figure 4.6, each bar corresponds to the average annual labor productivity growth rate across two-digit manufacturing sectors in the Latin American region for the latest decade with available data (post 1990). The sample corresponds to a baseline specification in Rodrik (2013). The growth rate is measured net of year-industry specific effects. The worldwide bar measures the average annual growth rate across all countries and two-digit manufacturing industries over a decade. An asterisk indicates that the growth rate in the region or country was statistically significantly different from the worldwide manufacturing labor productivity growth rate (that is, from 4.2 percent). LAC-large corresponds to Argentina, Brazil, Chile, Colombia, Mexico, and Peru. LAC excludes small island states (less than 200,000 people), Belize, French Guyana, Guyana, and Suriname.

Manufacturing labor productivity in the Latin American region overall is converging unconditionally (independent of policies, institutions, and educational levels) with the same convergence rate as the rest of the world. Table 4.1 shows the extent to which Latin American countries are catching up in manufacturing productivity with high-income countries. The table reports the three main estimation specifications from Rodrik (2013).[12] In all cases, the dependent variable is the (compound annual) growth rate of labor productivity for two-digit manufacturing industries. The regressors are the log of initial labor productivity and industry-year fixed effects.

The baseline estimation specification consists of a pooled sample that combines the latest 10-year period for each country, maximizing the number of countries covered (118). Since each country enters with around 20 industries, the total number of observations is 2,122. The second specification restricts the sample to post-1990, 10-year periods, while the third is a pure cross-section for 1995–2005. The second column replicates Rodrik's findings of a convergence rate of 2.9 percent, implying that industries that are a tenth of the way to the technology frontier (roughly the bottom 20 percent of industries in the sample) experience a convergence boost in their labor productivity growth of 6.7 percentage points per annum.

In columns 5 to 15 of table 4.1, we test whether the convergence rate was different in Latin America; that is, we include a region dummy and its interaction term with log initial labor productivity in the corresponding estimation specifications. The coefficient of the interaction term measures whether the convergence rate was different from the convergence rate across all other countries. Table 4.1 only reports cases in which the convergence rate was statistically significantly different from the rest of the world (the t-statistic of the interaction term is reported in brackets). The results show that the convergence rate in the Latin American region overall was the same as in the rest of the world.[13] The results for the region overall conceal substantial heterogeneity across countries.

Manufacturing labor productivity in Brazil, Chile, and Peru did not catch up (unconditionally) with high-productivity countries. The last three columns of table 4.1 show that the convergence rate in Brazil, Chile, and Peru was (statistically) significantly lower than in the rest of the world. The actual convergence rate (−2.9 percent plus the coefficient of the interaction term) was close to zero

Understanding the Income and Efficiency Gap in Latin America and the Caribbean
http://dx.doi.org/10.1596/978-1-4648-0450-2

Table 4.1 Is the Convergence Rate in Manufacturing Labor Productivity Different in Latin America?

	Rodrik (2013)			Is the speed of convergence in manufacturing labor productivity different in LAC?									
	All countries	Countries	Obs	LAC	LAC-large	Mexico	Argentina	Uruguay	Venezuela, RB	Costa Rica	Colombia	Peru	Brazil	Chile
Baseline	-0.029***	118	2,122	same	same	-0.048*	same	same	same	same	same	0.000***	-0.001**	0.016*
	(-6.95)					(-1.86)						(3.32)	(2.28)	(1.83)
Post-1990	-0.029***	104	1,861	same	same	-0.048*	same	same	same	same	same	0.000***	-0.001**	0.016*
	(-7.14)					(-1.92)						(3.45)	(2.37)	(1.90)
1995–2005	-0.0024***	58	955	same	-0.001**			same			0.006***	0.000***	same	0.004***
	(-6.17)				(2.18)						(3.51)	(3.33)		(3.08)

Source: World Bank calculations.

Note: LAC = Latin America and the Caribbean; LAC-large = Argentina, Brazil, Chile, Colombia, Mexico, and Peru.

and even diverging in Chile (not statistically different from zero). For all other larger Latin American countries in the sample except Mexico, the speed of convergence was not (statistically) different from the convergence rate in the rest of the world.

The convergence rate of manufacturing labor productivity in Mexico was significantly higher than in the rest of the world. The yearly convergence rate for manufacturing productivity in Mexico amounted to 4.8 percent between 1993 and 2003 (last year with available data), which is two-thirds larger than in the rest of the world. The Mexican manufacturing convergence rate is (statistically) different from the rate in the rest of the world (at the 10 percent level of significance). Thus, manufacturing firms in Mexico were able to catch up in terms of productivity with high-productivity countries (the United States) between 1993 and 2003.

In table 4.1, columns 2–4 replicate the baseline findings of Rodrik (2013). Columns 4 to 12 show whether the convergence rate in manufacturing labor productivity differed among (groups of) Latin American countries. Each cell is based on a regression of growth on initial productivity including year-industry dummies (analog to Rodrik 2013) and a region dummy, as well as the interaction term of the region dummy with initial productivity. The coefficients show the compound convergence coefficient (baseline-coefficient + coefficient interaction term), while the t-statistic tests whether the convergence coefficient is statistically different from the convergence coefficient in the full sample, that is, across all countries (for example, –0.029). Standard errors are clustered at the country level in all specifications.

Why Did Unconditional Convergence in Manufacturing for Most Latin American Countries Not Translate into Higher Manufacturing Productivity Growth?

Rodrik (2013) shows that unconditional convergence in (formal) manufacturing does not translate into aggregate convergence because of low (sometimes declining) manufacturing labor shares. He derives the following decomposition of aggregate productivity growth into a manufacturing convergence term and a reallocation term measuring the potentially negative effect of labor moving from the manufacturing sector to lower productivity non-manufacturing sectors:

$$\Delta Y = g + \left[\alpha\theta_m\beta(lny^* - lny_m)\right] + \left[(\theta_m - \theta_n)\Delta\alpha\right] \quad (4.2)$$

where aggregate labor productivity $Y = \alpha y_m - (1 - \alpha)y_n$ is the weighted average of labor productivity in these two activities, α is the share of the economy's labor force employed in manufacturing, ΔY is the aggregate labor productivity growth rate, g is the long-term balanced growth rate of the economy, $\theta_m = y_m/y$ and $\theta_n = y_n/y$ are the productivity premium/discounts for the manufacturing and non-manufacturing sectors, $\beta = 2\%$ is the convergence rate estimated for the full sample from 1995–2005 that is applied to all countries, and y^* is the productivity frontier in manufacturing. Rodrik (2013) quantifies equation 4.2 by combining the INDSTAT manufacturing data with data for aggregated GDP per worker from the Penn World Tables (nonmanufacturing productivity being the difference between the two for each country).

Annex table 4A.2 provides the details for the convergence terms in equation 4.2 for the Latin American countries with available data.[14] The table shows that aggregate productivity convergence was lagging in the region because of (i) small initial manufacturing labor shares (α), (ii) declining manufacturing labor shares over time $(\Delta\alpha)$, (iii) small productivity differentials relative to the rest of the economy (θ_m), or (iv) smaller productivity gaps relative to the world productivity frontier in manufacturing $(lny^* - lny_m)$. Moreover, we emphasize that tradable service sectors arguably have similar characteristics as manufacturing, but sufficiently detailed cross-country data for these service subsectors are not available, limiting the scope of the analysis to unconditional convergence in manufacturing.

To What Extent Do Patterns in Specialization within Manufacturing Help Explain the Declining Labor Shares and Slower Manufacturing Productivity Convergence in Some Countries in the Region?

Changing Production Structures in Manufacturing

In the following, we evaluate in detail the patterns of specialization within manufacturing observed in Latin American countries. These patterns help explain country-specific specialization trends, potentially leading to either declining labor shares or slow productivity growth.

The structural transformation that took place in Latin America's manufacturing sector is analyzed in detail through the lens of analyzing the evolution of export specialization patterns. We use the product space to capture the evolution of Latin America's manufacturing. Despite some notable limitations of the product space analysis (Hidalgo et al. 2007),[15] it is a relevant analytical tool for studying the dynamics of the manufacturing sector over the past 15–30 years.

The product space methodology measures the potential relatedness between production structures among 775 four-digit Standard International Trade Classification (SITC) products. The analysis is based on export data at the four-digit product level from the Comtrade database. The data are pooled for the corresponding three-year periods (for example, 2008–10) to minimize the impact of yearly outliers in export values. The product space is a graphical representation of the relatedness between every pair of the 775 four-digit SITC manufacturing products whereby distances between two products represent the similarity between their production structures. Figure 4.7 illustrates the product space for Brazil.

Comparison with the evolution of the production structures in East Asia reveals a lack of cluster formation among related manufacturing products or industries in Latin America. The findings are summarized in figure 4.8, which illustrates the product space among lower-middle-income countries (LMICs) in Latin America and East Asia and Pacific (EAP) today and 30 years ago. In particular, the product space reveals the existence of a densely connected industrial

Figure 4.7 Brazil's Product Space, 2008–10

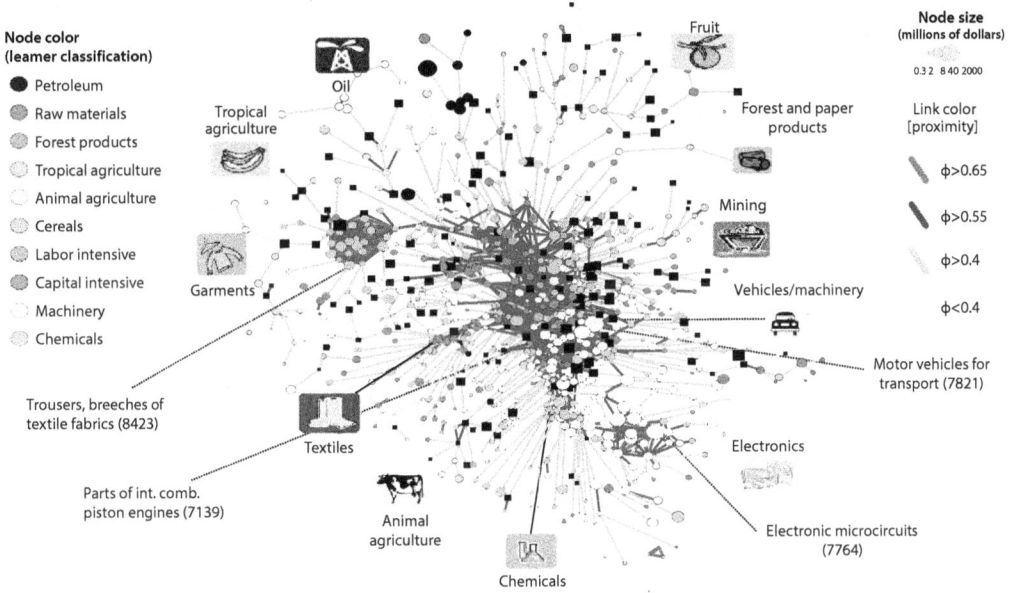

Source: World Bank calculations.

Figure 4.8 Product Space for Latin America and the Caribbean and East Asia and Pacific, 1976–78 and 2007–09

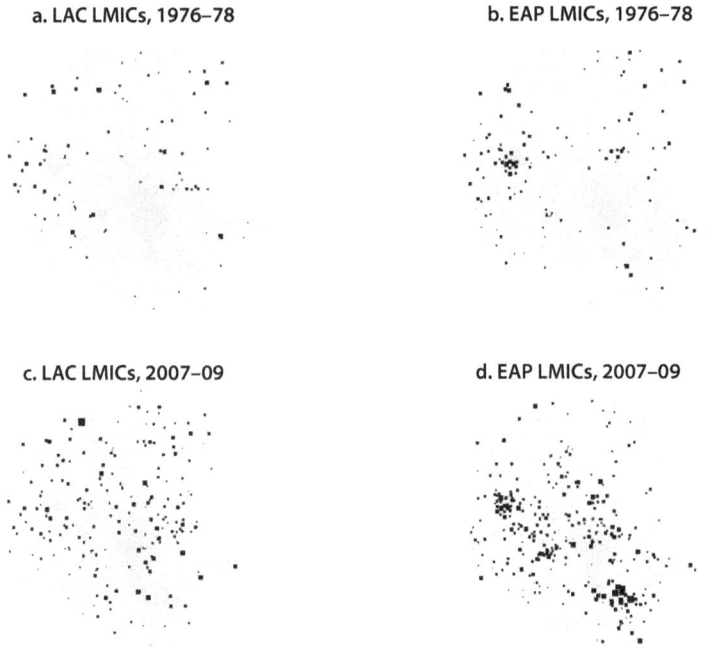

a. LAC LMICs, 1976–78

b. EAP LMICs, 1976–78

c. LAC LMICs, 2007–09

d. EAP LMICs, 2007–09

Source: World Bank calculations.
Note: EAP = East Asia and Pacific; LAC = Latin America and the Caribbean; LMICs = lower-middle-income countries.

Understanding the Income and Efficiency Gap in Latin America and the Caribbean
http://dx.doi.org/10.1596/978-1-4648-0450-2

core (center) and several peripheral clusters, such as garments, textiles, or electronics. Modern manufacturing clusters are typically located in the core (such as vehicles, machinery, or chemicals) or the bottom (electronics cluster). Products in which a country has a (revealed) comparative advantage (in exporting) are depicted as black squares.

Figure 4.8 shows that LMICs in Latin America succeeded in developing a relatively diversified manufacturing base over the past 30 years. Nevertheless, peripheral agricultural and natural resource–related products still make up the majority of revealed comparative advantages (RCAs). Moreover, figure 4.8 suggests that Latin America did not develop major industrial manufacturing clusters at the aggregate regional level. This situation contrasts with the development of electronics, machinery, or car parts clusters in East Asia. Figure 4.9 confirms the lack of cluster formation among related products or manufacturing subsectors for the largest Latin American countries; however, Mexico appears to differ from

Figure 4.9 Product Space for Selected Emerging Asian Economies, Latin America, and Selected High-Income Countries, 2008–10

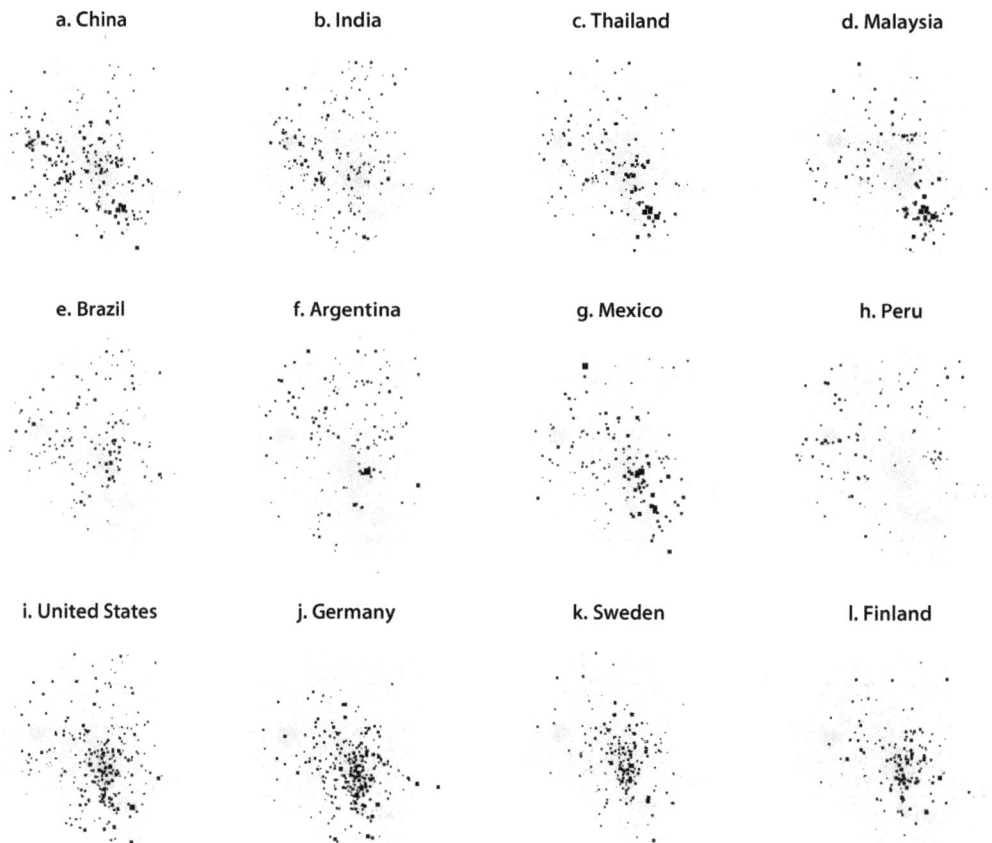

a. China   b. India   c. Thailand   d. Malaysia

e. Brazil   f. Argentina   g. Mexico   h. Peru

i. United States   j. Germany   k. Sweden   l. Finland

Source: World Bank calculations.

this pattern. In the following, we analyze the evolution of manufacturing production clusters in detail for selected Latin American countries.

Mexico. The product space for Mexico reveals the formation of industrial clusters in automobile as well as machinery and transport equipment (car parts). Mexico gained competitiveness in the machinery and transport equipment industry. As of 2008–10, Mexico has RCA in several product classes in the core of the product space (figure 4.10), such as the machinery and transport equipment industry and electronics (52 RCAs). Those are mostly medium technology engineering products (MT3, based on a classification from Lall 2000; see table 4.2) and electronics (HT1); in addition, the country displays a significant comparative advantage in automotive products (MT1) such as passenger motor cars (7810) and motor vehicles for transport of goods (7821).

Many of the products in the core, which Mexico successfully exports, are also successfully exported by the United States (or at least closely related to products with RCA in the United States). This suggests that some of the products with RCA in Mexico in potentially higher technology sectors, such as automobiles and electronics, could be merely assembled in Mexico and re-exported to the United States. The formation of automobile and electronics clusters in Mexico is closely related to the foreign direct investment of several U.S. electronics companies as well as major car producers from the United States or Germany producing in Mexico.

Nevertheless, figure 4.10 suggests that Mexico has developed a domestic car parts industry supplying intermediate goods ranging from tires to motor parts to foreign multinational enterprises (MNEs) operating in the country. That is, once domestic producers manage to satisfy the quality standards of MNEs in Mexico, the producers automatically obtain the accreditation to sell their intermediate

Figure 4.10 Mexico's Product Space, 2008–10

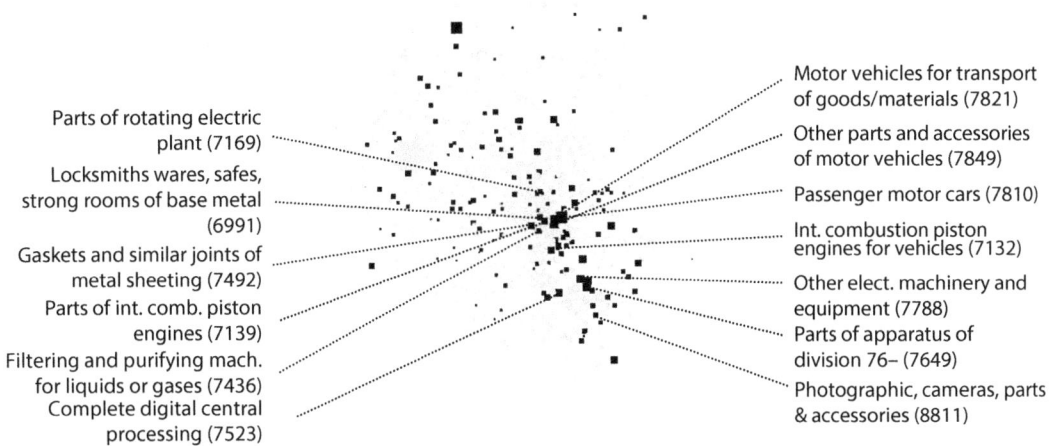

Parts of rotating electric plant (7169)
Locksmiths wares, safes, strong rooms of base metal (6991)
Gaskets and similar joints of metal sheeting (7492)
Parts of int. comb. piston engines (7139)
Filtering and purifying mach. for liquids or gases (7436)
Complete digital central processing (7523)

Motor vehicles for transport of goods/materials (7821)
Other parts and accessories of motor vehicles (7849)
Passenger motor cars (7810)
Int. combustion piston engines for vehicles (7132)
Other elect. machinery and equipment (7788)
Parts of apparatus of division 76– (7649)
Photographic, cameras, parts & accessories (8811)

Source: World Bank calculations. Codes are Standard International Trade Classification Rev.4.

Understanding the Income and Efficiency Gap in Latin America and the Caribbean
http://dx.doi.org/10.1596/978-1-4648-0450-2

Table 4.2 Commodity Technology Classification

PP	**Primary Products**
RB	**Resource-based Manufactures**
RB1	Resource-based Manufactures: Agro-Based
RB2	Resource-based Manufactures: Other
LT	**Low Technology Manufactures**
LT1	Low Technology Manufactures: Textiles, Garment, and Footwear
LT2	Low Technology Manufactures: Other Products
MT	**Medium Technology Manufactures**
MT1	Medium Technology Manufactures: Automotive
MT2	Medium Technology Manufactures: Process
MT3	Medium Technology Manufactures: Engineering
HT	**High Technology Manufactures**
HT1	High Technology Manufactures: Electronic and Electrical
HT2	High Technology Manufactures: Other

Source: Lall (2000).

Figure 4.11 Mexico's Dynamic Product Space, Mexico's Emerging Products, and Thailand's Product Space, 2008–10

a. Mexico's dynamic products   b. Mexico's emerging products   c. Thailand's product space

Source: World Bank calculations.
Note: Dynamic representation of Mexico's product space over the past decade (panel a). Four different categories of products as color coded; "classics" refer to products that have RCA in 2000–02 as well as 2008–10 and are represented by a blue triangle; "disappearing" reflect an RCA in 2000–02 but not in 2008–10, represented by a red square; "emerging" shows RCA in 2008–10 but not 2000–02, represented by a green diamond. "Marginals" reflect products where Mexico has not yet acquired an RCA (0.5 < RCA < 1), but experienced positive export growth (of 10 percent or higher) since 2000–02, represented by a yellow pentagon.

products to all other production facilities of that MNE around the world. As a consequence, Mexico gained RCAs in exporting machinery and transport equipment to the rest of the world.

Argentina also developed an export cluster in passenger motor cars (7810). However, figure 4.9 illustrates that Argentina has so far not developed similar production clusters in related upstream supplying industries.[16]

The dynamic representation of the product space (figure 4.11) reveals that Mexico already successfully exported automobiles, electronics, and several machinery and transport equipment products in 2000–02, while several new export successes have emerged in these clusters since 2008–10. Figure 4.11 shows the dynamic representation of Mexico's product space over the past decade. We distinguish between four different categories of products. First, classics refer to products that have RCA in 2000–02 as well as 2008–10 and are represented by a blue triangle. Second, disappearing reflect an RCA in 2000–02 but not in 2008–10, represented by a red square. Third, emerging shows RCA in 2008–10 but not 2000–02, represented by a green diamond. Finally, marginals reflect products where Mexico has not yet acquired an RCA (0.5 < RCA < 1), but experienced positive export growth (of 10 percent or higher) since 2000–02, represented by a yellow pentagon.

Figure 4.11, panel a, reveals that Mexico lost export competitiveness in several products in the garments cluster. At the same time, the country maintained RCAs in exporting automobiles, electronics, and several machinery and transport equipment products. Moreover, figure 4.11, panel b, highlights that additional export successes have emerged among in related products within these product classes (in the core of the product space) since 2000–02, including complete digital central processing (7523) and internal combustion piston engines (7132). The long-term picture points to a successful structural transformation of Mexico's manufacturing productive capabilities from resource-based products to automobiles and machinery. However, figure 4.11, panel c, puts this picture in perspective by comparing Mexico's product space with that of Thailand. Namely, Thailand has developed twice as many new RCAs as Mexico since 2000–02. In particular, Thailand managed to expand the number of new products with RCAs in the electronics cluster, while Mexico lost some competitiveness in electronics (as indicated by the red squares). Overall, however, the strong export growth of manufacturing clusters in the core of the product space in Mexico is consistent with a higher manufacturing convergence rate than in the rest of the world.

Costa Rica. Costa Rica's economy is fairly diversified, with export successes ranging from garments, food, and base metal products, to car parts, chemicals, and electronics. Figure 4.12 illustrates that Costa Rica has RCAs in several products in the densely connected core of the product space, including medicaments (5417), varnishes and lacquers (5334), tires (6251), internal combustion piston engines (7131), parts for office machines (7599), and electronic microcircuits (7764). The strong export growth in the latter two electronic products emerged over the past 20 years and has been triggered by the substantial investment of a foreign MNE (Intel).

Figure 4.12 shows that Costa Rica lost some competitiveness in garments as well as two major products located in the core of the product space (miscellaneous articles of materials [8939] and other electrical machinery & equipment [7788]) over the past decade. The figure also reveals many marginals, that is, products with strong export growth since 2000 for which Costa Rica is close to achieving RCA.

Understanding the Income and Efficiency Gap in Latin America and the Caribbean
http://dx.doi.org/10.1596/978-1-4648-0450-2

Figure 4.12 Costa Rica's Product Space, 2000–10

a. Dynamic products   b. Marginal products

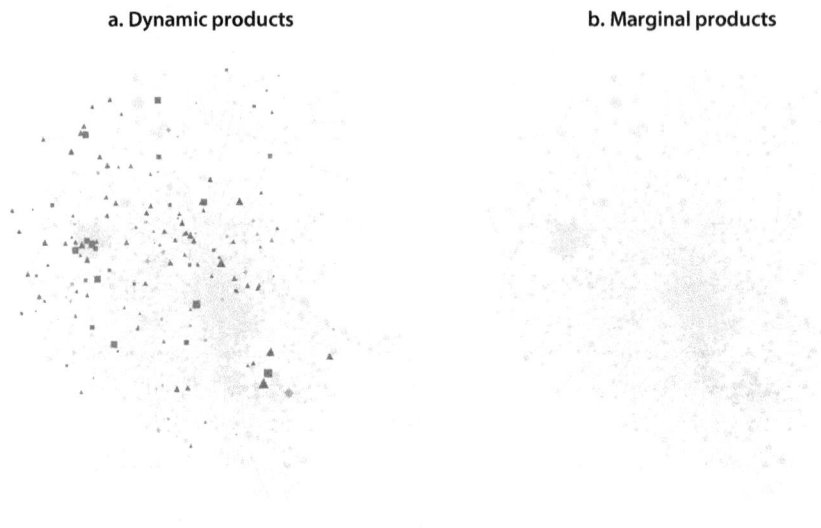

Source: World Bank calculations.
Note: Dynamic representation of Costa Rica's product space over the past decade. Four different categories of products as color coded; "classics" refer to products that have RCA in 2000–02 as well as 2008–10 and are represented by a blue triangle; "disappearing" reflect an RCA in 2000–02 but not in 2008–10, represented by a red square; "emerging" shows RCA in 2008–10 but not 2000–02, represented by a green diamond. "Marginals" reflect products where Costa Rica has not yet acquired an RCA (0.5 < RCA < 1), but experienced positive export growth (of 10 percent or higher) since 2000–02, represented by a yellow pentagon.

Brazil. The dynamic representation of the product space (figure 4.13) reveals that Brazil's export basket has shifted over time, but not significantly. Figure 4.13, panel a, shows that Brazil lost export competitiveness in products of various industries located in the core of the product space since 2000–02, including photographic film (8822); television tubes (7761); radio receivers of cars (7621); cast, rolled, drawn, or blown glass (6644); optical glass (6642); transmission shafts (7493); refractory bricks (6623); natural or artificial abrasive powder (6632); cut-to-size paper and paperboard (6424); and other furniture (8219). However, figure 4.13, panel b, highlights the following emerging products in the core of the product space since 2000–02: motor vehicles for transport (7821); road tractors and semitrailers (7832); machinery for sorting, screening, and separating (7283); larger aircrafts (7924); and other printing and writing paper, machine made (6412). While declining and emerging product categories are scattered across various industries, the recent decline of Brazil's television and photographic industry as well as glass manufacturing is evident. In contrast, emerging products in automotive and machinery clusters suggest that these industry clusters are expanding and gaining international competitiveness.

Peru. Figure 4.14 illustrates that Peru has RCA in many agricultural and mining-based products, including fresh or chilled vegetables (545), copper or zinc alloys, metallic salts (5232), and manufactures of asbestos (6638). The dynamic

Figure 4.13 Brazil's Product Space, 2000–10

a. Dynamic products   b. Emerging products

Source: World Bank calculations.
Note: Dynamic representation of Brazil's product space over the past decade. Four different categories of products as color coded; "classics" refer to products that have RCA in 2000–02 as well as 2008–10 and are represented by a blue triangle; "disappearing" reflect an RCA in 2000–02 but not in 2008–10, represented by a red square; "emerging" shows RCA in 2008–10 but not 2000–02, represented by a green diamond. "Marginals" reflect products where Brazil has not yet acquired an RCA (0.5 < RCA < 1), but experienced positive export growth (of 10 percent or higher) since 2000–02, represented by a yellow pentagon.

Figure 4.14 Peru's Revealed Comparative Advantage, 2008–10

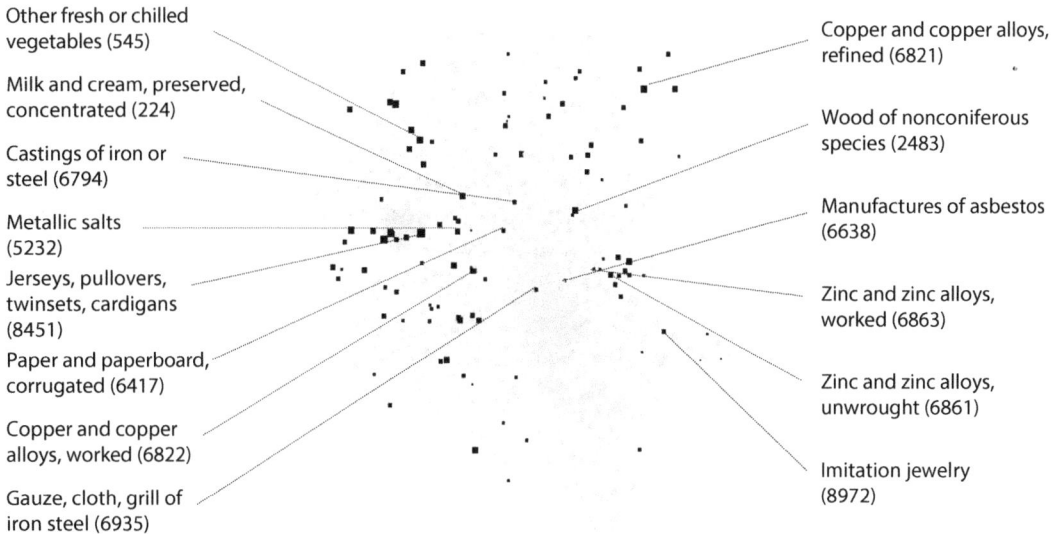

Other fresh or chilled vegetables (545)

Milk and cream, preserved, concentrated (224)

Castings of iron or steel (6794)

Metallic salts (5232)

Jerseys, pullovers, twinsets, cardigans (8451)

Paper and paperboard, corrugated (6417)

Copper and copper alloys, worked (6822)

Gauze, cloth, grill of iron steel (6935)

Copper and copper alloys, refined (6821)

Wood of nonconiferous species (2483)

Manufactures of asbestos (6638)

Zinc and zinc alloys, worked (6863)

Zinc and zinc alloys, unwrought (6861)

Imitation jewelry (8972)

Source: World Bank calculations.

Figure 4.15 Peru's Product Space, 2000–10

a. Dynamic products   b. Emerging products

Source: World Bank calculations.
Note: Dynamic representation of Peru's product space over the past decade. Four different categories of products as color coded; "classics" refer to products that have RCA in 2000–02 as well as 2008–10 and are represented by a blue triangle; "disappearing" reflect an RCA in 2000–02 but not in 2008–10, represented by a red square; "emerging" shows RCA in 2008–10 but not 2000–02, represented by a green diamond. "Marginals" reflect products where Peru has not yet acquired an RCA (0.5 < RCA < 1), but experienced positive export growth (of 10 percent or higher) since 2000–02, represented by a yellow pentagon.

representation of the product space in figure 4.15 shows that the export successes in garments emerged in the 1990s. Overall, however, few new products have emerged over the past 10 years.

Natural Resource–Rich Countries. Except for Chile, natural resource–rich countries in Latin America performed worse in economic growth than other countries that are resource rich in other parts of the world. For example, the product space of República Bolivariana de Venezuela reflects the dominance of natural resources, in particular petroleum and crude oil. República Bolivariana de Venezuela's economy is highly concentrated, with RCA only in 12 products. Although part of the decline in other manufacturing products might stem from a Dutch disease type of effect, a comparison with Canada, New Zealand, and Norway (figure 4.16) suggests that other forces might have played a more important role. That is, Canada, New Zealand, and Norway are major exporters of mining products but nevertheless developed a sound manufacturing base.

It should be stressed that the product space methodology does not imply that sustained growth necessarily requires an expanding manufacturing sector. Chile specialized in products that are typically not in the core of the product space (food processing and mining), having RCA in many agricultural and mining-based products (figure 4.17). Chile's export basket has barely shifted over the past decade. Moreover, Chile lost comparative advantage in a few manufactured products while few new products emerged, which is consistent

Figure 4.16 Natural Resource Leverage, Selected Economies, 2008–10

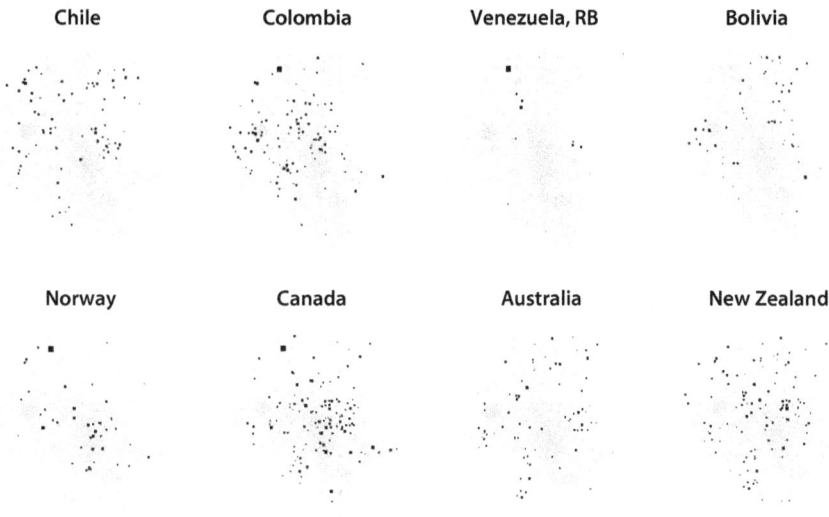

Chile	Colombia	Venezuela, RB	Bolivia

Norway	Canada	Australia	New Zealand

Source: World Bank calculations.

Figure 4.17 Chile's Product Space, 2008–10

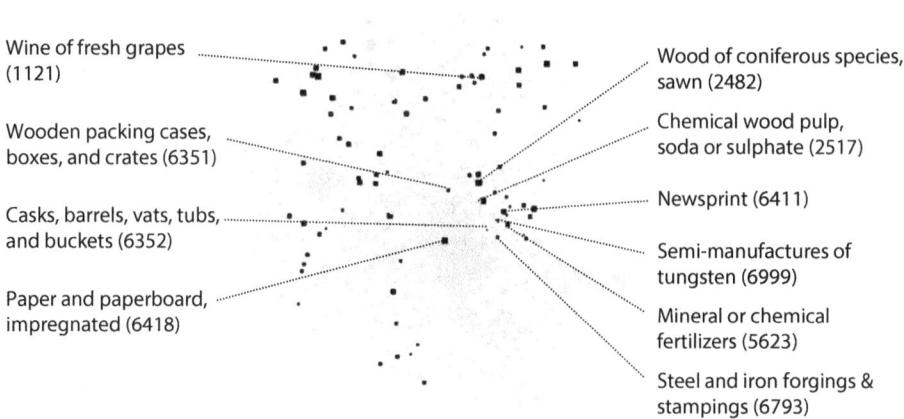

Wine of fresh grapes (1121)

Wooden packing cases, boxes, and crates (6351)

Casks, barrels, vats, tubs, and buckets (6352)

Paper and paperboard, impregnated (6418)

Wood of coniferous species, sawn (2482)

Chemical wood pulp, soda or sulphate (2517)

Newsprint (6411)

Semi-manufactures of tungsten (6999)

Mineral or chemical fertilizers (5623)

Steel and iron forgings & stampings (6793)

Source: World Bank calculations.

with the decline in the manufacturing labor share as well as the stagnant productivity growth in Chile.

However, these developments did not preclude strong economic growth in Chile over the past decade, suggesting an example of advancement from low-income to (higher) middle-income levels without a strong manufacturing base in the core of the product space. This situation means that there is not necessarily a unique economic structure suitable for growth. In addition, the historical experience of Canada, Finland, and Sweden shows that

Understanding the Income and Efficiency Gap in Latin America and the Caribbean
http://dx.doi.org/10.1596/978-1-4648-0450-2

diversification into non-resource industries from a strong resource base is possible (Lederman and Maloney 2012). Similarly, Colombia's manufacturing sector is concentrated in natural resource–based products (for example, crude oil and paper products) and several garments and textile products. Over the past 20 years, however, the country successfully started to export some chemicals as well as car parts.

Primary and resource-based products still dominate Latin America's exports. We use the classification of Lall (2000), presented in table 4.2, to classify countries' exports into primary; resource-based; and low-, medium-, and high-technology products. Table 4.3 (classics category) shows that exports of primary and resource-based products account for the lion's share of manufacturing exports among Latin American countries. The importance of these exports increased between 2005 and 2009 (see the emerging category, table 4.3). For instance, 60 percent of all products in which Brazil has an RCA are primary and resource-based products (table 4.3). The products in which Latin American countries are about to gain RCA (that is, products in the marginal category) are either primary, resource-based, or low technology, except for Costa Rica.

Does the Lack of Specialization Away from Primary or Resource-Based Manufacturing Products in Many Latin American Countries Matter?
Export Quality and Knowledge Spillovers

For economywide productivity, how goods are produced can often matter more than the sectors in which they are produced (Lederman and Maloney 2012). Identical goods can be produced at very different levels of sophistication and with very distinct long-term impacts on growth. That is, within each industry, the sophistication and novelty of the production process and potential for productivity growth matter.[17] For example, although Mexico and the Republic of Korea have reached a similar degree in manufacturing export sophistication, the manufacturing share of value added in Mexico was declining until recently, while it has been rising continuously in Korea (Jankowska, Nagengast, and Perea 2012). Moreover, the lack of technology absorption capacity in Chile at the turn of last century did not allow the country's copper industry to increase productivity to the degree it did in the United States, with wide-ranging externalities to the rest of the economy (Wright and Czelusta 2006).

The following analysis suggests that what and how countries produce might be correlated. The scope for learning and foreign knowledge and technology spillovers might depend on the specific product or industry. Cai and Li (2013) show that production technologies differ in the extent to which they are more or less widely applicable across products or industries. That is, some knowledge can be more readily adapted to be used in related production processes, while other knowledge is limited in its scope of application. Cai and Li find that U.S. firms using more applicable technologies are more likely to innovate. Thus, products or industries embodying more applicable technologies also embody a larger scope for knowledge spillovers. Primary and resource-based products might in fact embody less scope for knowledge spillovers, as their production processes

Table 4.3 PRODY, PATH, and Technological Sophistication

	TOTAL	PP	RB1	RB2	LT1	LT2	MT1	MT2	MT3	HT1	HT2	Average PRODY 0509	Average PATH 0509	Export share 2009 (percent)
CLASSICS						(RCA 05>=1, RCA 09>=1)								
Argentina	134	54	33	14	6	2	2	17	2		1	13,112	124	70.1
Brazil	137	36	29	17	8	8	4	18	12	2	3	12,874	122	67.1
Chile	75	28	23	12		4		7				13,010	118	89.8
Colombia	87	14	11	12	15	12		15	3	1		12,674	131	80.5
Costa Rica	95	19	24	4	8	15		12	7	3	2	13,007	133	88.0
Mexico	117	17	8	10	7	19	4	10	25	13	3	15,094	134	73.2
Peru	91	36	11	18	11	7		7				10,075	119	89.4
Venezuela, RB	11	3		2		3		3				12,820	111	96.6
EMERGING						(RCA 05<1, RCA 09>=1)								
Argentina	16	2	4	1			2	2	4		1	18,222	132	9.9
Brazil	20	9		3	1	1		2	3	1		13,060	127	3.6
Chile	12	5	3	3								12,703	120	1.1
Colombia	31	9		6	7	3		2	3		1	14,155	135	4.7
Costa Rica	18	7	3	2	1	3		1		1		13,349	126	2.0
Mexico	32	6	6	4	1	2		3	6	2		15,074	130	6.6
Peru	17	4	2	2	5	2		1				11,421	116	1.4
Venezuela, RB	4	1		1		1		1				16,329	124	0.4
MARGINALS					(RCA 05<1 or RCA 05 = ., 0.5<RCA 09<1 and RCA growth>= 10 percent)									
Argentina	9	2	2	1	1			2	1			16,339	140	0.3
Brazil	12	5	1	1		1		1	2	1		17,592	125	7.5
Chile	12	3	2		2	3		1	1			12,353	134	0.4
Colombia	13	3	2	1		2		1	4			14,225	124	1.4
Costa Rica	9		1	2	1				3		2	19,468	132	0.3
Mexico	24	3	5	3	2	3	1	5	2			13,828	120	1.2
Peru	14	2	3	1	1	4		2	1			12,914	132	0.8
Venezuela, RB	2	1		1								6,967	95	0.4
DISAPPEARING						(RCA 05>1, RCA 09<1)								
Argentina	27	2	5	5	2	4	1	4	2	1	1	15,170	125	2.4
Brazil	58	8	10	8	3	7	2	6	11	3		15,806	123	5.8
Chile	16	4	3	2	1			2	4			13,201	120	0.5
Colombia	41	12	8	1	6	5		4	1			11,046	130	2.9
Costa Rica	37	6	6	3	8		3	3	5	2	1	12,582	125	1.7
Mexico	44	2	5	3	11	5		4	2	10	2	14,155	128	5.2
Peru	17	2	2	4	2	3		2	1			12,352	129	1.3
Venezuela, RB	19	3	3	5	1	3		3	1			15,702	118	0.9

Source: World Bank calculations.

Note: See table 4.2 for the technology classifications. PRODY is used as a proxy for the capabilities embedded in a product. However, there are some limitations to using PRODY, since high-income countries export natural resources resulting in high PRODY values for certain goods not necessarily representative of the capabilities required for production. PRODY measures the revealed export sophistication for each product; it is a measure of the GDP per capita of the "typical" country that exports product *i*. A product is considered more sophisticated if it is exported more intensively by high-income countries, and less sophisticated if it is exported more intensively by low-income countries. PATH is a measure of the distance between any two products within the product space matrix. Calculating PATH gives an indication as to whether any given product is located in a particularly dense or sparse part of the product space: if the PATH is short, factors of production, skills or technologies can be more easily deployed from one product to another.

Understanding the Income and Efficiency Gap in Latin America and the Caribbean
http://dx.doi.org/10.1596/978-1-4648-0450-2

Figure 4.18 Average Annual Per Capita GDP Growth and Log (TA)

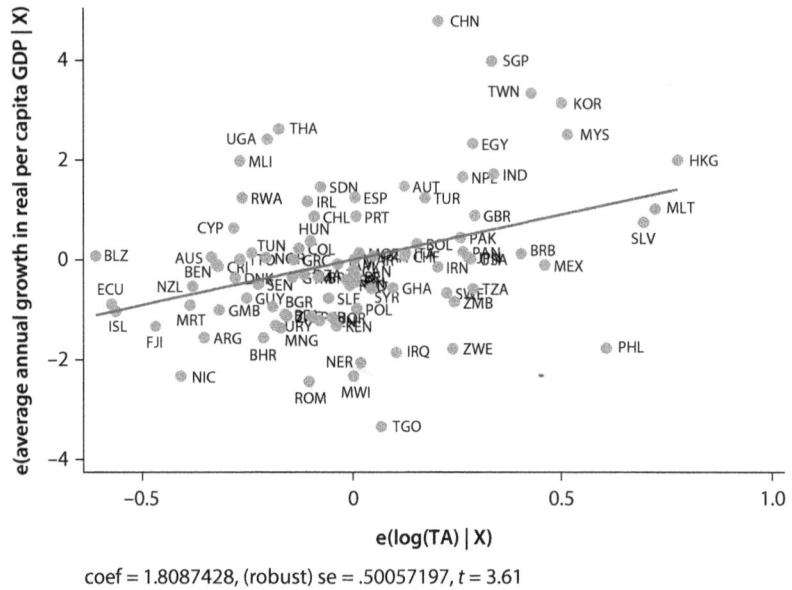

coef = 1.8087428, (robust) se = .50057197, t = 3.61

Source: World Bank calculations.
Note: TA = technological applicability.

and embodied technologies are more idiosyncratic and thus less widely applicable.

In the following, we analyze whether Latin American countries tend to be specialized in less widely applicable technologies and production processes. The analysis uses a quantitative measure of the knowledge applicability developed by Cai and Li (2013). The measure is based on patent citation data and can be aggregated to the country level by measuring a country's knowledge composition.

Latin America as a region appears to be less specialized in industries with high knowledge applicability. Cai and Li (2013) develop for each industry a quantitative measure of knowledge applicability. They use the 2006 patent citation database, provided by the U.S. Patent and Trade Office, to trace the direction and intensity of knowledge flows within and across technological classes. This process allows constructing indices of knowledge applicability for each industry. This measure is aggregated to the country level based on using countries' export structure to create industry weights. Cai and Li (2013) find that countries with a higher knowledge applicability index experience higher subsequent economic growth.[18] Figure 4.18 summarizes one of their main findings. The figure demonstrates that countries that initially specialize in exporting goods that embody highly applicable knowledge experience higher subsequent growth.

Despite substantial heterogeneity across countries, production structures in most countries in Latin America imply low knowledge applicability. Figure 4.19 represents the time trends for the knowledge applicability indices (log(TA)) for

Figure 4.19 Knowledge Applicability over Time for Selected Countries

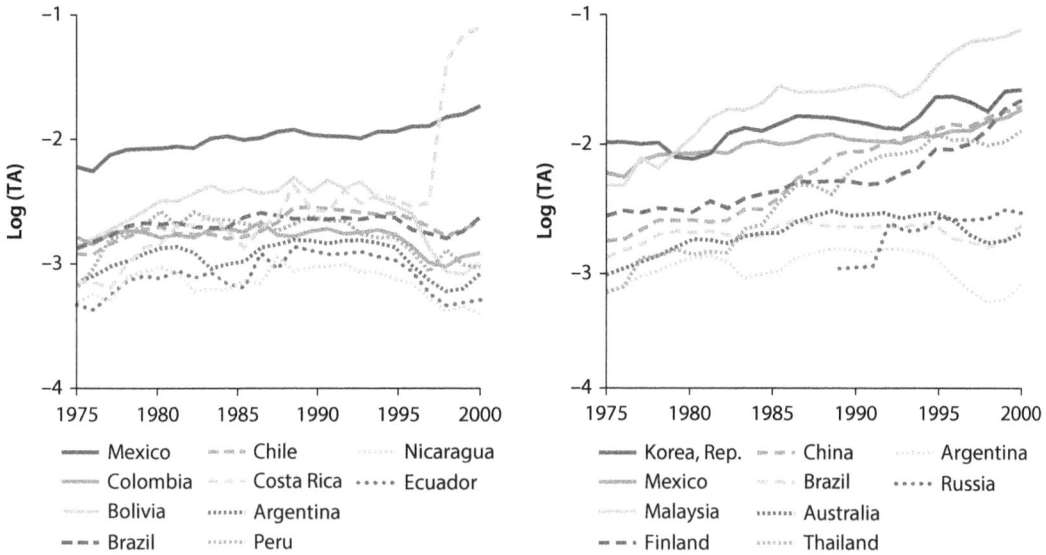

— Mexico	– – – Chile	·········· Nicaragua
— Colombia	– – Costa Rica	····· Ecuador
Bolivia	········ Argentina	
– – – Brazil	········ Peru	

— Korea, Rep.	– – · China	·········· Argentina
— Mexico	Brazil	····· Russia
Malaysia	········ Australia	
– – · Finland	········ Thailand	

Source: Cai and Li 2013.

a sample of 17 countries. The figure shows that China's and Thailand's export knowledge applicability has been growing steadily, rapidly converging to the index levels of Korea and the United States over the past decades. In contrast, the export baskets of most Latin American countries imply lower knowledge applicability in their embodied technologies. Thus, they are less specialized in sectors with high knowledge applicability.

The exceptions are Mexico and Costa Rica (because of the strong growth of electronics exports after the entry of Intel in the mid-1990s). For these countries, the knowledge applicability of their production structures is relatively high and has been rising since 1990. This finding is consistent with our results in the section on labor productivity and structural change, showing that manufacturing labor productivity converged unconditionally in both countries. Moreover, the section on changing production structures showed that both countries are the least specialized in primary and resource-based goods in the region. In contrast, Argentina, Colombia, Ecuador, Nicaragua, and Peru, which are all specialized in primary and resource-based goods, have the lowest knowledge applicability index. The knowledge applicability embodied in Chile's export basket was rising until the late 1990s and is higher than that of most other countries in Latin America.[19]

Conclusions and Potential Policy Implications

The findings of this chapter suggest that structural change in Latin America has often been accompanied by some degree of resource misallocation or inefficient resource use. Three distinct but related phenomena affecting countries in the region deserve particular attention: (i) structural change accompanied by decreased economywide value added per worker, (ii) manufacturing productivity growth below the world average, and (iii) the presence of idiosyncratic production structures.

First, in contrast to East Asia, the contribution of structural change to growth in value added per worker in Latin America has been small and even negative in some countries. More specifically, an increase in the employment shares of lower productivity sectors seems to have been the prevalent pattern across the countries in Latin America in recent decades. This phenomenon may be one factor behind the limited income convergence observed with respect to richer countries.[20] It is important to keep in mind, however, that in many instances high growth of within-sector value added per worker compensates for the adverse structural change effect.

Second, average manufacturing productivity growth in Latin America has been significantly lower than the worldwide average. Therefore, the region seems to have benefited less than others from the phenomenon of unconditional convergence in manufacturing. Two caveats are in order, however: (i) there is significant variation across countries in the region; and (ii) some service subsectors are acquiring manufacturing-like characteristics, which may propel them to display unconditional convergence properties as well. Thus, it is not all about manufacturing, but rather modern economic activities, which are subject to the forces of competition and exposed to incentives to innovate.

Third, idiosyncratic production structures may be limiting the ability of Latin American firms to absorb or imitate more productive foreign technologies. That is, the region appears to have specialized in technologies that are idiosyncratic or not well connected. This finding can be seen through the analysis of the product space and the knowledge applicability of a country's technology. However, there is not a one-to-one relationship between the results of the two methodologies: while Chile shows a lack of specialization in products within the core of the product space, its degree of knowledge applicability is among the highest in the region.

These findings highlight the difficulty in clearly separating the effects of two competing explanations of low TFP growth in Latin America: resource misallocation versus delays in technology adoption. At the sector level, structural change may be related to inefficiencies in the allocation and reallocation of resources in many economies in Latin America. At a more disaggregated level (for example, through the product space and knowledge applicability analyses), technology adoption patterns emerge as a potentially important explanatory factor. Ultimately, it might not be possible to disentangle completely the misallocation effects from the technology adoption effects, since the misallocation of resources may itself affect the pace of technological diffusion in the region.

Whereas manufacturing has some special characteristics, it does not follow that reversing the decline in manufacturing labor shares should be a development policy goal. To jump from the empirically observed phenomenon of unconditional convergence in manufacturing to an assertion that deindustrialization would have to be reversed somehow is a non sequitur. The reason is twofold. First, reversing the decline in manufacturing is not costless. Not only the potential benefits, but also the costs, of undertaking this kind of economic reengineering would need to be assessed. Second, certain subsectors within the services sector are becoming tradable and as such are potentially also subject to unconditional convergence.

Perhaps the main implication from the results reported here is that searching for an optimal economic structure is futile. A more sensible approach would be to look for productivity growth opportunities across different sectors. In other words, instead of attempting to protect existing manufacturing activities and preventing them from shedding labor, the key policy goals should involve (i) lifting productivity levels in lagging sectors that are absorbing labor; and (ii) upgrading skills across the board, so that newly unemployed workers can find jobs in more productive sectors that could potentially absorb labor.

Annex 4A Structural Change and Marginal Productivity of Labor

Structural Change

Gross domestic product per capita growth can be decomposed into the following components, as illustrated in figure 4A.1: (i) change in employment rate, (ii) change in demographic structure, and (iii) change in labor productivity.

Labor productivity can be further decomposed into two additional components: changes in sector-level productivity ("within" component) and changes arising from a reallocation of labor between sectors ("structural change" component). Following Pages (2010) and McMillan and Rodrik (2011), this can be written as:

$$\Delta Y_t = \sum_{i=n} s_{i,t-k}\Delta y_{it} + \sum_{i=n} y_{i,t}\Delta s_{it} \qquad (4A.1)$$

Figure 4A.1 GDP per Capita Growth Decomposition

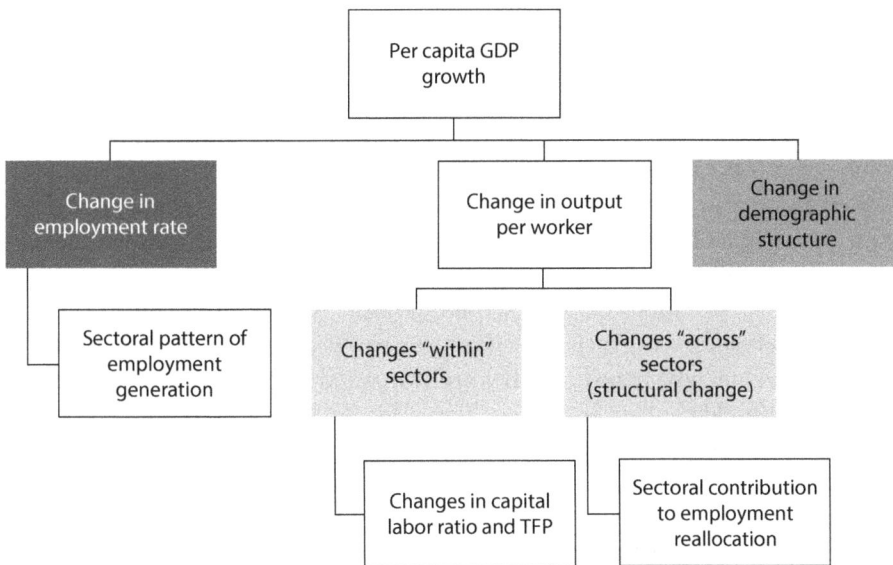

Source: World Bank calculations.
Note: GDP = gross domestic product; TFP = total factor productivity.

Understanding the Income and Efficiency Gap in Latin America and the Caribbean
http://dx.doi.org/10.1596/978-1-4648-0450-2

where ΔY_t is the change in aggregate labor productivity between t and $t-k$, s_{it} is the employment share in sector i at time t, and y_{it} is the productivity level in sector i at time t. The first term is the "within" component and the second term the "structural change" component. Alternatively, the decomposition can be conducted using the Shapley decomposition as follows:

$$\Delta y_t = \sum_{i=n} \frac{s_{i,t} + s_{i,t-k}}{2} \Delta y_{it} + \sum_{i=n} \frac{y_{i,t} + y_{i,t-k}}{2} \Delta s_{it} \qquad (4A.2)$$

whereby the main difference is that the Shapley decomposition assigns to each factor the average marginal contribution rather than the contribution of a specific year.

Marginal Productivity of Labor

The analysis of structural change has been based on average productivity. To pass judgment on whether this change was welfare improving and growth promoting, however, would require a more in-depth analysis.[21] An important step in this direction is to look at marginal productivity across sectors. Under perfect competition, marginal labor productivity—not average productivity—should be equalized across sectors. Assuming a constant returns production function, since labor shares are not necessarily negatively correlated with average productivity, large gaps in average productivity may reflect large gaps in marginal labor productivity. However, there are some caveats. For example, high average labor productivity in capital-intensive sectors, such as mining, may simply reflect that the labor share is low.

The marginal productivity of labor can be calculated by estimating the labor share of income. Using World Bank International Income Distribution Data Set (I2D2) data, we calculated the income share of labor using wage data for Chile and Peru, the only two countries with reliable wage data (McMillan and Verduzco-Gallo 2012; see annex table 4A.1). In a perfectly competitive market, wages equal the marginal product of labor. Labor markets are often not perfectly competitive, for example, in the presence of unionization or indexed contracts. Moreover, in many low- and middle-income countries, some workers, such as those in the agricultural sector or household employees, are only paid partially in wages. Finally, using wages to calculate labor's share of income automatically leads to the exclusion of the self-employed. To eliminate biases arising from unobserved heterogeneity, the data are narrowed down to a subset of workers. The marginal labor productivities are calculated for single males, ages 30 to 34 years, with elementary education. The wage data are adjusted for the rural-urban price differential.

Gaps in marginal productivities measured by average wages across sectors are smaller than gaps measured by value added per worker, but sectoral differences remain significant. In Chile in 1990, the gap between the highest productivity sector (public utilities) and the lowest productivity sector (agriculture) was 12, while the difference in raw wages between the minimum (agriculture) and

Table 4A.1 **Estimates of Labor's Share and Marginal Productivities Using Harmonized Household Survey Data from the World Bank**

Country	Year	Sector	Code	Value added per capita		Average wages (raw differences)*		Average wages (controlling for individual characteristics)*		Average wages (controlling for individual characteristics)**		% of labor force in paid employment (%)
				In 2005 PPP dollars	Employment share (%)	In 2005 PPP dollars	Implied labor share (%)	In 2005 PPP dollars	Implied labor share (%)	In 2005 labor PPP dollars	Implied labor share (%)	
Chile	**1990**	Agriculture	agr	5,546	18.1	2,837	51.2	2,716	58.0	2,699	58.0	66.4
		Mining	min	37,973	3.0	7,329	19.3	4,097	21.1	4,096	21.1	87.9
		Manufacturing	man	17,688	17.5	4,476	25.3	2,965	27.1	2,943	27.1	79.0
		Public utilities	pu	68,697	0.6	8,322	12.1	3,526	14.4	3,509	14.4	97.4
		Construction	con	19,918	7.4	4,479	22.5	3,033	24.3	3,011	24.3	69.6
		Commerce	wrt	9,226	17.1	3,913	42.4	2,528	44.7	2,511	44.8	51.7
		Transport and communications	tsc	13,610	6.8	5,013	36.8	2,877	38.8	2,861	38.9	72.2
		Financial and business-oriented services	fire	31,700	4.9	8,334	26.3	3,718	32.0	3,687	32.0	81.7
		Community and family-oriented services	cspsgs	12,159	24.8	5,304	43.6	2,309	49.2	2,293	49.2	90.3
	2003	Agriculture	agr	12,484	11.2	3,539	28.4	2,897	33.4	3,028	33.3	68.0
		Mining	min	147,720	1.3	11,637	7.9	4,848	9.5	5,076	9.5	92.5
		Manufacturing	man	30,341	12.4	5,664	18.7	3,092	22.1	3,236	22.1	75.5
		Public utilities	pu	111,641	0.6	7,864	7.0	3,626	8.2	3,788	8.1	95.6
		Construction	con	22,529	8.5	5,655	25.1	3,254	30.0	3,407	30.0	68.4
		Commerce	wrt	11,795	21.7	4,819	40.9	2,896	61.3	3,031	61.4	58.3
		Transport and communications	tsc	25,043	7.6	6,033	24.1	3,077	28.2	3,218	28.2	71.6
		Financial and business-oriented services	fire	26,428	11.4	8,132	30.8	3,347	40.0	3,501	40.0	81.0
		Community and family-oriented services	cspsgs	13,438	25.3	7,525	56.0	2,797	65.1	2,925	65.1	90.8
Peru	**1999**	Agriculture	agr	3,807	33.0	2,087	54.8	2,990	93.7	3,100	93.8	17.6
		Mining	min	80,849	0.9	7,746	9.6	6,462	10.0	6,707	10.0	90.1
		Manufacturing	man	19,622	10.2	3,518	17.9	3,075	19.8	3,172	19.7	52.9
		Public utilities	pu	89,894	0.3	5,390	6.0	3,062	8.0	3,164	7.9	81.1

table continues next page

Table 4A.1 Estimates of Labor's Share and Marginal Productivities Using Harmonized Household Survey Data from the World Bank (continued)

Country	Year	Sector	Code	Value added per capita		Average wages (raw differences)*		Average wages (controlling for individual characteristics)*		Average wages (controlling for individual characteristics)**		% of labor force in paid employment (%)
				In 2005 PPP dollars	Employment share (%)	In 2005 PPP dollars	Implied labor share (%)	In 2005 PPP dollars	Implied labor share (%)	In 2005 labor PPP dollars	Implied labor share (%)	
		Construction	con	25,209	3.0	4,120	16.3	3,546	19.8	3,661	19.8	67.0
		Commerce	wrt	11,770	21.3	3,352	28.5	3,014	30.5	3,114	30.5	25.2
		Transport and communications	tsc	19,610	5.6	6,052	30.9	4,389	36.2	4,572	36.4	44.1
		Financial and business-oriented services	fire	27,718	4.9	5,917	21.3	3,334	27.9	3,450	28.0	66.1
		Community and family-oriented services	cspsgs	10,225	20.7	4,809	47.0	2,287	48.5	2,366	48.5	79.9
	2005	Agriculture	agr	4,347	34.1	1,587	36.5	2,107	50.5	2,223	50.7	17.4
		Mining	min	90,987	1.2	8,217	9.0	6,070	10.0	6,362	10.0	89.3
		Manufacturing	man	26,104	9.7	3,512	13.5	3,037	13.9	3,208	13.9	55.2
		Public utilities	pu	125,931	0.3	7,095	5.6	4,079	6.4	4,286	6.4	96.8
		Construction	con	28,100	2.9	3,185	11.3	2,800	13.4	2,954	13.4	65.7
		Commerce	wrt	14,504	20.4	3,101	21.4	2,770	20.6	2,922	20.5	26.0
		Transport and communications	tsc	24,351	5.5	4,002	16.4	2,965	18.0	3,124	17.9	40.4
		Financial and business-oriented services	fire	30,910	4.9	5,605	18.1	3,491	22.0	3,683	21.9	71.8
		Community and family-oriented services	cspsgs	11,721	21.0	4,306	36.7	2,304	38.4	2,431	38.4	82.2

Source: World Bank International Income Distribution Data Set.
Note: * Regression results controlling for urban location, gender, age (6-year intervals), marital status, occupation, and education level (no education, primary, secondary, and post-secondary); ** Adds household size and number of working members to the previous controls.

maximum (public utilities and finance) wage was 3. The difference becomes even smaller when controlling for individual characteristics, shrinking to 1.8. This gap remained almost constant in Chile between 1990 and 2003. That is, in 2003, an individual with the same characteristics and education would have earned nearly 1.7 times more if she would have moved from community services (the lowest wage sector) to mining (the highest wage sector). In Peru in 1999, the gap between the highest productivity sector (public utilities) and the lowest productivity sector (agriculture) was 23, while the difference in wages after controlling for individual characteristics between the minimum (community services) and maximum (mining) wage was 2.8. In 2005, the difference in wages after controlling for individual characteristics between the minimum (agriculture) and maximum (mining) sector increased slightly to 2.9.

Manufacturing Convergence and Reallocation Effects

Table 4A.2 Predicted Aggregate Growth Rates Based on Manufacturing Convergence and Reallocation Effects

	(1)	(2)	(3)	(4)	(5)	(6)	(7)
				Manufacturing growth [β x (3)]	Aggregate convergence term		Predicted aggregate growth
	α	θ_m	$(lny^* - lny_m)$	(%)	(1) x (2) x (4) (%)	Δ (%)	(5) + (6) (%)
Brazil	0.0662	3.9088	0.7826	1.58	0.41	−0.03	0.38
Peru	0.0346	7.2648	0.971	1.96	0.49	0.38	0.87
Colombia	0.0441	3.7566	1.4963	3.02	0.50	−0.79	−0.29
Urugay	0.1196	2.3889	1.6237	3.27	0.94	−0.57	0.36
Ecuador	0.032	3.3488	1.9056	3.84	0.41	−0.15	0.26
Chile	0.0599	4.3842	0.8962	1.81	0.47	0.18	0.65
Costa Rica	0.1173	1.123	2.3018	4.64	0.61	−0.22	0.39
Mexico	0.0398	2.244	1.2578	2.54	0.23	0.31	0.53
Trinidad and Tobago	0.0658	0.1877	3.6921	7.44	0.09	−0.69	−0.60
Argentina	0.0684	3.2578	1.0709	2.16	0.48	−0.21	0.27
Bolivia	0.0129	11.0363	1.5602	3.15	0.45	0.00	0.45
China	0.0814	2.7279	3.745	7.55	1.68	0.04	1.72
India	0.0229	3.2179	3.0258	6.10	0.45	−0.08	0.37
Malaysia	0.1226	1.6098	1.8863	3.80	0.75	0.16	0.91
Thailand	0.0555	5.8818	1.5038	3.03	0.99	0.63	1.62
Turkey	0.046	3.2232	0.889	1.79	0.27	0.04	0.30

Source: World Bank calculations.

Notes

1. Trade data are only a proxy for the productive structure of an economy, and in some cases can substantially deviate from actual sectoral contributions to gross domestic product.

2. That is, excluding the mining and utilities sectors, which also suffer from methodological issues related to their capital intensity.

3. Structural change can be regarded as a convergence concept toward a long-term equilibrium with comparable marginal productivity levels across sectors.

4. It is possible that these differences in labor productivity growth stem almost entirely from differences in capital-labor ratios across sectors, implying that TFP is similar across sectors. However, Herrendorf and Valentinyi (2012) show that this is not the case for broader sector definitions. For service subsectors, we cannot directly test this hypothesis given the absence of sectoral time-series capital stock data. Nevertheless, we argue that it is unlikely that differences in capital intensities alone can explain the large differences in labor productivity levels and growth across service subsectors in Latin American countries.

5. The definition of structural change is consistent with Duarte and Restuccia (2010), McMillan and Rodrik (2011), and others. Alternatively, Hausman and Klinger (2006) use exports as a proxy for production to analyze structural change in the manufacturing sector only.

6. At the aggregate level, previous analysis was typically limited to measuring the reallocation of labor across three broad sectors only: agriculture, manufacturing, and services. The recent availability of new data sets, such as the Groningen 10-sector database and the UNIDO sector data, provides more detailed international time-series sector data for value added and employment that ensure a certain degree of consistency in cross-country sector definitions, making it possible to refine the previous approaches.

7. We emphasize that aggregate gross domestic product (GDP) growth depends not only on aggregate labor productivity growth, but also on changes in aggregate labor input and demographics. For example, if a redundant worker with zero productivity is laid off in agriculture and drops out of the labor force, labor productivity in agriculture increases, the contribution of the labor input to GDP growth declines, while structural change and aggregate GDP growth remain the same.

8. McMillan and Rodrik (2011) refer, for instance, to Mundlak, Butzer, and Larson (2012), who show that it is not clear that the labor share in agriculture is significantly lower than in manufacturing once the share of land is taken into account.

9. See Hsieh and Olken (2014), who discuss in detail under which conditions the average and marginal products of capital and labor move together.

10. These two countries have the most reliable wage data in the I2D2 in the region. To eliminate biases arising from unobserved heterogeneity, the data are narrowed to a subset of workers. The marginal labor productivities are calculated for single males, ages 30–34 years, with elementary education. The wage data are adjusted for the rural-urban price differential.

11. McMillan and Rodrik (2011) come to similar conclusions using a comparable approach for Mexico.

12. We thank Dani Rodrik for sharing the original data and Stata codes of Rodrik (2013) with us. We added regression specifications to test for differences in the speed of

unconditional manufacturing convergence in Latin America. All potential errors are our responsibility.

13. We find a lack of unconditional convergence in manufacturing labor productivity among the large Latin American countries for the 1995–2000 cross-sections (the convergence rate of 0.1 percent corresponds to the convergence coefficient in the rest of the world, –2.4 percent plus the coefficient of the interaction term of –2.3 percent, which is not reported explicitly here). This result is probably caused by the fact that data for Argentina, Costa Rica, Mexico, and República Bolivariana de Venezuela are not available for the 1995–2005 cross-section.

14. Brazil, Chile, and Peru are estimated to have benefitted from manufacturing convergence since we assumed the same convergence rate of 2 percent for all countries. Table 4.1 shows, however, that this assumption is rejected in the data for these three countries. Accordingly, manufacturing convergence terms should have amounted to zero instead ($\beta = 0$ cannot be rejected in the data for these three countries). In turn, table 4.1 shows that the actual speed of manufacturing convergence is estimated to have been higher in Mexico.

15. The product space analysis depends on several limiting assumptions. Trade data are only a proxy for the productive structure of an economy, and in some cases can substantially deviate from actual sectoral contributions to GDP. In addition, Lederman and Maloney (2012) highlight that there can be a substantial degree of heterogeneity in technology content of products even at the four-digit level.

16. However, Argentina recently gained RCA in exporting radio broadcast receivers for motor vehicles (7621). Other recent export successes have emerged in Argentina in the densely connected core of the product space, including dairy machinery (7213); agricultural and horticulture machinery (7211); polyamides (5824); chemical products and preparations (5989); transmission, conveyor/elevator belts (6282); and photographic film (8822).

17. Lederman and Maloney (2012) also highlight that there can be a substantial degree of heterogeneity in the technology content of products, even at the four-digit level. For instance, a country that successfully exports microchips might host high-tech firms engaging in research and development and product design or low-tech firms simply assembling the microchips without adding much value. Therefore, detailed sector case studies or value chain analysis would be necessary to supplement the analysis.

18. The applicability of a country's knowledge portfolio (revealed through its exports) indeed predicts its subsequent growth. Cai and Li (2013) find that the coefficients on log (TA) are always positive and highly significant across all specifications, suggesting that specializing in sectors with large knowledge spillovers brings growth in the future. The size of the estimated effect is large. The estimated coefficients vary from 1.1 to 4.7, implying that a 10 percent increase in log (TA0), which is approximately what Thailand achieved between 1975 and 1980, on average enhances a country's subsequent growth by 1/4 percent per year. In addition, all the other initial control variables have the correct signs. Notably, the initial investment-to-GDP ratio, export diversification, and openness do not seem to enter in a robustly significant way, and including institutional quality does not have much of an effect on the significance of log initial TA.

19. This result is quite different from the measure of export sophistication developed in Hausman, Hwang, and Rodrik (2007).

Understanding the Income and Efficiency Gap in Latin America and the Caribbean
http://dx.doi.org/10.1596/978-1-4648-0450-2

20. Silva and Ferreira (2013) argue that low growth in the tertiary sector explains much of the divergence between Latin America and the United States after 1980.

21. Not all structural change is good. For example, productivity may be higher in sectors with monopoly power. A reallocation to these sectors would contribute positively to structural change, but would not necessarily promote growth or enhance welfare.

Bibliography

Aghion, P., and P. Howitt. 1992. "A Model of Growth through Creative Destruction." *Econometrica* 60: 323–51.

Baumol, W. 1967. "Macroeconomics of Unbalanced Growth: The Anatomy of the Urban Crisis." *American Economic Review* 57: 415–26.

Borchert, I., B. Gootiiz, and A. Mattoo. 2012. "Policy Barriers to International Trade in Services: Evidence from a New Database." Policy Research Working Paper 6109, World Bank, Washington, DC.

Cai, J., and N. Li. 2013. "The Composition of Knowledge and Economic Growth in a Path-Dependent World." Society for Economic Dynamics, 2013 Meeting Papers No. 336.

Duarte, M., and D. Restuccia. 2010. "The Role of the Structural Transformation in Aggregate Productivity." *Quarterly Journal of Economics* 125: 129–73.

Echevarria, C. 1997. "Changes in Sectoral Composition Associated with Economic Growth." *International Economic Review* 38: 431–52.

Hausman, R., J. Hwang, and D. Rodrik. 2007. "What You Export Matters." *Journal of Economic Growth* 12: 1–25.

Hausman, R., and B. Klinger. 2006. "Structural Transformation and Patterns of Comparative Advantage in the Product Space." CID Working Paper No. 128, Center for International Development, Harvard University, Cambridge, MA.

Herrendorf, B., R. Rogerson, and A. Valentinyi. 2013a. "Growth and Structural Transformation." In *Handbook of Economic Growth*, edited by Philippe Aghion and Steven N. Durlauf. San Diego, CA: Elsevier.

———. 2013b. "Two Perspectives on Preferences and Structural Transformation." *American Economic Review* 103 (7): 2752–89.

Herrendorf, B., and A. Valentinyi. 2012. "Which Sectors Make Poor Countries So Unproductive?" *Journal of the European Economic Association* 10: 323–41.

Hidalgo, C. A., B. Klinger, A. L. Barabasi, and R. Hausman. 2007. "The Product Space Conditions and the Development of Nations." *Science* 317: 482.

Hsieh, C., and B. Olken. 2014. "The Missing 'Missing Middle.'" NBER Working Paper 19966, National Bureau of Economic Research, Cambridge, MA.

Jankowska, A., A. Nagengast, and J. R. Perea. 2012. "The Product Space and the Middle-Income Trap: Comparing Asian and Latin American Experiences." OECD Development Centre Working Papers 311, OECD Publishing.

Kongsamut, P., S. Rebelo, and D. Xie. 2002. "Beyond Balanced Growth." *Review of Economic Studies* 68: 869–82.

Lall, S. 2000. "The Technological Structure and Performance of Developing Country Manufactured Exports, 1985–98." *Oxford Development Studies* 28 (3): 337–69.

Lederman, D., and W. Maloney. 2012. "Does What You Export Matter? In Search of Empirical Guidance for Industrial Policies." World Bank, Washington, DC.

McMillan, M., and D. Rodrik. 2011. "Globalization, Structural Change and Productivity Growth." NBER Working Paper 17143, National Bureau of Economic Research, Cambridge, MA.

McMillan, M., and I. Verduzco-Gallo. 2012. "Measuring the Impact of Structural Change on Labor's Share of Income." Background Paper, World Development Report 2013, World Bank, Washington, DC.

Mundlak, Y., R. Butzer, and D. Larson. 2012. "Heterogeneous Technology and Panel Data: The Case of the Agricultural Production Function." *Journal of Development Economics* 99 (1): 139–49.

Ngai, R., and C. Pissarides. 2007. "Structural Change in a Multisector Model of Growth." *American Economic Review* 97: 429–43.

Pages, C. 2010. *The Age of Productivity: Transforming Economies from the Bottom Up.* Inter-American Development Bank, Palgrave Macmillan.

Pasinetti, L. 1981. *Structural Change and Economic Growth.* Cambridge: Cambridge University Press.

Rodrik, Dani. 2013. "Unconditional Convergence in Manufacturing." *Quarterly Journal of Economics* 128 (1): 165–204.

Romer, Paul M. 1990. "Endogenous Technological Change." *Journal of Political Economy* 98 (5): S71–S102.

Silva, L. F., and P. C. Ferreira. 2013. "Structural Transformation and Productivity in Latin America." Mimeo, Fundação Getúlio Vargas, Rio de Janeiro, Brazil.

Timmer, M., and G. de Vries. 2009. "Structural Change and Growth Accelerations in Asia and Latin America: A New Sectoral Data Set." *Cliometrica* 3 (2): 165–90.

Wright, Gavin, and Jesse Czelusta. 2006. "Resource-Based Growth Past and Present." In *Neither Curse nor Destiny: Natural Resources and Development,* edited by Daniel Lederman and William Maloney. Stanford University Press and World Bank Publications.

CHAPTER 5

Productivity Convergence at the Firm Level: New Evidence from the Americas

J. David Brown, Gustavo A. Crespi, Leonardo Iacovone, and Luca Marcolin

Introduction

Since 2003, Latin America has experienced a period of economic resurgence, with strong output growth and generally favorable macroeconomic conditions (Sosa, Tsounta, and Kim 2013). Growth in the Latin America and the Caribbean (LAC) Region reached an average of 4.2 percent per year from 2003 to 2012; after a slowdown in 2013 (2.75 percent) and 2014 (projected at 2.25 percent), growth is expected to pick up again to 3 percent in 2015 (IMF 2014). These outcomes stand in contrast to the chronic low rates of economic growth registered in most Latin American countries in the past 50 years. In particular, the ratio of average income per capita in Latin America to that in the United States decreased from one-fourth in 1960 to one-sixth in the early 2000s (IDB 2010). Analysis of the roots of such underperformance highlights the role of low-productivity growth in the region, despite nonnegligible rates of investment in physical and human capital. However, the positive aggregate performance in recent years has been found to be disproportionately caused by factor accumulation rather than increases in factor productivity (Sosa, Tsounta, and Kim 2013), which marks a clear distinction between Latin America and emerging Asia. As a consequence, there is general consensus that faster productivity growth in the region needs to be achieved for output growth to be sustainable in the future.

Adopting a microeconomic lens, this chapter explores the reasons why countries in LAC have been lagging behind in their rate of productivity growth. Recent economic literature has linked low aggregate productivity growth to either the performance of firms or that of markets. Bartelsman, Haltiwanger, and Scarpetta (2013)

Any opinions and conclusions expressed herein are those of the authors and do not necessarily reflect the views of the U.S. Census Bureau. All results have been reviewed to ensure that no confidential information on individual firms is disclosed.

and Hsieh and Klenow (2009), for instance, highlight two distinct channels driving cross-country differences in productivity: the capacity of markets to allocate resources efficiently among firms or establishments[1] and the evolution of firm productivity itself. In other words, differences in growth rates of aggregate productivity can be pinned down to changes in the average firm-level productivity and changes in the relative importance of firms in their sector or market.

In the presence of distortions in the efficient allocation of resources across firms or establishments and the process of entry into and exit from the market, more productive units may fail to grow and be limited in their share, thus reducing aggregate productivity. This chapter investigates both channels of aggregate productivity growth using firm-level data from the manufacturing sector in Colombia, Mexico, and the United States, in the past decade. We find that the allocation of employment in productive establishments has improved in the aggregate manufacturing sector during the 2000s, but that this aggregate picture hides notable heterogeneity across industries and even more firm-level heterogeneity. This heterogeneity is evident in figure 5.1, where the distribution of the growth rate of labor productivity at the firm level is more widespread than at the industry level.[2]

The analysis decomposes productivity growth and confirms the predominance of within-firm productivity in determining overall aggregate productivity. Therefore, we further investigate the process of productivity growth at the plant level, by analyzing the determinants of productivity convergence. More importantly, we distinguish between convergence with the domestic frontier and convergence with the "global" frontier.[3] In a second stage, we explore what factors influence the speed of convergence at the plant level. Our results suggest that in Colombia and Mexico, as well as the United States, there is evidence of productivity convergence, but this is only the case for convergence with the domestic frontier.[4] We also find that the degree of "integration" of the plants with the

Figure 5.1 Density of Industry and Firm-Level Productivity Growth

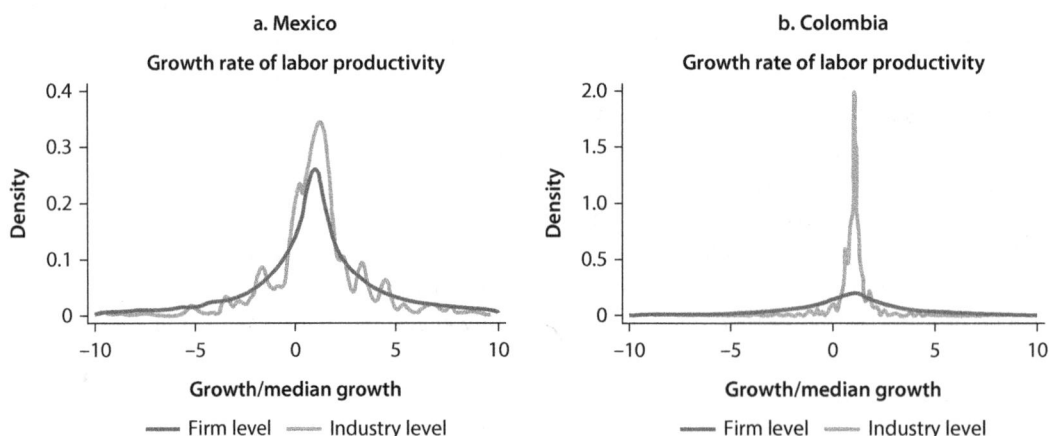

a. Mexico — Growth rate of labor productivity

b. Colombia — Growth rate of labor productivity

— Firm level — Industry level

Source: World Bank calculations.

global economy does not influence the speed of convergence for Colombia and Mexico, but it does increase the speed of convergence with the local frontier for U.S. companies.

In addition, we find that for all countries analyzed, the most important determinant of productivity convergence at the firm level is innovation effort. Innovation effort is measured as the firm-level expenditure shares in innovation and investment in capital equipment. We also find that faster growth in the domestic frontier translates into higher productivity growth at the plant level, which suggests the existence of productivity spillovers. However, these spillovers appear to be weaker for those plants that are far away from the frontier, which is consistent with the idea that companies lacking absorptive capabilities are less able to take advantage of potential knowledge spillovers.

The chapter is divided into four main sections aside from introduction and conclusion. The first section presents the most important economic literature that inspired the current work. The second section presents the data at hand, the first descriptive evidence of the catch-up in firm labor productivity, and the results of the productivity decomposition. This is followed by the discussion of our estimation strategy and the results of the econometric analysis. The annexes provide further estimation results (annex 5A), estimation results with the local frontier only (annex 5B), and details on data construction (annex 5C).

Literature

Aggregate productivity growth is normally estimated as the part of gross domestic product (GDP) growth that cannot be explained by the growth in the inputs of production (employment, physical capital, and human capital). This unexplained component measures the country's efficiency in the use of inputs for producing one unit of output. Recent analyses, by contrast, have investigated aggregate productivity as the result of firm-level processes, where firms are assumed to be heterogeneous in their productivity even within narrowly defined sectors (Bartelsman, Haltiwanger, and Scarpetta 2004, 2009; Foster, Haltiwanger, and Syverson 2008; Syverson 2004). This heterogeneity in firm-level productivity can reflect misallocation of resources across firms: as low-productivity firms have lower survival than high-productivity firms, aggregate (industry) productivity can improve by reallocating resources among incumbents with different productivity levels, or between incumbents and firms entering or exiting the market. (For a recent survey of this literature, see Restuccia and Rogerson 2013.) Moreover, cross-country differences in output per capita can be at least partially explained by the extent of such misallocation (Banerjee and Duflo 2005; Hsieh and Klenow 2009; Restuccia and Rogerson 2008).

The availability of micro-level data now permits the investigation of the extent of such differences in the link between misallocation and productivity at the cross-country level (Bartelsman, Haltiwanger, and Scarpetta 2004, 2013). In this chapter, we do so for Colombia and Mexico and compare the results with the United States, exploiting the industry-level productivity decomposition proposed by Olley and Pakes (1996). This decomposition divides aggregate productivity into an unweighted average of firm-level productivity in the sector and a covariance term picturing the joint distribution of firms' (or establishments') productivity and market share. The extent of resource misallocation is inferred by the covariance term; larger positive values indicate that more productive firms use higher shares of industry inputs. Increases in the covariance term would therefore imply improvements in the allocation of productive inputs (such as workers) across firms (within the industry).

However, this decomposition does not distinguish between reallocation between incumbents and reallocation caused by churning (that is, the entry and exit of firms). By neglecting that entrants and exiters can have substantially different productivity than incumbents, the Olley-Pakes decomposition therefore understates the importance of creative destruction in the market. The literature has proposed several measures to overcome this limitation, which usually break down productivity growth into four components: growth in productivity of the incumbents, changes in market shares of the incumbents, contribution of entrants, and contribution of exiters (Baily et al. 1992; Foster, Haltiwanger, and Krizan 2001; Griliches and Regev 1995).

In our analysis, we rely on the dynamic decomposition proposed by Melitz and Polanec (2012). The authors propose a clear extension of the Olley-Pakes static decomposition that takes into account entry and exit. Further, they show that previous dynamic decompositions suffer from biases by construction, and therefore fail to account appropriately for the contribution of entry and exit in aggregate productivity. Although the sign of such bias is theoretically ambiguous, the authors show that previous decompositions underestimate the role of survivors and overestimate that of entrants in the aggregate productivity of fast-growing economies.

The second part of this chapter extends our analysis of the process of creative destruction by investigating the determinants of firm-level productivity catch-up. Earlier literature on productivity convergence has traditionally focused on countries or regions as the units of observation (Sala-i-Martin 1996), and their capability to bridge the gap with the highest productivity growth among all other units, or the global technological frontier. In Acemoglu, Aghion, and Zilibotti (2006), efficiency improvements are driven by changes in the frontier and the speed of catch-up of firms to it. Our study takes a more micro-level approach instead, and evaluates the process of productivity convergence toward the national and international frontiers. This is the strategy followed by Girma and Kneller (2005) to study the convergence process of the UK service sector, as well as by Alvarez and Crespi (2007) for the Chilean manufacturing sector and Iacovone and Crespi (2010) for Mexico. Contrary to Griffith, Redding, and Simpson (2009) or Alvarez and Crespi (2007), however, we do not define the catch-up process only with respect to the national frontier, but with the international frontier as well (Bartelsman, Haskel, and Martin 2008; Griffith et al. 2004; Iacovone and Crespi 2010).

It seems implausible, especially for fast-developing countries in the 2000s, to define the technological frontier as the national one. Although it may be true that many firms in these countries cannot compete with their best international peers, it is very likely that several of them are exposed to the international market either through trade or foreign direct investment. For these firms, in light of the firm-level differences in degree of internationalization, the process of convergence to the frontier may be substantially different across firms. Further, in the presence of differences in the evolution of the national and global technological frontiers, within-country convergence to the national frontier may be biased by the absence of the term for convergence toward the international frontier, which may be especially problematic for firms integrated with the global economy. Therefore, we explore the extent to which convergence differs when in relation to the local or global frontier.

In doing so, we also investigate how the catch-up of plants with the best practice in their industry is affected by different firm-level capabilities, and in particular the degree of trade integration and innovation, technological investment, and investment in human capital of the firm. We focus our analysis on Latin American countries, thus building on the contributions of IDB (2010) and Pages, Pierre, and Scarpetta (2009), among others, which explore several aspects of productivity evolution in the region. Previous studies selectively tested some of these channels, such as foreign ownership (Alvarez and Crespi 2007; Griffith, Redding, and Simpson 2009), R&D expenditure (Griffith, Redding, Simpson and Van Reenen 2004), or trade and innovation (Iacovone and Crespi 2010). Similarly Vandenbussche, Aghion, and Meghir (2006) show that skilled human capital increases growth when countries are closer to the frontier, while unskilled human capital increases growth when the country is lagging behind the frontier. A recent investigation of the role of human capital for the speed of productivity catch up, though at the country level, is proposed by Madsen (2014) as well.[5] Our study will test the effect of these firm-level capabilities simultaneously, short of foreign ownership, for which we have no information in the Mexican and Colombian datasets.

As a consequence, our analysis relates to the long-lasting literature exploring the linkages between trade and firm-plant level productivity, albeit ignoring the role of the firm's distance from the technological frontier. While it is clear that exporters are more productive than nonexporters (Bernard and Jensen 1995; Tybout and Westbrook 1995; Bernard et al. 2007), early works find that the direction of causality goes from firm productivity to exports. Bernard and Jensen (1999) show that future U.S. exporters performed better than future nonexporters before entering the export market. After entry, they display higher survival and growth in sales and employment, but not higher productivity growth. Clerides, Lach and Tybout (1998) explicitly test whether the correlation between exporting and plant productivity is driven by the self-selection of firms into the export market, or by learning-by-exporting. Their sample of Mexican, Colombia and Moroccan plants supports only the former hypothesis. Vice versa, Van Biesebroeck (2005) finds evidence of both effects in nine sub-Saharan countries.

Exporters increase their productivity advantage after entry in the export market, possibly due to higher intensity in capital or training of the workforce, or access to better technology. Further evidence of the learning-by-exporting hypothesis is provided by De Loecker (2007), who finds significant productivity premia for Slovenian firms entering the export market. These gains are driven by exports towards developed economies, which provide better learning opportunities for Slovenian firms and a more competitive environment. Our empirical specification, by looking at the role of trade for productivity convergence, implicitly assumes a role for exports in shaping firms' productivity growth.

Descriptive Statistics

Data Characteristics

This study focuses on the analysis of productivity growth and convergence in Colombia, Mexico, and the United States, using establishment-level data from the manufacturing sector.[6] For Mexico, we rely on an unbalanced, establishment-level panel data set, known as the Annual Industrial Survey (EIA), which tracks manufacturing plants, for the years 2003 to 2011. The survey is collected annually by the Mexican National Institute of Statistics (INEGI). The survey excludes establishments with fewer than 15 employees, and aims at covering at least 85 percent of output in the whole manufacturing sector.[7]

For Colombia, plant-level information was obtained from the Manufacturing Survey (EAM) collected by the Departamento Administrativo Nacional de Estadística (DANE). The survey covers the universe of manufacturing establishments with at least 10 employees or at least Col$136.4 million in revenues from sales, for the years 2000 to 2011.[8]

Plants were selected into the sample for the census year (2003) for Mexico and on a yearly basis for Colombia, then followed over time. For Mexico, while this process allows us to construct a plant-level panel, it also implies that the sample allows for limited entry in noncensus years (usually when new plants are especially relevant in size). In Colombia, DANE revised the sample on the basis of other sources of information in 2008. However, exit is reported consistently in both cases. The resulting sample (after cleaning) for Mexico contains 5,782 plants in 2003 and 4,499 in 2011; for Colombia, the sample covers 6,925 plants in 2000 and 8,988 in 2011.[9] Plants are distributed in 231 four-digit industries according to the Système de classification des industries de l'Amérique du Nord (SCIAN) classification (2002 and 2007) for Mexico, in 142 four-digit International Standard Industrial Classification (ISIC) 3.1 sectors for Colombia, and in 473 six-digit North American Industry Classification System (NAICS) industries for the United States.[10]

The surveys provide access to information on all inputs of production and sources of revenues, by breaking them down according to their international versus domestic origin or destination. The main outcome variable of interest is labor productivity or value added per worker, where value added is computed as revenues from sales minus the cost of intermediate inputs and electricity.

Information on capital stock at book value and investment is also reported in the manufacturing surveys, which allows us to construct a measure of investment in technology (or net investment in capital equipment that is not buildings). The Mexican survey also includes data on expenditure on certain forms of external innovation (patents, consultancy services, advisory services, etc.). We do not have information on research and development (R&D) expenditure for Mexico, but we do have such information for Colombia by merging the EAM with the Innovation Survey,[11] and for the United States by merging the Business Research and Development and Innovation Survey.[12] All variables are deflated with the most disaggregated deflator at our disposal, then transformed into U.S. dollars.[13]

Table 5.1 reports basic statistics for our sample for Colombia and Mexico, pooling all years. It highlights significant differences in the types of surveyed establishments. While the Mexican sample covers relatively large plants, with 220 employees and US$30.5 million in revenues per year on average, plants in the Colombian data set are significantly smaller on average (70 employees and US$5 million). The within-country heterogeneity in productivity is also high,

Table 5.1 Sample Description

	Count	Mean	sd	p5	p10	p25	p50	p75	p90	p99
Mexico										
Sales	47,868	31,626	183,192	193	404	1,297	4,982	18,604	60,040	333,675
Employment	47,868	221	389	10	17	39	98	242	512	1,936
Capital	47,868	11,648	71,296	30	68	229	1,027	4,943	20,398	163,975
Value added	47,868	15,019	76,334	84	180	601	2,294	8,685	29,956	179,814
Value added/Employment	47,868	45.28	83.46	4.51	6.65	11.90	22.62	46.81	94.04	394.68
Export/Sales	47,408	0.11	0.23	0.00	0.00	0.00	0.00	0.07	0.43	0.99
Import/Sales	47,413	0.07	0.14	0.00	0.00	0.00	0.00	0.09	0.28	0.60
External innovation/Sales	47,865	0.04	0.20	0.00	0.00	0.00	0.00	0.00	0.04	0.82
Investment/Sales	47,866	0.02	0.26	0.00	0.00	0.00	0.00	0.02	0.06	0.27
Equipment investment/Sales	47,522	0.02	0.24	0.00	0.00	0.00	0.00	0.02	0.05	0.23
Colombia										
Sales	84,815	5,207	55,208	74	106	224	624	2,256	9,197	68,030
Employment	84,815	70	153	5	7	12	24	64	162	713
Capital	82,050	2,396	20,787	9	19	57	179	684	3,142	40,375
Value added	84,815	2,523	31,005	35	52	114	328	1,150	4,110	33,567
Value added/Employment	84,815	22.94	74.25	3.58	4.98	7.91	13.16	22.95	42.36	162.88
Export/Sales	84,389	0.06	0.16	0.00	0.00	0.00	0.00	0.00	0.19	0.89
Import/Sales	84,356	0.03	0.11	0.00	0.00	0.00	0.00	0.00	0.10	0.53
Internal innovation/Sales	51,972	0.00	0.18	0.00	0.00	0.00	0.00	0.00	0.00	0.03
External innovation/Sales	51,972	0.00	0.33	0.00	0.00	0.00	0.00	0.00	0.00	0.05
Investment/Sales	84,389	0.10	12.33	0.00	0.00	0.00	0.01	0.03	0.10	0.57
Equipment investment/Sales	84,389	0.08	12.32	0.00	0.00	0.00	0.00	0.03	0.08	0.40

Source: World Bank calculations.

Note: All statistics are constructed using deflated values in the clean sample. Sales, capital, and value added (per employee) are reported in thousands of US$. The Mexican sample covers 2003–11; the Colombian sample covers 2000–11. sd = standard deviation; p = percentile.

with low-productivity plants (bottom decile) producing US$5,000 per employee in Mexico (US$3,600 in Colombia) compared with almost US$400,000 in high-productivity plants at the top decile (US$163,000 in Colombia).

Differences in plants' labor productivity are unsurprisingly correlated to exposure to international trade and innovation. Only a fraction of establishments engages in exporting (36 percent of plants export on average each year in our Mexican sample, and 23 percent in the Colombian sample), and for those that export, only 11 percent of revenues are from exports on average for Mexico and 6 percent for Colombia.[14] In Mexico, 39 percent of plants import on average in a given year; in Colombia, 19 percent import on average. But expenditure on imported intermediate inputs is a much lower fraction of revenues from sales: on average 7 percent in Mexico and 3 percent in Colombia. Furthermore, engagement in innovation is even more limited, with expenditure on consulting services and patents reaching 4 percent of revenues in Mexico, and essentially zero for Colombian plants on average.[15]

In tables 5.2 to 5.4, we show similar statistics but for the sample of plants that engage in two-way trade (table 5.2), external innovation (table 5.3), and

Table 5.2 Sample Description by Activity: Two-Way Trade

	Count	Mean	sd	p5	p10	p25	p50	p75	p90	p99
Mexico										
Sales	11,893	59,834	196,624	1,344	2,322	6,055	17,442	47,838	121,583	705,810
Employment	11,893	386	501	35	55	112	229	445	878	2,835
Capital	11,893	20,725	71,579	194	389	1,233	4,454	15,508	42,111	292,945
Value added	11,893	28,132	75,829	627	1,097	2,865	8,530	24,397	63,224	314,827
Value added/Employment	11,893	63.36	96.78	9.03	12.00	19.60	35.76	69.85	131.85	452.70
Export/Sales	11,893	0.32	0.31	0.01	0.02	0.06	0.20	0.53	0.85	1.00
Import/Sales	11,893	0.19	0.16	0.01	0.02	0.05	0.15	0.29	0.43	0.65
External innovation/Sales	11,893	0.07	0.24	0.00	0.00	0.00	0.00	0.00	0.24	0.97
Investment/Sales	11,893	0.02	0.06	0.00	0.00	0.00	0.01	0.03	0.06	0.24
Equipment investment/Sales	11,829	0.02	0.05	0.00	0.00	0.00	0.01	0.02	0.05	0.21
Colombia										
Sales	9,201	16,851	51,161	445	738	1,778	5,253	16,035	40,453	160,653
Employment	9,201	212	295	18	26	53	114	255	504	1,331
Capital	9,151	8,626	30,371	67	145	407	1,507	6,369	19,480	119,217
Value added	9,201	8,087	22,038	209	368	927	2,677	7,844	19,721	73,904
Value added/Employment	9,201	36.7	65.33	6.6	8.55	13.31	21.5	39.26	72.3	238.92
Export/Sales	9,201	0.24	0.24	0.01	0.01	0.05	0.15	0.35	0.61	0.96
Import/Sales	9,201	0.19	0.23	0.00	0.01	0.04	0.13	0.28	0.46	0.85
Internal innovation/Sales	5,221	0.00	0.01	0.00	0.00	0.00	0.00	0.00	0.00	0.04
External innovation/Sales	5,221	0.00	0.05	0.00	0.00	0.00	0.00	0.00	0.00	0.06
Investment/Sales	9,201	0.05	0.33	0.00	0.00	0.01	0.02	0.05	0.10	0.42
Equipment investment/Sales	9,201	0.04	0.24	0.00	0.00	0.00	0.01	0.04	0.08	0.31

Source: World Bank calculations.
Note: All statistics are constructed using deflated values in the clean sample. Sales, capital, and value added (per employee) are reported in thousands of US$. The Mexican sample covers 2003–11; the Colombian sample covers 2000–11. sd = standard deviation; p = percentile.

Table 5.3 Sample Description by Activity: External Innovation

	Count	Mean	sd	p5	p10	p25	p50	p75	p90	p99
Mexico										
Sales	6,131	69,175	272,270	1,891	3,210	7,925	23,011	59,024	138,142	659,067
Employment	6,131	436	565	32	51	101	256	521	1,018	3,094
Capital	6,131	24,257	105,265	155	316	1,230	5,357	20,224	50,756	246,422
Value added	6,131	36,622	125,849	996	1,728	4,133	12,322	32,660	79,435	328,112
Value added/Employment	6,131	79.29	103.42	11.72	15.95	26.87	49.18	89.27	165.65	501.22
Export/Sales	6,124	0.18	0.27	0.00	0.00	0.00	0.03	0.26	0.64	0.99
Import/Sales	6,124	0.14	0.17	0.00	0.00	0.00	0.07	0.24	0.40	0.62
External innovation/Sales	6,131	0.31	0.48	0.00	0.01	0.05	0.17	0.40	0.72	1.82
Investment/Sales	6,131	0.02	0.10	0.00	0.00	0.00	0.01	0.03	0.06	0.21
Equipment investment/Sales	6,097	0.02	0.07	0.00	0.00	0.00	0.01	0.02	0.05	0.17
Colombia										
Sales	8,148	15,627	140,469	97	176	496	1,803	7,806	25,986	138,866
Employment	8,148	134	263	8	11	21	55	140	319	1,182
Capital	7,993	7,072	47,225	16	37	121	462	2,429	10,206	117,855
Value added	8,148	8,111	85,241	55	95	279	973	3,673	11,612	70,738
Value added/Employment	8,148	36.86	199.82	4.21	5.7	9.49	17.06	32.44	64.46	289.47
Export/Sales	8,052	0.09	0.18	0.00	0.00	0.00	0.00	0.07	0.33	0.89
Import/Sales	8,052	0.05	0.16	0.00	0.00	0.00	0.00	0.03	0.20	0.59
Internal innovation/Sales	8,052	0.02	0.47	0.00	0.00	0.00	0.00	0.00	0.01	0.14
External innovation/Sales	8,052	0.03	0.84	0.00	0.00	0.00	0.00	0.01	0.03	0.26
Investment/Sales	8,052	0.07	0.66	0.00	0.00	0.00	0.02	0.05	0.12	0.66
Equipment investment/Sales	8,052	0.06	0.64	0.00	0.00	0.00	0.01	0.04	0.09	0.50

Source: World Bank calculations.
Note: All statistics are constructed using deflated values in the clean sample of plants displaying nonzero expenditure on external innovation. Sales, capital, and value added (per employee) are reported in thousands of US$. The Mexican sample covers 2003–11; the Colombian sample covers 2000–11. sd = standard deviation; p = percentile.

investment in machinery and at least one type of innovation (internal or external) (table 5.4). Previous literature has already established that trade and innovation are strongly correlated with productivity, a fact we exploit in our econometric analysis. Our sample confirms the stylized fact that plants engaged in international trade (in particular here, plants that import and export goods) are larger than average in sales, capital stock, and employment on average, and they are more productive.

Furthermore, plants that are engaged in international trade spend more on external innovation than the average plant in Mexico (expenditure reaches 7 percent of revenues on average), and this is driven by the intensity of investment at the top of the distribution (the intensity of investments among plants in the top decile is six times higher than the overall Mexico average, while a difference can be observed only at the top percentile of the distribution in Colombia). Two-way traders also invest more often than plants in the entire population in both countries of interest, although the traders do not invest more on average, at least in machinery. Colombian plants seem to invest a greater portion of their

Table 5.4 Sample Description by Activity: Innovation and Investment in Equipment

	Count	Mean	sd	p5	p10	p25	p50	p75	p90	p99
Mexico										
Sales	4,515	75,611	309,956	2,456	3,962	8,923	25,451	63,597	142,286	692,207
Employment	4,515	464	590	39	57	116	276	556	1,070	3,201
Capital	4,515	27,832	119,345	222	431	1,623	6,540	23,250	56,815	299,745
Value added	4,515	40,049	143,122	1,284	1,992	4,729	13,642	34,471	81,596	337,299
Value added/Employment	4,515	77.84	97.80	12.30	16.46	27.32	49.64	88.94	163.14	482.34
Export/Sales	4,512	0.19	0.27	0.00	0.00	0.00	0.04	0.29	0.66	0.98
Import/Sales	4,512	0.14	0.17	0.00	0.00	0.00	0.08	0.24	0.41	0.64
External innovation/Sales	4,515	0.30	0.50	0.00	0.01	0.05	0.18	0.39	0.69	1.96
Investment/Sales	4,515	0.03	0.11	0.00	0.00	0.01	0.02	0.04	0.07	0.24
Equipment investment/Sales	4,515	0.03	0.07	0.00	0.00	0.00	0.01	0.03	0.06	0.20
Colombia										
Sales	6,603	18,374	153,836	195	323	786	2,622	10,139	31,050	148,845
Employment	6,603	153	282	11	15	29	68	168	359	1,235
Capital	6,511	8,289	51,952	41	70	190	672	3,234	12,346	130,998
Value added	6,603	9,321	91,916	93	157	407	1,261	4,460	13,253	74,746
Value added/Employment	6,603	36.6	163.34	4.8	6.57	10.55	18.32	33.98	65.36	274.89
Export/Sales	6,603	0.10	0.19	0.00	0.00	0.00	0.00	0.10	0.35	0.90
Import/Sales	6,510	0.06	0.17	0.00	0.00	0.00	0.00	0.05	0.22	0.61
Internal innovation/Sales	6,603	0.01	0.21	0.00	0.00	0.00	0.00	0.00	0.01	0.10
External innovation/Sales	6,603	0.03	0.89	0.00	0.00	0.00	0.00	0.01	0.03	0.24
Investment/Sales	6,603	0.09	0.73	0.00	0.00	0.01	0.02	0.06	0.14	0.74
Equipment investment/Sales	6,603	0.07	0.71	0.00	0.00	0.01	0.02	0.05	0.10	0.59

Source: World Bank calculations.
Note: All statistics are constructed using deflated values in the clean sample of plants displaying nonzero expenditure on external innovation and purchases of equipment. Sales, capital, and value added (per employee) are reported in thousands of US$. The Mexican sample covers 2003–11; the Colombian sample covers 2000–11. sd = standard deviation; p = percentile.

revenues from sales than Mexican plants do, in the complete sample and the sample of two-way traders.

Similar characteristics are displayed by plants that do some external innovation (through purchasing patents or consulting services), with even more pronounced differences with respect to the average plant in the entire population (table 5.3). The same can be said if the plant invests in new machinery and innovates, with the exception of labor productivity in Mexico. The distribution of value added per employee in the latter type of plants is slightly to the left of that of innovators.[16] This is not the case for Colombia, where the average plant investing in new equipment and in at least one of the two innovation activities is twice as productive as the average plant in the entire sample, and the entire distribution is shifted to the right.

Distance from the Frontier

Our analysis relies on the possibility of identifying a technological frontier serving as a benchmark for firm productivity. We compute the national frontier as the mean of the top quartile of the distribution of value added per employee in the four-digit industry and year. The global frontier is similarly computed on the basis of the survey of U.S. manufacturing plants collected by the U.S. Census Bureau.[17] Figures 5.2 and 5.3 show the ratio between the global and local frontiers at the (two-digit) sector level.[18] Unsurprisingly, the U.S. frontier is above the Mexican and Colombian frontiers in all sectors, with the Colombian frontier lagging further behind than the Mexican frontier. At the same time, the distance between the two frontiers does not seem to have changed in a relevant way in the considered time span, with the exception of the crisis years in Mexico in particular, where the most productive plants (as an average of those at or above the top quartile) lost ground[19] with respect to their U.S. peers.[20] In Colombia, the distance between the global and local frontiers displays a distinct inverted-U shape in most sectors. More importantly, in both countries substantial cross-industry heterogeneity is also evident in the level of the distance, with sectors where the global frontier is a higher multiple of the national one than others (for Mexico: leather, medical equipment, and wood; for Colombia: chemicals, communications equipment, and medical equipment).[21]

Although the Mexican and Colombian frontiers are far from the global frontier, in both countries a few plants are highly productive at the "global" level. Figure 5.4 reports the number of plants more productive than the global frontier (blue bars), by year. The orange bars show instead the number of plants above the global frontier, as a percentage of the total number of plants in the same year. The latter figure never exceeds 1 percent, and it has clearly been affected by the global economic crisis of 2008–09. The relatively high percentage in 2008 in Mexico reflects the decrease in value of the global frontier caused by the decrease in output in the United States.[22] Though the number (and percentage) of plants above the global frontier has reached the precrisis level in Colombia but not in Mexico, these numbers are still considerably lower in Colombia than in Mexico.

The aggregate values display substantial industry heterogeneity. Figure 5.5 shows that the percentage of plants more productive than the global frontier is substantially different across two-digit industries in a given year.[23] Each bar represents the number of plants with higher productivity than the frontier as a percentage of the total number of plants in the same two-digit industry. It is clear that several sectors do not have any plant that performs better than the frontier, while others have up to 2 and 5 percent of such plants, respectively, in Mexico and Colombia.

Another way to show the relative standing of Mexican and Colombian establishments with respect to the frontier is to calculate the distance between the frontier and the median plant's productivity.[24] Figures 5.6 and 5.7 display this ratio for the five largest and smallest sectors in the economy (in gross deflated value added), as well as aggregating over all industries. In all cases, the left vertical axis measures the distance to the global frontier; the right axis measures the distance to the domestic frontier. Although both distances often seem to move together, the magnitude of the distance is clearly different, with the distance with

Figure 5.2 Trend in the Ratio of Global to Domestic Frontiers, by Sector: Mexico

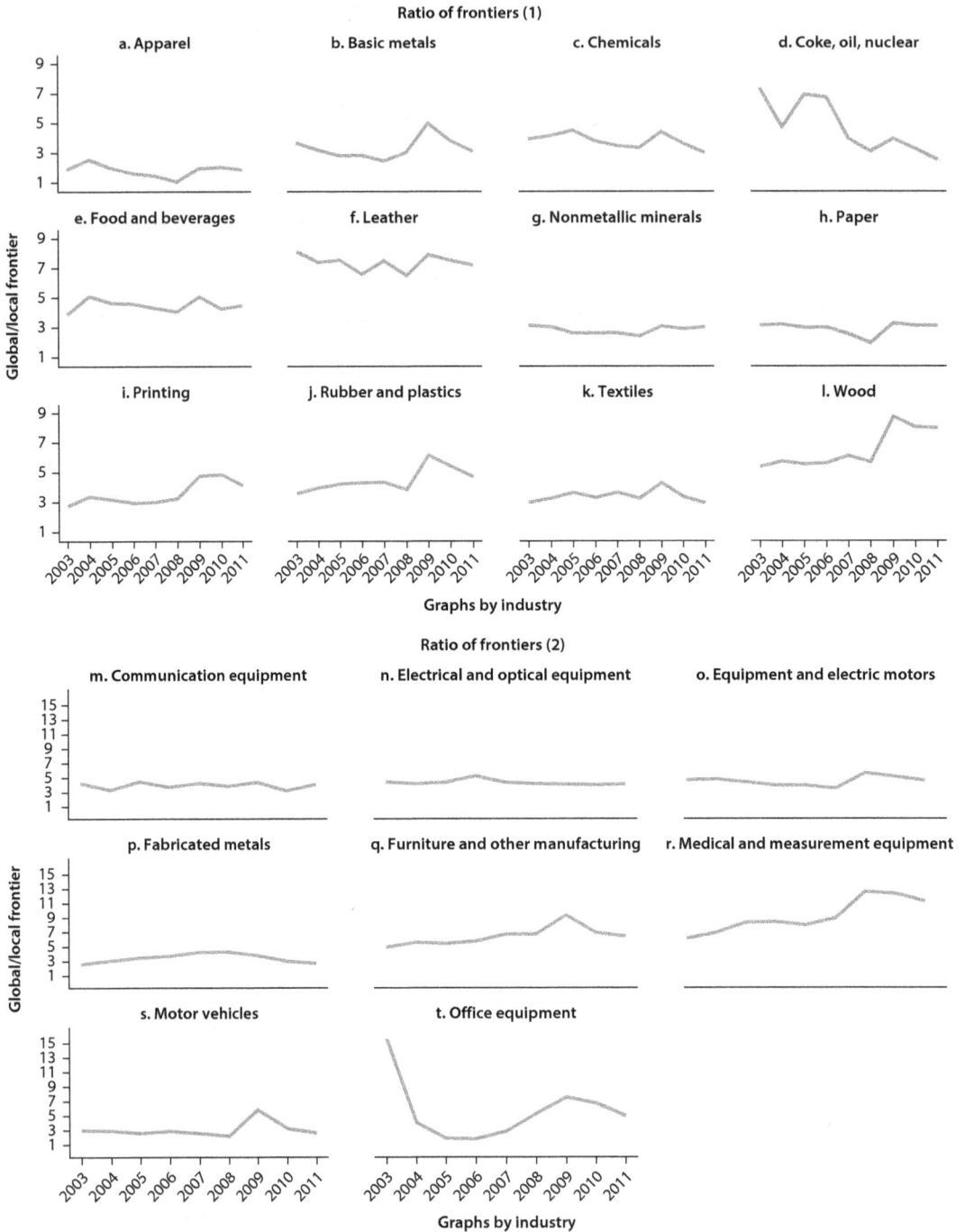

Ratio of frontiers (1)

Graphs by industry

Ratio of frontiers (2)

Graphs by industry

Source: World Bank calculations.

Figure 5.3 Trend in the Ratio of Global to Domestic Frontiers, by Sector: Colombia

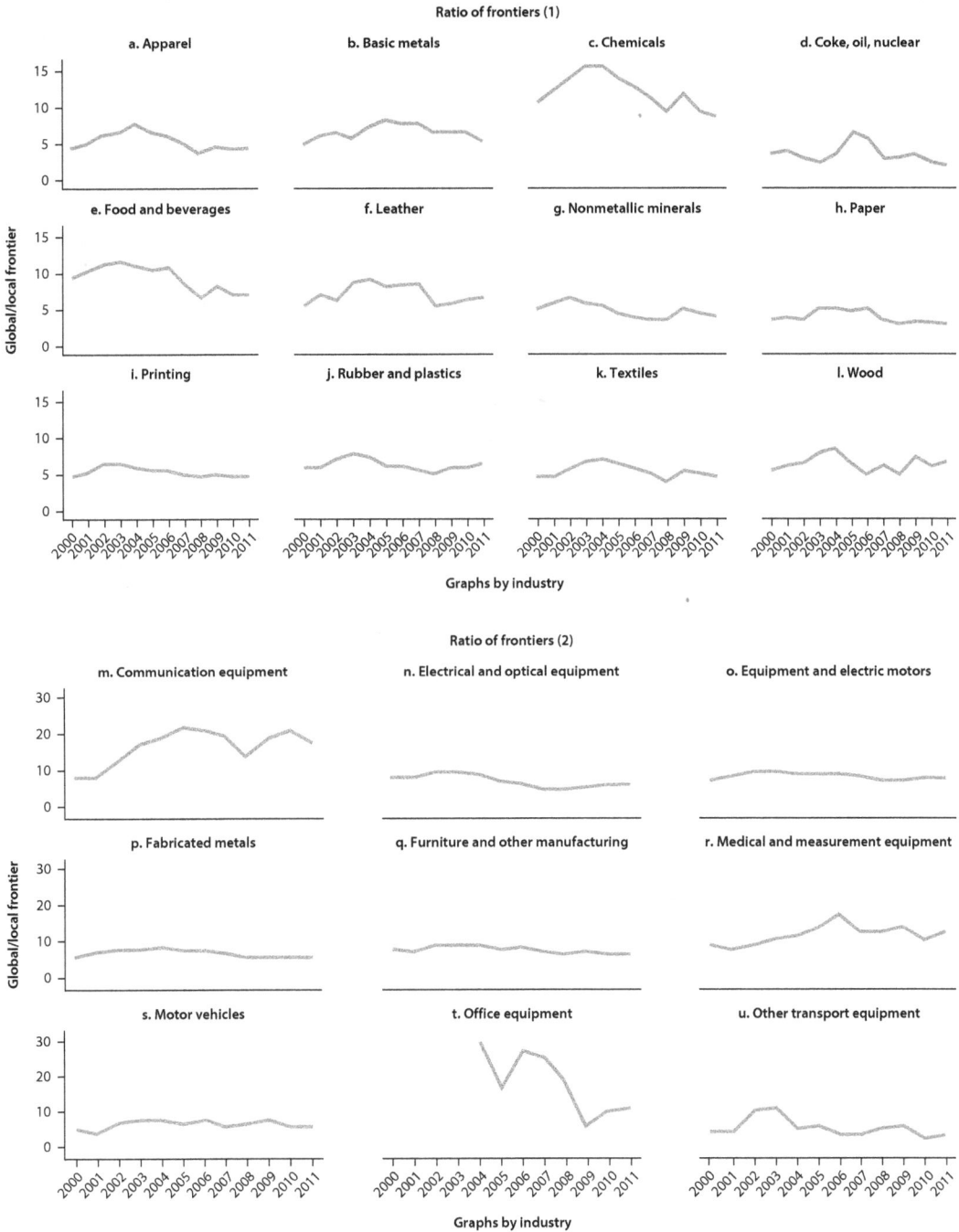

Source: World Bank calculations.

Figure 5.4 Exceeding the Global Frontier, by Year

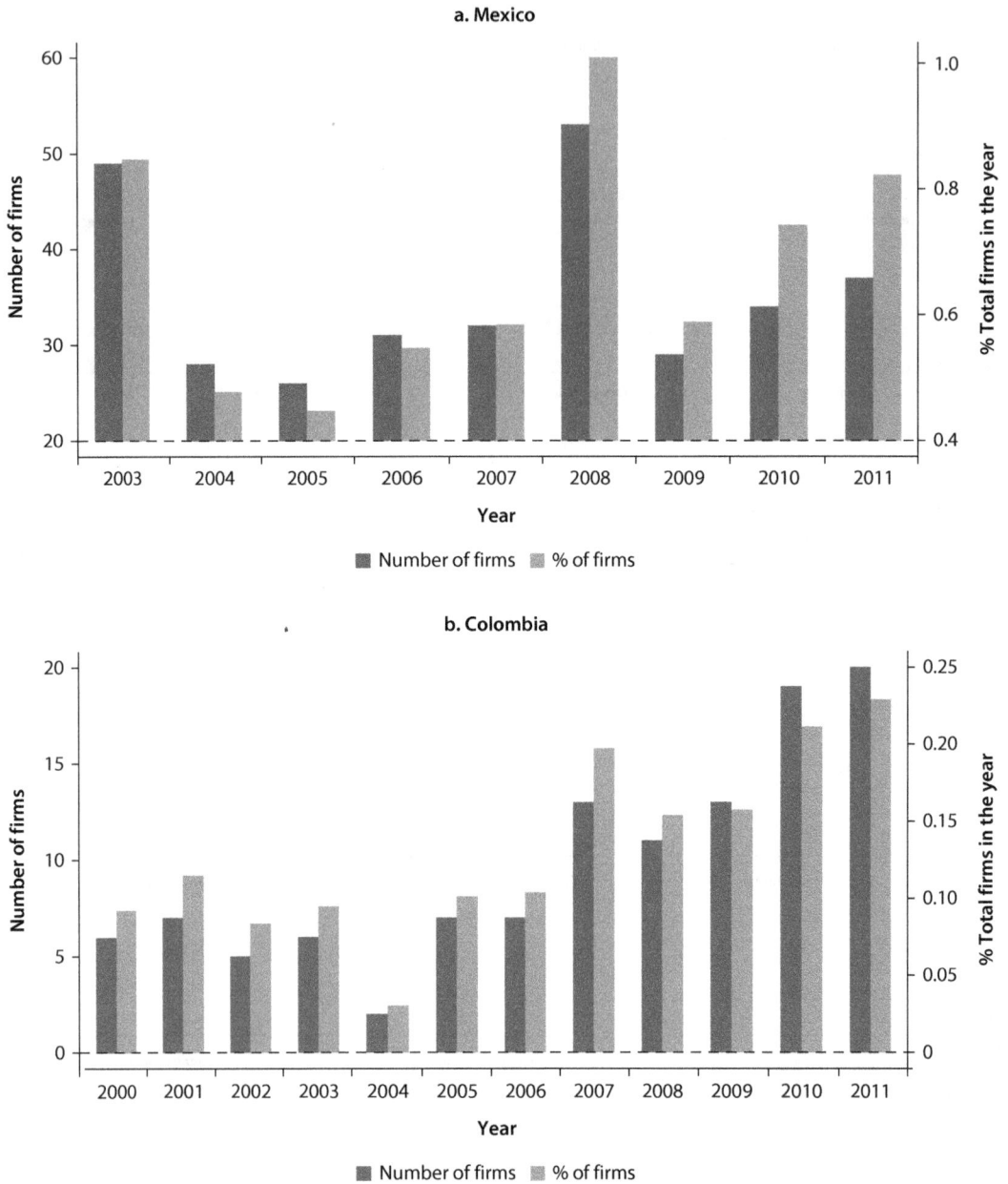

a. Mexico

■ Number of firms   ■ % of firms

b. Colombia

■ Number of firms   ■ % of firms

Source: World Bank calculations.

Figure 5.5 Exceeding the Global Frontier, by Sector

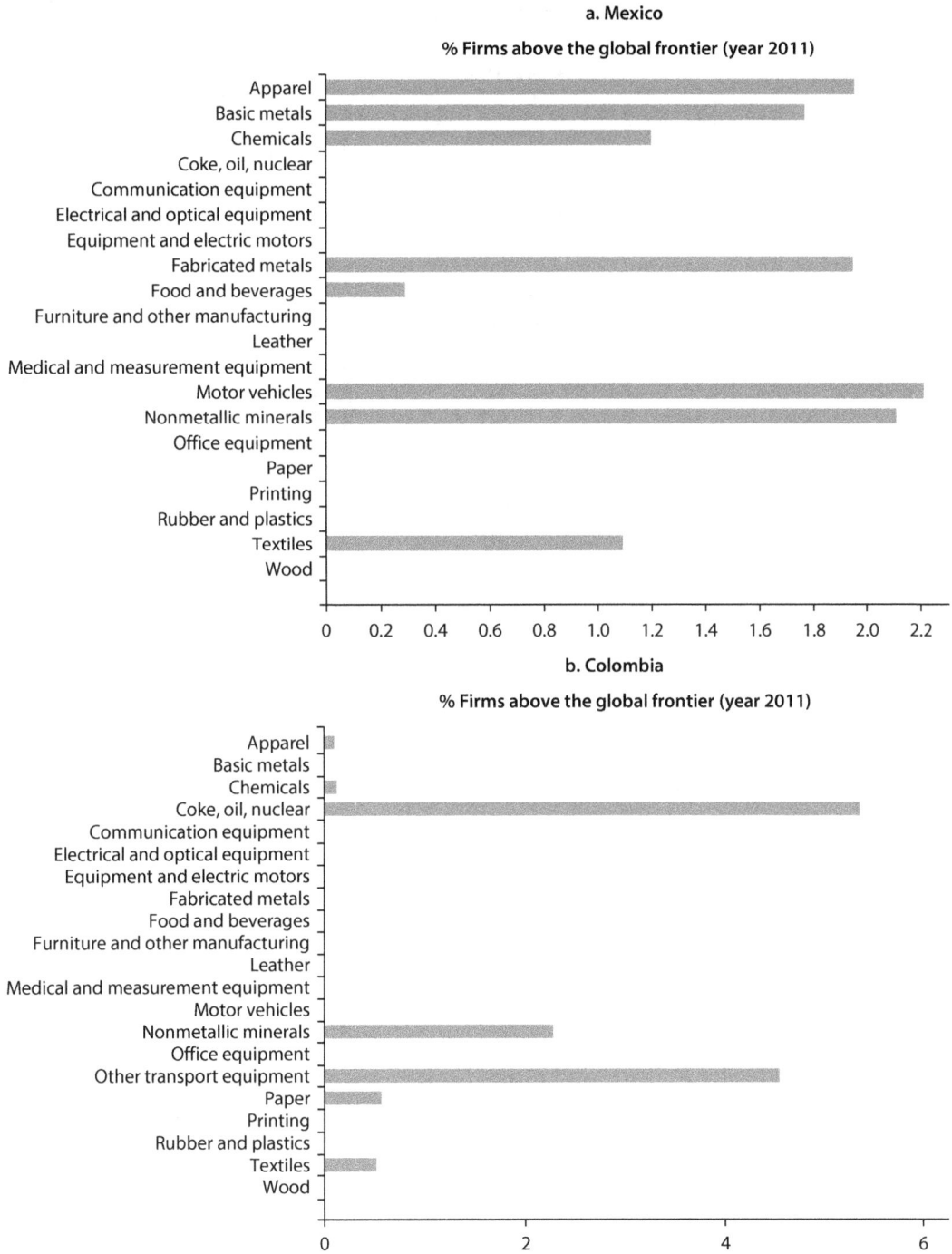

a. Mexico

% Firms above the global frontier (year 2011)

b. Colombia

% Firms above the global frontier (year 2011)

Source: World Bank calculations.

Understanding the Income and Efficiency Gap in Latin America and the Caribbean
http://dx.doi.org/10.1596/978-1-4648-0450-2

Figure 5.6 Distance between Frontier and Plants, by Sector: Mexico

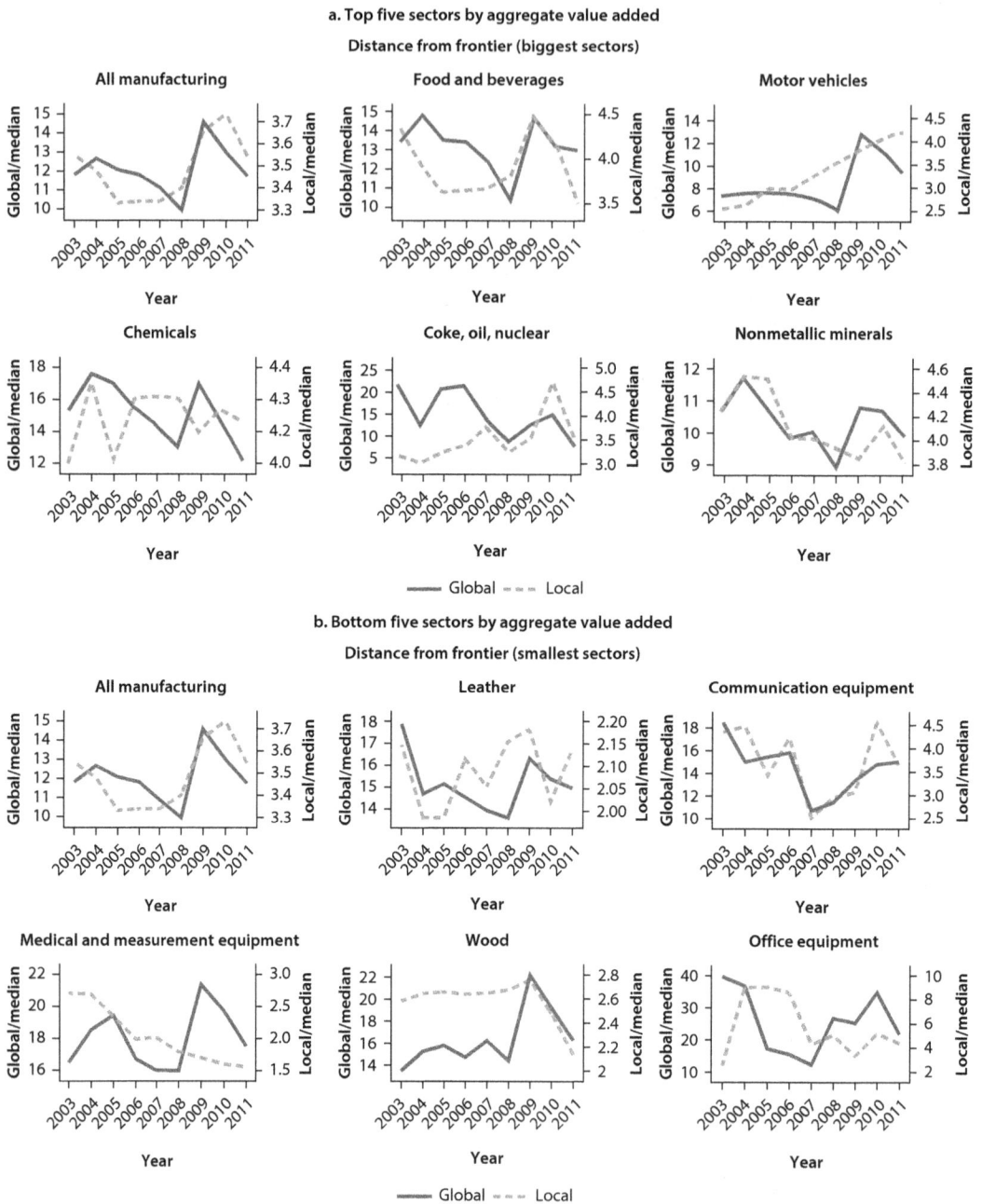

a. Top five sectors by aggregate value added

Distance from frontier (biggest sectors)

All manufacturing

Food and beverages

Motor vehicles

Chemicals

Coke, oil, nuclear

Nonmetallic minerals

—— Global - - - Local

b. Bottom five sectors by aggregate value added

Distance from frontier (smallest sectors)

All manufacturing

Leather

Communication equipment

Medical and measurement equipment

Wood

Office equipment

—— Global - - - Local

Source: World Bank calculations.

Figure 5.7 Distance between Frontier and Plants, by Sector: Colombia

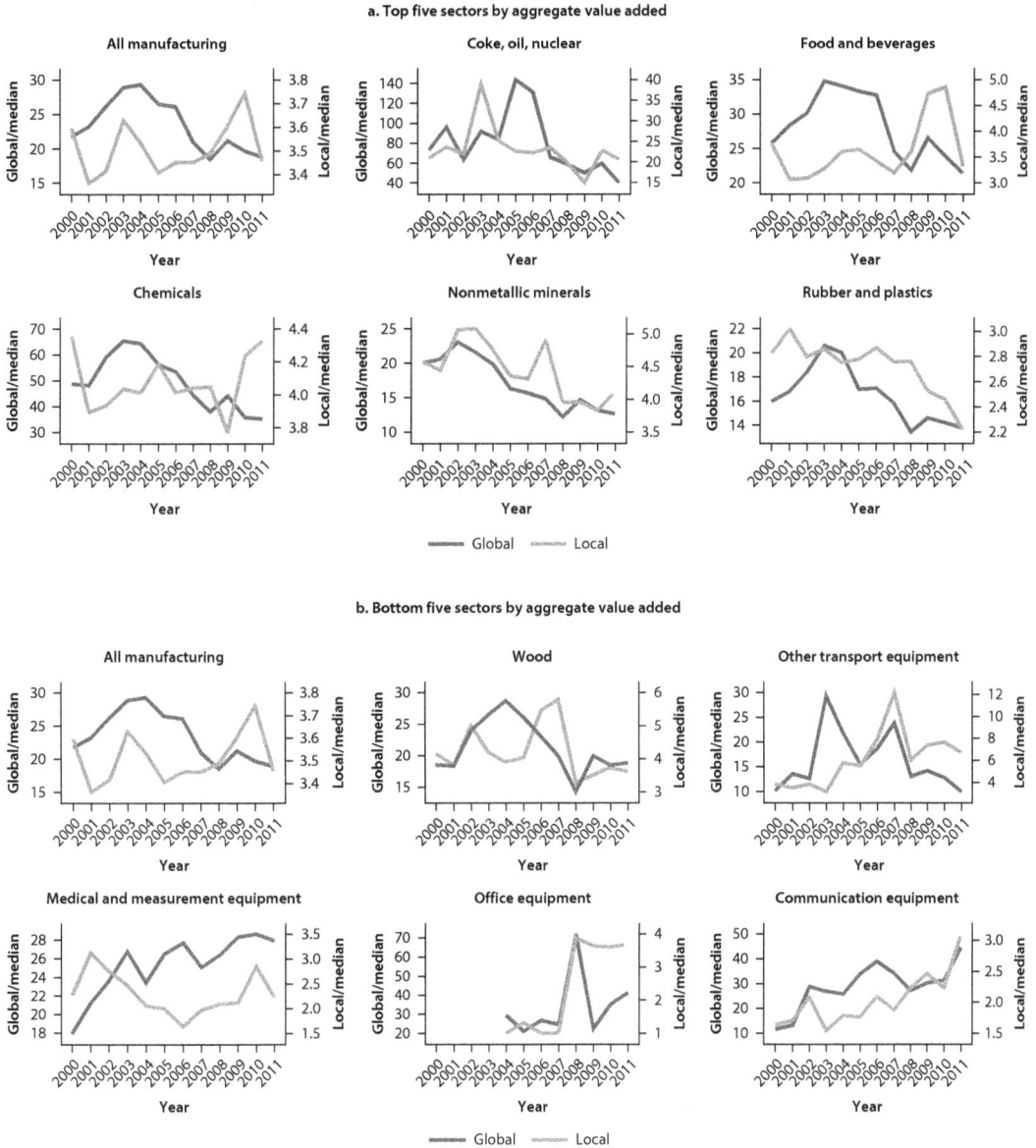

a. Top five sectors by aggregate value added

b. Bottom five sectors by aggregate value added

Source: World Bank calculations.

respect to the global frontier always exceeding the distance with the domestic one by a multiple of three to four times.

At the aggregate level, this picture suggests a small decrease in the distance from the global frontier for Mexico and a relatively more noticeable decrease for Colombia, especially after 2003. The patterns of convergence to the domestic frontier are less clear. Overall, in Mexico the convergence process seems to have been negatively affected by the Great Recession, as shown by the sudden increase in distance from the frontier during the crisis years. However, distances clearly differ across industries in both countries, ranging for Mexico from 2 to 5 for the local frontier, and from 5 to 20 for the global one; in Colombia, the average distance of the median plant from the global frontier can be more sizeable, reaching 60 in chemicals or communications equipment.

Similarly, patterns of convergence through time differ between sectors. In some sectors, there is clear evidence of divergence relative to the local and global frontiers (for example, motor vehicles in Mexico and communications equipment in Colombia). In other sectors, there is evidence of convergence with respect to both (for example, nonmetallic minerals in Mexico and fabricated metals in Colombia). In still other sectors, there is evidence of convergence toward only one of the two frontiers (for example, chemicals in Mexico and medical equipment in Colombia).

Figure 5.8 plots the distance (with respect to the local frontier only) for U.S. establishments. In the aggregate, the distance from the frontier was lower in 2011 than in 1995, but the downward trend seems to have reversed since 2004. However, the distance has been increasing throughout the sample for four of five of the largest sectors in the economy, and mostly decreasing for as many among the smallest sectors.

Figure 5.8 Distance between Frontier and Plants, by Sector: United States

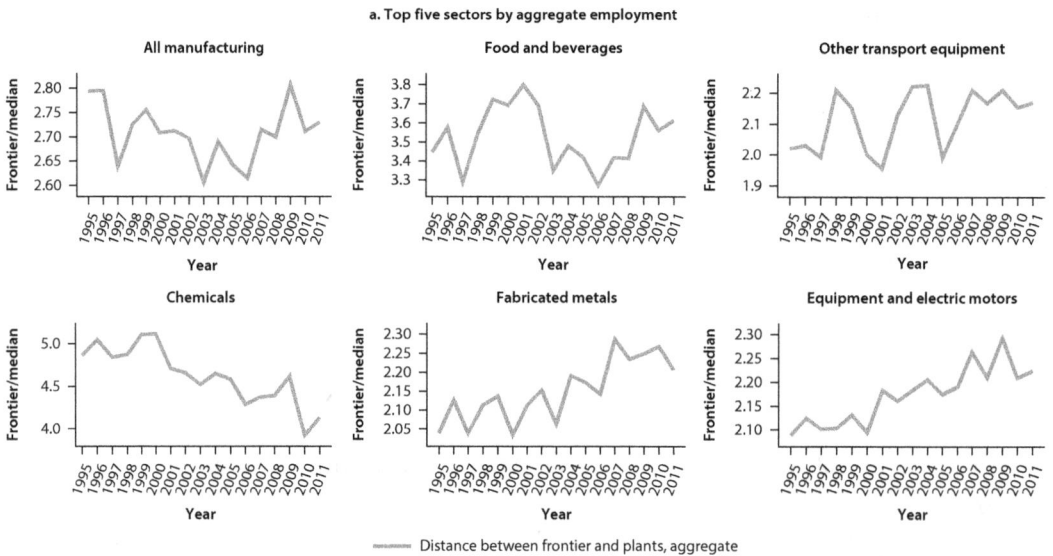

a. Top five sectors by aggregate employment

———— Distance between frontier and plants, aggregate

figure continues next page

Figure 5.8 Distance between Frontier and Plants, by Sector: United States *(continued)*

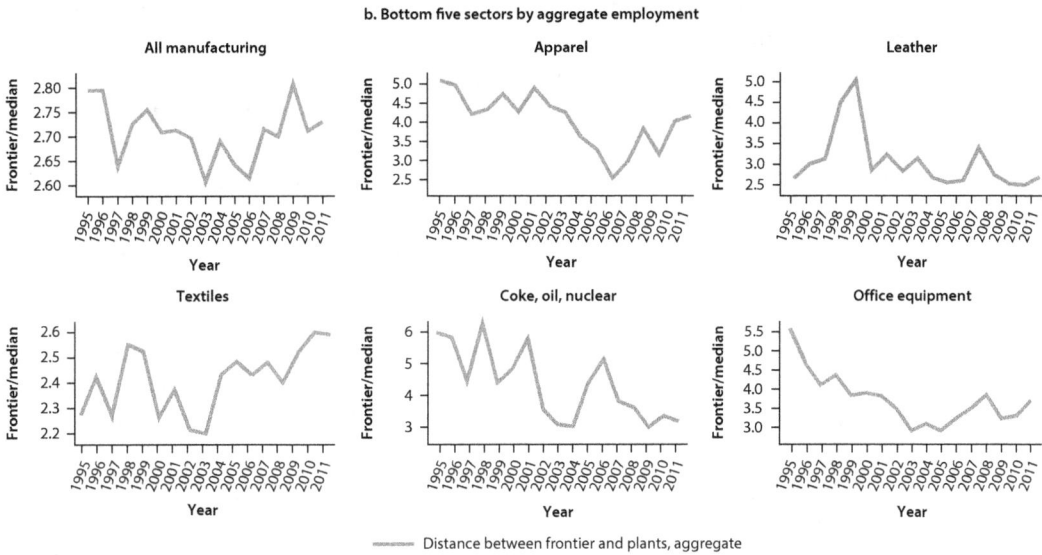

b. Bottom five sectors by aggregate employment

Source: World Bank calculations.

Productivity Decomposition

In this section, we explore another aspect of industry heterogeneity, that is, the extent to which the allocation of market shares toward more productive plants can explain the pattern of aggregate productivity. We can redefine the aggregate labor productivity of industry j at time t, Ω_{jt}, as the weighted average of firm-level labor productivity, where the weights are calculated as the share of firm employment in total industry employment.[25] Aggregate industry productivity can then be decomposed into unweighted mean productivity, $\bar{\omega}_{jt} = \frac{1}{n_{jt}}\sum \omega_{ijt}$, and a term capturing the covariance between firm productivity and firm size $\sum(S_{ijt} - \bar{S}_{jt})(\omega_{ijt} - \bar{\omega}_{jt})$. With $S_{ijt} \geq 0$ representing the weight (that is, the importance) of firm i in industry j, and $\bar{S}_{jt} = \frac{1}{n_{jt}}$, one can write:

$$\Omega_{jt} = \bar{\omega}_{jt} + \sum\left(S_{ijt} - \bar{S}_{jt}\right)\left(\omega_{ijt} - \bar{\omega}_{jt}\right) \tag{5.1}$$

This productivity decomposition was first proposed by Olley and Pakes (1996)[26] and has the advantage of being easily interpretable. Aggregate productivity will grow because average productivity grows ("within-firm component") or because market reallocation increases the size (weight) of more productive plants. The higher the covariance between productivity and size is, the higher is market efficiency, because a larger share of employment in industry is attributed to the most productive plants. Given a fixed number of plants with heterogeneous productivity, shifting employment away from low-productivity to high-productivity plants increases aggregate productivity and the covariance between firm efficiency and size.

Figure 5.9 plots the trend in aggregate productivity (value added per employee) for the Mexican, Colombian, and U.S. manufacturing sector (left vertical axis) as well as the relative size of the covariance term as a percentage of aggregate productivity (right vertical axis).[27] With the exception of the dip caused by the Great Recession, the Mexican manufacturing sector experienced (on aggregate) substantial growth in labor productivity in the period considered (from US$55,000 per employee in 2003 to US$88,000 in 2011, approximately). The same can be said for the United States, which displays almost double the value added per employee as Mexico, and which suffered a smaller decrease in labor productivity during the crisis years. Colombian aggregate productivity also increased, from US$35,000 to US$50,000 per employee between 2000 and 2011.

In Mexico, this growth in labor productivity was associated with an increase in the covariance term between employment and productivity, thus signaling a general improvement in the allocation of employment shares across plants in the manufacturing sector. The same cannot be said for Colombia, where the past few years have seen a deterioration of the allocative efficiency of

Figure 5.9 Firm-Level Static Decomposition (Manufacturing)

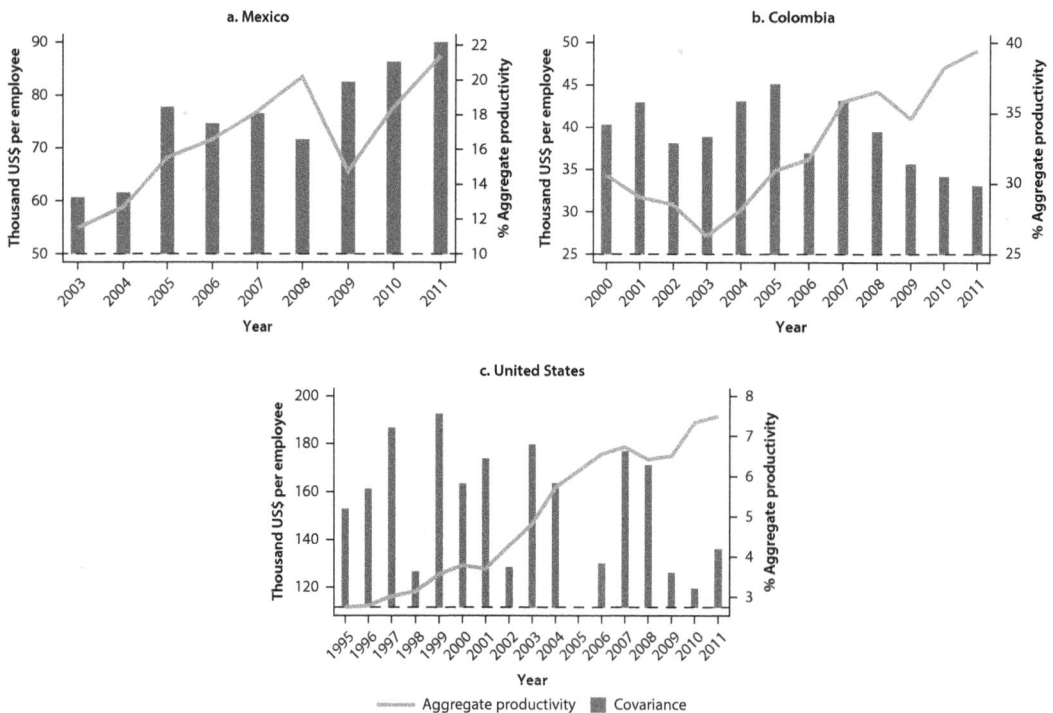

Source: World Bank calculations.

Figure 5.10 Industry-Level Static Decomposition (Manufacturing)

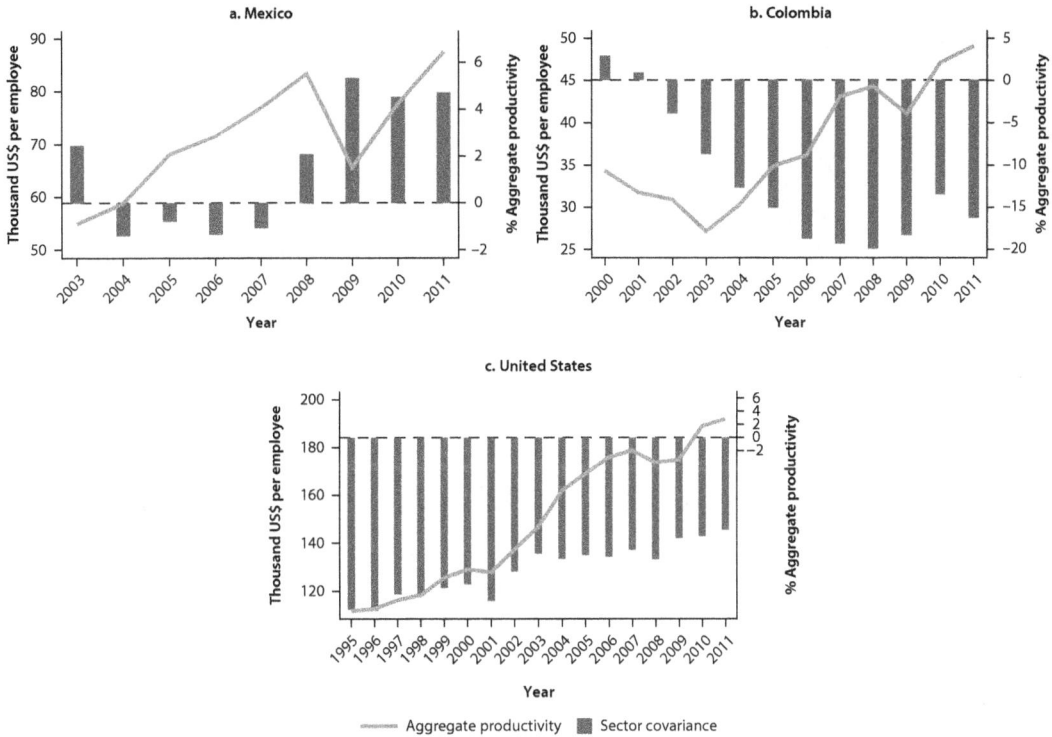

Source: World Bank calculations.

the markets. No clear pattern is identifiable for the United States. The covariance term is generally relatively small in Mexico (at most 22 percent in the aggregate) and even smaller in the United States (at most 8 percent of aggregate productivity), so that productivity growth in the country seems to be driven mainly by improvements in the within-firm component. The covariance term in Colombia always represents at least 30 percent of aggregate productivity throughout the sample.

Very similar conclusions can be drawn from the analysis of the economy-wide decomposition, which we report in figure 5.10 and which takes the industry level as the point of observation. In these graphs, we explore whether aggregate productivity (the same as in the previous decomposition graphs) is mostly determined by the (unweighted) average productivity growth of sectors, or by an improvement in the allocation of employment across sectors.[28] We find that the contribution of cross-sector reallocation to aggregate productivity in Mexico is even lower than in the within-industry case reported in figure 5.9, reaching at most 5 percent of aggregate productivity in Mexico. For Colombia and the United States, this covariance is negative in most years, suggesting that employment moved from more productive manufacturing sectors to less productive ones.[29]

Figure 5.11 Firm-Level Static Decomposition for Selected Sectors: Mexico

Decreasing covariance

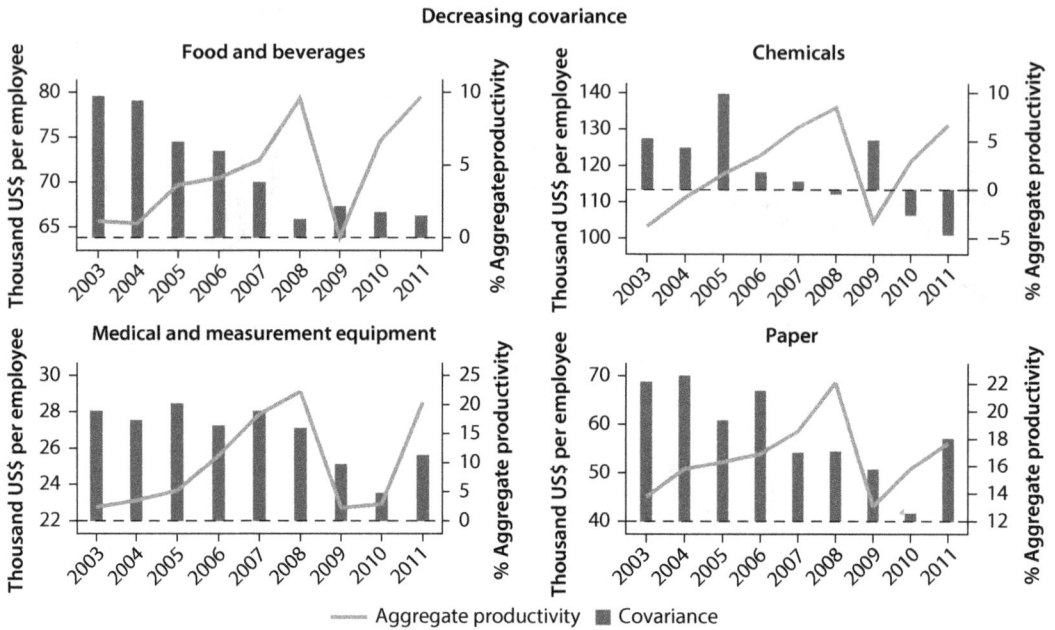

Aggregate productivity ▬▬▬   Covariance ■

Source: World Bank calculations.

However, figure 5.9 hides significant heterogeneity across sectors, in aggregate industry productivity and the extent of within-sector misallocation. Figures 5.11 to 5.13 focus on the within-sector reallocation process. Graphs are provided for a few sectors by way of example, while grouping them with respect to the trend in their covariance term. Aggregate industry productivity is upward sloping in almost all sectors, but it obviously differs in levels.[30] Despite an overall positive trend, covariances can still significantly decrease in selected sectors, or even turn negative (for example, in apparel and chemicals in Mexico, apparel and leather in Colombia, and food and rubber in the United States).

With the exception of very few sectors (such as motor vehicles), the covariance term remains relatively small with respect to within-firm productivity in all Mexican sectors. In Colombia, almost all sectors experienced a decrease in the covariance term except for the production of coke and oil, and transportation equipment (hence the omission of the graph with increasing covariance sectors). In the United States, only one sector (other transportation equipment) shows a clear upward trend in the covariance term (figure not reported).

We look for confirmation of this descriptive evidence by adopting an alternative decomposition for productivity growth rather than for productivity levels, as this allows us to take into account the role of entry and exit. Equation 5.1 keeps the number of firms or establishments constant and analyzes productivity in levels.

Figure 5.12 Firm-Level Static Decomposition for Selected Sectors: Colombia

Decreasing covariance

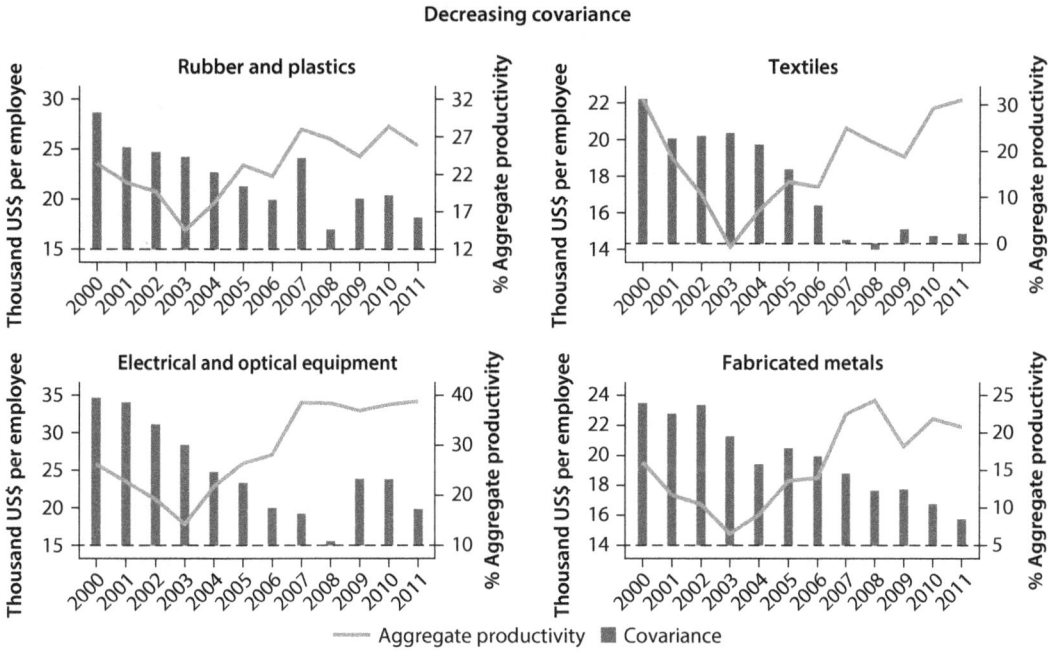

—— Aggregate productivity ■ Covariance

Source: World Bank calculations.

Figure 5.13 Firm-Level Static Decomposition for Selected Sectors: United States

Decreasing covariance

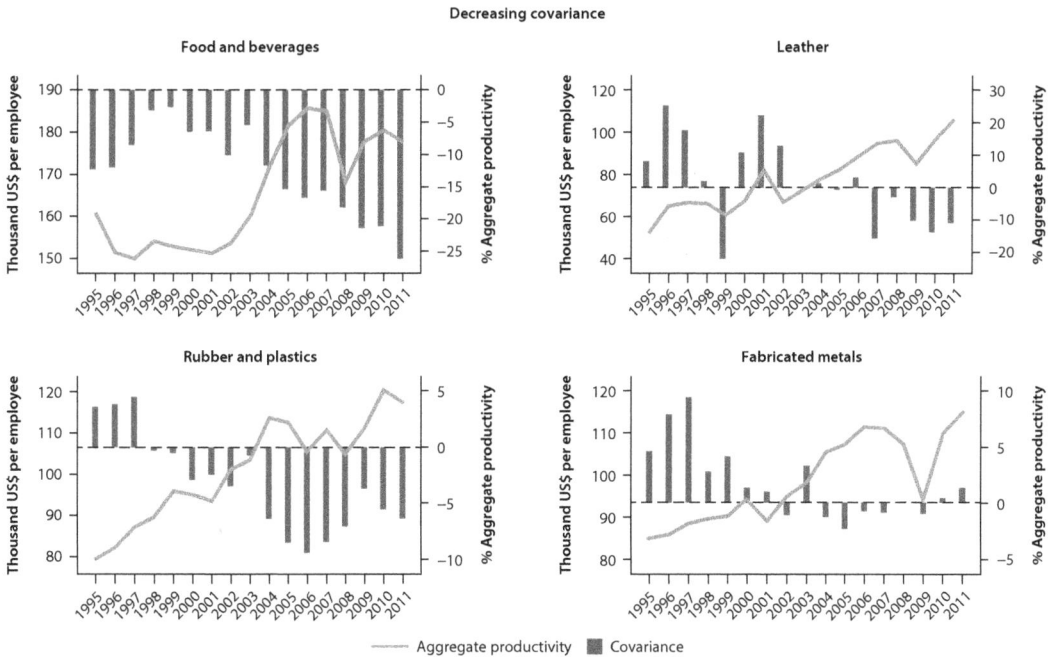

—— Aggregate productivity ■ Covariance

Source: World Bank calculations.

Understanding the Income and Efficiency Gap in Latin America and the Caribbean
http://dx.doi.org/10.1596/978-1-4648-0450-2

When not controlling for entry and exit, however, it would be possible to observe changes in the covariance term that do not appropriately reflect changes in the allocative efficiency of the economy. Consider, for instance, the exit of a low-productivity firm, whose employees are hired by a high-productivity firm: aggregate productivity would increase, while the covariance term would decrease.

In the dynamic form of decomposition, by contrast, changes in aggregate productivity can be decomposed into a term capturing the performance of incumbent plants, that of plants entering and exiting the market, and the consequent changes in market shares of each firm in the sector. Accordingly, aggregate productivity shifts can be broken down into four components: (i) changes in the average productivity of the incumbents that stay in the market in all years (or "survivors"); (ii) changes in market shares among these survivors; (iii) the contribution of entrants in the second period; and (iv) the contribution of exiting plants. We follow Melitz and Polanec (2012) and extend the Olley and Pakes (1996) decomposition, so that:

$$\Delta\Omega_{jt} = \Delta\bar{\omega}_{pjt} + \Delta Cov_{pt} + \left(\sum_{i\in E} S_{ijt}\right)\left(\Omega_{Ejt} - \Omega_{Pjt}\right) + \left(\sum_{i\in X} S_{ijt-1}\right)\left(\Omega_{Pjt-1} - \Omega_{Xjt-1}\right) \quad (5.2)$$

where subscript p refers to survivors, e to entrants in t, and x to exiters in $t-1$. The first and second terms on the right-hand side measure the contribution of survivors to aggregate (sectoral) productivity, which is decomposed according to Olley and Pakes (1996) into a change in average productivity of the survivors between t and $t-1$, and a term for the change in covariance between market share and productivity for the same category of plants and timeline. The contribution of entrants (respectively, exiters) is a function of the share of the firm's output in total entrants' (respectively, exiters') output in the industry, $\sum_{i\in E} S_{ijt}$ and $\sum_{i\in X} S_{ijt-1}$, and the difference between aggregate productivity of entrants and that of survivors $\left(\Omega_{Ejt} - \Omega_{Pjt}\right)$, and the difference between the aggregate productivity of survivors and exiters $\left(\Omega_{Pjt-1} - \Omega_{Xjt-1}\right)$.[31]

Figure 5.14 reports the dynamic decomposition of the overall manufacturing sector in Mexico, Colombia, and the United States, by year. Each component of the decomposition is made scale-independent and expressed in aggregate productivity growth, following the appendix in Melitz and Polanec (2012). Once again, we find that the within-firm productivity component (the change in productivity of the incumbents or survivors) is more important than all other components. For Mexico and the United States, it is also positive in all years except the crisis years. For Colombia, by contrast, the pattern is much less clear.

The contribution of the survivors' covariance term is relatively small and can change in sign in both Latin American countries, but it is consistently positive (albeit small) in the United States. The positive sign in the crisis year, especially in Mexico, hints at a pro-competitive effect of the crisis on incumbents. While we refrain from interpreting the results for entrants in light of the data limitation, we note that the contribution of exiters to aggregate productivity growth is usually small and volatile for Mexico and Colombia, with the exception, once again,

Figure 5.14 Dynamic Decomposition (Manufacturing)

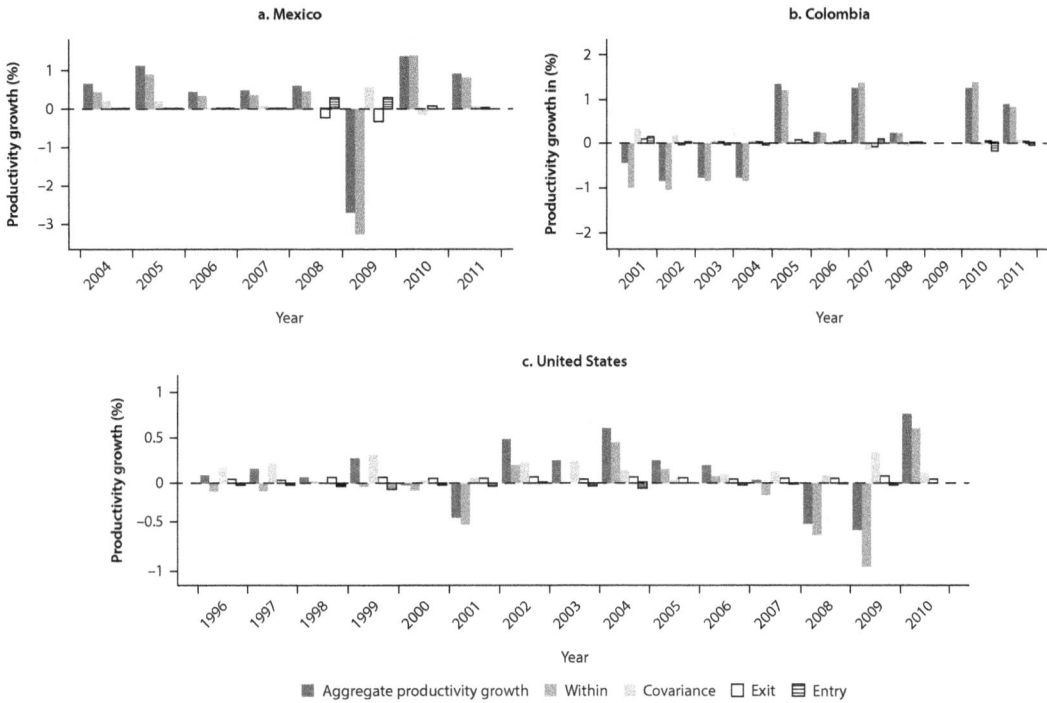

a. Mexico

b. Colombia

c. United States

■ Aggregate productivity growth   ▨ Within   ▨ Covariance   □ Exit   ▤ Entry

Source: World Bank calculations.

of the crisis years for Mexico, where their component is negative. This suggests that the crisis has negatively affected high-productivity plants as well, so that the aggregate productivity of exiters is higher than that of survivors. Exit in the United States, by contrast, is consistently productivity-enhancing throughout the sample period, while entrants decrease productivity growth as their productivity is lower than that of the average incumbent.

Econometric Estimation

The importance of the within-firm component of aggregate productivity growth motivates the second part of our analysis, where we investigate the process of convergence of firm-level productivity to the technological frontier, where the latter is defined at the national and global levels. With this micro-level approach, we stress the heterogeneity of productivity growth between plants in the same industry. The further away a plant lies with respect to the frontier, the higher its growth potential: plants which are further away from the frontier can grow more because there is greater scope for potential technology transfer. This depends on the firm's capacity to absorb knowledge, however. This situation is consistent with a model where firms make strategic decisions about integrating with the global economy and investing in knowledge acquisition, and where they have varying capacities to absorb knowledge, resulting in different speeds of convergence toward the technological frontier. We define the production function at the firm (plant) level in a standard way, as:

$$Y_{ijt} = A_{ijt} F(L_{ijt}, K_{ijt}) \qquad (5.3)$$

where $F(.)$ is the plant's production function transforming labor and capital inputs (L and K) into output (Y), and A_{ijt} is an index capturing technical efficiency or, equivalently, the plant's stock of knowledge capital.[32] Following Griffith et al. (2004) and Griffith, Redding, and Simpson (2009), we consider a very general specification of knowledge spillover linking the stock of knowledge in (nonfrontier) firm i in sector j at time t with the frontier. This reads

$$A_{ijt} = \phi(A_{jt-1}; A_{jt}^{NF}; A_{jt}^{GF}; Z_{ijt-1}) \qquad (5.4)$$

The plant's productivity this year (A_{ijt}) is a function of the same outcome last year (A_{jt-1}), the domestic technological frontier (A_{jt}^{NF}) and the global one (A_{jt}^{GF}), and a set of plant characteristics the previous year (Z_{ijt-1}), the most important of which is innovation effort. The productivity gap between plant i and the frontier is the measure of potential technological transfer. Assuming a Cobb-Douglas functional form and constant returns to scale for production and knowledge formation, log-linearizing and taking first differences, we can derive our estimation equation:

$$\Delta log(A_{ijt}) = \beta_1 \left(\frac{A_{jt-1}^{NF} - A_{ijt-1}}{A_{jt-1}^{NF}} \right) + \beta_2 \left(\frac{A_{jt-1}^{GF} - A_{ijt-1}}{A_{jt-1}^{GF}} \right) + \beta_3 \Delta \, log \left(\frac{K_{ijt}}{L_{ijt}} \right) + \qquad (5.5)$$

$$+ \lambda_1 \Delta \, log \left(A_{jt}^{NF} \right) + \lambda_2 \Delta \, log \left(A_{jt}^{GF} \right) + \theta_i + \chi_j + \gamma_t + \varepsilon_{ijt}$$

where the outcome variable is proxied by value added per worker in the plant $A_{ijt} = \frac{Y_{ijt}}{L_{ijt}}$, $log \left(\frac{K_{ijt}}{L_{ijt}} \right)$ is the logarithm of the ratio of capital and labor endowments of the plant, and $\frac{A_{jt-1}^{NF} - A_{ijt-1}}{A_{jt-1}^{NF}}$ is the distance between the plant's labor productivity and the sector efficiency frontier.[33] The change in the (domestic or global) frontier, $\Delta \, log \left(A_{jt-1}^{NF} \right)$, is a technological shifter. χ_j is a series of industry dummies capturing time-invariant industry-specific determinants of changes in value added per worker, γ_t for year dummies capturing macroeconomic fluctuations, and θ_i reflects unobserved plant-specific, time-invariant characteristics. The main coefficients of interest are therefore β_1 and β_2, which estimate the response of convergence to the plant's distance from the technological frontier, that is, the speed of plant catch-up to the productivity frontier. We then consider what factors at the plant level may influence the catch-up process. Equation 5.5 can be expanded as:

$$\Delta log(A_{ijt}) = \beta_1 \left(\frac{A_{jt-1}^{NF} - A_{ijt-1}}{A_{jt-1}^{NF}} \right) + \beta_2 \left(\frac{A_{jt-1}^{GF} - A_{ijt-1}}{A_{jt-1}^{GF}} \right) + \beta_3 \left(\frac{A_{jt-1}^{NF} - A_{ijt-1}}{A_{jt-1}^{NF}} \right)(log(Z_{ijt-1})) +$$

$$+ \beta_4 \left(\frac{A_{jt-1}^{GF} - A_{ijt-1}}{A_{jt-1}^{GF}} \right)(log(Z_{ijt-1})) + \beta_5 \, log(Z_{ijt-1}) + [\dots] + \varepsilon_{ijt} \qquad (5.6)$$

Following previous studies (Griffith, Redding, and Simpson 2009; Iacovone and Crespi 2010), we assess whether catch-up changes in magnitude and sign (through β_3 and β_4) when plants invest in innovation, engage in international trade, or invest in human capital or new capital equipment, activities that are captured by Z_{ijt-1}. Technological upgrade (either in the form of innovation or investment in capital equipment) can indeed increase the speed of convergence to the frontier (Griffith et al. 2004). It also seems likely that establishments exposed to international competition and having access to international technology are more likely to converge faster to the frontier than establishments that are not. Finally, plants that employ a more skilled workforce are also likely to manage the process of technological upgrade more successfully. All regressors in our specifications are lagged once in respect of the functional assumptions stated in equation 5.6. This lag also helps in reducing the possibility of endogeneity (reverse causality) between labor productivity and the main regressors of interest.

We estimate equation 5.6 with ordinary least squares (OLS) and fixed effects (FE). The latter specification has the advantage of providing estimates of the main coefficients of interest that are net of plant-specific, time-invariant unobservable characteristics. Furthermore, reporting OLS and FE specifications is especially important in our context, where the existence of a lagged dependent variable on the right-hand side can result in inconsistent estimates for OLS and FE estimators. Indeed, the distance term (which enters alone and in interaction with other plant-level covariates) is a (reverse) function of the plant's productivity in the previous year. For OLS, this form of endogeneity biases the coefficient downward, according to Bond (2002). The FE estimator, by contrast, is upward biased, as the technology gap and the error term are positively correlated. Lacking an appropriate instrumental variable specification to take care of the lagged dependent variable endogeneity, we report OLS and FE estimates, highlighting that the "true" coefficient should lie between the OLS (lower bound) and the FE (upper bound) estimates.

Equations 5.5 and 5.6 are estimated separately for each country covered in this study, as we cannot stack information from the various countries in one single data set.[34]

Estimation Results

Tables 5.5 to 5.7 report the results of estimating equation 5.5 with OLS and FE, respectively, for Mexico, Colombia, and the United States.[35] For the first two specifications (columns 1 to 4) for Mexico and Colombia, we show that including only one distance term (distance from the local or global frontier, respectively) would lead to biased estimates for the convergence parameter. Plants would appear to converge toward the domestic and global frontiers.[36] When both distances are introduced (columns 5 and onward), the coefficient on firm distance from the global frontier becomes insignificant or negative, thus suggesting lack of convergence with respect to the global frontier. By contrast, the

Table 5.5 Baseline Estimation Results: Mexico

Variable	OLS1	FE1	OLS2	FE2	OLS3	FE3	OLS4	FE4	OLS5	FE5	OLS6	FE6
Distance (Local)	0.078***	0.585***			0.102***	0.583***	0.125***	0.695***	0.115***	0.667***	0.125***	0.664***
	(0.008)	(0.043)			(0.008)	(0.039)	(0.008)	(0.037)	(0.008)	(0.036)	(0.008)	(0.036)
Distance (Global)			0.098**	0.833***	−0.058***	0.006	−0.101***	−0.217	−0.098***	−0.219*	−0.105***	−0.218*
			(0.038)	(0.258)	(0.017)	(0.188)	(0.011)	(0.138)	(0.012)	(0.131)	(0.011)	(0.130)
Delta log frontier (Local)							0.535***	0.556***	0.534***	0.552***	0.535***	0.552***
							(0.023)	(0.023)	(0.023)	(0.023)	(0.023)	(0.023)
Delta log frontier (Global)							−0.013	−0.009	−0.017	−0.012	−0.014	−0.013
							(0.021)	(0.022)	(0.021)	(0.022)	(0.021)	(0.022)
Delta log (K/L)									0.166***	0.171***	0.164***	0.169***
									(0.013)	(0.013)	(0.013)	(0.013)
Log size (Medium)											0.053***	0.036***
											(0.005)	(0.014)
Log size (Large)											0.075***	0.050***
											(0.006)	(0.019)
Observations	40,545	40,545	40,545	40,545	40,545	40,545	40,545	40,545	40,216	40,216	40,216	40,216
R-squared	0.154	0.235	0.150	0.200	0.154	0.235	0.196	0.282	0.210	0.296	0.214	0.296
Number of id		6,197		6,197		6,197		6,197		6,157		6,157

Source: World Bank calculations.

Note: The dependent variable is the change in the logarithm of value added per employee. Delta log frontier (Local) = change in value of local frontier (in logs) between t and $t − 1$; Distance (Local) = lagged difference between plant's productivity and (domestic) frontier over value of frontier, as expressed in equation 5.5. All other terms are lagged once. FE = fixed effects; K/L = capital-labor ratio in the plant; Log size (Medium, Large) = dummy with value 1 if firm has between 50 and 200 employees (medium) or more than 200 employees (large) in year $t − 1$; OLS = ordinary least squares. All specifications include time dummies, two-digit industry dummies, and the cross product of the two. The Mexican sample covers 2003–11. Clustered standard errors are in parentheses.

***$p < .01$; **$p < .05$; *$p < .1$.

144

Table 5.6 Baseline Estimation Results: Colombia

Variable	OLS1	FE1	OLS2	FE2	OLS3	FE3	OLS4	FE4	OLS5	FE5	OLS6	FE6
Distance (Local)	0.208***	0.685***			0.208***	0.689***	0.219***	0.731***	0.189***	0.620***	0.199***	0.628***
	(0.009)	(0.035)			(0.016)	(0.059)	(0.016)	(0.059)	(0.014)	(0.036)	(0.014)	(0.036)
Distance (Global)			0.817***	2.446***	-0.004	-0.021	-0.051	-0.197	0.011	0.358	0.003	0.348
			(0.082)	(0.519)	(0.091)	(0.497)	(0.088)	(0.483)	(0.074)	(0.262)	(0.075)	(0.263)
Delta log frontier (Local)							0.145***	0.215***	0.128***	0.181***	0.128***	0.181***
							(0.014)	(0.019)	(0.014)	(0.015)	(0.014)	(0.015)
Delta log frontier (Global)							-0.068***	-0.059**	-0.064***	-0.038**	-0.065***	-0.038**
							(0.017)	(0.023)	(0.017)	(0.019)	(0.017)	(0.019)
Delta log (K/L)									0.286***	0.259***	0.282***	0.259***
									(0.008)	(0.008)	(0.008)	(0.008)
Log size (Medium)											0.028***	-0.023**
											(0.004)	(0.011)
Log size (Large)											0.064***	-0.035*
											(0.006)	(0.021)
Log age											0.003	-0.012
											(0.003)	(0.018)
Observations	68,533	68,533	68,533	68,533	68,533	68,533	68,533	68,533	66,119	66,119	65,996	65,996
R-squared	0.105	0.192	0.093	0.143	0.105	0.192	0.107	0.197	0.155	0.241	0.157	0.242
Number of id		11,924		11,924		11,924		11,924		11,681		11,667

Source: World Bank calculations.

Note: The dependent variable is the change in the logarithm of value added per employee. Delta log frontier (Local) = change in value of local frontier (in logs) between t and $t - 1$; Distance (Local) = lagged difference between plant's productivity and (domestic) frontier over value of frontier, as expressed in equation 5.5. All other terms are lagged once. FE = fixed effects; K/L = capital-labor ratio in the plant; Log age = logarithm of plant's age increased by one (so that entrants would not be dropped from the sample); Log size (Medium, Large) = dummy with value 1 if firm has between 50 and 200 employees (medium) or more than 200 employees (large) in year $t - 1$; OLS = ordinary least squares. All specifications include time dummies, two-digit industry dummies, and the cross product of the two. Data availability for Colombia also permits controlling for age and regional dummies. The Colombian sample covers 2000–11. Clustered standard errors are in parentheses.

***$p < .01$; **$p < .05$; *$p < .1$.

Table 5.7　Baseline Estimation Results: United States

Variable	OLS1	FE1	OLS2	FE2	OLS3	FE3	OLS4	FE4
Distance (Local)	0.275***	0.744***	0.278***	0.751***	0.250***	0.711***	0.251***	0.712***
	(0.003)	(0.007)	(0.003)	(0.007)	(0.003)	(0.006)	(0.003)	(0.006)
Delta log frontier (Local)			0.222***	0.266***	0.199***	0.254***	0.198***	0.254***
			(0.007)	(0.008)	(0.008)	(0.009)	(0.008)	(0.009)
Delta log (K/L)					0.273***	0.256***	0.269***	0.257***
					(0.004)	(0.004)	(0.004)	(0.005)
Log size (Medium)							0.027***	0.005
							(0.002)	(0.005)
Log size (Large)							0.032***	−0.011
							(0.002)	(0.007)
Log age							0.009***	0.000
							(0.001)	(0.005)
Observations	~650,000	~650,000	~650,000	~650,000	~490,000	~490,000	~490,000	~490,000
R-squared	0.064	0.159	0.067	0.162	0.114	0.202	0.115	0.202
Number of id		~140,000		~140,000		~110,000		~110,000

Source: World Bank calculations.
Note: The dependent variable is the change in the logarithm of value added per employee. Delta log frontier (Local) = change in value of local frontier (in logs) between t and $t-1$; Distance (Local) = lagged difference between plant's productivity and (domestic) frontier over value of frontier, as expressed in equation 5.5. No global frontier is available for the United States (by definition). All other terms are lagged once. FE = fixed effects; K/L = capital-labor ratio in the plant, Log age = logarithm of plant's age increased by one (so that entrants would not be dropped from the sample); Log size (Medium, Large) = dummy with value 1 if firm has between 50 and 200 employees (medium) or more than 200 employees (large) in year $t-1$; OLS = ordinary least squares. All specifications include time dummies, two-digit industry dummies, and the cross product of the two. Data availability for the United States also permits controlling for age and regional (state-level) dummies. The U.S. sample covers 1995–2011. The number of observations is not precisely reported to respect disclosure constraints. Clustered standard errors are in parentheses.
***p < .01; **p < .05; *p < .1.

coefficient of the domestic distance is always positive and significant, even in more complex specifications where we include our most important controls (lagged firm size and capital-labor ratio). Mexican and Colombian plants appear to converge toward the domestic most productive plants, but not toward the absolute (international) best practices. Catch-up with the (local and only) frontier is found for U.S. plants as well.[37]

Columns 6 to 12 in tables 5.5 and 5.6, as well as columns 3 to 8 in table 5.7, are estimated including the change in industry (local or global) frontier between t and $t-1$, as in equations 5.5 and 5.6. The estimates of these technological shifters should be interpreted as the spillovers from the frontier itself and the plant's productivity: the general level of productivity in the domestic or international market can only influence the productivity of the firm if there are technological spillovers. From tables 5.5 to 5.7, it is evident that spillovers from the domestic frontier are positive and strong, unlike spillovers from the global frontier. For Colombia, a faster change in the global frontier has a negative impact on productivity growth at the plant level.

In another specification, we introduce an interaction term between the distance from the frontier and the spillover term. The results confirm the absence of any significant effect as far as spillovers from the global frontier are concerned, but not from the domestic frontier: when further away from the domestic frontier, the spillover effect on productivity growth is significantly lower.[38] This result is consistent with the concept of absorptive capabilities and the idea that establishments that are further away from the technology frontier may be unable to benefit from spillovers.[39] We conclude the analysis of tables 5.5 to 5.7 by highlighting that more capital-intensive plants seem to enjoy higher productivity growth in all countries, while there is a positive premium for size (relative to small plants) in Mexico only.

A key objective of our analysis is to identify whether certain firm characteristics alter the speed of convergence. In particular, we focus on the degree to which plants invest in knowledge and technological upgrade, and the extent to which these are integrated with the global economy. We do so by including an interaction term between the plant's distance from the frontier and these covariates of interest, as in equation 5.6.

Tables 5.8 to 5.10 highlight that innovation effort and investment in new equipment influence plants' productivity convergence. In fact, plants' productivity convergence in Mexico is increased by greater investments in machinery (specifications 1 and 3) and in expenses to purchase external knowledge (specification 3). However, convergence toward the global frontier is not influenced by investment in innovation. For Colombia, the speed of convergence to the domestic frontier is positively affected by innovation only (specifications 2 to 5), and not by purchases of capital equipment (specifications 1, 4, and 5). Internal innovation efforts are more effective in increasing the speed of productivity convergence toward the domestic frontier than the purchase of external innovation (specifications 4 and 5). For the United States, on the one hand, we find a positive (but not very robust) role of investment in stimulating productivity catch-up. On the other hand, innovation reduces the speed of convergence for establishments that are far from the frontier. When establishments display frontier productivity (distance is zero), internal innovation positively contributes to productivity growth.[40]

Table 5.11 reports only the estimates for the interaction terms, across multiple specifications, when only one interaction variable is introduced in each specification.[41] In Mexico and Colombia, paying workers more (on average) while holding all other plant features constant (and in particular capital intensity and distance from the frontier) significantly decreases the speed of catch-up toward the local frontier. In Colombia, the same applies for convergence to the global frontier. The differences in cost of skilled versus unskilled employees impact productivity growth positively in the United States and negatively in Colombia.[42] These signs are confirmed when only interactions with the local frontier are included (see annex table 5B.2). In a context where the supply of skills is especially limited, such as in Colombia, this ratio captures this scarcity and the fact that firms have to pay a high premium to hire skilled workers, which increases firms' costs. In the United States, where the skill supply constraints are much less binding, this ratio is likely to capture the decision of establishments to invest in a more skilled workforce.[43]

Trade does not influence the speed of convergence toward the global frontier in Colombia or Mexico. However, trade decreases the speed of convergence to the local frontier in Colombia, while it increases this convergence in the

Table 5.8 Estimation Results for Innovation and Technology Interactions: Mexico

	OLS1	FE1	OLS2	FE2	OLS3	FE3
Distance (Local)	0.181***	0.845***	0.171***	0.873***	0.237***	1.029***
	(0.017)	(0.048)	(0.023)	(0.059)	(0.030)	(0.072)
Distance (Global)	−0.166***	−0.483***	−0.174***	−0.293	−0.292***	−0.542**
	(0.022)	(0.145)	(0.053)	(0.193)	(0.069)	(0.214)
Delta log frontier (Local)	0.538***	0.562***	0.535***	0.551***	0.537***	0.560***
	(0.024)	(0.024)	(0.023)	(0.023)	(0.024)	(0.024)
Delta log frontier (Global)	−0.011	−0.014	−0.014	−0.009	−0.011	−0.010
	(0.022)	(0.022)	(0.021)	(0.021)	(0.022)	(0.022)
Delta log (K/L)	0.168***	0.182***	0.164***	0.168***	0.168***	0.182***
	(0.014)	(0.013)	(0.013)	(0.013)	(0.014)	(0.013)
Log (Investment/Sales)	0.011***	0.024*			0.012***	0.020*
	(0.003)	(0.013)			(0.003)	(0.012)
Distance (Local)*Log (Investment/Sales)	0.011***	0.028***			0.011***	0.026***
	(0.003)	(0.006)			(0.003)	(0.006)
Distance (Global)*Log (Investment/Sales)	−0.012***	−0.035**			−0.014***	−0.030*
	(0.004)	(0.018)			(0.004)	(0.016)
Log (Ext Inno/Sales)			0.006*	0.012	0.010**	0.015*
			(0.004)	(0.008)	(0.004)	(0.008)
Distance (Local)*Log (Ext Inno/Sales)			0.006**	0.028***	0.007***	0.027***
			(0.002)	(0.006)	(0.003)	(0.006)
Distance (Global)*Log (Ext Inno/Sales)			−0.008	−0.012	−0.013**	−0.014
			(0.005)	(0.012)	(0.006)	(0.012)
Log size (Medium)	0.054***	0.037***	0.056***	0.042***	0.057***	0.043***
	(0.005)	(0.014)	(0.005)	(0.014)	(0.005)	(0.014)
Log size (Large)	0.077***	0.037**	0.080***	0.063***	0.080***	0.050***
	(0.006)	(0.019)	(0.006)	(0.019)	(0.006)	(0.019)
Observations	36,847	36,847	40,214	40,214	36,846	36,846
R-squared	0.218	0.303	0.214	0.300	0.218	0.307
Number of id		6,138		6,157		6,138

Source: World Bank calculations.
Note: The dependent variable is the change in the logarithm of value added per employee. Delta log frontier (Local) = change in value of local frontier (in logs) between t and $t − 1$; Distance (Local) = lagged difference between plant's productivity and (domestic) frontier over value of frontier, as expressed in equation 5.5. All other terms are lagged once. Ext Inno = expenditure on external innovation (patents) over revenue from sales; FE = fixed effects; Investment = net investment in machinery over sales; K/L = capital-labor ratio in the plant; Log size (Medium, Large) = dummy with value 1 if firm has between 50 and 200 employees (medium) or more than 200 employees (large) in year $t − 1$; OLS = ordinary least squares. All specifications include time dummies, two-digit industry dummies, and the cross product of the two. Clustered standard errors are in parentheses.
*** $p < .01$; ** $p < .05$; * $p < .1$.

United States (even if the two estimated models are different).[44] These results are robust to alternative measures of integration and separating imports from exports. This difference in the results could be explained by the different patterns of trade between the United States on the one side, and Colombia and Mexico on the other, in terms of technological content, product diversification, and destinations or origin of trade.[45] The lack of a general productivity-enhancing effect of trade at the firm level is at odds with some of the results in the literature

Table 5.9 Estimation Results for Innovation and Technology Interactions: Colombia

	OLS1	FE1	OLS2	FE2	OLS3	FE3	OLS4	FE4	OLS5	FE5
Distance (Local)	0.204***	0.706***	0.440***	0.985***	0.481***	1.102***	0.509***	1.137***	0.490***	1.178***
	(0.032)	(0.052)	(0.054)	(0.088)	(0.055)	(0.100)	(0.058)	(0.106)	(0.065)	(0.116)
Distance (Global)	0.037	0.101	-0.019	1.098**	-0.034	0.480	-0.038	0.858	-0.052	0.710
	(0.127)	(0.419)	(0.225)	(0.497)	(0.234)	(0.489)	(0.257)	(0.604)	(0.287)	(0.716)
Delta log frontier (Local)	0.128***	0.182***	0.114***	0.168***	0.115***	0.171***	0.115***	0.168***	0.115***	0.168***
	(0.014)	(0.015)	(0.016)	(0.017)	(0.016)	(0.017)	(0.016)	(0.017)	(0.016)	(0.017)
Delta log frontier (Global)	-0.063***	-0.039**	-0.062***	-0.039*	-0.062***	-0.042*	-0.062***	-0.040*	-0.062***	-0.039*
	(0.017)	(0.019)	(0.020)	(0.022)	(0.020)	(0.022)	(0.020)	(0.022)	(0.020)	(0.022)
Delta log (K/L)	0.283***	0.263***	0.278***	0.247***	0.277***	0.248***	0.277***	0.247***	0.278***	0.251***
	(0.007)	(0.008)	(0.008)	(0.008)	(0.008)	(0.008)	(0.008)	(0.008)	(0.008)	(0.008)
Log (Investment/Sales)	0.002	0.044							0.008	0.028
	(0.020)	(0.040)							(0.023)	(0.033)
Distance (Local)*Log (Investment/Sales)	0.001	0.014*							-0.004	0.010
	(0.006)	(0.007)							(0.007)	(0.009)
Distance (Global)*Log (Investment/Sales)	0.007	-0.042							0.002	-0.025
	(0.024)	(0.046)							(0.028)	(0.039)
Log (Ext Inno/Sales)			0.002	-0.022			0.007	-0.046	0.004	-0.051*
			(0.019)	(0.038)			(0.023)	(0.031)	(0.023)	(0.031)
Distance (Local)*Log (Ext Inno/Sales)			0.033***	0.048***			0.017**	0.026***	0.017**	0.025***
			(0.006)	(0.009)			(0.008)	(0.010)	(0.008)	(0.010)
Distance (Global)*Log (Ext Inno/Sales)			-0.007	0.032			-0.007	0.059	-0.004	0.064*
			(0.024)	(0.045)			(0.028)	(0.037)	(0.028)	(0.037)

table continues next page

Table 5.9 Estimation Results for Innovation and Technology Interactions: Colombia *(continued)*

	OLS1	FE1	OLS2	FE2	OLS3	FE3	OLS4	FE4	OLS5	FE5
Log (Int Inno/Sales)					-0.003	0.042	-0.009	0.058	-0.005	0.065
					(0.021)	(0.044)	(0.024)	(0.040)	(0.025)	(0.044)
Distance (Local)*Log (Int Inno/Sales)					0.037***	0.062***	0.024***	0.043***	0.025***	0.044***
					(0.006)	(0.011)	(0.008)	(0.011)	(0.008)	(0.012)
Distance (Global)*Log (Int Inno/Sales)					-0.009	-0.041	-0.003	-0.059	-0.008	-0.068
					(0.025)	(0.051)	(0.029)	(0.047)	(0.030)	(0.052)
Log size (Medium)	0.027***	-0.026**	0.049***	-0.000	0.044***	0.001	0.047***	0.004	0.043***	0.000
	(0.004)	(0.011)	(0.005)	(0.013)	(0.005)	(0.013)	(0.005)	(0.013)	(0.005)	(0.013)
Log size (Large)	0.060***	-0.045**	0.083***	0.002	0.074***	0.013	0.079***	0.016	0.069***	0.008
	(0.006)	(0.021)	(0.008)	(0.025)	(0.009)	(0.025)	(0.009)	(0.025)	(0.009)	(0.025)
Log age	0.005*	-0.003	0.006*	-0.025	0.005*	-0.023	0.005*	-0.021	0.006**	-0.013
	(0.003)	(0.018)	(0.003)	(0.026)	(0.003)	(0.026)	(0.003)	(0.026)	(0.003)	(0.026)
Observations	65,684	65,684	46,131	46,131	46,131	46,131	46,131	46,131	46,131	46,131
R-squared	0.158	0.244	0.164	0.281	0.164	0.281	0.165	0.283	0.165	0.284
Number of id		11,637		9,510		9,510		9,510		9,510

Source: World Bank calculations.

Note: The dependent variable is the change in the logarithm of value added per employee. Delta log frontier (Local) = change in value of local frontier (in logs) between *t* and *t* − 1; Distance (Local) = lagged difference between plant's productivity and (domestic) frontier over value of frontier, as expressed in equation 5.5. All other terms are lagged once. Ext Inno = expenditure on external innovation (patents) over revenue from sales; Int Inno = expenditure on research and development over revenues from sales; Investment = net investment in machinery over sales; *K/L* = capital–labor ratio in the plant; Log age = logarithm of plant's age increased by one (so that entrants would not be dropped from the sample); Log size (Medium, Large) = dummy with value 1 if firm has between 50 and 200 employees (medium) or more than 200 employees (large) in year *t* − 1; OLS = ordinary least squares. All specifications include time dummies, two–digit industry dummies, and the cross product of the two. Clustered standard errors are in parentheses.

***p < .01; **p < .05; *p < .1.

Table 5.10 Estimation Results for Innovation and Technology Interactions: United States

	OLS1	FE1	OLS2	FE2	OLS3	FE3	OLS4	FE4	OLS5	FE5
Distance (Local)	0.274***	0.761***	0.189***	0.590***	0.169***	0.566***	0.182***	0.580***	0.191***	0.628***
	(0.007)	(0.011)	(0.009)	(0.016)	(0.007)	(0.012)	(0.009)	(0.016)	(0.014)	(0.019)
Delta log frontier (Local)	0.198***	0.254***	0.239***	0.300***	0.239***	0.301***	0.239***	0.301***	0.238***	0.301***
	(0.008)	(0.009)	(0.013)	(0.015)	(0.013)	(0.015)	(0.013)	(0.015)	(0.013)	(0.015)
Delta log (K/L)	0.270***	0.258***	0.277***	0.273***	0.277***	0.272***	0.277***	0.272***	0.278***	0.274***
	(0.004)	(0.005)	(0.008)	(0.008)	(0.008)	(0.008)	(0.008)	(0.008)	(0.008)	(0.008)
Log (Investment/Sales)	0.002**	-0.001							0.005***	0.001
	(0.001)	(0.001)							(0.001)	(0.001)
Distance (Local)*Log (Investment/Sales)	0.005***	0.010***							0.002	0.010***
	(0.001)	(0.002)							(0.002)	(0.002)
Log (Ext Inno/Sales)			0.001***	0.001			-0.001	-0.000	-0.001	-0.000
			(0.000)	(0.001)			(0.000)	(0.001)	(0.000)	(0.001)
Distance (Local)*Log (Ext Inno/Sales)			-0.001*	-0.001			0.002*	0.002	0.002*	0.002
			(0.001)	(0.001)			(0.001)	(0.001)	(0.001)	(0.001)
Log (Int Inno/Sales)					0.003***	0.002***	0.003***	0.002***	0.003***	0.002***
					(0.000)	(0.001)	(0.000)	(0.001)	(0.000)	(0.001)
Distance (Local)*Log (Int Inno/Sales)					-0.005***	-0.005***	-0.006***	-0.006***	-0.006***	-0.006***
					(0.001)	(0.001)	(0.001)	(0.001)	(0.001)	(0.001)

table continues next page

Table 5.10 Estimation Results for Innovation and Technology Interactions: United States *(continued)*

	OLS1	FE1	OLS2	FE2	OLS3	FE3	OLS4	FE4	OLS5	FE5
Log size (Medium)	0.026***	0.004	0.023***	0.003	0.022***	0.002	0.022***	0.002	0.019***	0.001
	(0.002)	(0.005)	(0.003)	(0.011)	(0.003)	(0.011)	(0.003)	(0.011)	(0.003)	(0.011)
Log size (Large)	0.030***	−0.013*	0.026***	−0.007	0.025***	−0.007	0.025***	−0.007	0.020***	−0.009
	(0.002)	(0.007)	(0.004)	(0.013)	(0.004)	(0.013)	(0.004)	(0.013)	(0.004)	(0.013)
Log age	0.010***	0.002	0.004**	0.000	0.004**	−0.000	0.004**	−0.000	0.004***	0.001
	(0.001)	(0.005)	(0.002)	(0.009)	(0.002)	(0.009)	(0.002)	(0.009)	(0.002)	(0.009)
Observations	~490,000	~490,000	~200,000	~200,000	~200,000	~200,000	~200,000	~200,000	~200,000	~200,000
R-squared	0.116	0.202	0.095	0.170	0.095	0.170	0.095	0.170	0.096	0.171
Number of id		~110,000		~50,000		~50,000		~50,000		~50,000

Source: World Bank calculations.

Note: The dependent variable is the change in the logarithm of value added per employee. Delta log frontier (Local) = change in value of local frontier (in logs) between *t* and *t* − 1; Distance (Local) = lagged difference between plant's productivity and (domestic) frontier over value of frontier, as expressed in equation 5.5. All other terms are lagged once. Ext Inno = expenditure on external innovation (patents) over revenue from sales; Int Inno = expenditure on research and development over revenues from sales; Investment = net investment in machinery over sales; *K/L* = capital-labor ratio in the plant; Log age = logarithm of plant's age increased by one (so that entrants would not be dropped from the sample); Log size (Medium, Large) = dummy with value 1 if firm has between 50 and 200 employees (medium) or more than 200 employees (large) in year *t* − 1; OLS = ordinary least squares. All specifications include time dummies, two-digit industry dummies, and the cross product of the two. Clustered standard errors are in parentheses.

***p < .01; **p < .05; *p < .1.

Table 5.11 Estimation Results: One Interaction per Specification

	Log(Ext Inno/Sales)		Log(Int Inno/Sales)		Log(Investment/Sales)		Log(Trade/Sales)		Log(Avg Wage)		Log(Avg Wage Sk/Unsk)	
	OLS	FE	OLS	FE	OLS	FE	OLS	FE	OLS	FE	OLS	FE
Mexico												
X	0.006*	0.012			0.011***	0.024*	0.002	0.020*	0.008	-0.152**		
	(0.004)	(0.008)			(0.003)	(0.013)	(0.003)	(0.011)	(0.024)	(0.074)		
Distance (Local)*X	0.006**	0.028***	0.037***	0.062***	0.011***	0.028***	-0.001	0.002	-0.082***	-0.253***		
	(0.002)	(0.006)	(0.006)	(0.011)	(0.003)	(0.006)	(0.002)	(0.006)	(0.016)	(0.035)		
Distance (Global)*X	-0.008	-0.012			-0.012***	-0.035**	0.003	-0.015	0.077**	0.346***		
	(0.005)	(0.012)			(0.004)	(0.018)	(0.005)	(0.014)	(0.036)	(0.087)		
Observations	40,214	40,214			36,847	36,847	39,763	39,763	35,687	35,687		
Number of id		6,157				6,138		6,137		5,725		
Colombia												
X	0.002	-0.022	-0.003	0.042	0.002	0.044	-0.010	-0.009	0.341***	0.375**	0.004	0.004
	(0.019)	(0.038)	(0.021)	(0.044)	(0.020)	(0.040)	(0.014)	(0.024)	(0.116)	(0.188)	(0.008)	(0.012)
Distance (Local)*X	0.033***	0.048***	0.037***	0.062***	0.001	0.014*	-0.011***	-0.012**	-0.093***	-0.183***	-0.006***	-0.014***
	(0.006)	(0.009)	(0.006)	(0.011)	(0.006)	(0.007)	(0.004)	(0.005)	(0.021)	(0.037)	(0.002)	(0.003)

table continues next page

Table 5.11 Estimation Results: One Interaction per Specification *(continued)*

	Log(Ext Inno/Sales)		Log(Int Inno/Sales)		Log(Investment/Sales)		Log(Trade/Sales)		Log(Avg Wage)		Log(Avg Wage Sk/Unsk)	
	OLS	FE	OLS	FE	OLS	FE	OLS	FE	OLS	FE	OLS	FE
Distance (Global)*X	−0.007	0.032	−0.009	−0.041	0.007	−0.042	0.019	0.022	−0.306**	−0.401*	0.000	0.002
	(0.024)	(0.045)	(0.025)	(0.051)	(0.024)	(0.046)	(0.016)	(0.028)	(0.132)	(0.216)	(0.009)	(0.014)
Observations	46,131	46,131	46,131	46,131	65,684	65,684	65,684	65,684	65,986	65,986	65,996	65,996
Number of id		9,510		9,510		11,637		11,637		11,667		11,667
U.S.A.												
X	0.001***	0.001	0.003***	0.002***	0.002**	−0.001	0.000	−0.002**	0.045***	−0.014*	0.001*	−0.000
	(0.000)	(0.001)	(0.000)	(0.001)	(0.001)	(0.001)	(0.001)	(0.001)	(0.004)	(0.007)	(0.001)	(0.001)
Distance (Local)*X	−0.001*	−0.001	−0.005***	−0.005***	0.005***	0.010***	0.000	0.005***	−0.076***	−0.263***	0.005***	0.005**
	(0.001)	(0.001)	(0.001)	(0.001)	(0.001)	(0.002)	(0.001)	(0.002)	(0.006)	(0.010)	(0.002)	(0.002)
Observations	~200,000	~200,000	~200,000	~200,000	~490,000	~490,000	~270,000	~270,000	~490,000	~490,000	~490,000	~490,000
Number of id		~50,000		~50,000		~110,000		~60,000		~110,000		~110,000

Source: World Bank calculations.

Note: Avg Wage = average wage in the plant in $t-1$; Avg Wage Sk/Unsk = ratio of cost of employment of all skilled workers in the plant over that of unskilled workers in $t-1$; Distance (Local) = lagged difference between plant's productivity and (domestic) frontier over value of frontier, as expressed in equation 5.5; Ext Inno = expenditure on external innovation (patents) over revenue from sales; FE = fixed effects; Int Inno = expenditure on research and development over revenues from sales; Investment = net investment in machinery over sales; OLS = ordinary least squares; Trade = sum of expenditure on imports and revenue from exports over revenue from sales, in $t-1$. Each column corresponds to a different specification in which the lagged value of the variable at the top of the column (X) is interacted with the firm's distance from the global and local frontiers. The following regressors are also included in each specification: the distance from the global and local frontiers, the one-year change in the global and local frontiers, change in the capital-labor ratio; and dummies for size, industry, time, and industry-time. For Colombia and the United States, regional (state) dummies and a control for the firm's age are also included. For the United States, no global frontier is available (by definition). Clustered standard errors are in parentheses.

***$p < .01$; **$p < .05$; *$p < .1$.

(Bai, Krishna, and Ma 2015; Bastos and Silva 2010; De Loecker 2007; Van Biesebroeck 2005), but is in line with other previous studies, as in Bernard and Jensen (1999), where firms may be selecting themselves into trade because of their pre-existing productivity advantage. Changes in the intensive margin of exports may thus be insufficient to identify an impact of trade on productivity convergence. Future extension of this analysis may explore, for instance, the role of the destination market for exports for productivity convergence.[46] While an extensive literature finds within-firm productivity gains of trade liberalization because of increased competition on the import side (e.g., Pavcnik 2002; Amiti and Konings 2007; Fernandes 2007; Topalova and Khandelwal 2011), these may not arise in countries which lowered trade barriers on manufacturing years before the time span considered in the sample. Furthermore, to our knowledge, the literature is silent on the productivity-enhancing effect of trade on firms at the frontier. If one considers that firms at the frontier connect to the international market not only through trade but also through changes in the boundaries of the firm, frontier firms may not rely on trade to grow in productivity. Last, the absence of a trade effect may relate to the estimators used for distance. Trade may matter for productivity growth in a different way for firms at different distance from the frontier, in the spirit of Acemoglu, Aghion, and Zilibotti (2006). By estimating the average effect of distance only, we may be failing to capture such a heterogenous effect. The exploration of this venue is left to future research.

Tables 5.12 and 5.13 include trade and innovation interaction terms in the same specification (specification 1), and all interactions together (specifications 2 and 3). In this horse race between trade and innovation, we find that trade does not seem to affect the speed of productivity convergence with either the global or domestic frontier in Mexico or Colombia, but it does so in the United States. Further, greater expenditure on innovation (relative to sales) increases the speed of catch-up toward the domestic frontier in both countries, whether measured as purchase of external knowledge (Mexico) or R&D (Colombia).[47] These results confirm that the convergence of plant productivity to the domestic frontier is slowed by higher average wages in all three countries of analysis, and by the higher wage gap between skilled and unskilled workers in Colombia but not in the United States.

As a robustness check, to control for the possibility that our results are driven by reversion to the mean,[48] we reestimate equations 5.5 and 5.6 using four-year changes (see annex 5A for the relevant tables). The sign on the main coefficients of interest remains the same, with the exception of the speed of convergence toward the global frontier, which turns insignificant for Mexico as well.[49] Once again, the only firm-level characteristic that still has a positive impact on plant-level productivity convergence is innovation effort (external innovation for Mexico, internal innovation for Colombia). The negative impact of higher wages is robust to this specification. The results for the United States are somewhat less consistent for the specifications looking at year-on-year changes: investment seems to be the only significant determinant of catch-up in this scenario.

To conclude, we also reestimate equation 5.6, where Z_{jt} is measured at the industry level (rather than the plant level). In particular, we are interested in

Table 5.12 Estimation Results for Multiple Interactions per Specification: Mexico and Colombia

	Mexico 1		Mexico 2		Colombia 1		Colombia 2		Colombia 3	
	OLS	FE	OLS	FE	OLS	FE	OLS	FE	OLS	FE
Log (Trade/Sales)	-0.001	0.018	-0.003	0.009	-0.003	-0.023	0.010	-0.017	0.001	-0.019
	(0.003)	(0.011)	(0.004)	(0.009)	(0.015)	(0.024)	(0.017)	(0.022)	(0.017)	(0.023)
Distance (Local)*Trade	-0.003	-0.001	-0.000	0.002	-0.007**	-0.012**	-0.002	-0.008	-0.005	-0.009
	(0.002)	(0.005)	(0.003)	(0.006)	(0.003)	(0.006)	(0.003)	(0.005)	(0.004)	(0.006)
Distance (Global)*Trade	0.007	-0.010	0.007	-0.002	0.008	0.035	-0.009	0.027	0.003	0.030
	(0.005)	(0.014)	(0.006)	(0.012)	(0.018)	(0.029)	(0.020)	(0.026)	(0.020)	(0.028)
Log (Investment/Sales)	0.014***	0.013	0.010	0.004	0.010	0.028	0.008	0.030	0.009	0.034
	(0.004)	(0.010)	(0.007)	(0.013)	(0.022)	(0.033)	(0.027)	(0.030)	(0.022)	(0.031)
Distance (Local)*Investment	0.012***	0.022***	0.011***	0.021***	-0.003	0.011	0.001	0.013	-0.002	0.014*
	(0.003)	(0.005)	(0.004)	(0.007)	(0.007)	(0.009)	(0.006)	(0.009)	(0.006)	(0.008)
Distance (Global)*Investment	-0.017***	-0.021	-0.011	-0.008	-0.001	-0.025	-0.001	-0.029	-0.001	-0.034
	(0.005)	(0.015)	(0.010)	(0.018)	(0.027)	(0.040)	(0.032)	(0.037)	(0.026)	(0.036)
Log (Ext Inno/Sales)	0.010**	0.013*	0.015***	0.009	0.004	-0.048	0.013	-0.044	-0.002	-0.055*
	(0.004)	(0.008)	(0.005)	(0.009)	(0.023)	(0.031)	(0.022)	(0.030)	(0.023)	(0.030)
Distance (Local)*Ext Inno	0.006**	0.023***	0.008***	0.026***	0.016**	0.026***	0.011	0.016*	0.014*	0.024***
	(0.002)	(0.006)	(0.003)	(0.006)	(0.008)	(0.009)	(0.008)	(0.009)	(0.008)	(0.009)
Distance (Global)*Ext Inno	-0.013**	-0.012	-0.021***	-0.008	-0.004	0.060	-0.013	0.059*	0.004	0.068*
	(0.006)	(0.011)	(0.007)	(0.013)	(0.028)	(0.037)	(0.027)	(0.035)	(0.029)	(0.036)
Log (Int Inno/Sales)					-0.005	0.059	-0.006	0.046	-0.007	0.052
					(0.025)	(0.042)	(0.022)	(0.036)	(0.025)	(0.041)
Distance (Local)*Int Inno					0.024***	0.043***	0.018**	0.031***	0.023***	0.039***
					(0.008)	(0.011)	(0.007)	(0.010)	(0.008)	(0.011)

table continues next page

Table 5.12 Estimation Results for Multiple Interactions per Specification: Mexico and Colombia *(continued)*

	Mexico 1		Mexico 2		Colombia 1		Colombia 2		Colombia 3	
	OLS	FE	OLS	FE	OLS	FE	OLS	FE	OLS	FE
Distance (Global)*Int Inno					-0.008	-0.060	-0.005	-0.043	-0.005	-0.052
					(0.030)	(0.049)	(0.027)	(0.042)	(0.030)	(0.048)
Log (Avg Wage)			0.025	-0.180***			0.305**	0.471**		
			(0.027)	(0.064)			(0.135)	(0.239)		
Distance (Local)*Avg W			-0.072***	-0.234***			-0.082***	-0.144***		
			(0.017)	(0.035)			(0.027)	(0.050)		
Distance (Global)*Avg W			0.044	0.360***			-0.267*	-0.511*		
			(0.039)	(0.079)			(0.156)	(0.277)		
Log (Avg Wage Sk/Unsk)									0.005	0.011
									(0.008)	(0.010)
Distance (Local)*Avg Wage (Sk/Unsk)									-0.005**	-0.013***
									(0.002)	(0.003)
Distance (Global)*Avg Wage (Sk/Unsk)									-0.002	-0.005
									(0.009)	(0.012)
Observations	36,415	36,415	32,308	32,308	46,131	46,131	46,122	46,122	46,131	46,131
Number of id		6,116		5,671		9,510		9,510		9,510

Source: World Bank calculations.

Note: Avg Wage = average wage in the plant in $t - 1$; Avg Wage Sk/Unsk = ratio of the cost of employment of all skilled workers in the plant over that of unskilled workers in $t - 1$; Distance (Local) = lagged difference between the plant's productivity and the (domestic) frontier over the value of the frontier, as expressed in equation 5.5; Ext Inno = expenditure on external innovation (patents) over revenue from sales; FE = fixed effects; Int Inno = expenditure on research and development over revenues from sales; Investment = net investment in machinery over sales; OLS = ordinary least squares; Trade = sum of expenditure on imports and revenue from exports over revenue from sales, in $t - 1$. The following regressors are also included in each specification: the distance from the global and local frontiers, the one-year change in the global and local frontiers, change in the capital-labor ratio; and dummies for size, industry, time, and industry-time. For Colombia, regional (state) dummies and a control for the firm's age are also included. Clustered standard errors are in parentheses.

***$p < .01$; **$p < .05$; *$p < .1$.

157

Table 5.13 Estimation Results for Multiple Interactions per Specification: United States

	USA1		USA2		USA3	
	OLS	FE	OLS	FE	OLS	FE
Log (Trade/Sales)	−0.003***	−0.003**	−0.004***	−0.006***	−0.003***	−0.003**
	(0.001)	(0.001)	(0.001)	(0.001)	(0.001)	(0.001)
Distance (Local)*Trade	0.007***	0.011***	0.009***	0.017***	0.007***	0.011***
	(0.002)	(0.002)	(0.002)	(0.002)	(0.002)	(0.002)
Log (Investment/Sales)	0.005***	0.001	0.004***	0.001	0.005***	0.001
	(0.001)	(0.001)	(0.001)	(0.001)	(0.001)	(0.001)
Distance (Local)*Investment	0.002	0.010***	0.002	0.011***	0.001	0.010***
	(0.002)	(0.003)	(0.002)	(0.003)	(0.002)	(0.003)
Log (Ext Inno/Sales)	0.000	0.001	0.001	0.001	0.000	0.001
	(0.000)	(0.001)	(0.000)	(0.001)	(0.000)	(0.001)
Distance (Local)*Ext Inno	−0.001	−0.001	−0.001	−0.001	−0.001	−0.001
	(0.001)	(0.001)	(0.001)	(0.001)	(0.001)	(0.001)
Log (Int Inno/Sales)	0.003***	0.003***	0.003***	0.003***	0.003***	0.003***
	(0.001)	(0.001)	(0.001)	(0.001)	(0.001)	(0.001)
Distance (Local)*Int Inno	−0.007***	−0.008***	−0.007***	−0.008***	−0.007***	−0.008***
	(0.001)	(0.001)	(0.001)	(0.001)	(0.001)	(0.001)
Log (Avg Wage)			0.026***	−0.009		
			(0.006)	(0.011)		
Distance (Local)*Avg Wage			−0.049***	−0.210***		
			(0.009)	(0.015)		
Log (Avg Wage Sk/Unsk)					0.000	0.002
					(0.001)	(0.002)
Distance (Local)*Avg Wage (Sk/Unsk)					0.007***	0.004
					(0.002)	(0.003)
Observations	~180,000	~180,000	~180,000	~180,000	~180,000	~180,000
Number of id		~40,000		~40,000		~40,000

Source: World Bank calculations.

Note: Avg Wage = average wage in the plant in $t − 1$; Avg Wage Sk/Unsk = ratio of the cost of employment of all skilled workers in the plant over that of unskilled workers in $t − 1$; Distance (Local) = lagged difference between the plant's productivity and the (domestic) frontier over the value of the frontier, as expressed in equation 5.5; Ext Inno = expenditure on external innovation (patents) over revenue from sales; FE = fixed effects; Int Inno = expenditure on research and development over revenues from sales; Investment = net investment in machinery over sales; OLS = ordinary least squares; Trade = sum of expenditure on imports and revenue from exports over revenue from sales, in $t − 1$. The following regressors are also included in each specification: the distance from the global and local frontiers, the one-year change in the global and local frontiers, change in the capital-labor ratio; and dummies for size, industry, time, and industry-time. State dummies and a control for the firm's age are also included. Clustered standard errors are in parentheses.
***$p < .01$; **$p < .05$; *$p < .1$.

assessing whether higher levels of allocative efficiency at the industry level affect plants' speed of convergence toward the technology frontier. We find no evidence in this direction (tables 5.14 to 5.16): the coefficient on the covariance interaction term is never significant for OLS or FE for any of the countries. However, higher levels of productivity dispersion in the industry (as captured by the coefficient of variation) significantly reduce the speed of catching up toward the local frontier in all countries. The catch-up is toward the global frontier in Colombia only (and not in Mexico). At the frontier, higher productivity

Understanding the Income and Efficiency Gap in Latin America and the Caribbean
http://dx.doi.org/10.1596/978-1-4648-0450-2

Table 5.14 Estimation Results for Covariance Interaction: Mexico

	OLS1	FE1	OLS2	FE2
Distance (Local)	0.133***	0.641***	0.146***	0.771***
	(0.011)	(0.030)	(0.016)	(0.044)
Distance (Global)	−0.132***	−0.144*	−0.097***	0.080
	(0.023)	(0.075)	(0.032)	(0.105)
Delta log frontier (Local)	0.539***	0.560***	0.548***	0.581***
	(0.023)	(0.023)	(0.024)	(0.024)
Delta log frontier (Global)	−0.014	−0.012	−0.010	0.008
	(0.021)	(0.021)	(0.021)	(0.021)
Delta log (K/L)	0.164***	0.168***	0.164***	0.168***
	(0.013)	(0.012)	(0.013)	(0.013)
Covariance	−0.000	−0.002**		
	(0.000)	(0.001)		
Distance (Local)*Covariance	−0.000	0.003**		
	(0.000)	(0.001)		
Distance (Global)*Covariance	−0.000	−0.002***		
	(0.000)	(0.001)		
Coeff variation			0.034***	0.212***
			(0.008)	(0.034)
Distance (Local)*Coeff variation			−0.032**	−0.184***
			(0.013)	(0.042)
Distance (Global)*Coeff variation			0.024**	0.039
			(0.011)	(0.024)
High dispersion dummy				
Distance (Local)*High dispersion dummy				
Distance (Global)*High dispersion dummy				
Log size (Medium)	0.052***	0.037***	0.053***	0.036***
	(0.005)	(0.014)	(0.005)	(0.014)
Log size (Large)	0.074***	0.050***	0.077***	0.049***
	(0.006)	(0.019)	(0.006)	(0.019)
Observations	40,216	40,216	40,214	40,214
Number of id		6,157		6,156

Source: World Bank calculations.

Note: Covariance = covariance of productivity and size in percentage terms of aggregate productivity in the sector-year; Coeff variation = coefficient of variation; Delta log frontier (Local) = the change in the value of the local frontier (in logs) between t and $t − 1$; Distance (Local) = lagged difference between the plant's productivity and the (domestic) frontier over the value of the frontier, as expressed in equation 5.5; FE = fixed effects; K/L is the capital-labor ratio in the plant; Log size (Medium, Large) is a dummy with value 1 if the firm has between 50 and 200 employees (medium) or more than 200 employees (large) in year $t − 1$; OLS = ordinary least squares. Clustered standard errors at the establishment level are in parentheses.
***$p < .01$; **$p < .05$; *$p < .1$.

Table 5.15 Estimation Results for Covariance Interaction: Colombia

	OLS1	FE1	OLS2	FE2
Distance (Local)	0.221***	0.633***	0.254***	0.733***
	(0.019)	(0.045)	(0.035)	(0.065)
Distance (Global)	−0.058	0.315	0.453***	1.340***
	(0.088)	(0.280)	(0.169)	(0.333)
Delta log frontier (Local)	0.127***	0.175***	0.119***	0.163***
	(0.014)	(0.015)	(0.014)	(0.015)
Delta log frontier (Global)	−0.067***	−0.039**	−0.058***	−0.026
	(0.017)	(0.019)	(0.017)	(0.018)
Delta log (K/L)	0.282***	0.259***	0.281***	0.258***
	(0.007)	(0.008)	(0.008)	(0.008)
Covariance	−0.001	−0.002		
	(0.002)	(0.005)		
Distance (Local)*Covariance	−0.001*	−0.000		
	(0.001)	(0.001)		
Distance (Global)*Covariance	0.002	0.003		
	(0.002)	(0.006)		
Coeff variation			0.228***	0.496**
			(0.085)	(0.202)
Distance (Local)*Coeff variation			−0.080***	−0.167***
			(0.029)	(0.059)
Distance (Global)*Coeff variation			−0.212**	−0.439*
			(0.107)	(0.246)
High dispersion dummy				
Distance (Local)*High dispersion dummy				
Distance (Global)*High dispersion dummy				
Log size (Medium)	0.027***	−0.023**	0.030***	−0.024**
	(0.004)	(0.011)	(0.004)	(0.011)
Log size (Large)	0.059***	−0.036*	0.067***	−0.034*
	(0.006)	(0.021)	(0.006)	(0.020)
Log age	0.003	−0.013	0.002	−0.010
	(0.003)	(0.018)	(0.003)	(0.018)
Observations	65,996	65,996	65,990	65,990
Number of id		11,667		11,667

Source: World Bank calculations.

Note: Covariance = covariance of productivity and size in percentage terms of aggregate productivity in the sector-year; Coeff variation = coefficient of variation; Delta log frontier (Local) = the change in the value of the local frontier (in logs) between t and $t − 1$; Distance (Local) = lagged difference between the plant's productivity and the (domestic) frontier over the value of the frontier, as expressed in equation 5.5; FE = fixed effects; K/L is the capital-labor ratio in the plant; Log age = logarithm of plant's age increased by one (so that entrants would not be dropped from the sample); Log size (Medium, Large) = dummy with value 1 if the firm has between 50 and 200 employees (medium) or more than 200 employees (large) in year $t − 1$; OLS = ordinary least squares. Clustered standard errors at the establishment level are in parentheses.
***$p < .01$; **$p < .05$; *$p < .1$.

Table 5.16 Estimation Results for Covariance Interaction: United States

	OLS1	FE1	OLS2	FE2
Distance (Local)	0.251***	0.712***	0.326***	0.922***
	(0.003)	(0.006)	(0.008)	(0.017)
Delta log frontier (Local)	0.196***	0.246***	0.194***	0.243***
	(0.008)	(0.009)	(0.008)	(0.009)
Delta log (K/L)	0.269***	0.257***	0.268***	0.255***
	(0.004)	(0.005)	(0.004)	(0.005)
Covariance	0.000**	0.001***		
	(0.000)	(0.000)		
Distance (Local)*Covariance	−0.000	−0.000		
	(0.000)	(0.000)		
Coeff variation			−0.011	0.097***
			(0.008)	(0.018)
Distance (Local)*Coeff variation			−0.083***	−0.241***
			(0.010)	(0.021)
High dispersion dummy				
Distance (Local)*High dispersion dummy				
Log size (Medium)	0.027***	0.005	0.027***	0.003
	(0.002)	(0.005)	(0.002)	(0.005)
Log size (Large)	0.032***	−0.011	0.033***	−0.014**
	(0.002)	(0.007)	(0.002)	(0.007)
Log age	0.009***	0.001	0.009***	0.002
	(0.001)	(0.005)	(0.001)	(0.005)
Observations	~490,000	~490,000	~490,000	~490,000
Number of id		~110,000		~110,000

Source: World Bank calculations.
Note: Covariance = covariance of productivity and size in percentage terms of aggregate productivity in the sector-year; Coeff variation = coefficient of variation; Delta log frontier (Local) = the change in the value of the local frontier (in logs) between t and $t − 1$; Distance (Local) = lagged difference between the plant's productivity and the (domestic) frontier over the value of the frontier, as expressed in equation 5.5; FE = fixed effects; K/L is the capital-labor ratio in the plant; Log age = logarithm of plant's age increased by one (so that entrants would not be dropped from the sample); Log size (Medium, Large) = dummy with value 1 if the firm has between 50 and 200 employees (medium) or more than 200 employees (large) in year $t − 1$; OLS = ordinary least squares. Clustered standard errors at the establishment level are in parentheses.
***$p < .01$; **$p < .05$; *$p < .1$.

dispersion implies higher productivity growth for Colombia and Mexico, but not (unambiguously) for the United States.

Conclusions

Understanding the drivers of productivity growth is a first-order question in Latin America, as growth in the past decade has been driven mostly by favorable external conditions that may not continue forever. Historically, productivity growth in Latin America has been sluggish and the region has not been able to keep the pace of productivity growth of its northern neighbor, the United States.

For the first time, we have performed a comparative analysis of productivity convergence at the firm level for various Latin American countries and the

United States. Our analysis has focused on the decade of the 2000s and has been organized around two main questions.

First, we evaluated the extent to which aggregate productivity growth (in the manufacturing sector) is driven by growth in productivity at the firm level or by reallocation of employment shares across establishments. Our results are very clear and show that if we want to understand productivity growth during the 2000s, we need to focus on firm-level productivity growth, as this has contributed the most to overall productivity growth. Reallocation between plants, within sectors, is a weak force of productivity growth. Further, reallocation between sectors is an even weaker source of growth.

Second, building on the previous result, we zoomed in on the determinants of productivity catch-up at the firm level to evaluate the extent to which establishments converge with the "technology frontier," and even more to analyze the "drivers" of productivity catch-up. Uniquely, for the Latin American countries in this study, we are able to assess not only convergence toward the "domestic frontier," measured as the average productivity of the most productive establishments in the sector (at four-digit ISIC), but also convergence toward the "global frontier," measured by the average productivity of the most productive U.S. establishments in the sector (at four-digit ISIC).

Our results suggest that although establishments converge toward the domestic frontier and there are spillovers arising from the growth of the domestic frontier, unfortunately no convergence happens with respect to the global frontier. Finally, an especially crucial result is that what seems to be increasing the speed of convergence with the domestic frontier is investment to expand the innovation and technological capabilities of firms. No effect comes from integration with trade for Latin American countries, while trade appears beneficial for U.S. companies to accelerate their convergence with the domestic frontier.

From our analysis, the picture that emerges for Mexico and Colombia is that of a situation where there exist very few establishments at the "global frontier" and catch-up is limited to converging toward the local frontier. In a context where the local frontier is not converging with the global frontier, this is an especially worrying situation for manufacturing firms in Latin America.

In conclusion, given the importance of innovation and technological capabilities for productivity catch-up at the firm level, our results point toward an agenda to understand how to develop technological capabilities to speed up the convergence with the frontier in Mexico and Colombia. At the same time, these results raise the question of why reallocation appears to be so limited in explaining overall productivity growth.

Annex 5A Further Estimation Results

Table 5A.1 Four-Year Changes: Mexico

	OLS1	FE1	OLS2	FE2	OLS3	FE3	OLS4	FE4
Distance (Local)	0.408***	1.524***	0.374***	1.454***	0.570***	1.894***	1.460***	3.094***
	(0.027)	(0.100)	(0.036)	(0.113)	(0.089)	(0.181)	(0.252)	(0.492)
Distance (Global)	-0.404***	-0.535	-0.337***	-0.339	-0.496**	0.052	-0.999	-0.917
	(0.068)	(0.414)	(0.074)	(0.472)	(0.246)	(0.545)	(0.947)	(2.674)
Delta log frontier (Local)	0.560***	0.532***	0.553***	0.526***	0.564***	0.510***	0.534***	0.486***
	(0.028)	(0.033)	(0.028)	(0.033)	(0.029)	(0.032)	(0.029)	(0.032)
Delta log frontier (Global)	-0.082*	-0.180***	-0.090**	-0.163***	-0.059	-0.156***	-0.079*	-0.114**
	(0.043)	(0.050)	(0.044)	(0.050)	(0.045)	(0.048)	(0.046)	(0.046)
Delta log (K/L)	0.135***	0.134***	0.136***	0.145***	0.130***	0.140***	0.140***	0.133***
	(0.014)	(0.018)	(0.015)	(0.018)	(0.015)	(0.020)	(0.015)	(0.020)
Log (Trade/Sales)			-0.001	-0.016				
			(0.012)	(0.024)				
Distance (Local)*Log (Trade/Sales)			-0.010	-0.008				
			(0.007)	(0.015)				
Distance (Global)*Log (Trade/Sales)			0.021	0.040				
			(0.017)	(0.029)				
Log (Investment/Sales)					-0.007	-0.077***		
					(0.013)	(0.029)		
Distance (Local)*Log (Investment/Sales)					0.001	-0.005		
					(0.008)	(0.013)		
Distance (Global)*Log (Investment/Sales)					0.018	0.107***		
					(0.019)	(0.041)		
Log (Ext Inno/Sales)					0.019	0.035		
					(0.014)	(0.030)		

table continues next page

163

Table 5A.1 Four-Year Changes: Mexico (*continued*)

	OLS1	FE1	OLS2	FE2	OLS3	FE3	OLS4	FE4
Distance (Local)*Log (Ext Inno/Sales)					0.020**	0.060***		
					(0.008)	(0.018)		
Distance (Global)*Log (Ext Inno/Sales)					−0.023	−0.026		
					(0.021)	(0.039)		
Log (Avg Wage)							0.053	−0.045
							(0.131)	(0.408)
Distance (Local)*Log (Avg Wage)							−0.215***	−0.368***
							(0.049)	(0.098)
Distance (Global)*Log (Avg Wage)							0.131	0.217
							(0.173)	(0.501)
Log size (Medium)	0.080***	0.061**	0.071***	0.064**	0.090***	0.071**	0.079***	0.054*
	(0.015)	(0.030)	(0.015)	(0.031)	(0.016)	(0.032)	(0.016)	(0.031)
Log size (Large)	0.143***	0.085*	0.122***	0.087*	0.158***	0.109**	0.139***	0.076*
	(0.017)	(0.044)	(0.018)	(0.045)	(0.018)	(0.047)	(0.018)	(0.044)
Observations	23,259	23,259	22,874	22,874	21,301	21,301	21,017	21,017
R-squared	0.207	0.397	0.211	0.396	0.208	0.408	0.215	0.406
Number of id		5,528		5,495		5,492		5,123

Source: World Bank calculations.

Note: The dependent variable is the four-year change in the logarithm of value added per employee. Delta log frontier (Local) = four-year change in value of local frontier (in logs) between t and t −4; Distance (Local) = lagged difference between plant's productivity and (domestic) frontier over value of frontier, all lagged four years. Avg Wage = average wage in the plant in t − 1; Ext Inno = expenditure on external innovation (patents) over revenue from sales; Invest = net investment in machinery over sales; K/L = capital-labor ratio in the plant; Log size (Medium, Large) = dummy with value 1 if firm has between 50 and 200 employees (medium) or more than 200 employees (large) in year t − 1; OLS = ordinary least squares; Trade = sum of expenditure on imports and revenue from exports over revenue from sales, in t − 1. All specifications include time dummies, two-digit industry dummies, and the cross product of the two. The Mexican sample covers 2003–11. Clustered standard errors are in parentheses.

***p < .01; **p < .05; *p < .1.

Table 5A.2 Four-Year Changes: Colombia

	OLS1	FE1	OLS2	FE2	OLS3	FE3	OLS4	FE4	OLS5	FE5
Distance (Local)	0.476***	1.335***	0.439***	1.325***	1.182***	1.937***	3.194***	4.398***	0.390***	1.165***
	(0.036)	(0.063)	(0.050)	(0.075)	(0.171)	(0.214)	(0.503)	(0.654)	(0.038)	(0.060)
Distance (Global)	-0.120	0.457	-0.093	0.203	0.138	2.129*	5.069	9.294**	-0.068	0.594
	(0.188)	(0.415)	(0.263)	(0.503)	(0.732)	(1.098)	(3.121)	(3.990)	(0.185)	(0.376)
Log (Trade/Sales)			-0.002	0.037						
			(0.030)	(0.035)						
Distance (Local)*Log (Trade/Sales)			-0.011	-0.008						
			(0.008)	(0.009)						
Distance (Global)*Log (Trade/Sales)			0.014	-0.027						
			(0.036)	(0.041)						
Log (Investment/Sales)					-0.058	-0.034				
					(0.044)	(0.058)				
Distance (Local)*Log (Investment/Sales)					-0.000	0.003				
					(0.017)	(0.021)				
Distance (Global)*Log (Investment/Sales)					0.076	0.054				
					(0.055)	(0.071)				
Log (Ext Inno/Sales)					0.035	-0.118***				
					(0.055)	(0.045)				
Distance (Local)*Log (Ext Inno/Sales)					0.038**	0.021				
					(0.016)	(0.016)				
Distance (Global)*Log (Ext Inno/Sales)					-0.032	0.152***				
					(0.065)	(0.053)				
Log (Ext Inno/Sales)					-0.020	0.060				
					(0.064)	(0.071)				

table continues next page

Table 5A.2 Four-Year Changes: Colombia (continued)

	OLS1	FE1	OLS2	FE2	OLS3	FE3	OLS4	FE4	OLS5	FE5
Distance (Local)*Log (Int Inno/Sales)					0.064***	0.085***				
					(0.018)	(0.021)				
Distance (Global)*Log (Int Inno/Sales)					−0.003	−0.069				
					(0.075)	(0.083)				
Log (Avg Wage)							0.631**	0.794**		
							(0.254)	(0.333)		
Distance (Local)*Log (Avg Wage)							−0.286***	−0.328***		
							(0.048)	(0.064)		
Distance (Global)*Log (Avg Wage)							−0.458	−0.823**		
							(0.291)	(0.380)		
Avg Wage (Sk/Unsk)									0.013	−0.009
									(0.019)	(0.023)
Distance (Local)*Avg Wage (Sk/Unsk)									−0.015***	−0.031***
									(0.004)	(0.005)
Distance (Global)*Avg Wage (Sk/Unsk)									−0.003	0.027
									(0.022)	(0.027)
Observations	38,055	38,055	37,850	37,850	22,392	22,392	38,052	38,052	38,055	38,055
Number of id		6,975		6,947		6,103		6,974		6,975

Source: World Bank calculations.

Note: The dependent variable is the four-year change in the logarithm of value added per employee. The coefficients for the changes in local and global frontiers, size dummies, capital-labor ratio, and plants' age are omitted for layout purposes. Distance (Local) = lagged difference between plant's productivity and (domestic) frontier over value of frontier, all lagged four years. All other terms are lagged four years. Avg Wage = average wage in the plant in $t − 1$; Avg Wage Sk/Unsk = ratio of the cost of employment of all skilled workers in the plant over that of unskilled workers in $t − 1$; Ext Inno = expenditure on external innovation (patents) over revenue from sales; Int Inno = expenditure on research and development over revenues from sales; Investment = net investment in machinery over sales; OLS = ordinary least squares; Trade = sum of expenditure on imports and revenue from exports over revenue from sales, in $t − 1$. All specifications include time dummies, two-digit industry dummies, and the cross product of the two. Regional (state) dummies and a control for the firm's age are also included. The Colombian sample covers 2000–11. Clustered standard errors are in parentheses.

***$p < .01$; **$p < .05$; *$p < .1$.

Table 5A.3 Four-Year Changes: United States

	OLS1	FE1	OLS2	FE2	OLS3	FE3	OLS4	FE4	OLS5	FE5
Distance (Local)	0.616***	1.493***	0.596***	1.538***	0.598***	1.602***	1.509***	3.191***	0.623***	1.499***
	(0.007)	(0.013)	(0.012)	(0.020)	(0.030)	(0.041)	(0.054)	(0.088)	(0.008)	(0.014)
Delta log frontier (Local)	0.339***	0.465***	0.340***	0.469***	0.374***	0.527***	0.342***	0.465***	0.338***	0.466***
	(0.012)	(0.016)	(0.015)	(0.020)	(0.018)	(0.024)	(0.012)	(0.016)	(0.012)	(0.016)
Delta log (K/L)	0.147***	0.149***	0.145***	0.151***	0.149***	0.159***	0.150***	0.139***	0.147***	0.149***
	(0.004)	(0.006)	(0.006)	(0.009)	(0.007)	(0.009)	(0.004)	(0.006)	(0.004)	(0.006)
Log (Trade/Sales)			0.000	−0.008***						
			(0.001)	(0.002)						
Distance (Local)*Log (Trade/Sales)			−0.003	0.022***						
			(0.002)	(0.003)						
Log (Investment/Sales)					0.000	0.000				
					(0.002)	(0.002)				
Distance (Local)*Log (Investment/Sales)					0.021***	0.028***				
					(0.004)	(0.005)				
Log (Ext Inno/Sales)					−0.003**	0.000				
					(0.001)	(0.001)				
Distance (Local)*Log (Ext Inno/Sales)					0.002	0.002				
					(0.002)	(0.002)				
Log (Int Inno/Sales)					0.012***	−0.000				
					(0.001)	(0.001)				
Distance (Local)*Log (Int Inno/Sales)					−0.015***	0.002				
					(0.002)	(0.003)				
Log (Avg Wage)							0.168***	0.065***		
							(0.009)	(0.015)		

table continues next page

167

Table 5A.3 Four-Year Changes: United States *(continued)*

	OLS1	FE1	OLS2	FE2	OLS3	FE3	OLS4	FE4	OLS5	FE5
Distance (Local)*Log (Avg Wage)							-0.234***	-0.453***		
							(0.014)	(0.022)		
Avg Wage(Sk/Unsk)									0.003*	-0.000
									(0.002)	(0.003)
Distance (Local)*Avg Wage(Sk/Unsk)									0.008**	0.007
									(0.003)	(0.005)
Log size (Medium)	0.019***	-0.055***	-0.020**	-0.075***	-0.025**	-0.072***	0.023***	-0.067***	0.019***	-0.055***
	(0.005)	(0.012)	(0.008)	(0.021)	(0.010)	(0.025)	(0.005)	(0.012)	(0.005)	(0.012)
Log size (Large)	0.016***	-0.098***	-0.034***	-0.122***	-0.051***	-0.122***	0.018***	-0.125***	0.016***	-0.098***
	(0.006)	(0.017)	(0.009)	(0.027)	(0.010)	(0.028)	(0.006)	(0.017)	(0.006)	(0.017)
Log age	-0.017***	-0.022*	-0.026***	-0.037**	-0.030***	-0.034	-0.019***	-0.014	-0.018***	-0.022*
	(0.003)	(0.012)	(0.004)	(0.017)	(0.004)	(0.021)	(0.003)	(0.012)	(0.003)	(0.012)
Observations										
R-squared	0.187	0.354	0.193	0.353	0.191	0.351	0.191	0.363	0.187	0.354
Number of id										

Source: World Bank calculations.

Note: The dependent variable is the four-year change in the logarithm of value added per employee. The coefficients for the changes in local and global frontiers, size dummies, capital-labor ratio, and plants' age are omitted for layout purposes. Delta log frontier (Local) = four-year change in value of local frontier (in logs) between t and $t − 4$; Distance (Local) = lagged difference between plant's productivity and (domestic) frontier over value of frontier, all lagged four years. All other terms are lagged four years. Avg Wage = average wage in the plant in $t − 1$; Avg Wage Sk/Unsk = ratio of the cost of employment of all skilled workers in the plant over that of unskilled workers in $t − 1$; Ext Inno = expenditure on external innovation (patents) over revenue from sales; FE = fixed effects; Int Inno = expenditure on research and development over revenues from sales; Investment = net investment in machinery over sales; K/L = capital-labor ratio in the plant; Log age = logarithm of plant's age in the plant; Log age = logarithm of plant's age increased by one (so that entrants would not be dropped from the sample); Log size (Medium, Large) = dummy with value 1 if firm has between 50 and 200 employees (medium) or more than 200 employees (large) in year $t − 1$; OLS = ordinary least squares; Trade = sum of expenditure on imports and revenue from exports over revenue from sales, in $t − 1$. All specifications include time dummies, two-digit industry dummies, and the cross product of the two. State dummies and a control for the firm's age are also included. The U.S. sample covers 1995–2011. The numbers of observations and firms are omitted due to disclosure concerns. Clustered standard errors are in parentheses.

*** $p < .01$; ** $p < .05$; * $p < .1$.

Table 5A.4 GMM: Mexico

	1	2	3	4a	4b	5	6	7
Distance (Local)	0.436***	0.401***	0.368***	0.739***	0.819***	0.790***	0.981***	0.264
	(0.088)	(0.080)	(0.098)	(0.167)	(0.209)	(0.226)	(0.274)	(0.504)
Distance (Global)	−0.232*	−0.224***	−0.231	−0.867**	−0.946**	−1.674**	−2.065**	1.580
	(0.131)	(0.065)	(0.240)	(0.342)	(0.454)	(0.743)	(0.815)	(1.344)
Log (Trade/Sales)			0.020					
			(0.032)					
Distance (Local)*Log (Trade/Sales)			0.028					
			(0.018)					
Distance (Global)*Log (Trade/Sales)			−0.031					
			(0.047)					
Log (Investment/Sales)				0.061*	0.064		0.113**	
				(0.035)	(0.048)		(0.048)	
Distance (Local)*Log (Investment/Sales)				0.088***	0.088**		0.083***	
				(0.029)	(0.038)		(0.026)	
Distance (Global)*Log (Investment/Sales)				−0.118**	−0.125*		−0.181***	
				(0.053)	(0.074)		(0.068)	
Log (Ext Inno/Sales)						0.103*	0.056	
						(0.053)	(0.037)	
Distance (Local)*Log (Ext Inno/Sales)						0.044**	0.022	
						(0.021)	(0.018)	
Distance (Global)*Log (Ext Inno/Sales)						−0.145**	−0.079	
						(0.073)	(0.052)	
Log (Avg Wage)								0.309
								(0.230)

table continues next page

Table 5A.4 GMM: Mexico (continued)

	1	2	3	4a	4b	5	6	7
Distance (Local)*Log (Avg Wage)								0.032
								(0.110)
Distance (Global)*Log (Avg Wage)								−0.437
								(0.313)
Hansen p-value	0.475	0.416	0.355	0.026	0.188	0.365	0.181	0.667
AB p-value	0.640	0.605	0.606	0.387	0.351	0.566	0.360	0.156
Number of IVs	177	182	200	200	193	200	226	200
Observations	40,545	40,216	39,763	36,847	36,847	40,214	36,846	35,687
Number of id	6,197	6,157	6,137	6,138	6,138	6,157	6,138	5,725

Source: World Bank calculations.

Note: The dependent variable is the four-year change in the logarithm of value added per employee. Avg Wage = average wage in the plant in $t - 1$; Distance (Local) = lagged difference between plant's productivity and (domestic) frontier over value of frontier; Ext Inno = expenditure on external innovation (patents) over revenue from sales; Investment = net investment in machinery over sales; IVs = instrumental variables; Trade = sum of expenditure on imports and revenue from exports over revenue from sales, in $t - 1$. The following regressors are included in the estimation but omitted from the table: change in capital-labor ration, size dummies, and change in frontiers. All specifications include time dummies, two-digit industry dummies, and the cross product of the two. Hansen is the p-value of the test of joint validity of the instruments in the presence of heteroskedastic errors; AB is the p-value of the Arellano Bond test for the absence of autocorrelation in the errors of order higher than one. All models except for 4b use the same number of lags as instruments for the endogenous variables, where the growth in the frontier and the level variable for the interaction variable (such as trade) are considered predetermined, while the distances and the cross products between distances and the interaction variable are considered endogenous. Specification 4b is included to improve on the failure of specification 4a to pass the Hansen test. Standard errors (in parentheses) are robust and corrected to account for small sample biases. GMM = Generalized Method of Moments.

*** $p < .01$; ** $p < .05$; * $p < .1$.

Annex 5B Estimation Results with Local Frontier Only

Table 5B.1 Estimation Results: Baseline, with Local Frontier Only

	Mexico				Colombia			
	OLS1	FE1	OLS2	FE2	OLS1	FE1	OLS2	FE2
Distance (Local)	0.083***	0.618***	0.080***	0.587***	0.210***	0.697***	0.199***	0.682***
	(0.009)	(0.045)	(0.009)	(0.045)	(0.009)	(0.036)	(0.008)	(0.022)
Delta log frontier (Local)	0.529***	0.542***	0.529***	0.538***	0.134***	0.201***	0.119***	0.187***
	(0.023)	(0.022)	(0.023)	(0.022)	(0.014)	(0.015)	(0.014)	(0.014)
Delta log (K/L)			0.164***	0.168***			0.282***	0.260***
			(0.013)	(0.013)			(0.008)	(0.008)
Log size (Medium)			0.052***	0.037***			0.028***	−0.021**
			(0.005)	(0.014)			(0.004)	(0.011)
Log size (Large)			0.074***	0.051***			0.064***	−0.035*
			(0.006)	(0.019)			(0.006)	(0.021)
Log age							0.003	−0.012
							(0.003)	(0.018)
Observations	40,545	40,545	40,216	40,216	68,533	68,533	65,996	65,996
R-squared	0.194	0.281	0.213	0.295	0.107	0.197	0.156	0.242
Number of id		6,197		6,157		11,924		11,667

Source: World Bank calculations.

Note: The dependent variable is the logarithm of value added per employee. Delta log frontier (Local) = change in value of local frontier (in logs) between t and $t - 1$; Distance (Local) = lagged difference between plant's productivity and (domestic) frontier over value of frontier, as expressed in equation 5.5. All other terms are lagged once. FE = fixed effects; K/L = capital-labor ratio in the plant; Log age = logarithm of plant's age increased by one (so that entrants would not be dropped from the sample); Log size (Medium, Large) = dummy with value 1 if firm has between 50 and 200 employees (medium) or more than 200 employees (large) in year $t - 1$; OLS = ordinary least squares. All specifications include time dummies, two-digit industry dummies, and the cross product of the two. Data availability permits controlling for age and regional dummies for Colombia but not for Mexico. The Colombian sample covers 2000–11; the Mexican sample covers 2003–10. Clustered standard errors are in parentheses.
***$p < .01$; **$p < .05$; *$p < .1$.

Table 5B.2 Estimation Results: One Interaction per Specification, with Local Frontier Only

	Log(Ext Inno/Sales)		Log(Int Inno/Sales)		Log(Investment/Sales)		Log(Trade/Sales)		Log(Avg Wage)		Log(Avg Wage Sk/Unsk)	
	OLS	FE	OLS	FE	OLS	FE	OLS	FE	OLS	FE	OLS	FE
Mexico												
X	0.000	0.004			0.003*	−0.001	0.004***	0.010***	0.060***	0.084***		
	(0.001)	(0.002)			(0.002)	(0.003)	(0.001)	(0.003)	(0.009)	(0.030)		
Distance (Local)*X	0.005***	0.026***			0.005	0.018***	−0.000	−0.002	−0.057***	−0.144***		
	(0.002)	(0.004)			(0.003)	(0.005)	(0.002)	(0.005)	(0.011)	(0.042)		
Observations	40,214	40,214			36,847	36,847	39,763	39,763	35,687	35,687		
Number of id		6,157				6,138		6,137		5,725		
Colombia												
X	−0.004	0.005	−0.010***	0.009*	0.007***	0.010**	0.006***	0.010***	0.079***	0.028	0.004***	0.006***
	(0.003)	(0.004)	(0.003)	(0.005)	(0.003)	(0.004)	(0.001)	(0.002)	(0.009)	(0.018)	(0.001)	(0.001)
Distance (Local)*X	0.031***	0.051***	0.035***	0.054***	0.002	0.006	−0.007***	−0.008**	−0.139***	−0.230***	−0.006***	−0.013***
	(0.003)	(0.006)	(0.004)	(0.009)	(0.005)	(0.007)	(0.002)	(0.004)	(0.010)	(0.020)	(0.001)	(0.002)
Observations	46,131	46,131	46,131	46,131	65,684	65,684	65,684	65,684	65,986	65,986	65,996	65,996
Number of id		9,510		9,510		11,637		11,637		11,667		11,667

Source: World Bank calculations.

Note: Avg Wage = average wage in the plant in $t - 1$; Avg Wage Sk/Unsk = ratio of cost of employment of all skilled workers in the plant over that of unskilled workers in $t - 1$; Distance (Local) = lagged difference between plant's productivity and (domestic) frontier over value of frontier, as expressed in equation 5.5; Ext Inno = expenditure on external innovation (patents) over revenue from sales; FE = fixed effects; Int Inno = expenditure on research and development over revenues from sales; Investment = net investment in machinery over sales; OLS = ordinary least squares; Trade = sum of expenditure on imports and revenue from exports over revenue from sales, in $t - 1$. Each column corresponds to a different specification in which the lagged value of the variable at the top of the column (X) is interacted with the firm's distance from the local frontier. The following regressors are also included in each specification: the distance from the local frontier, the one-year change in the local frontier, change in the capital-labor ratio; and dummies for size, industry, time, and industry-time. For Colombia, regional dummies and a control for the firm's age are also included. Clustered standard errors are in parentheses.

***p < .01; **p < .05; *p < .1.

Table 5B.3 Estimation Results: Multiple Interactions per Specification, with Local Frontier Only

	Mexico				Colombia					
	OLS1	FE1	OLS2	FE2	OLS1	FE1	OLS2	FE2	OLS3	FE3
Log (Trade/Sales)	0.004***	0.011***	0.001	0.009***	0.004***	0.007***	0.003*	0.006***	0.003**	0.006***
	(0.001)	(0.003)	(0.001)	(0.003)	(0.001)	(0.002)	(0.001)	(0.002)	(0.002)	(0.002)
Distance (Local)*Trade	−0.000	−0.005	0.003*	0.000	−0.005**	−0.008*	−0.004	−0.006	−0.005*	−0.006
	(0.002)	(0.005)	(0.002)	(0.006)	(0.003)	(0.004)	(0.003)	(0.004)	(0.003)	(0.004)
Log (Investment/Sales)	0.003*	−0.001	0.001	−0.003	0.009***	0.008**	0.007**	0.007*	0.008***	0.007**
	(0.002)	(0.002)	(0.001)	(0.003)	(0.003)	(0.004)	(0.003)	(0.004)	(0.003)	(0.003)
Distance (Local)*Investment	0.005*	0.017***	0.009***	0.022***	−0.003	0.006	0.000	0.007	−0.002	0.007
	(0.003)	(0.005)	(0.002)	(0.005)	(0.005)	(0.007)	(0.005)	(0.006)	(0.005)	(0.006)
Log (Ext Inno/Sales)	0.000	0.004*	0.000	0.004	0.001	0.003	0.003	0.005	0.001	0.002
	(0.001)	(0.002)	(0.001)	(0.003)	(0.003)	(0.004)	(0.003)	(0.003)	(0.003)	(0.004)
Distance (Local)*Ext Inno	0.004**	0.021***	0.002	0.025***	0.016***	0.034***	0.008*	0.024***	0.014***	0.034***
	(0.002)	(0.004)	(0.002)	(0.005)	(0.005)	(0.007)	(0.005)	(0.006)	(0.005)	(0.006)
Log (Int Inno/Sales)					−0.011***	0.008*	−0.009***	0.010**	−0.011***	0.008*
					(0.003)	(0.005)	(0.003)	(0.004)	(0.003)	(0.005)
Distance (Local)*Int Inno					0.023***	0.033***	0.017***	0.025***	0.022***	0.031***
					(0.005)	(0.009)	(0.005)	(0.008)	(0.006)	(0.009)
Log (Avg Wage)			0.054***	0.064**			0.080***	0.028		
			(0.009)	(0.027)			(0.011)	(0.025)		

table continues next page

173

Table 5B.3 Estimation Results: Multiple Interactions per Specification, with Local Frontier Only *(continued)*

	Mexico				Colombia					
	OLS1	FE1	OLS2	FE2	OLS1	FE1	OLS2	FE2	OLS3	FE3
Distance (Local)*Avg Wage			-0.056***	-0.116***			-0.126***	-0.201***		
			(0.011)	(0.037)			(0.016)	(0.033)		
Log (Avg Wage Sk/Unsk)									0.003***	0.007***
									(0.001)	(0.001)
Distance (Local)*Avg Wage (Sk/Unsk)									-0.005***	-0.013***
									(0.001)	(0.002)
Observations	36,415	36,415	32,308	32,308	46,131	46,131	46,122	46,122	46,131	46,131
Number of id		6,116		5,671		9,510		9,510		9,510

Source: World Bank calculations.

Note: The dependent variable is the logarithm of value added per employee. Avg Wage = average wage in the plant in $t-1$; Avg Wage Sk/Unsk = ratio of cost of employment of all skilled workers in the plant over that of unskilled workers in $t-1$; Distance (Local) = lagged difference between plant's productivity and (domestic) frontier over value of frontier, as expressed in equation 5.5; Ext Inno = expenditure on external innovation (patents) over revenue from sales; Int Inno = expenditure on research and development over revenues from sales; Investment = net investment in machinery over sales; OLS = ordinary least squares; Trade = sum of expenditure on imports and revenue from exports over revenue from sales, in $t-1$. The following regressors are also included in each specification: the distance from the local frontier, the one-year change in the local frontier, change in the capital-labor ratio; and dummies for size, industry, time, and industry-time. For Colombia, regional dummies and a control for the firm's age are also included. Clustered standard errors are in parentheses.

***$p < .01$; **$p < .05$; *$p < .1$.

Annex 5C Data Construction

We have access to three establishment-level panel data sets, one for Colombia (Encuesta Anual Manufacturera, EAM), one for Mexico (Encuesta Industrial Anual, EIA), and one for the United States (U.S. Annual Survey of Manufacturers [ASM]). This was possible thanks to the respective national institutes of statistics (DANE and INEGI) and the U.S. Census Bureau. These data sets contain accounting information on plants in the manufacturing sector for 2000–11 for Colombia, 2003–11 for Mexico, and 1995–2011 for the U.S. We also match the plant-level information from EAM with the annual survey on innovation activities of Colombian manufacturing establishments (Encuesta de Desarrollo e Innovación Tecnológica en la Industria Manufacturera) for 2003–10. In this annex, we supplement the information on eligibility and coverage of the manufacturing surveys that was provided in the main text.

Data Cleaning

To proceed with our analysis, we needed our main variable of interest to be non-missing in all plants. That is why we dropped all observations without information for value added per employee, as well as industry classification (which is needed for descriptive statistics and to merge the values of the global frontier). We made sure that our data are reliable by eliminating observations in which employment was reported to be negative. We treated the presence of extreme values in the resulting sample by truncating the distribution of value added and growth in value added at 1 and 99 percent.

Further, we made sure that the sample used for the descriptive statistics and productivity decompositions was the same as the one used for the baseline regressions in tables 5.5 and 5.6. Since these regressions take value added per employee in logarithmic form, we also excluded observations with negative or zero value added. In a further effort to limit the extent of misreporting, we also dropped observations with positive value added but zero employment; as a consequence, we excluded the possibility of sole proprietorship, which we deemed more unlikely in manufacturing.

A final constraint in the Colombian and Mexican data was imposed after merging the values for the global frontier. Evidently, there were four-digit sectors for which a value of the global frontier was available, but that did not exist in Colombia and Mexico (in a given year or throughout the sample): the values of the global frontier in these sectors were discarded without loss of information for the Colombian or Mexican data. There were also cases (3 percent of the cleaned sample) in which the four-digit industry code was available in the main data sets of interest, but not in the global frontier data. This situation mostly happened in sector-year pairs for which a value of the frontier could not be issued, in compliance with the U.S. Census Bureau data protection rules.

Industry Classification and Conversion

We relied on industry information contained in the EAM for Colombia, the EIA for Mexico, and the AMS for the United States. Each of these surveys follows a different industry classification. The EAM classifies plants according to a four-digit International Standard Industrial Classification (ISIC3) specifically adapted to the Colombian context. The EIA uses a six-digit classification inspired by the North American Industry Classification System (NAICS) for 2002 and 2007 (Système de classification des industries de l'Amérique du Nord [SCIAN] 2002 and 2007). We use U.S. data based on the six-digit NAICS 2002 classification.

The use of three different industry classifications would have hindered the cross-country comparison of descriptive statistics and productivity decompositions. Further, we needed the U.S.-based information to calculate Mexican and Colombian plant-level distances from the global frontier, where the value of the frontier was computed from a statistical moment of the firm productivity distribution at the industry level. As the NAICS 2002-ISIC3 (or 3.1) conversion implies numerous many-to-many correspondences, we created a new industry classification for manufacturing, which could include all national classifications, on the basis of existing NAICS 2002-NAICS 2007, NAICS-SCIAN, ISIC3 (Colombia)-ISIC 3.1 (international), and NAICS 2002-ISIC3.1 (international) conversion tables.

We obtain a single classification inspired by (but not coinciding with) the international ISIC 3.1 classification, which contains 104 four-digit classes and which we call NewInd hereafter. One ISIC 3.1 four-digit class (of 122) and seven six-digit NAICS 2002 classes (of 473) have no correspondence in the new classification. All statistics in the chapter requiring an industry declination (including the computation of the global frontier) are calculated with NewInd.

In constructing NewInd, we first converted the national classifications into either NAICS 2002 or ISIC 3.1. This proved to be a relatively straightforward task, beccause of the existence of one-to-one conversions for almost all industries in each country. A one-to-many correspondence between a four-digit ISIC 3.1 and a six-digit NAICS 2002 code also resulted in the use of the ISIC 3.1 code (this happened for 281 of 473 NAICS manufacturing classes). In taking into consideration the many-to-many correspondences between NAICS 2002 and ISIC 3.1, we followed these priciples:

1. When one of the multiple ISIC 3.1 codes corresponding to a single NAICS 2002 code was not classified as manufacturing in the ISIC 3.1 classification, we dropped this ISIC 3.1 code altogether. This happened for eight six-digit NAICS codes.
2. When the NAICS 2002 classification was specific enough, we searched for the corresponding products in the ISIC 3.1. A description table for the ISIC 3.1 code can be found at http://unstats.un.org/unsd/statcom/doc02/isic.pdf.
3. When in doubt about the attribution of a certain six-digit NAICS code to an ISIC code, we also took into consideration the meaning of the five- and four-digit NAICS codes.
4. When the "predominant meaning" of an NAICS code was clear once aggregating two or more of the proposed four-digit ISIC codes in the NAICS-ISIC conversion table, we merged the different ISIC codes. We limited the number

of cases in which this happened, as it reduced the number of final available industry codes in NewInd. In most cases, the merged ISIC codes refer to the same two- or three-digit ISIC classes.

5. We dropped seven NAICS six-digit codes, whose meaning could not be linked to any single ISIC or combination of ISIC codes.

Deflation

All financial information in the different manufacturing surveys is reported in nominal terms. We therefore deflate these values with an appropriate deflator in base 2005. We then convert them to thousands of U.S. dollars using the appropriate (yearly) exchange rate from the World Bank. As the values of the global frontier were computed in thousands of U.S. dollars, we converted them into the national currencies before merging them and calculating the plant-frontier distance.

To deflate domestic sales and export sales, we use six-digit producer index prices for Mexico,[50] and a manufacturing-level producer price index for Colombia.[51] For domesticly sourced material inputs, we use the appropriate four-digit producer price index (based on the Mexican Catalog of Economic Activities classification) for Mexico, and a manufacturing-wide deflator for Colombia. Imported materials in Colombia and Mexico are deflated using the manufacturing-wide U.S. price of exports of nonagricutural supplies and intermediate goods (available on the U.S. Census webpage) once adjusted by the US$/country currency exchange rate. Expenditure for electricity was deflated using the producer price index for the electricity sector in both countries. Finally, we used the consumer price index to deflate labor costs and expenditure for innovation.

For both countries, the deflation of most capital investment is based on three-digit price indexes for investment from the U.S. Bureau of Labor Statistics (BLS) (http://www.bls.gov/mfp/mprtech.pdf), which we adjust by the exchange rate between US$ and the country currency. The BLS provides price deflators for different types of investment: all capital goods, equipment, structures, land, intellectual property products, and inventories. We exploit the first three prices for, respectively, all investments, investment in machinery, and investment in buildings. For information and communications technology (ICT) capital investment, we use the price of gross output for the "information-communications-technology-producing industries" elaborated by the Bureau of Economic Analysis[52] and adjusted by the exchange rate. We deflated investment in transportation equipment by the country-specific producer price index for the transportation sector.

Variable Construction

Our main outcome variable relies on the existence of value added at the plant level. As this is not directly reported in the data set, we constructed it as the sum between (deflated) revenues from sales, minus the (deflated) cost of raw (either domestic or imported) materials and the (deflated) cost of electricity. If any component of this sum is missing, the result is also missing.

The EAM and EIA report the plant's capital stock at book value. However, this is not the actual use value of the capital for the plant, but rather the result of the depreciated value at which such capital was purchased. A better measure of the value of capital would be its replacement value, but we do not have access to it. This is why we assume that the book value in the first year of the sample (1995 for the United States, 2000 for Colombia, and 2003 for Mexico) corresponds to the capital replacement value. We then construct the value of capital for the following years using the perpetuary inventory method (PIM) according to the following equation:

$$K_{ijt} = K_{ijt-1}(1 - \delta_{jt-1}) + I_{ijt-1}$$

for $t \in [1996, 2011]$ for the United States, $t \in [2001, 2011]$ for Colombia, and $t \in [2004, 2011]$ for Mexico. I_{ijt-1} denotes investment, or the purchase of new capital goods (which is reported in the data sets), and K_{ijt} is the result of the calculation of capital stocks in the year. δ_{jt} is the depreciation rate of capital. EAM and EIA contain information on depreciation rates by type of capital. To limit the impact of possible misreporting, in the PIM we use the median of the two-digit sector depreciation rate from the data, where values above 100 percent and below 0 percent of capital stock were winsorized. Once we obtained a time series for the capital stock of each type of capital (buildings, equipment, ICT, and transportation), we aggregated them into two variables, one for total capital and another for total capital except buildings and structures.

A final note is allocated to the creation of the innovation variables. We have information on expenditure for research and development (R&D) (new and improved processes or products, which we call internal innovation) only for Colombia and the United States. In Mexico, the external innovation variable covers the expenditure for the exploitation of the rights connected to a copyright, patent, brand, or know-how. In Colombia, the external innovation variable is obtained as the sum of expenditure for the purchase of R&D that was carried out by others, expenditure for patents and copyrights, fees for technical assistance, and consulting on technological know-how. The U.S. external innovation variable is the sum of the expenditure for R&D carried out by foreign affiliates of the firm and by entities outside the boundaries of the firm.

Entry and Exit

We define a plant appearing for the first time in the unclean sample as an entrant. However, the Mexican EIA does not take into account entry in a systematic way: updates to the sample are done for sizeable plants entering the market, or in case the number and coverage of plants in a sector drop below the mandatory minimums for the year. We therefore observe very limited entry in years other than the first year of the sample (2003). Accounting for entry in the Colombian survey is also problematic, as the methodology to update the sample changed in 2008. Until 2007, the EAM was updated on the basis of mini-surveys that were conducted by DANE's regional offices; starting in 2008, the central DANE cross-referenced its sample with other sources of information (Superintendence of Companies, Chambers of Commerce, Free Export Zones, and the exporter's database). A plant is identified as exiter in the last year of operation in the data set before cleaning.

Notes

1. We use the terms "establishment" and "firm" or "plant" interchangeably in this paper, but it should be noted that our data are based on establishment-level surveys.

2. At the firm level, we graph the ratio between the plant's growth rate in a year over the median growth rate of all plants in the same four-digit sector. At the industry level, we graph the ratio between the median growth rate in the four-digit sector over the median growth rate in the economy.

3. We use the U.S. productivity frontier as our measure for the global frontier.

4. This latter result is not relevant for the United States, for which we do not have a global frontier.

5. In order to contain the size of the literature review, we restricted it as much as possible to the analysis of firm-level dynamics (rather than country-level) which explicitly accounted for the interactions between some of the firm-level outcomes we are also investigating, and a measure of distance from the frontier. A synthesis of the related literatures on endogenous growth (e.g., Aghion and Howitt 2006) and on the link between competition, innovation, and growth (e.g., Aghion and Schankerman 2004 and Aghion et al. 2005) is therefore omitted here.

6. Unfortunately, no information is available on nonmanufacturing firms, while manufacturing firms are associated to a single industry code. Furthermore, data availability for Mexico makes it impossible to distinguish between single-product and multi-product firms. As the units of observation are establishments, it is assumed that they operate in a single sector.

7. These statistics are for 2005. In 2009, the survey covered 90 percent of manufacturing sales in Mexico.

8. This is the threshold for 2012, and it changes yearly on the basis of the producer price index.

9. For more information on entry and exit and for the cleaning procedure, please refer to annex 5C.

10. Mexican data are reported at the six-digit SCIAN level, and Colombian data at the four-digit level. To be able to compare Colombian, Mexican, and U.S. data in the descriptive statistics, we constructed a conversion table between the SCIAN/NAICS 2002 and ISIC 3.1 classifications. This is discussed in greater detail in annex 5C.

11. This survey covers 2003–10 and reports firm-level information. In consideration of the fact that only 8 percent of observations are multi-plant firms, we do not believe that the use of firm-level expenditure at the plant level is severely biasing our results.

12. The innovation surveys in Colombia and the United States collect information at the firm level, while our main accounting data refer to establishments as observational units. In light of the relative scarcity of multi-plant firms in Colombia (contrary to the United States), we performed all our econometric analysis again on a sample of single-plant firms (tables are not reported). The inference does not change with respect to the complete sample.

13. For further details on the construction of the capital variable and deflation, please refer to annex 5C.

14. A similar proportion is found in Iacovone (2012), where the proportion of manufacturing plants engaged in exports vary from 25 percent in 1994 to 37 percent in 2003. For Colombia, this proportion reached 13.5 percent in 1989 (Roberts and Tybout, 1997). Similarly, the U.S. Census of Manufacturers in 2002 reported 18 percent of manufacturing *firms* to be exporting in 2002, while restricting the sample to firms appearing in both the Census of Manufacturers and the Linked-Longitudinal Firm Trade Transaction Database raised this proportion to 27 percent for 1997 (Bernard, Jensen, Redding, and Schott 2007). Countries can therefore differ in the intensity of exporters in the manufacturing sectors, depending on the covered period, reporting threshold to enter the database under analysis, and definition of the observational unit at the establishment versus firm level. More generally, a higher proportion of exporting firms in smaller developing economies could reflect the relatively smaller domestic market, and the search for economies of scale through internationalization.

15. Note that the number of observations for the innovation variables falls, because information on innovation is altogether absent for some years in the sample (2000 to 2002 and 2011).

16. We define innovators as those plants engaged in the purchase of patents or consulting services.

17. Choosing the mean of the top quartile is consistent with Bartelsman, Haskel, and Martin (2008). Alternatively, computing the frontier based on the top decile would have reduced the number of available sector-year pairs for which a value for the global (U.S.) frontier could be issued, in light of the confidentiality constraints imposed by data distribution.

18. Sectors are divided into two graphs to enhance readability. Part 1 includes sectors that roughly correspond to ISIC 3.1 codes 15 to 28; part 2 contains the other manufacturing sectors.

19. Although it is a general pattern, this does not apply to all sectors, as in the case of communications and electrical equipment for Mexico.

20. In principle, this increase in the distance could be caused by an increase in the value of the global frontier or a decrease in the domestic frontier. The value of the global frontier decreased on average across all sectors between 2007 and 2008, but it increased again starting in 2008. For Mexico and Colombia, the decrease in the domestic frontier takes place between 2008 and 2009, that is, one year later.

21. There are no graphs for the United States here because the global and local frontiers coincide by definition.

22. This result does not necessarily contradict what is shown in the previous figure, as it may still be that more firms exceed the international frontier despite a general decrease in the relative value of the local frontier with respect to the global one.

23. The last year of the sample was chosen arbitrarily, but the same can be shown for other years in the sample.

24. Domestic and global frontiers are calculated per each four-digit industry and year. The two-digit graphs in this section are obtained as weighted averages of the ratio of frontier and median productivity in the four-digit Mexican sector, where the weights are

the employment shares of the four-digit sectors in the two-digit sectors in the same year. For the aggregate graph, the weight is the employment share of each four-digit sector in total manufacturing in each year.

25. An important part of the literature computes this decomposition using output instead of employment weights. It is mostly the case, however, that output weights are used when productivity is estimated as total factor productivity (Bartelsman, Haltiwanger, and Scarpetta 2009, 2013). As we are focusing our analysis on labor productivity only, we prefer using employment weights. In our context, the weights measure the extent to which the labor input is allocated across firms.

26. The subscript for the country is omitted to simplify the notation.

27. This is the aggregate productivity in overall manufacturing, that is, the weighted average of the aggregate two-digit sector productivity Ω_{jt} across sectors, where the weights are constructed as the share of sector employment in total manufacturing employment. Consistent with this, the covariance term is also measured as the weighted average of the two-digit sector covariances.

28. In formal terms, the covariance here is a function of the difference between the aggregate productivity at the industry level Ω_{jt} and its average across industries $\bar{\Omega}_t$ on the one side, and the difference between the employment share of the industry in total manufacturing $S_{jt} = \dfrac{n_j t}{n_t}$ and the cross-industry average of such shares $\bar{S}_t = \dfrac{1}{J}(S_{jt})$. Hence, covariance $= \Sigma_j(\Omega_{jt} - \bar{\Omega}_t)(S_{jt} - \bar{S}_t)$.

29. Negative values for the covariance term imply that more productive establishments are downsizing (or doing so faster than less productive ones). When this is associated with aggregate productivity growth, such growth is achieved by the job destruction process. For a thorough analysis of the meaning and likelihood of negative covariances when investigating labor productivity using employment weights, see Nishida, Petrin, and Polanec (2013).

30. The covariance term here is at the two-digit sector level and is rescaled by Ω_{jt}.

31. To compute changes in productivity between $t-1$ and t, the fact that a firm enters in $t-1$ or that a firm exits in t is irrelevant, as both cases will be captured by the terms referring to surviving establishments.

32. In the notation of the previous section, $\omega_{ijt} = A_{ijt}$, that is, in this study we consider only labor productivity and not total factor productivity.

33. The expression for the distance from the frontier we report here cannot be directly derived from 5.4, contrary to previous estimators derived in the literature (e.g., Griffith, Redding, and Simpson 2009). Our measure, which one also finds in Madsen (2014), is motivated by the presence of observations with very small firm-level labor productivity in our data, typically when the firm is hit by a shock which reduces its value added much faster than it is possible for the firm to reduce employment (or because of measurement errors). Our estimator has the advantage of being increasing in the distance, which simplifies the interpretation of the estimation results.

34. This is because of confidentiality reasons and rules governing access to data for each of the countries analyzed.

35. The reported number of observations and establishments is approximated to comply with restrictions in data distribution at the U.S. Census.

36. A comparison of the speed of convergence between the global and local frontiers is invalidated by the fact that the "true" coefficient lies between the OLS and FE coefficients, and we cannot assess whether endogeneity biases the coefficient on the distance from the local frontier differently than that on the distance from the global frontier.

37. To enhance the comparability between the Mexican and Colombian results on the one side, and the U.S. results on the other, we ran our estimation with a single frontier for Mexico and Colombia as well. The results are reported in annex 5B.

38. For reasons of space, these results have not been included but are available upon request.

39. This result is also consistent with the work of Griffith, Redding, and Simpson (2003).

40. In the specifications where "internal innovation" is missing but "external innovation" is not, it cannot be excluded that the coefficient on purchases of innovation services are partially capturing the effect of doing R&D. The coexistence of a positive cross product for both external and internal innovation for Colombia seems to provide support for this hypothesis. More importantly, the two activities have been found to be positively correlated and complementary, with each form of innovation stimulating investment in the other (Cassiman and Veugelers 2006), albeit in a Western European country context. This is less problematic for Colombia and the U.S. than for Mexico, where controlling for both capabilities at the same time is not possible, in light of data availability on R&D expenditure at the firm level.

41. For example, the first two columns (the interaction terms for external innovation) report the same results as in specification 2 of the previous tables.

42. This metric is computed as the ratio of the costs of all skilled employees in the plant over the costs of all unskilled employees.

43. Ideally we would like to control for local availability of skilled workers to confirm our interpretation, but these data are not available.

44. Our measure for trade is the ratio of revenues generated by international trade over total revenues from sales, where trade is either import or export.

45. Differences may of course derive also from the differences in the estimated models. However, in annex table 5B.2, where we only include interactions with the local frontier for Mexico and Colombia, we find different significance and signs compared with the United States.

46. Bernard, Jensen, Redding, and Schott (2007) find that more productive firms export to more destinations, sell more widely in any given market, and make up for a larger share of total exports from the U.S. A similar, but somewhat less regular pattern is supported also in Eaton, Kortum, and Kramarz (2011), whereby more efficient firms can sell more than inefficient ones in any single market: for a given fixed cost, larger sales translate into higher value added per input used. However, among the studies highlighting the existence of "learning by exporting," only De Loecker (2007), to our knowledge, finds that export premia are bigger for firms exporting to high-income countries. This result can be explained by the greater set of learning opportunities generated by exports to developed countries, or by the generally tougher level of market competition when selling in those markets. For other stylized facts on export dynamics and firm-level outcomes besides productivity, see, for instance, Eaton et al. (2008) on Colombian firms. Unfortunately, we cannot explore these phenomena with the data at hand, as for Mexico and Colombia we only observe the value of the establishments' overall exports.

47. In view of the strong correlation between R&D and external innovation, it is possible that the coefficient on external innovation in Mexico is capturing the effect of internal innovation as well, which is absent in the Mexican specifications. As R&D expenditure information is unavailable in the Mexican data, we cannot improve on these results.

48. After receiving a productivity shock, a plant may move back to its long-term productivity pattern (mean reversion). Exploiting year-on-year changes may increase the probability that our coefficients attribute the effect of mean reversion to convergence.

49. The estimates for some covariates were omitted from the Colombian table (but not from the estimation) for layout purposes.

50. These are published on the INEGI website.

51. At the time of writing, a more disaggregated producer price index time series was available from 2006 onward only.

52. This is a synthetic sector covering hardware- and software-producing industries, including computer and electronics production, software publishing, telecommunications, data processing, Internet publishing, web portals, computer system designs, and related services.

Bibliography

Acemoglu, Daron, Philippe Aghion, and Fabrizio Zilibotti. 2006. "Distance to Frontier, Selection, and Economic Growth." *Journal of the European Economic Association* 4 (1): 37–74.

Aghion, Philippe, and Peter Howitt. 2006. "Appropriate Growth Policy: a Unifying Framework," *Journal of the European Economic Association* 4 (2–3): 269–314.

Aghion, Philippe, Nick Bloom, Richard Blundell, Rachel Griffith, and Peter Howitt. 2005. "Competition and Innovation: An Inverted-U Relationship." *The Quarterly Journal of Economics* 120 (2): 701–28.

Aghion, Philippe, and Mark Schankerman. 2004. "On the Welfare Effects and Political Economy of Competition-Enhancing Policies." *The Economic Journal* 114 (498): 800–824.

Alvarez, Roberto, and Gustavo Crespi. 2007. "Multinational Firms and Productivity Catching-Up: The Case of Chilean Manufacturing." *International Journal of Technological Learning, Innovation and Development* 1 (2): 136–52.

Amiti, Mary, and Jozef Konings. 2007. "Trade Liberalization, Intermediate Inputs, and Productivity: Evidence from Indonesia." *American Economic Review* 97(5): 1611–38.

Baily, Martin Neil, Charles Hulten, David Campbell, Timothy Bresnahan, and Richard E. Caves. 1992. "Productivity Dynamics in Manufacturing Plants." *Brookings Papers on Economic Activity: Microeconomics*, 187–267.

Bai, Xue, Kala Krishna, and Hong Ma. 2015. "How You Export Matters: Export Mode, Learning and Productivity in China." NBER Working Paper 21164, National Bureau of Economic Research, Cambridge, MA.

Banerjee, Abhijit V., and Esther Duflo. 2005. "Growth Theory through the Lens of Development Economics." In *Handbook of Economic Growth*, volume 1, edited by Philippe Aghion and Steven N. Durlauf, 473–552. San Diego, CA: Elsevier.

Bartelsman, Eric, John C. Haltiwanger, and Stefano Scarpetta. 2004. "Microeconomic Evidence of Creative Destruction in Industrial and Developing Countries." IZA Discussion Papers 1374, Institute for the Study of Labor (IZA), Bonn, Germany.

———. 2009. "Measuring and Analyzing Cross-country Differences in Firm Dynamics." In *Producer Dynamics: New Evidence from Micro Data*, edited by Timothy Dunne, J. Bradford Jensen, and Mark J. Roberts, 15–76. Chicago: University of Chicago Press.

———. 2013. "Cross-Country Differences in Productivity: The Role of Allocation and Selection." *American Economic Review* 103 (1): 305–34.

Bartelsman, Eric J, Jonathan Haskel, and Ralf Martin. 2008. "Distance to Which Frontier? Evidence on Productivity Convergence from International Firm-Level Data." CEPR Discussion Papers 7032, Center for Economic and Policy Research, Washington, DC.

Bastos, Paulo, and Joana Silva. 2010. "The Quality of a Firm's Exports: Where You Export to Matters." *Journal of International Economics* 82 (2): 99–111.

Bernard, Andrew B., and J. Bradford Jensen. 1995. "Exporters, Jobs, and Wages in U.S. Manufacturing: 1976–1987." *Brookings Papers on Economic Activity, Microeconomics*: 67–119.

———. 1999. "Exceptional Exporter Performance: Cause, Effect, or Both?" *Journal of International Economics* 47(1): 1–25.

Bernard, Andrew B., J. Bradford Jensen, Stephen J. Redding, and Peter K. Schott. 2007. "Firms in International Trade." *Journal of Economic Perspectives* 21 (3): 105–30.

Bond, Steve. 2002. "Dynamic Panel Data Models: A Guide to Microdata Methods and Practice." CeMMAP working papers CWP09/02, Centre for Microdata Methods and Practice, Institute for Fiscal Studies, London.

Cassiman, Bruno, and Reinhilde Veugelers. 2006. "In Search of Complementarity in Innovation Strategy: Internal R&D and External Knowledge Acquisition." *Management Science* 52 (1): 68–82.

De Loecker, Jan. 2007. "Do Exports Generate Higher Productivity? Evidence from Slovenia." *Journal of International Economics* 73 (1): 69–98.

Eaton, Jonathan, Marcela Eslava, Maurice Kugler, and James Tybout. 2008. "Export Dynamics in Colombia: Transaction-Level Evidence." In *The Organization of Firms in a Global Economy*, edited by Elhanan Helpman, Marin Dalia, and Verdier Thierry. Cambridge, MA: Harvard University Press.

Eaton, Jonathan, Samuel Kortum, and Francis Kramarz. 2011. "An Anatomy of International Trade: Evidence From French Firms." *Econometrica* 79 (5): 1453–98.

Fernandes, Ana M. 2007. "Trade Policy, Trade Volumes and Plant-Level Productivity in Colombian Manufacturing Industries." *Journal of International Economics* 71: 52–71.

Foster, Lucia, John C. Haltiwanger, and C. J. Krizan. 2001. "Aggregate Productivity Growth. Lessons from Microeconomic Evidence." In *New Developments in Productivity Analysis*, edited by Charles R. Hulten, Edwin R. Dean, and Michael J. Harper, 303–372. Chicago: University of Chicago Press.

Foster, Lucia, John Haltiwanger, and Chad Syverson. 2008. "Reallocation, Firm Turnover, and Efficiency: Selection on Productivity or Profitability?" *American Economic Review* 98 (1): 394–425.

Girma, Sourafel, and Richard Kneller. 2005. "Convergence in the UK Service Sector: Firm Level Evidence, 1988–1998." *Scottish Journal of Political Economy* 52 (5): 736–46.

Griffith, Rachel, Stephen Redding, and Helen Simpson. 2003. "Productivity Convergence and Foreign Ownership at the Establishment Level." CEP Discussion Papers dp0573, Centre for Economic Performance, London School of Economics.

———. 2009. "Technological Catch-Up and Geographic Proximity." *Journal of Regional Science* 49 (4): 689–720.

Griffith, Rachel, Stephen Redding, Helen Simpson, and John Van Reenen. 2004. "Mapping the Two Faces of R&D: Productivity Growth in a Panel of OECD Industries." *Review of Economics and Statistics* 86 (4): 883–95.

Griliches, Zvi, and Haim Regev. 1995. "Firm Productivity in Israeli Industry 1979–1988." *Journal of Econometrics* 65 (1): 175–203.

Hsieh, Chang-Tai, and Peter J. Klenow. 2009. "Misallocation and Manufacturing TFP in China and India." *Quarterly Journal of Economics* 124 (4): 1403–48.

Iacovone, Leonardo. 2012. "The Better You Are The Stronger It Makes You: Evidence on the Asymmetric Impact of Liberalization." *Journal of Development Economics* 99 (2): 474–85.

Iacovone, Leonardo, and Gustavo A. Crespi. 2010. "Catching Up with the Technological Frontier: Micro-Level Evidence on Growth and Convergence." *Industrial and Corporate Change* 19 (6): 2073–96.

IDB (Inter-American Development Bank). 2010. *The Age of Productivity*. Washington, DC: Palgrave MacMillan.

IMF (International Monetary Fund). 2014. "Regional Economic Outlook Update: Western Hemisphere - Latin America and the Caribbean." Technical Report, International Monetary Fund, Washington, DC.

Madsen, Jakob B. 2014. "Human Capital and the World Technology Frontier." *The Review of Economics and Statistics* 96 (3): 676–92.

Melitz, Marc J., and Sašo Polanec. 2012. "Dynamic Olley-Pakes Productivity Decomposition with Entry and Exit." NBER Working Paper 18182, National Bureau of Economic Research, Cambridge, MA.

Nishida, Mitsukuni, Amil Petrin, and Sašo Polanec. 2013. "Exploring Reallocation's Apparent Weak Contribution to Growth." NBER Working Paper 19012, National Bureau of Economic Research, Cambridge, MA.

Olley, G. Steven, and Ariel Pakes. 1996. "The Dynamics of Productivity in the Telecommunications Equipment Industry." *Econometrica* 64 (6): 1263–97.

Pages, Carmen, Gaëlle Pierre, and Stefano Scarpetta. 2009. *Job Creation in Latin America: Recent Trends and Policy Challenges*. Washington, DC: World Bank.

Pavcnik, Nina. 2002. "Trade Liberalization, Exit, and Productivity Improvements: Evidence from Chilean Plants." *Review of Economic Studies* 69 (1): 245–76.

Restuccia, Diego, and Richard Rogerson. 2008. "Policy Distortions and Aggregate Productivity with Heterogeneous Plants." *Review of Economic Dynamics* 11 (4): 707–20.

———. 2013. "Misallocation and Productivity." *Review of Economic Dynamics* 16 (1): 1–10.

Roberts, Mark J., and James R. Tybout. 1997. "The Decision to Export in Colombia: An Empirical Model of Entry with Sunk Costs." *American Economic Review* 87 (4): 545–64.

Sala-i-Martin, Xavier. 1996. "The Classical Approach to Convergence Analysis." *Economic Journal* 106 (437): 1019–36.

Sosa, Sebastian, Evridiki Tsounta, and Hye S Kim. 2013. "Is the Growth Momentum in Latin America Sustainable?" IMF Working Papers 13/109, International Monetary Fund, Washington, DC.

Syverson, Chad. 2004. "Product Substitutability and Productivity Dispersion." *Review of Economics and Statistics* 86 (2): 534–50.

Topalova, Petia, and Amit Khandelwal. 2011. "Trade Liberalization and Firm Productivity: The Case of India." *The Review of Economics and Statistics* 93 (3): 995–1009.

Tybout, James R., and M. Daniel Westbrook. 1995. "Trade Liberalization and the Dimensions of Efficiency Change in Mexican Manufacturing Industries." *Journal of International Economics* 39 (1–2): 53–78.

Van Biesebroeck, Johannes. 2005. "Exporting Raises Productivity in Sub-Saharan African Manufacturing Firms." *Journal of International Economics* 67 (2): 373–91.

Vandenbussche, Jerome, Philippe Aghion, and Costas Meghir. 2006. "Growth, Distance to Frontier and Composition of Human Capital." *Journal of Economic Growth* 11 (2): 97–127.

CHAPTER 6

Institutions and Returns to Firm Innovation: Focus on Latin America

Ha Nguyen and Patricio A. Jaramillo

Introduction

Firms' innovation and technology adoption are widely considered as the key drivers of economic growth. Google and Apple are prime examples, where their innovation and new products not only contribute to the economy, but also fundamentally change the way we work, entertain, and communicate. Many low- and middle-income countries, via different means, such as foreign direct investment, also try to encourage firms to adopt new technologies and management practices.

Yet many firms do not innovate or adopt new technology. In seeking explanations for this, the conventional focus has been on the obstacles to firms. For example, firms might not have the ability to innovate: they might not have the know-how or access to new technologies.[1] Even if they do have the ability to innovate, firms might not have access to finance for research or adoption of new technology. Girma, Gong, and Görg (2008) show that private and collectively owned firms without foreign capital participation and those with poor access to domestic bank loans innovate less than other firms do.

In this chapter, we do not follow the conventional path to examine the obstacles to firms' innovation, but rather turn our focus to firms' incentives to innovate. This angle, although more neglected, deserves more attention in our view. We argue that in many low- and middle-income countries, firms might not have the incentive to innovate because the reward to innovation is small. For instance, in an environment where property rights are not well protected, a firm's new product can be easily copied.[2] This will significantly reduce the returns to innovation. Lin, Lin, and Song (2010) use the 2003 World Bank Enterprise Survey, which contains more than 2,400 firms in 18 Chinese cities, to show that firms' perception about property rights protection is positively and significantly related to corporate research and development (R&D) activity. Another example is that in a monopolized sector, the incumbent might not need to innovate: its products, good or bad, are the only ones available in the market.

To make our point, we proceed in two steps. In the first step, we estimate the returns to firms' innovation across many low- and middle-income countries. We measure quantitative returns in sales and sales per worker. We find that the returns are low, which implies that the incentive to innovate is small. In the second step, we compare the returns to innovation across countries with different institutional quality. We find that in countries with lower institutional quality (in particular, rule of law, regulatory quality, and property rights protection), the returns to firms' innovation are lower.

Estimating the returns to firms' product innovation is not entirely new. Other studies measure the sales and employment returns to product innovation, but mostly are limited to a single country. Earlier studies focus on the manufacturing sector, such as Van Reene (1997) for the United Kingdom, Greenan and Guellec (2000) for France, Hall, Lotti, and Mairesse (2008) for Italy, and Guadalupe, Kuzmina, and Thomas (2012) for Spain. Recent studies have begun to quantify the returns in low- and middle-income countries, including Benavente and Lauterbach (2008) for Chile, Aboal et al. (2011) for Uruguay, and Crespi and Tacsir (2012) for four Latin American countries.

The main contribution of this chapter is at the second step, where we are the first to show that the returns to innovation are positively correlated with countries' institutional quality. In other words, in countries with lower levels of institutional quality, the returns to product innovation are lower. This is an interesting result, because it implies that an important element for the lack of innovation in low- and middle-income countries is the incentive to innovate. Related to our findings, Goni and Maloney (2014) find that at the country level, the rates of return to R&D expenditures follow an inverted U: they rise with distance to the frontier and then fall thereafter, potentially turning negative for the poorest countries.

The comparison across countries is made possible thanks to the World Bank's Enterprise Surveys. The Enterprise Survey is a firm-level survey of a stratified representative sample of firms. It covers a large set of countries. This survey has been conducted since 2002 and is typically answered by business owners and top managers. The survey covers a broad range of business environment topics, including access to finance, corruption, infrastructure, crime, competition, and performance measures.[3] Enterprise Surveys are stratified with random sampling, where the strata are firm size, business sector, and geographic region within a country. Firm size levels are 5–19 (small), 20–99 (medium), and 100+ employees (large firms).

This chapter focuses on product innovation. A firm is understood to innovate if it introduced a new product or service or upgraded an existing product or service. In our data, only firms in the Latin America (LA) and Europe and Central Asia (ECA) Regions are surveyed about their product innovation. We estimate the percentage change in sales per worker *within* a firm if it has introduced or upgraded its products or services in the three years prior to the survey. The idea is that if a firm innovates, its sales and sales per worker should increase. Ideally one should look at firms' profits as the best measure of returns.

Unfortunately, data on reported profit are much more infrequent than data on sales, and we are concerned about the problem of firms underreporting profits.

Overall, we find that after a firm innovates, its sales per worker increase by 18 percent, although this finding is only significant at the 10 percent level. Focusing on Latin America, we find that the returns to innovation in terms of sales and sales per worker are not statistically different from zero. This finding implies that within a country, the returns to innovation in Latin America are very small. Obviously, without the appropriate instrument to capture the exogenous component of product innovation, the results suffer from biases. We discuss the sources of biases and how we deal with them in more detail in the section on the model. We argue that if the biases are not systematically correlated with countries' institutions, the cross-country comparison of the impacts of institutions—our ultimate interest—is valid.

We find that the returns to innovation are higher in countries with better institutions. Overall, if a country is ranked 1 percentile higher in the world's rule of law and regulatory quality rankings, the sales return to innovation is about 1.7–1.9 percent higher and the sales per worker return is about 0.85–0.95 percent higher. This finding implies that in countries with better rule of law and regulatory quality, firms have greater incentives to innovate. We also zoom in on an important component of the returns to innovation: property rights protection and patent rights protection. We find that in countries with good property rights protection, the return to innovation is higher. We find that in countries with good property and patent rights protection, the returns to innovation are also higher, with about the same magnitude. If we restrict the analysis to Latin America only, the relationship between the returns to innovation and a country's institutional quality is even larger. However, because of the small sample problem, we should take the results with caution. We will return to these points in greater detail.

Data and Variables

The data are the from the World Bank Enterprise Survey, which is a rich, firm-level survey database that provides information about firms' characteristics, such as ownership, size, sector, region in which they are located, annual sales, capacity utilization, employment, competition, etc. To analyze change within a firm, we select firms that appear in at least two surveys (that is, panel data). In our sample, 6,191 firms appear in two surveys and 256 firms appear in three. There are 44 countries with 6,447 unique firms. Annex table 6A.1 provides a list of countries and the number of firms included in the analysis. The innovation module in the survey only exists in LA and ECA. At the end, only LA and ECA countries remain. The data are for 2002 to 2010.

The innovation module for LA is quite different from that for ECA. For LA, we use the following question to obtain data for innovation:

> During the last three years, did the establishment introduce onto the market any new or significantly improved products? (Yes/No/Don't know)

We define a firm as innovating if it answers yes to this question.

For ECA, we use the following two questions in the survey to obtain data for innovation:

Q1: In the last three years, has this establishment introduced new products or services? (Yes/No/Don't answer)

Q2: In the last three years, has this establishment upgraded an existing product line or service? (Yes/No/Don't answer)

We define a firm as innovating if the answer to either of the questions is yes. In this way, we can harmonize the innovation variable between LA and ECA and hence increase the sample size. The downside of this procedure is that for ECA, we mix the returns to an upgraded product and those of a completely new product.[4]

Of the 3,798 observations, 1,855 firms answered yes to either of the innovation questions. Figure 6.1 summarizes the profile of innovating firms by size and region. Large firms are more likely to innovate than small firms. ECA firms are more likely to innovate than LA firms.

We use the following two proxies for firms' performance: real sales and real sales per worker. The proxies are admittedly not ideal measures. The ideal measure would be firms' profit. We do not use firms' profit because data on profits are much spottier,[5] and firms' profit might be underreported in many low- and middle-income countries.

Sales can go up or down with a new product. A new product may cannibalize the business; that is, new products may replace and drive out old products from the market. Or a new product on the market could be a complement for an old product. In any case, successful introduction of a new or upgraded product

Figure 6.1 Firms' Innovation in Emerging Markets Economies
number of firms

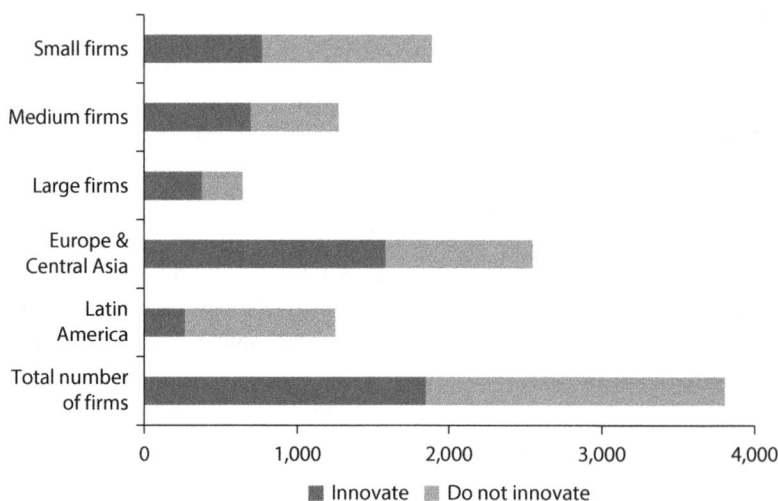

Source: Based on World Bank Enterprise Surveys.

should increase sales. Between the two measures of sales, in our view, sales per worker is a more precise measure of returns to innovation than total sales. A sharper increase in sales per worker implies higher returns.

A firm can answer *yes* to these questions even if the firm just slightly modified its product or adopted a new product from overseas. The firm could also simply copy a product from another domestic firm. As long as the product is new or improved for that firm, the firm can answer *yes* to the questions. In this sense, the understanding of "innovation" is broader than usual, but the implication for the returns to innovation is unchanged: in an environment where a firm can freely copy a product and claim it as a new innovating product, the return to the firm's innovation is not likely high. The return is not high for those that originally come up with the product and it is not high for those that copy it.

Choosing control variables is not straightforward, because we need to find factors that potentially affect firm sales. In addition to change in manager, we found two variables in the questionnaire: whether a firm became an exporter between the two waves of the survey, and whether the number of a firm's competitors increased or decreased. We expect that becoming an exporter will boost the firm's sales and employment, and an increase in competitors will reduce sales and employment. We also include firm size, industry, and country*time fixed effects. The detailed rationale and data sources for these variables are discussed in the next section.

We use rule of law and regulatory quality to proxy for institutional quality. Rule of law reflects perceptions of the extent to which agents have confidence in and abide by the rules of society, and in particular the quality of contract enforcement, property rights, the police, and the courts, as well as the likelihood of crime and violence. Regulatory quality reflects perceptions of the ability of the government to formulate and implement sound policies and regulations that permit and promote private sector development.

The data are from the Worldwide Governance Indicators (WGI). WGI is a research data set that summarizes the views on the quality of governance provided by a large number of enterprises, citizens, and expert survey respondents in high-income and low- and middle-income countries (Kaufmann, Kraay, and Mastruzzi 2010). We use the property rights index from the Heritage Foundation[6] to proxy for property rights protection. The property rights index assesses the extent to which private economic activity is facilitated by an effective legal system and rule-based governance structure in which property and contract rights are reliably respected and enforced. For patent rights protection, we use the patent rights index from Park (2008).

Model

Model Setup
The baseline weighted regression is the following:

$$\Delta y_{ijt} = \alpha + \delta D_{ijt}^{innov} + \beta X_{ijt} + \mu_{jt}\left(f_j \cdot f_t\right) + \mu_s\left(f_s\right) + \varepsilon_{it}$$

where $\Delta y_{ijt} = \ln(y_{ijt}) - \ln(y_{ijt-1})$ is the dependent variable, and y_{ijt} are sales, employment, and sales per worker of firm i in country j at time t. D_{ijt}^{innov} equals 1 if firm i in country j innovates between time t and time $t-1$. The interactive dummy $f_j \cdot f_t$ captures the macroeconomic conditions for country j at time t. The dummy f_s captures the sector fixed effects. X_{jit} are different firm-level control variables.

The extended regression (to interact with various institutional variables) is the following:

$$\Delta y_{ijt} = \alpha + \delta\, D_{ijt}^{innov} + \mu\left(D_{ijt}^{innov} \cdot Ins_j\right) + \beta X_{ijt} + \mu_{jt}\left(f_j \cdot f_t\right) + \mu_s\left(f_s\right) + \varepsilon_{it}$$

where Ins_j is the institutional variable for country j. Note that institutional variables here are time-invariant. Since the surveys are typically very close together, the institutional quality rarely changes. $D_{ijt}^{innov} \cdot Ins_j$ is the interaction between a country's institutional variables and a firm's innovation. We ultimately are interested in μ.

Since the data are collected by the stratified random sampling method, all the regressions are weighted accordingly to restore representativeness. In addition, we cluster the standard errors at the country level to capture potential correlations between the error terms, and allow for heteroscedasticity (that is, having robust standard errors).

Dependent variables:

- Log of real sales (sales divided by the price level)
- Log of real sales per full-time employee

Explanatory variables:

- *Innovation:* whether a firm introduced products or services or upgraded its products or services in the past three years. This is problematic for our regression if the two rounds of the survey are less than three years apart. For this reason, we only keep countries that have surveys more than three years apart.
- *Changing manager:* if a firm changed its manager between the two waves of the survey. This variable captures potential other restructuring activities in addition to innovation. There is no direct way to know if a firm changes its manager. We indirectly guess by using the manager's experience (as the firms are asked about the manager's experience). We identify whether a firm changed managers by comparing the change in the experience of the managers and the years between the two surveys. If the change in experience years is different from the change in years, we conclude that the firm changed its manager. For example, at the first round of the survey in 2005, the firm's manager had 10 years of experience; at the second round of survey in 2009, the firm's manager had 20 years of experience. Since $\Delta year_{EXPERIENCE}$ is greater than $\Delta year_{SURVEY}$, we conclude that the firm must have changed its manager between the two rounds of the survey.

We acknowledge that there is a possibility that the manager might not remember exactly his or her years of experience. As a robustness check, we allow for that possibility by loosening the restriction: only when $year_{EXPERIENCE}$ is greater than $year_{SURVEY} + 1$ or smaller than $year_{SURVEY} - 1$ can we conclude that the firm changed its manager. The variable is quite robust: if we follow the original criteria, we find that 3,495 of 6,447 (54.2 percent) firms changed their managers; if we follow the less restrictive criteria, we find that 2,616 (40.5 percent) of the firms changed their managers. In the regression, we use the original criteria.

- *Becoming an exporter:* this dummy variable equals 1 if a firm becomes an exporter between the two waves of the survey; it equals 0 otherwise.
- *Increasing number of competitors:* this dummy variable equals 1 if the firm's number of competitors increases between the two waves of the survey; it equals 0 otherwise.
- *Firm size:* small (0–20 full-time employees), medium (21–100 employees), and large (more than 100 employees).
- *Rule of law:* percentile rank of the country. We calculate the ranking from the entire population of countries provided by the WGI. The rank is 100 for the highest ranked countries and 1 for the lowest ranked. The detailed rankings of countries for rule of law and other institutional variables are shown in annex table 6A.2.
- *Regulatory quality:* percentile rank of the country. We calculate the ranking from the entire population of countries provided by the WGI. The rank is 100 for the highest ranked countries and 1 for the lowest ranked.
- *Property rights:* percentile rank of the country. We calculate the ranking from the entire population of countries provided by the Heritage Foundation. The rank is 100 for the highest ranked countries and 1 for the lowest ranked.
- *Patent protection:* percentile rank of the country (by our own calculation from the entire population of countries). The rank is 100 for the highest ranked countries and 1 for the lowest ranked. The data are a proxy for how well a patent is protected in a country. The data are from Park (2008). The variable is the sum of five separate scores for coverage (inventions that are patentable), membership in international treaties, duration of protection, enforcement mechanism, and restrictions (Park 2008).
- *Sector fixed effects:* two-digit International Standard Industrial Classification revision 3. This variable captures industry-specific characteristics that may affect returns to innovation. For example, it might be argued that a new product in electronics is likely to have better sales than a new line of shoes.
- *Country*time fixed effects:* captures a country's macroeconomic context.

Potential Estimation Biases

It is difficult to isolate and capture exogenous sources of innovation. There are several issues when it comes to measuring the impact of innovation. The first

Understanding the Income and Efficiency Gap in Latin America and the Caribbean
http://dx.doi.org/10.1596/978-1-4648-0450-2

is a concern that inherently good firms in general will do better than bad firms in sales, and at the same time be more likely to innovate. In other words, the correlation between innovation and firm performance might be driven by unobserved characteristics of the firms. We address this issue with the use of panel data: we only consider change in sales within the same firm, not across firms. By looking for change within a firm, we effectively control for firms' time-invariant characteristics.

The second issue is that of omitted variables. We will not be able to capture any unobserved change in firms' characteristics between the two waves of the survey. For example, a firm might go through a restructuring and at the same time introduce a new product. The observed change in sales and employment could then be the result of innovation and restructuring. In our regression, we try our best to capture unobserved changes by controlling for change in the top manager. We include a dummy that equals 1 if the firm changes the manager between the two waves of the survey. Many changes in a firm's structure, management style, or marketing strategies come from a new manager (see Bloom and Van Reenen 2010).

Another concern is the issue of reverse causality between change in sales and innovation. It could be argued that perhaps changes in sales also affect innovation. For example, when a firm witnesses declines in sales and market share, it might want to introduce a new product or service to halt the declines. In this case, the correlation between innovation and the change in sales would tend to be negative (a negative change in sales leads to a positive change in innovation). The ordinary least squares results then would underestimate the true impacts of innovation on sales and employment. The reverse causality is more severe if the innovation process is quick; for example, when sales decline, the decision to innovate and the introduction of a new product take place in the same period. The reverse causality is less severe if the innovation process takes time. If there is a "time-to-build" period between when the innovation decision is made and when a new product is introduced, the introduction of a new or improved product is likely too late for and hence uncorrelated with the decline in sales.

None of the variables available in the survey can serve as a good instrumental variable for innovation. An ideal instrument should capture firms' perception about protection of *intellectual* rights. Unfortunately, the variable is not available. The best two candidates for the instrument that we can find are (1) firms' concern about competition practice in the informal sector and (2) the amount of R&D a firm invested in the previous wave of the survey. These instruments are still flawed because they violate the exclusion restriction. Regarding instrument 1, although a large part of the concern about the informal sector has to do with infringement of intellectual property rights, there may also be concern about labor or tax practices, which can affect the firm's non-innovation investment activities. Regarding instrument 2, it is not a good instrument if the decision to do R&D also correlates with other non-innovation activities of the firm.

Having discussed all the drawbacks of the estimation, it is important to note that we are not interested in the precision of the return per se. We are instead interested in comparing the returns across countries. To the extent that the biases are not systematically correlated with countries' institutional characteristics, the comparison across countries is valid.

Regression Results

Returns to Innovation

Table 6.1 presents the overall results when we pool all countries in ECA and LA together, for a total of 1,879 unique firms. Overall, only sales per worker is marginally significant at the 10 percent level: an innovating firm sees its sales per worker increase by 18.3 percent. Since there are biases, it is safer to consider this as an association, not causation. The dummy variables more competitors and firm size are significant and have the expected signs. Firms that have more competitors between the two surveys see weaker growth in sales than those that have fewer competitors. In addition, small and medium firms see significantly weaker growth in sales than large firms do. This finding is counterintuitive if it is expected that firms should converge to an optimal size. Our conjecture is that in low- and middle-income countries, many obstacles (such as connection to politicians) prevent small firms from growing as fast as larger firms. The dummy for

Table 6.1 Returns to Innovation: All Countries

Variable	$\Delta ln(sales)$		$\Delta ln(sales/labor)$	
Innovation	0.242	0.147	0.198*	0.183*
	(0.146)	(0.149)	(0.109)	(0.0967)
New top manager		−1.308***		−1.475***
		(0.328)		(0.366)
Exporter		0.0550		0.0274
		(0.101)		(0.166)
More competitors		−0.902***		−0.697***
		(0.169)		(0.0990)
Small size		−1.483***		−0.541**
		(0.324)		(0.215)
Medium size		−1.136***		−0.555***
		(0.170)		(0.160)
Constant	1.355	4.142***	−0.0582	1.959***
	(1.202)	(1.365)	(0.109)	(0.568)
Year*Country FE	Yes	Yes	Yes	Yes
Industry FE	Yes	Yes	Yes	Yes
No. of observations	1,879	1,874	1,870	1,870
R-Squared	0.456	0.493	0.450	0.462

Source: World Bank calculations.
Note: FE = fixed effects.
***$p < 0.01$, **$p < 0.05$, *$p < 0.1$.
Clustered robust standard errors by country in parentheses.

new top manager is significant and negative. This could reflect adjustment costs to the restructuring associated with a new manager.[7]

Focusing on Latin America, table 6.2 shows that the returns to innovation in terms of sales and sales per worker for Latin American firms are not statistically different from zero. This finding implies that within a country, the returns to innovation in Latin America are very small. We interact innovation with the LA dummy, but the interacting coefficient is not significant, implying that the return to innovation in LA is not significantly different from that in ECA (results not shown).

An important exercise is to examine the returns to innovation for monopolists. It is usually argued that monopolists have little incentive to innovate: their product, good or bad, is the only one available in the market and they have already captured the market anyway. For example, if poor flight service is the only option available for travelers, improved flight service will not generate much return to an airline monopolist because it will not bring in many new passengers. Table 6.3 shows the returns to innovation to monopolists compared with non-monopolists. We define monopolists as those that have zero competitors. We show that the conventional wisdom is correct: after a monopolist innovates, its percentage increase in sales per worker is 90 percent (exp(−2.27)) lower than the percentage increase for a nonmonopolist. We expect the result to be

Table 6.2 Returns to Innovation: Latin American Countries

Variable	$\Delta ln(sales)$		$\Delta ln(sales/labor)$	
Innovation	−0.379	−0.597	−0.541	−0.435
	(0.254)	(0.325)	(0.319)	(0.362)
New top manager		−1.466***		−1.677***
		(0.197)		(0.224)
Exporter		0.180***		0.0433*
		(0.0353)		(0.0161)
More competitors		−1.054***		−0.795***
		(0.00106)		(0.000562)
Small size		−2.157***		−0.919***
		(0.0842)		(0.0386)
Medium size		−1.266***		−0.713***
		(0.00970)		(0.00747)
Constant	0.394	5.252***	0.681	2.922***
	(0.254)	(1.130)	(0.319)	(0.425)
Year*Country FE	Yes	Yes	Yes	Yes
Industry FE	Yes	Yes	Yes	Yes
No. of observations	547	546	546	543
R-Squared	0.147	0.224	0.224	0.163

Source: World Bank calculations.
Note: FE = fixed effects.
***$p < 0.01$, **$p < 0.05$, *$p < 0.1$.
Clustered robust standard errors by country in parentheses.

Table 6.3 Returns to Innovation for Monopolists

Variable	Δln(sales)		Δln(sales/labor)	
Innovation	0.111	−0.00814	−0.0483	−0.0451
	(0.288)	(0.323)	(0.252)	(0.283)
Monopolist*Innovation	−2.819*	−2.463	−2.472**	−2.376**
	(1.434)	(1.561)	(1.043)	(1.076)
Monopolist	1.614	1.258	1.005	0.848
	(1.357)	(1.526)	(0.892)	(0.969)
New top manager		−1.497***		−1.710***
		(0.337)		(0.383)
Exporter		0.0163		−0.125
		(0.129)		(0.112)
More competitors		−1.029***		−0.826***
		(0.0971)		(0.0555)
Small size		−1.569***		−0.656**
		(0.445)		(0.250)
Medium size		−1.151***		−0.584***
		(0.0891)		(0.0707)
Constant	−0.0967	−1.497	0.188	2.604***
	(0.288)	(1.255)	(0.252)	(0.432)
Year*Country FE	Yes	Yes	Yes	Yes
Industry FE	Yes	Yes	Yes	Yes
No. of observations	970	969	965	965
R-Squared	0.261	0.317	0.248	0.270

Source: World Bank calculations.
Note: FE = fixed effects.
***$p < 0.01$, **$p < 0.05$, *$p < 0.1$.
Clustered robust standard errors by country in parentheses.

stronger if we consider upgraded products alone, as we think that an improved product does not likely improve a monopolist's profits, whereas a completely new product might do so.

Returns to Innovation with Institutional Quality

This section focuses on whether the returns to innovation are higher in countries with better institutional quality. The argument is that in a better institutional environment, where property rights are protected, the courts are reliable, regulatory uncertainty is small, etc., firms' investment in bringing new products and services to the market will yield a good return. By contrast, in an environment where a new product can easily be copied at little enforceable punishment or the government's policy is highly volatile, the returns to innovation will likely be small. We proxy for institutional quality by rule of law and regulatory quality. These two variables are highly correlated and commonly used to capture institutional quality.

We show that, in general, in a country with better rule of law, the return to innovation is higher. Table 6.4 shows that if a country is placed 1 percentile

Table 6.4 Returns to Innovation with Rule of Law: All Countries

Variable	Δln(sales)		Δln(sales/labor)	
Innovation	−0.778*	−0.865**	−0.315	−0.330
	(0.443)	(0.407)	(0.256)	(0.234)
Rule of law*Innovation	0.0192**	0.0191***	0.00965**	0.00967**
	(0.00723)	(0.00682)	(0.00421)	(0.00388)
New top manager		−1.274***		−1.457***
		(0.371)		(0.389)
Exporter		0.0381		0.0187
		(0.0989)		(0.161)
More competitors		−0.902***		−0.697***
		(0.170)		(0.0991)
Small size		−1.480***		−0.540**
		(0.322)		(0.214)
Medium size		−1.139***		−0.557***
		(0.167)		(0.158)
Constant	1.716*	4.463***	1.714	3.720***
	(0.946)	(1.180)	(1.033)	(1.283)
Year*Country FE	Yes	Yes	Yes	Yes
Industry FE	Yes	Yes	Yes	Yes
No. of observations	1,879	1,874	1,870	1,870
R-Squared	0.458	0.495	0.450	0.462

Source: World Bank calculations.
Note: FE = fixed effects.
***$p < 0.01$, **$p < 0.05$, *$p < 0.1$.
Clustered robust standard errors by country in parentheses.

higher in the world's rule-of-law ranking (better rule of law), the sales return to a new and improved product is 1.91 percent higher, and the sales per worker return—which is our focus—is 0.97 percent higher. Similarly, if a country is placed 1 percentile higher in the world's regulatory quality, the sales return to innovation is 1.77 percent higher, and the sales per worker return is 0.86 percent higher (table 6.5).

The coefficients for the innovation variable become negative or insignificant. The first row in tables 6.4 and 6.5 shows that the sales per worker return to innovation for the lowest ranked country is essentially zero.

Focusing on LA, the impacts of rule of law and regulatory quality are more significant and of a larger magnitude compared with the pooled sample (tables 6.6 and 6.7). If a country in LA is placed 1 percentile higher in the world's rule-of-law ranking, the sales return to innovation is 12.7 percent higher and the sales per worker return is 11.4 percent higher (table 6.6). If a country in LA is placed 1 percentile higher in the world's rule-of-law ranking, the sales return to innovation is 3.9 percent higher, whereas the sales per worker return is 5.98 percent higher. The results imply a more detrimental impact of poor rule of law and regulatory quality on firms' incentive to innovate in LA. However, the results should be taken with caution given the small number of countries covered in Latin America.[8]

Table 6.5 Returns to Innovation with Regulatory Quality: All Countries

Variable	Δln(sales)		Δln(sales/labor)	
Innovation	−0.848	−0.975*	−0.339	−0.360
	(0.621)	(0.572)	(0.348)	(0.312)
RegQual*Innovation	0.0172*	0.0177**	0.00846	0.00857*
	(0.00865)	(0.00802)	(0.00521)	(0.00472)
New top manager		−1.222***		−1.432***
		(0.424)		(0.414)
Exporter		0.0445		0.0222
		(0.0975)		(0.162)
More competitors		−0.903***		−0.697***
		(0.170)		(0.0991)
Small size		−1.485***		−0.542**
		(0.320)		(0.214)
Medium size		−1.141***		−0.558***
		(0.166)		(0.158)
Constant	1.746*	4.461***	1.725	3.711***
	(0.941)	(1.203)	(1.027)	(1.295)
Year*Country FE	Yes	Yes	Yes	Yes
Industry FE	Yes	Yes	Yes	Yes
No. of observations	1,879	1,874	1,870	1,870
R-Squared	0.458	0.495	0.450	0.462

Source: World Bank calculations.
Note: FE = fixed effects.
***$p < 0.01$, **$p < 0.05$, *$p < 0.1$.
Clustered robust standard errors by country in parentheses.

Table 6.6 Returns to Innovation with Rule of Law: Latin America

Variable	Δln(sales)		Δln(sales/labor)	
Innovation	−2.246***	−2.476***	−2.236***	−2.130***
	(0.268)	(0.355)	(0.220)	(0.247)
Rule of law*Innovation	0.126***	0.127***	0.114***	0.114***
	(0.0142)	(0.0136)	(0.0233)	(0.0225)
New top manager		−1.467***		−1.678***
		(0.196)		(0.224)
Exporter		0.179***		0.0424*
		(0.0355)		(0.0164)
More competitors		−1.054***		−0.795***
		(0.00107)		(0.000567)
Small size		−2.157***		−0.920***
		(0.0840)		(0.0383)
Medium size		−1.266***		−0.713***
		(0.00977)		(0.00754)
Constant	0.495	5.303***	0.773	3.015***
	(0.340)	(1.147)	(0.367)	(0.494)

table continues next page

Table 6.6 **Returns to Innovation with Rule of Law: Latin America** *(continued)*

Variable	Δln(sales)		Δln(sales/labor)	
Year*Country FE	Yes	Yes	Yes	Yes
Industry FE	Yes	Yes	Yes	Yes
No. of observations	547	546	543	543
R-Squared	0.147	0.224	0.135	0.163

Source: World Bank calculations.
Note: FE = fixed effects.
***p < 0.01, **p < 0.05, *p < 0.1.
Clustered robust standard errors by country in parentheses.

Table 6.7 **Returns to Innovation with Regulatory Quality: Latin America**

Variable	Δln(sales)		Δln(sales/labor)	
Innovation	−1.220*	−1.427*	−1.851**	−1.718**
	(0.454)	(0.555)	(0.459)	(0.547)
RegQual*Innovation	0.0393**	0.0388**	0.0612***	0.0598***
	(0.00956)	(0.00974)	(0.00759)	(0.00860)
New top manager		−1.456***		−1.660***
		(0.209)		(0.245)
Exporter		0.185***		0.0505***
		(0.0311)		(0.00902)
More competitors		−1.054***		−0.796***
		(0.000990)		(0.000442)
Small size		−2.156***		−0.918***
		(0.0850)		(0.0397)
Medium size		−1.266***		−0.714***
		(0.00955)		(0.00722)
Constant	0.605	5.343***	1.012*	3.224***
	(0.372)	(1.142)	(0.426)	(0.616)
Year*Country FE	Yes	Yes	Yes	Yes
Industry FE	Yes	Yes	Yes	Yes
No. of observations	547	546	543	543
R-Squared	0.147	0.224	0.135	0.164

Source: World Bank calculations.
Note: FE = fixed effects.
***p < 0.01, **p < 0.05, *p < 0.1.
Clustered robust standard errors by country in parentheses.

Returns to Innovation with Property Rights Protection

Since rule of law and regulatory quality are too general to imply specific policy recommendations, this section zooms in on one particular component of institutional quality that we think is most obvious in affecting the returns to innovation. It is property rights protection. For our analysis, we use the property rights index from the Heritage Foundation[9] to proxy for property rights protection. The property rights index assesses the extent to which private economic activity is facilitated by an effective legal system and rule-based governance structure in which property and contract rights are reliably respected and enforced.

The property rights here include intellectual property rights and more general property rights. Although laws and enforcement for intellectual property rights provide necessary protection of the fruits of R&D (patents, copyrights, trademarks, etc.), broader property rights protection and contract enforcement protect investments that are complementary to R&D expenditures, especially during the post-R&D stage, and hence help realize the commercial value of R&D. In a country where property rights are not well protected, a new product or service that is deemed profitable will be easily copied; thus, the return to the innovating firm is reduced. By contrast, if property rights are well protected, the firm can extract a good return from its new products or services.

Tables 6.8 and 6.9 present the overall results across countries and those for Latin America, respectively. Overall, if a country is placed 1 percentile higher in the ranking, the sales per worker return to innovation for an innovating firm will be 0.91 percent higher and the sales return is 1.53 percent higher. Overall, the magnitude of the impact is similar to that in the regulatory quality and rule of law regressions. Across Latin American countries, we do not see a significant impact of property rights protection on the sales return to innovation.

Table 6.8 Innovation with Property Rights Protection: All Countries

Variable	$\Delta ln(sales)$		$\Delta ln(sales/labor)$	
Innovation	−0.635	−0.676	−0.307	−0.305
	(0.466)	(0.445)	(0.274)	(0.249)
PRP*Innovation	0.0163**	0.0153**	0.00937**	0.00909**
	(0.00748)	(0.00728)	(0.00428)	(0.00396)
New top manager		−1.274***		−1.454***
		(0.368)		(0.391)
Exporter		0.0406		0.0188
		(0.101)		(0.163)
More competitors		−0.901***		−0.696***
		(0.170)		(0.0990)
Small size		−1.477***		−0.538**
		(0.325)		(0.215)
Medium size		−1.137***		−0.556***
		(0.169)		(0.159)
Constant	1.643	4.372***	1.698	3.694***
	(0.996)	(1.226)	(1.042)	(1.294)
Year*Country FE	Yes	Yes	Yes	Yes
Industry FE	Yes	Yes	Yes	Yes
No. of observations	1,879	1,874	1,870	1,870
R-Squared	0.458	0.495	0.450	0.462

Source: World Bank calculations.
Note: FE = fixed effects; PRP = property rights protection.
***$p < 0.01$, **$p < 0.05$, *$p < 0.1$.
Clustered robust standard errors by country in parentheses.

Table 6.9 Returns to Innovation with Property Rights Protection: Latin America

Variable	$\Delta ln(sales)$		$\Delta ln(sales/labor)$	
Innovation	−1.039**	−1.235**	−2.038***	−1.883**
	(0.349)	(0.350)	(0.420)	(0.463)
PRP*Innovation	0.0336	0.0325	0.0763*	0.0737*
	(0.0270)	(0.0277)	(0.0297)	(0.0311)
New top manager		−1.460***		−1.662***
		(0.205)		(0.243)
Exporter		0.183***		0.0504***
		(0.0320)		(0.00910)
More competitors		−1.054***		−0.796***
		(0.00100)		(0.000442)
Small size		−2.156***		−0.918***
		(0.0848)		(0.0398)
Medium size		−1.266***		−0.714***
		(0.00957)		(0.00718)
Constant	0.481*	5.287***	0.881**	3.095***
	(0.204)	(1.106)	(0.249)	(0.449)
Year*Country FE	Yes	Yes	Yes	Yes
Industry FE	Yes	Yes	Yes	Yes
No. of observations	547	546	543	543
R-Squared	0.147	0.224	0.135	0.164

Source: World Bank calculations.
Note: FE = fixed effects; PRP = property rights protection.
***$p < 0.01$, **$p < 0.05$, *$p < 0.1$.
Clustered robust standard errors by country in parentheses.

However, property rights protection has a positive and significant impact on the sales per worker return to innovation. In Latin America, if a country is placed 1 percentile higher in the ranking, we expect the sales per worker return to increase by 7.37 percent. The magnitude is also much larger than that obtained from the sample for all countries. However, the coefficient is only significant at the 10 percent level.

Returns to Innovation with Patent Protection

In this section, we focus on what is arguably the most relevant factor that affects innovation: patent protection. The index is provided in Park (2008). It is "the unweighted sum of five separate scores for: coverage (inventions that are patentable); membership in international treaties; duration of protection; enforcement mechanisms; and restrictions (for example, compulsory licensing in the event that a patented invention is not sufficiently exploited)" (Park 2008, 761).

Table 6.10 shows the relationship between the returns to innovation and patent rights ranking (where 1 is for the lowest ranked country and 100 is for the highest ranked). We can see that the sales return for innovating firms is significantly smaller for countries with lower patent rights protection: if a country is 1 rank lower, the sales return is 3.49 percent lower. The magnitude is relatively

Table 6.10 Returns to Innovation with the Index of Patent Rights: All Countries

Variable	Δln(sales)		Δln(sales/labor)	
Innovation	−2.266	−2.584*	−0.0674	0.0140
	(1.389)	(1.329)	(1.071)	(1.027)
Patents rights*Innovation	0.0320	0.0349*	0.00197	0.00253
	(0.0183)	(0.0172)	(0.0148)	(0.0141)
New top manager		−1.484***		−1.700***
		(0.194)		(0.184)
Exporter		0.0407		−0.0374
		(0.112)		(0.169)
More competitors		−0.918***		−0.709***
		(0.167)		(0.0961)
Small size		−1.597***		−0.598**
		(0.355)		(0.222)
Medium size		−1.209***		−0.598***
		(0.123)		(0.127)
Constant	1.575	3.014***	1.535	3.841**
	(1.057)	(0.377)	(1.186)	(1.294)
Year*Country FE	Yes	Yes	Yes	Yes
Industry FE	Yes	Yes	Yes	Yes
No. of observations	1,198	1,193	1,189	1,189
R-Squared	0.306	0.359	0.262	0.280

Source: World Bank calculations.
Note: FE = fixed effects.
***$p < 0.01$, **$p < 0.05$, *$p < 0.1$.
Clustered robust standard errors by country in parentheses.

large, compared with the findings for the other institutional variables. However, the return in terms of sales per worker is not significantly correlated with the patent rights ranking, although the sign is correct. It is possible that measurement errors inflate the standard errors, making the coefficient insignificant. It is also possible that patent rights protection indeed has a smaller impact on the return compared with other components of property rights protection. For example, if firms in low- and middle-income countries do not habitually file for patent protection, the index would be irrelevant. We repeated the exercise for countries in LA; however, probably because of the small sample size, the results are not significant and have the wrong sign and therefore are not shown here.

Conclusion

Why firms do not innovate or adopt new technologies remains an important and interesting question. In this chapter, we did not take the usual route of examining the obstacles to firms' innovation, but focused on firms' incentives to innovate. We estimated the returns to innovation across countries and compared the returns in countries with different levels of institutional quality. The analysis found that in poorer countries, a large part of the lack of innovation is caused by firms' unwillingness to innovate: the poor institutional environment discourages firms from investing in researching new products.

The magnitude of the estimated gain is large. If a country can improve by 10 ranks in the world percentile ranking, the return to innovation in terms of sales per worker for firms in that country could be 8 to 10 percent higher. This finding calls for policies that go beyond addressing obstacles to firms' ability to innovate. Policies also have to place a strong focus on institutional factors (such as property rights protection) to address firms' incentive problem.

Annex 6A

Table 6A.1 List of Countries

	Country name	Number of unique firms	Percent
Latin America		1,229	32.73
	Brazil	426	11.34
	Ecuador	142	3.78
	Guatemala	210	5.59
	Honduras	194	5.17
	Nicaragua	213	5.67
	Venezuela, RB	44	1.17
Europe and Central Asia		2,526	67.27
	Albania	48	1.28
	Armenia	107	2.85
	Azerbaijan	107	2.85
	Belarus	77	2.05
	Bosnia and Herzegovina	51	1.36
	Bulgaria	131	3.49
	Croatia	72	1.92
	Czech Republic	40	1.07
	Estonia	87	2.32
	Georgia	68	1.81
	Hungary	75	2.00
	Kazakhstan	86	2.29
	Kyrgyz Republic	73	1.94
	Latvia	53	1.41
	Lithuania	58	1.54
	Macedonia, FYR	88	2.34
	Moldova	114	3.04
	Montenegro	4	0.11
	Poland	114	3.04
	Romania	95	2.53
	Russian Federation	61	1.62
	Serbia	90	2.40
	Slovak Republic	35	0.93
	Slovenia	80	2.13
	Tajikistan	55	1.46

table continues next page

Table 6A.1 List of Countries *(continued)*

	Country name	Number of unique firms	Percent
	Turkey	391	10.41
	Ukraine	173	4.61
	Uzbekistan	93	2.48
Total		3,755	100.00

Source: World Bank calculations.

Table 6A.2 Percentile Ranking by Country for Different Variables

Country	Rule of law	Regulatory quality	Property right protection	Patent right protection
Brazil	56	56	67	60
Ecuador	14	16	17	64
Guatemala	15	48	37	44
Honduras	20	50	37	34
Nicaragua	30	40	10	34
Venezuela, RB	2	7	1	48
Albania	38	59	37	–
Armenia	43	59	37	–
Azerbaijan	22	38	23	–
Belarus	15	10	88	–
Bosnia and Herzegovina	46	52	17	–
Bulgaria	52	71	37	90
Croatia	61	70	56	–
Czech Republic	81	86	82	83
Estonia	86	91	89	–
Georgia	51	74	62	–
Hungary	73	82	78	88
Kazakhstan	32	43	49	–
Kyrgyz Republic	10	45	17	–
Latvia	74	80	67	–
Lithuania	73	79	75	70
Macedonia, FYR	49	60	49	–
Moldova	45	51	56	–
Montenegro	56	52	56	–
Poland	72	80	75	78
Romania	57	75	56	75
Russian Federation	26	39	23	62
Serbia	47	53	56	–
Slovak Republic	69	81	67	78
Slovenia	84	73	75	–
Tajikistan	11	19	17	–
Turkey	58	66	67	71
Ukraine	23	32	37	62
Uzbekistan	6	4	10	–

Sources: World Governance Indicators (for rule of law and regulatory quality); calculations based on data from the World Bank's Doing Business Survey (for the cost of starting a business) and on the Heritage Foundation (for property rights protection).

Understanding the Income and Efficiency Gap in Latin America and the Caribbean
http://dx.doi.org/10.1596/978-1-4648-0450-2

Notes

1. Burstein and Monge-Naranjo (2009) show that low- and middle-income countries' output can grow significantly when they eliminate all barriers to foreign know-how.

2. See Branstetter, Fisman, and Foley (2006).

3. Methodological details can be found at http://www.enterprisesurveys.org/~/media /FPDKM/EnterpriseSurveys/Documents/Methodology.

4. See Akcigit and Kerr (2010) for a discussion of the innovation implications of completely new products and improved products.

5. In the data set, 33 percent of the firms do not report labor costs, and 60 percent of firms do not report costs of intermediate inputs and raw materials. The vast majority of firms do not report costs of fuel, electricity, and water.

6. http://www.heritage.org/index/property-rights.

7. Alternatively, reverse causality might be at play: firms with declining performance hire new managers.

8. For sales and sales per worker, there are five countries in the sample: Brazil, Ecuador, Guatemala, Honduras, and Nicaragua. For employment there are six countries: these five and República Bolivariana de Venezuela.

9. http://www.heritage.org/index/property-rights.

Bibliography

Aboal, D., P. Garda, B. Lanzilotta, and M. Perera. 2011. "Innovation, Firm Size, Technology Intensity, and Employment Generation in Uruguay: The Microeconometric Evidence." IDB Technical Notes No. IDB-TN-314, Inter-American Development Bank, Washington, DC.

Akcigit, U., and W. Kerr. 2010. "Growth through Heterogenous Innovations." NBER Working Paper 16433, National Bureau of Economic Research, Cambridge, MA.

Benavente, J. M., and Rodolfo Lauterbach. 2008. "Technological Innovation and Employment: Complements or Substitutes?" *European Journal of Development Research* 20 (2): 318–29.

Bloom, Nicholas, and John Van Reenen. 2010. "Why Do Management Practices Differ across Firms and Countries?" *Journal of Economic Perspectives* 24 (1): 203–24.

Branstetter, Lee G., Raymond Fisman, and C. Fritz Foley. 2006. "Do Stronger Intellectual Property Rights Increase International Technology Transfer? Empirical Evidence from U.S. Firm-Level Panel Data." *Quarterly Journal of Economics* 121 (1): 321–49.

Burstein, Ariel T., and Alexander Monge-Naranjo. 2009. "Foreign Know-How, Firm Control, and the Income of Developing Countries." *Quarterly Journal of Economics* 124 (1): 149–95.

Crespi, G., and Ezequiel Tacsir. 2012. "Effects of Innovation on Employment in Latin America." *IDB Publications* 78759, Inter-American Development Bank, Washington DC.

Girma, Sourafel, Yundan Gong, and Holger Görg. 2008. "Foreign Direct Investment, Access to Finance, and Innovation Activity in Chinese Enterprises." *World Bank Economic Review* 22 (2): 367–82.

Goni, Edwin, and William F. Maloney. 2014. "Why Don't Poor Countries Do R&D?" Policy Research Working Paper 6811, World Bank, Washington, DC.

Greenan, N., and D. Guellec. 2000. "Technological Innovation and Employment Reallocation." *LABOUR* 14 (4): 547–90.

Guadalupe, M., Olga Kuzmina, and Catherine Thomas. 2012. "Innovation and Foreign Ownership." *American Economic Review* 102 (7): 3594–627.

Hall, B. H., F. Lotti, and J. Mairesse. 2008. "Employment, Innovation, and Productivity: Evidence from Italian Microdata." *Industrial and Corporate Change* 17: 813–39.

Kaufmann, Daniel, Aart Kraay, and Massimo Mastruzzi. 2010. "The Worldwide Governance Indicators: A Summary of Methodology, Data and Analytical Issues." Policy Research Working Paper 5430, World Bank, Washington, DC.

Lin, Chen, Ping Lin, and Frank Song. 2010. "Property Rights Protection and Corporate R&D: Evidence from China." *Journal of Development Economics* 93 (1): 49–62.

Park, Walter G. 2008. "International Patent Protection: 1960–2005." *Research Policy* 37 (4): 761–66.

Van Reene, John. 1997. "Employment and Technological Innovation: Evidence from UK Manufacturing Firms." *Journal of Labor Economics* 15 (2): 255–84.

CHAPTER 7

Convergence, Poverty, and Macroeconomic Volatility: A Latin American Perspective

Konstantin M. Wacker

> *Until recently, inequality was not seen as having major implications for macroeconomic developments. This belief is increasingly called into question.*
>
> —Olivier Blanchard

Introduction

Historically, the Latin America and the Caribbean (LAC) Region has been notorious for macroeconomic volatility and inequality, with the latter reflected in a high poverty incidence given LAC's income level. Previous research has argued that both these factors can hamper income growth.[1] More recently, Crespo-Cuaresma, Klasen, and Wacker (henceforth CCKW 2013) suggest that the interaction of these two effects prevents countries from converging in poverty rates (it prevents countries with higher poverty from achieving faster progress in poverty reduction than those with lower poverty). Moreover, CCKW argue that this effect operates via income convergence (that is, poverty and macroeconomic volatility prevent income convergence).

Based on these findings, high poverty and volatility are potential factors that have prevented LAC from converging toward higher income levels. To investigate this possible explanation for LAC's income gap, this chapter adds to previous research in three regards. First, the chapter explores in more detail the economic rationale for why the interaction of poverty and volatility may prevent income convergence. Second, the chapter substantiates the findings of CCKW (2013) by using conventional macroeconomic instead of microeconomic data, and poverty gaps instead of the headcount ratio.[2] Third, the chapter assesses in more detail what these results imply for LAC.

A key argument of this chapter is that poverty, as a lack of opportunity, and volatility/uncertainty decrease the capacity and incentives to invest, which undermines the otherwise high returns to investment in countries at lower income levels and hence subverts the argument for convergence in neoclassical growth models. In such an environment, constrained households and firms (especially those at the bottom of the distribution) find it difficult and suboptimal to upgrade their productive capacities. This weighs on their opportunity to innovate, adopt newer technologies, or move into more productive sectors. The key rationale of this chapter is thus complementary and not conflicting with other explanations for LAC's income gap presented in this report.

In line with this reasoning, the empirical findings show that controlling for the poverty gap is sufficient to observe income convergence and that poverty and volatility drag on convergence, thereby broadly confirming the previous household data–based findings of CCKW (2013) on a national account macro level. The estimated results imply that LAC would converge about 20–35 percent faster if its poverty gap was at a level that would be appropriate for its income level.

Although empirically identifying the exact causal effect of poverty and volatility on growth and convergence is inherently difficult, these results highlight that not taking poverty into account will lead to biased results for convergence models. The latter assume that low initial income is beneficial for growth, but the models mostly neglect that low initial income is also correlated with higher poverty levels that hamper growth and undermine the "advantages of backwardness." Not simultaneously controlling for these related factors will thus blur the estimated convergence effects.

From a policy perspective, the results obtained in this chapter indicate that overcoming the constraints that are associated with poverty has potentially large payoffs for unleashing a country's productive capacity. Policy makers are hence well advised to address such constraints. The chapter suggests that providing a stable economic environment in which poor households are widely shielded from falling below a minimum income level could be one option to approach this challenge.

Poverty and Volatility as Limitations to Convergence

Differentials in Marginal Returns to Investment Should Lead Countries to Converge

The most basic neoclassical growth model (Solow 1956; Swan 1956) assumes a Cobb-Douglas production function of output Y:

$$Y_t = K_t^\alpha \left(A_t L_t \right)^{1-\alpha}, \tag{7.1}$$

where K and L are capital and labor inputs, respectively, A captures technology/productivity, $0 < \alpha < 1$ is the output elasticity of capital, and t indexes observations over time or cross-sections. This implies decreasing returns to capital K as:

$$\frac{\partial Y}{\partial K} = \alpha \left(\frac{A_t L_t}{K_t} \right)^{1-\alpha}. \tag{7.2}$$

Assuming that countries share common features (such as the production function, technology, and population growth), the model identifies a steady-state level of capital per effective unit of labor, k^*. Countries at lower income levels with associated lower capital stock will thus increase their capital stock to reach the steady state[3] and the model thus predicts that growth is related to the distance to the steady-state level of income:

$$\frac{d\ln(y)}{dt} = \lambda \left[\ln(y^*) - \ln(y_t) \right], \tag{7.3}$$

that is, countries at lower income levels should grow at higher rates than higher-income countries, the underlying rationale being that lower-income countries have a higher marginal return to capital. Empirically, it is well-known that this unconditional convergence does not hold—or holds only for a very limited set of countries—but requires controlling for several factors (conditional convergence).

But Poverty and Volatility Might Prevent Such Investments

This basic neoclassical model provides a very aggregate and schematic picture of the economy. For example, it does not consider credit constraints for investment or how investment barriers differ across individuals (or firms). A relatively poor household, however, is likely to be credit constrained and would thus have to finance an investment by lowering current consumption. The closer a household finds itself to the subsistence minimum (or the absolute poverty line), the more difficult such an investment hence becomes, despite the potentially high payoff. Apparently, this is the implicit underlying rationale that Ravallion (2012) provides for poverty not converging across countries.

The problem becomes potentially aggravated in the presence of uncertainty over the investment outcome, which is illustrated in figure 7.1: a relatively poor household (below the moderate poverty line but above the absolute poverty line equivalent to the subsistence minimum) can decide in period $t = 1$ whether or not to make an investment that will potentially pull it out of poverty (figure 7.1, panel a). The expected payoff to such an investment may be large, but even neglecting the above problem of financing the investment from current consumption, it can become unfavorable if its outcome in period $t = 2$ is uncertain. For example, the outcome may be uncertain because it depends on the economy being in a good state ($X = h$) or a bad state ($X = l$) and if the assumed utility function is sufficiently concave (that is, the utility gain from moving from the expected return to the return under $X = h$ is sufficiently small relative to the utility loss from falling from the expected return to the return under $X = l$, which is reasonable for households close to the poverty line).[4]

Understanding the Income and Efficiency Gap in Latin America and the Caribbean
http://dx.doi.org/10.1596/978-1-4648-0450-2

Figure 7.1 Escaping Poverty through an Investment Decision

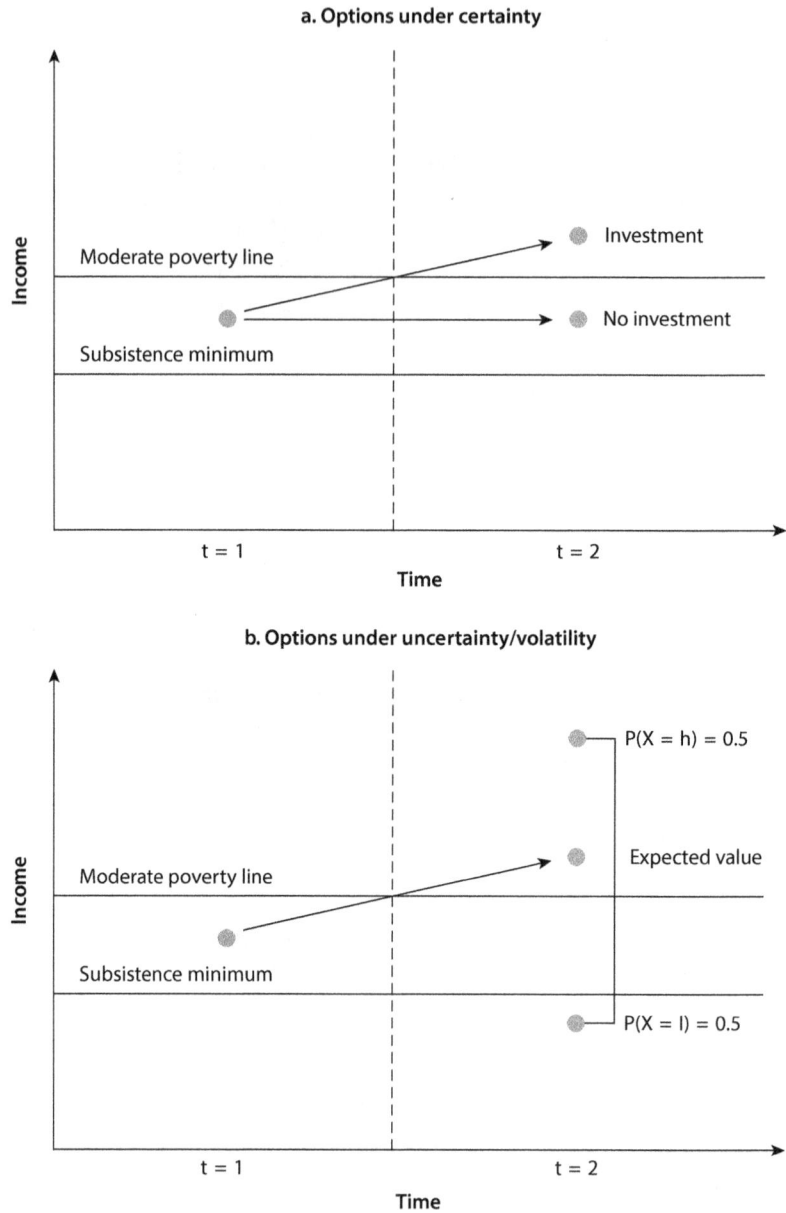

a. Options under certainty

b. Options under uncertainty/volatility

The nature of such investments by poor households and the uncertainty about their outcomes can vary in low- and middle-income economies. An example related to technology adoption[5] is the application of more productive fertilizers by farmers. Although such fertilizer investments provide potentially high returns, the returns are also more prone to weather-related shocks. There is thus ample empirical evidence documenting underinvestment of poor agricultural households, which is explained by high levels of risk and risk aversion.[6]

Figure 7.2 Difference in Utilities between Investment (Option 2) and No Investment (Option 1)

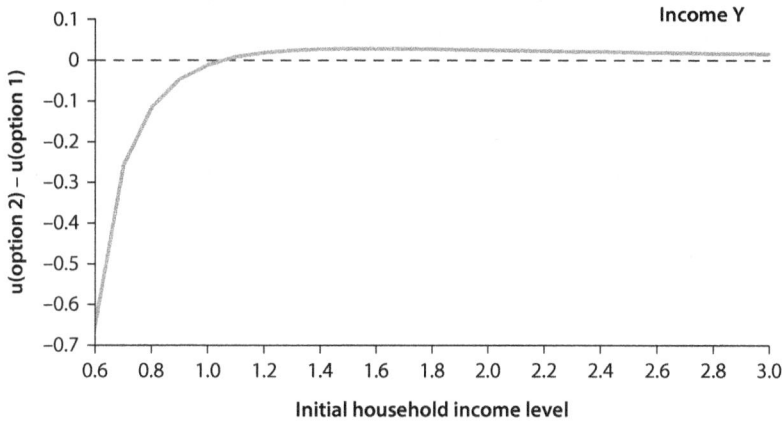

Similar rationales may certainly apply to other sectors and innovations[7] and associated economic (instead of weather-related) shocks.

Another interpretation of such investments is the decision to move into another business line or sector,[8] which might then comprise the costs for education, physical capital, or moving from rural to urban areas. Uncertainty about the payoff can arise from economic fluctuations, because the behavior of other agents and their external effects are unknown, or because the payoff depends on external factors such as the realization of infrastructure projects.[9] To overcome high initial poverty and low income levels via growth-promoting structural change, countries such as China and Vietnam thus combined stabilizing market conditions with high equity by providing "access to opportunity" despite high initial poverty.[10,11]

Finally, a numerical example of how poverty and volatility can deplete the neoclassical "advantages of backwardness" is depicted in figure 7.2. The figure compares the expected utility of not investing and staying in a state of relative poverty (option 1) with the expected utility under making an investment that is subject to uncertainty/volatility (option 2) in a two-period setup assuming an isoelastic utility function and diminishing marginal returns to investment (which gives rise to convergence in the neoclassical growth model). The details and parameterization are given in annex 7A.

In figure 7.2, to the right of a critical household income level, the utility of investing is higher than for not investing. The difference between the two is declining, thus reflecting higher incentives to invest in poorer countries that should give rise to convergence. However, with income falling below a certain level, the expected utility from not investing (option 1) is higher, as it is considered a safe strategy despite expected consumption being lower.

Implications and Empirical Hypotheses

The considerations discussed in the previous section suggest that despite diminishing returns to capital that underlie the rationale for convergence in neoclassical growth models, poverty and volatility might counteract the "advantages of backwardness." Although poor households would see high marginal returns to investment, constraints to financing these investments from current consumption (and associated credit market imperfections) and uncertainty about their future payoffs make it rational for poor households to opt for a "safe strategy" of not investing. Otherwise the households would run the risk of falling below the subsistence minimum and facing relatively large utility losses (as the utility decline from losing a certain amount of consumption is high at the poverty line compared with the utility increase from gaining the same amount of consumption). These considerations lead to a set of empirical hypotheses:

> **H1:** *Poverty is expected to have a hampering effect on growth*, as has been demonstrated in previous empirical studies. More precisely, it would be expected that the poverty *gap* would exercise this effect, as the poverty gap is a measure of how far the poor are from the poverty line on average and, thus, how close they are to the subsistence minimum.[12] As they approach this subsistence minimum, the poor will no longer be able to reduce consumption and invest; that is, they will no longer be able to benefit from the "advantages of backwardness."
>
> **H2:** *Controlling for poverty is expected to increase the speed of convergence.* This aspect has been widely ignored in the previous literature. Convergence means that in the model $\Delta \ln Y_{it} = \alpha_i + \beta_i \ln Y_{i,t-1}$, countries with lower initial income $\ln Y_{t-1}$ will see higher growth rates $\Delta \ln Y_t$ (that is, $\beta < 0$). However, since lower-income countries on average suffer from larger poverty gaps, not controlling for the latter will induce an omitted variable bias that reduces the convergence parameter β (in absolute terms).[13]
>
> **H3:** *These effects are expected to be reinforced by uncertainty/volatility.* As volatility increases the risk of a low payoff in the future, opting for a safe strategy becomes more advantageous, reinforcing the above-mentioned effects.
>
> **H4:** *The speed of convergence is directly influenced by the poverty gap.* In the strictest formulation, controlling for poverty will not only increase the speed of convergence (*H2*), but the speed of convergence will be a function of the poverty gap.

Empirical Investigation

Econometric Model and Data
The main model underlying this investigation is a standard neoclassical convergence specification, given by

$$\Delta \ln Y_{it} = \alpha_i + \beta_i \ln Y_{i,t-1} + \varepsilon_{it}, \tag{7.4}$$

where Y_{it} denotes gross domestic product (GDP) per capita in country i and period t, and ε_{it} is a standard disturbance term assumed to fulfill the usual assumptions of the error term in linear regression models. Subscript $t - 1$ refers to a value at the beginning of a period (initial level). If β_i is negative, countries converge in GDP levels, that is, countries starting out with a lower initial GDP grow faster in subsequent periods.

Several control variables, which are summarized in matrix X, can be added to the model:

$$\Delta \ln Y_{it} = \alpha_i + \beta_i \ln Y_{i,t-1} + X_{i,t-1}\theta_i + \varepsilon_{it}, \tag{7.5}$$

where X_i may include interactions among variables and can in principle be measured at various points in time. It should be noted that the interpretation of interaction models might not be straightforward. For example, in the model

$$\Delta \ln Y_{it} = \alpha_i + \beta_i \ln Y_{i,t-1} + \theta_{i1}x_{i1} + \theta_{i2}x_{i2} + \theta_{i3}x_{i1} \times x_{i2} + \varepsilon_{it}, \tag{7.6}$$

the marginal effect of x_{i1} on $\Delta \ln Y_{it}$ is given by

$$\frac{\partial \Delta \ln Y_{it}}{\partial x_{i1}} = \theta_{i1} + \theta_{i3}x_{i2}. \tag{7.7}$$

That is, the marginal effect of x_{i1} depends on the level of x_{i2}, and the statistical significance of the influence has to be evaluated over the relevant range of x_{i2}.

Data for GDP are taken from the Penn World Table (PWT) 7.1 in constant purchasing power parity (PPP) per capita. These data also underlie the calculation of the (five-year) GDP growth standard deviation. Aggregate data for the poverty gap[14] at PPP US$2 a day are retrieved from the World Bank World Development Indicators (WDI). For each country where data are available, I take the earliest and last observations that have a poverty data point. For robustness checks, I also add data on life expectancy, primary school completion rates, and agricultural exports, which are taken from WDI as well. The poverty gap and additional control variables enter the model with the values recorded at the beginning of the period (initial values). Data for up to 102 low- and middle-income countries are available for 1978–2010. More details on the data are provided in annex 7A and annex table 7A.1.

In line with the studies of Ravallion (2012) and CCKW (2013), I focus on ordinary least squares (OLS) estimation of the outlined equations, well aware of the fact that this might induce an endogeneity bias. However, the purpose of this chapter is less to identify an exact causal relationship running from poverty and volatility to growth, but to see how taking these variables into account changes convergence patterns. Furthermore, the chapter discusses endogeneity issues, which are partially addressed using instrumental variable (IV) regressions.

Results

Column 1 in table 7.1 displays the estimation results of the unconditional convergence equation 7.4. There are no signs of unconditional convergence among the 102 low- and middle-income countries included, and this approach virtually explains nothing of the variation in growth rates among them (as indicated by the low R-squared). When adding the initial poverty gap to the equation

Table 7.1 OLS Estimation Results

Variable	(1) $\Delta ln(Y)$	(2) $\Delta ln(Y)$	(3) $\Delta ln(Y)$	(4) $\Delta ln(Y)$	(5) $\Delta ln(Y)$	(6) $ln(povgap)$
$ln(GDP)_{t-1}$	0.000647	−0.00830*	0.000945	−0.00685*	−0.0164**	−1.826***
	(0.00288)	(0.00451)	(0.00266)	(0.00380)	(0.00797)	(0.184)
$ln(poverty\ gap)_{t-1}$		−0.00548***		−0.00368**	−0.0268	
		(0.00185)		(0.00185)	(0.0167)	
σ(growth)			−0.161	−0.0607	−0.149	
			(0.136)	(0.0896)	(0.114)	
$ln(poverty\ gap)_{t-1}$ × σ(growth)				−0.0347		
				(0.0272)		
$ln(poverty\ gap)_{t-1}$ × $ln(GDP)_{t-1}$					0.00243	
					(0.00180)	
LAC dummy						1.292***
						(0.401)
Constant	0.0203	0.102**	0.0238	0.0914***	0.179**	16.09***
	(0.0230)	(0.0387)	(0.0223)	(0.0337)	(0.0721)	(1.293)
Observations	102	102	102	102	102	102
R-squared	0.001	0.095	0.032	0.126	0.133	0.572

Note: Robust standard errors are in parentheses. GDP = gross domestic product; LAC = Latin America and the Caribbean; OLS = ordinary least squares; Y = income.
***$p < .01$, **$p < .05$, *$p < .1$.

(column 2), the picture changes: the explanatory power of the model increases (R-squared = 9.5 percent), conditional convergence is present (and significant at the 10 percent level), and initial poverty exercises a statistically highly significant negative impact on subsequent growth. Confirming hypothesis *H1*, these findings suggest that poverty impedes growth, as already pointed out by previous studies. More importantly, the findings suggest that when controlling for the fact that lower-income countries face higher poverty gaps, countries would actually converge in income levels, as stated in hypothesis *H2*.

When volatility is added to the convergence equation instead of poverty (column 3), volatility has a negative effect—in line with previous literature—that is somewhat beyond conventional levels of statistical significance (but the standard error is smaller than the estimated coefficient). The overall model does not fit the data as well as when including poverty instead. Interestingly, the inclusion of volatility also does not significantly alter the convergence parameter.[15] When adding the poverty gap and volatility and allowing them to interact (column 4), poverty exercises a statistically significant impact that is potentially aggravated by volatility (although the interaction is not statistically different from 0, its standard error is smaller than the estimated coefficient).

To understand the effect implied by the estimated model, figure 7.3 evaluates the impact of poverty on growth at different levels of volatility (following the rationale discussed for equations 7.6 and 7.7). The figure shows that the effect

Figure 7.3 Marginal Effect of Poverty on Growth for Different Levels of Volatility

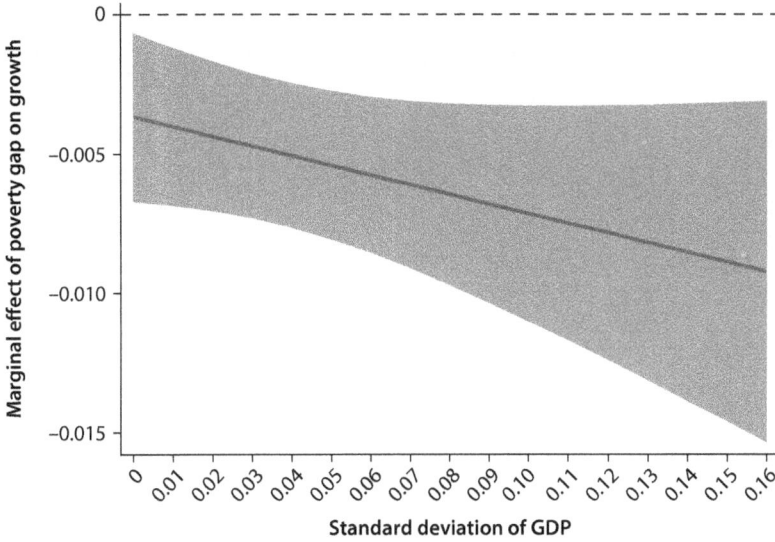

Source: World Bank staff calculations based on World Development Indicators and Penn World Table data.
Note: The blue area in the figure displays a 90 percent confidence interval. GDP = gross domestic product.

of poverty becomes severely more negative the higher volatility is, as suggested in this chapter and by CCKW (2013). Furthermore, column 4 in table 7.1 highlights that, controlling for the effects of poverty, volatility, and their interaction, convergence in income levels is taking place. Interestingly, in table 7.1, convergence appears slower in column 4 than when only controlling for the poverty gap (column 2); however, the two convergence coefficients are not significantly different from each other (in a statistical sense; p-value = .732). This finding suggests that controlling for poverty captures the main share for obtaining conditional convergence.

Finally, to test for hypothesis *H4*, I allow this convergence parameter to depend on the poverty gap by interacting the two relevant variables (column 5 in table 7.1). The evaluation of the effect is depicted in figure 7.4. The figure suggests that the smaller the poverty gap is, the faster a country converges in terms of the income level.[16] Once the poverty gap increases, it becomes less likely for a country to converge. This finding is in line with the consideration that poverty diminishes the "advantages of backwardness," as poor people will find it difficult to invest in assets, although the investments should provide a high marginal return.

These fairly frugal OLS estimates highlight that it is sufficient to control for the poverty gap to observe statistically significant (conditional) convergence in income levels in a broad sample of 102 low- and middle-income countries, in line with hypotheses *H1* and *H2*. So far, the evidence for the additional role of volatility (hypothesis *H3*) and for the speed of convergence to depend on the poverty

Figure 7.4 Convergence Parameter with Respect to Different Poverty Gaps: OLS

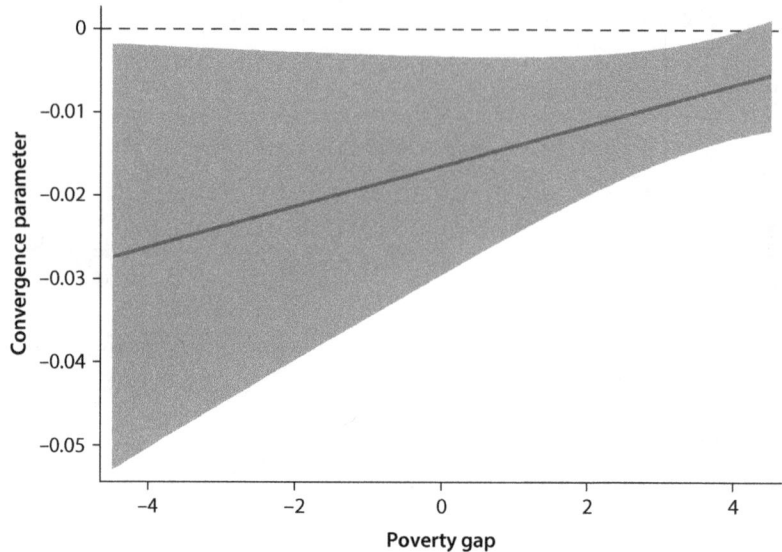

Source: World Bank staff calculations based on World Development Indicators and Penn World Table data.
Note: The blue area in the figure displays a 90 percent confidence interval. OLS = ordinary least squares.

gap (hypothesis *H4*) is rather weak, as the results are marginally beyond conventional levels of statistical significance.

Endogeneity Concerns and Instrumental Variable Results

The OLS results might be subject to an endogeneity bias. However, a key objective of this chapter is not to identify an exact causal relationship running from the poverty gap (and volatility) to growth, but to see how taking these variables into account changes convergence patterns. Furthermore, the specification is unlikely to suffer from reverse causality, as there is no reason to believe that growth over a certain time period would affect initial poverty at the beginning of the same period. The remaining endogeneity issues thus relate to a potential omitted variable bias and measurement error, which are addressed by adding additional control variables and an IV approach.

An omitted variable bias would reflect the possibility that a negative effect of poverty on convergence may also capture other underlying channels. For example, weak institutions and associated lack of redistributive capacity and/or low human capital endowment might simultaneously increase initial poverty and lower growth prospects. However, there are qualified reasons not to control for other standard variables in the first place, as the exact linkages and causalities between these variables and poverty are unclear. For example, is poverty high because institutional quality is low? Or do institutions not improve *because* the poor are systematically excluded from political participation? Similarly, are people poor because of low education? Or is it the case that poor people cannot invest in human capital *because* of a poverty trap, as suggested in this chapter?

Table 7.2 Results for Further Control Variables and IV Estimation

Variable	(1) $\Delta ln(Y)$	(2) $\Delta ln(Y)$	(3) $\Delta ln(Y)$	(4) $\Delta ln(Y)$
$ln(GDP)_{t-1}$	−0.0137**	−0.00830*	−0.00578	−0.0297**
	(0.00556)	(0.00485)	(0.00408)	(0.0148)
$ln(poverty\ gap)_{t-1}$	−0.00340*		−0.00574***	−0.0653*
	(0.00183)		(0.00199)	(0.0345)
$ln(poverty\ gap)_{t-1}$ x $ln(GDP)_{t-1}$				0.00670*
				(0.00380)
σ(growth)	0.00129	−0.0471		−0.0330
	(0.136)	(0.134)		(0.140)
ln(primary education)	−0.000393	0.000169		
	(0.0120)	(0.0130)		
ln(life expectancy)	0.0713**	0.0791**		
	(0.0331)	(0.0345)		
ln(primary exports)	0.00224	0.00295*		
Constant	(0.00172)	(0.00156)		
	−0.159	−0.243**	0.0893**	0.302**
	(0.119)	(0.119)	(0.0357)	(0.134)
Estimation	OLS	OLS	IV	IV
Observations	51	51	88	88
R-squared	0.284	0.209	0.101	0.098

Note: Robust standard errors are in parentheses. GDP = gross domestic product; IV = instrumental variable; Y = income.
***$p < .01$, **$p < .05$, *$p < .1$.

By not controlling for other variables, the full impact of initial poverty will be captured, although it might operate through various channels and capture the effects of variables correlated with poverty. Finally, it is important to note that the effect of poverty is estimated conditional on initial income. The latter and the poverty gap are strongly negatively correlated (correlation coefficient −0.72 in the sample), reflecting that poverty is generally lower the higher a country's income is (which will also correlate with factors such as education and institutions). The conditional poverty effect can thus be interpreted as a measure of how much emphasis a country at a certain income level puts on equity and poverty reduction.

Column 1 in table 7.2 nevertheless controls for further variables that are likely to induce omitted variable bias, which leaves the negative effect of the poverty gap nearly unaffected. In addition, the specification controls for education and health, which are likely to be alternative channels affecting poverty and growth outcomes, as well as for the share of primary exports, as resource-rich economies might face institutional and redistributive constraints that might affect poverty while at the same time affecting growth ("resource curse").

Although this specification changes the underlying sample (because of data availability) and induces some multicollinearity,[17] the negative effect of the poverty gap remains statistically significant but becomes somewhat smaller in

Understanding the Income and Efficiency Gap in Latin America and the Caribbean
http://dx.doi.org/10.1596/978-1-4648-0450-2

size compared with the unconditional specification in column 2 in table 7.1. Furthermore, the inclusion of poverty in addition to the other control variables (comparing column 1 with column 2 in table 7.2) considerably increases the explanatory power (R-squared) and leads to a substantial increase in the speed of convergence.[18] This finding confirms hypotheses H1 and H2 concerning the hampering effect of poverty on growth and that controlling for poverty increases the speed of convergence. Including the additional control variables renders no support for hypotheses H3 and H4, as the results for volatility, its interaction with poverty, and the interaction of poverty with the convergence parameter are not statistically significant (and thus are excluded from the specification).

As another way to tackle potential endogeneity, columns 3 and 4 in table 7.2 apply an IV approach. However, finding a credible instrument for the poverty gap is nearly impossible. Although it is relatively straightforward in the present cross-country setting to find some instruments that are relevant to poverty and that are not suspicious for reverse causality (that is, for depending on actual growth rates), such as variables related to geography or legal origins, none of the potential instruments is likely to meet the exclusion restriction. I thus opt for a pragmatic approach and use the first available poverty data point as an instrument for the second poverty data point available. This somewhat limits the sample size (as countries with only two observations have to be dropped) and shortens the timespan for each observation.

With this approach, the instrument relevance is strong (F-statistic of the first-stage regression: 221.6) and the results concerning the negative effect of poverty reported in column 3 in table 7.2 are nearly identical to the OLS results in column 2 in table 7.1, although the convergence parameter becomes slightly smaller and statistically insignificant. Column 4 in table 7.2 is equivalent to the OLS specification in column 5 in table 7.1. Including the interaction of poverty and the convergence parameter as another potentially endogenous variable requires the inclusion of another instrument, for which I take the first observed (lagged) poverty headcount ratio. The results show all the features expected from hypotheses H1, H2, and H4: controlling for poverty leads to (conditional) convergence, poverty hampers growth, and the convergence parameter depends on the poverty gap.

The dependence of the convergence parameter on the poverty gap is depicted in figure 7.5, which is the IV equivalent to the OLS-based figure 7.4. Figure 7.5 adds the distribution of poverty gaps in the sample to the picture. The figure shows that the bulk of sampled countries (light grey)—including the LAC subsample (dark grey)—have a relatively high poverty gap, implying that their conditional convergence parameter is small. These countries converge only very slowly (already controlling for the direct effect of the poverty gap on growth) and since they constitute the majority of countries, it is not surprising that unconditional convergence of income levels is not found in conventional samples. Finally, the results in column 4 of table 7.2 do not lend support for hypothesis H3 concerning the effect of volatility.

Figure 7.5 Convergence Parameter with Respect to Different Poverty Gaps: IV

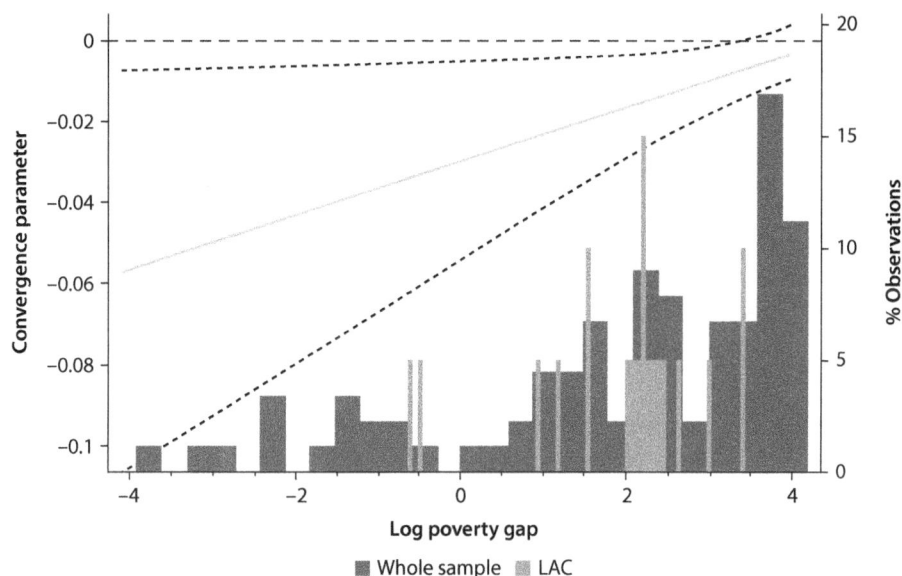

Source: World Bank staff calculations based on World Development Indicators and Penn World Table data.
Note: The figure shows the dependence of the convergence parameter (left scale) on the poverty gap (solid line) together with the respective 90 percent confidence interval (dashed lines), based on the IV regression. A more negative parameter implies faster convergence. The right scale and bar chart show the distribution of poverty gaps for the whole sample (blue) and countries in LAC (orange). IV = instrumental variable; LAC = Latin America and the Caribbean.

Overall, the results highlight the relevance of poverty gaps for growth and associated income convergence: countries facing higher poverty gaps grow slower and presumably also converge slower. The evidence for the additional role of growth volatility is more limited: some weak evidence from the OLS regressions could not be confirmed in the IV regression. This result calls for a more thorough analysis of this channel, maybe using more detailed measures of volatility and/or controlling for other factors.[19]

What Do the Results Imply for Lack of Convergence and Policy Options in LAC?

Controlling for poverty, countries that have lower initial income levels are expected to grow faster and converge. High poverty conditional on initial income level, by contrast, slows down this effect. Historically, LAC has been notorious for high levels of inequality and, relatedly, for considerable poverty incidence considering the level of income. This point is depicted in figure 7.6. The figure shows (the logarithm of) the poverty gap on the vertical axis and (the logarithm of) GDP per capita on the horizontal axis, outlining a clear negative relationship between income and poverty, as expected. Given this relationship, however, countries in LAC (depicted in full black) have larger poverty gaps than what would be expected considering their income level. This finding is also confirmed

Figure 7.6 Relation between Poverty and Income

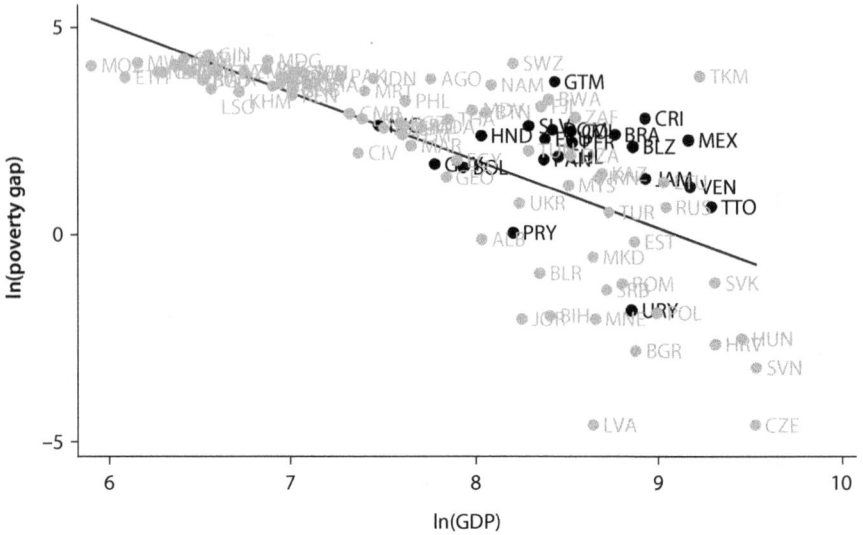

Source: World Bank staff calculations based on World Development Indicators data.
Note: GDP = gross domestic product.

parametrically in column 6 in table 7.1, showing (with a dummy variable for LAC), that LAC's poverty gap is significantly higher than that of the rest of the low- and middle-income countries after controlling for the level of GDP per capita: the poverty gap in LAC has been 129 percent higher than it should have been (considering the region's income level). This means that LAC is over-proportionally burdened with poverty given its income level, which potentially causes a drag on the region's convergence process.[20]

Following the rationale of equation 7.7 and figures 7.4 and 7.5, the (conditional) convergence speed can be expressed as

$$\frac{\partial \Delta \ln Y_{it}}{\partial \ln(Y)_{i,t-1}} = \beta + \delta \times \ln(poverty\ gap)_{i,t-1}, \qquad (7.8)$$

where β is the parameter for initial income and δ the interaction term of initial income with poverty. The OLS (column 5 in table 7.1) and IV (column 4 in table 7.2) results imply the following parameters for equation 7.8:[21]

$$\frac{\partial \Delta \ln Y_{it}}{\partial \ln(Y)_{i,t-1}} = \begin{matrix} -0.0164 + 0.00243 \times \ln(poverty\ gap)_{i,t-1} \ [OLS] \\ -0.0297 + 0.00670 \times \ln(poverty\ gap)_{i,t-1} \ [IV] \end{matrix}$$

The actually observed log poverty gap in the OLS (IV) sample is 1.84 (2.08) for countries in LAC. This implies a convergence speed of −0.012 (−0.016) for the average country in LAC. However, the poverty gap could be expressed as:

$$\ln(poverty\ gap)_{i,t-1} = a + b\ln(Y)_{i,t-1} + c\ LAC\ dummy_i + e_{it},$$

according to column 6 in table 7.1, with $c = 1.29$, suggesting that the poverty gap in LAC has been 129 percent higher than it should have been considering its income level. Subtracting 1.29 from LAC's actually observed log poverty gap would thus bring the poverty gap down to the level that would be "appropriate" for the region's income level. Using this corrected level would lead to a convergence speed of -0.015 with OLS (-0.024 with IV). This suggests that if LAC closed its poverty gap to a level appropriate for its income level, it would have (conditionally) converged 20.8 (35.5) percent faster.

This effect should not be seen as a sole poverty effect on top of other factors (such as lagging technology adoption, lacking innovation, or unfavorable technological change), as those factors are likely to interact with each other and the empirical identification strategy does not allow for retrieving a clear causal effect exclusively attributable to poverty. Nevertheless, this result suggests that a considerable fraction of LAC's lack of convergence might be caused by *factors associated with large poverty gaps* and that the benefits of closing the poverty gaps may be large.[22]

The causal link from poverty to growth and convergence may remain opaque and differ across countries. In any case, it would be naïve to assume that a mere closing of the poverty gap per se, for example, by a monetary transfer that brings every household to the US$2-a-day income level, would suffice to take care of the problem and obtain convergence. Despite the need for more fiscal redistribution in many countries in LAC, such a view would not reflect the multidimensional aspect of poverty that can only be *approximated* in monetary terms, whereas there are other factors limiting access to opportunity for poor households.

For some countries in LAC, equity in access to quality education and health services or creating more stable and diversified employment opportunities will be a priority, while other countries will have to improve institutions to make them more accessible to the poor. To the extent that volatility and uncertainty limit the opportunity of households to escape poverty, improvements in macroeconomic stabilization policies, allowing the poor to overcome credit constraints, and/or more comprehensive social safety nets will have a role to play as well. However, even controlling for some of these factors (like health, education, and volatility), the poverty gap retains a significant negative impact on growth and convergence. Finally, while countries are well advised to identify their most constraining factors, in no case will a single measure suffice to close the poverty and income gaps, given that poverty interacts with other factors and is by itself a multidimensional phenomenon. Policy makers should thus strive to assess the most relevant links between poverty and income gaps and address them appropriately.

Taking a historical perspective, two issues would deserve further attention in the future. First, several countries in LAC have seen quite fast growth since World War II, when poverty was worse than it has been over the past decades, raising the question how the region overcame constraints from large poverty gaps. A hypothesis could be that patterns of rural-urban migration and structural change (from the primary sector to manufacturing and services) during that period allowed labor to flow into activities with higher value added (thus boosting income). At the same time, those patterns did not over-proportionally constrain the poor, since these sectors intensively required lower-skilled labor. Institutional factors during that period most likely contributed as well. The fact that this potential of structural change will be exhausted at some point (or was even overrun during import-substituting industrialization) while less emphasis was given to (within-sector and within-firm) productivity increases could help explain the stagnation of this development model and the widening income gap vis-à-vis the United States after 1980. The resulting supply constraints and associated inflation patterns kept poverty (which is measured in real terms) relatively high. Such a pattern would imply that LAC did not effectively manage to overcome some sort of a "middle-income trap."

Second, LAC has achieved considerable progress concerning poverty reduction over the past decade, mostly caused by positive growth effects (Dollar, Kleinebert, and Kraay 2013; World Bank 2014). Moreover, CCKW (2013) show that LAC has seen poverty convergence, that is, LAC is one of the few regions where countries starting out with a higher poverty incidence have seen faster subsequent success in poverty reduction. This situation raises the hope that the potential drag of poverty on income convergence will be somewhat attenuated in the future, as the analysis in this chapter for LAC mostly covers earlier observations.[23]

However, the situation in the future will also depend on whether poverty reduction is mainly temporary, for example, driven by booms in the commodity and related sectors that have a high demand for unskilled labor, potentially benefitting poor households (de la Torre, Messina, and Pienknagura 2012), or has truly enlarged socioeconomic opportunities for the poor, which would potentially allow them to move up the ladder toward higher-productivity activities over time. World Bank (2014) highlights that equality of access to basic childhood goods and services has improved in recent years, while serious issues remain concerning the quality of those goods and services, particularly in education and housing infrastructure. Concerning volatility, most countries in the region have managed to stabilize output and inflation, and to support overall stability (Araujo et al. 2014). Overall, this situation should give rise to a somewhat more optimistic growth outlook for the region going forward, on top of the intrinsic benefits of reducing poverty.

Conclusion

This chapter has argued that poverty can override the "advantages of backwardness" that underlie the convergence rationale in neoclassical growth models. Poor households may come close to or fall below an essential minimum consumption level if their investment does not materialize profitably in volatile environments. Therefore, countries with deep poverty cannot easily benefit from high marginal returns to capital.

The empirical results of the chapter show that, taking into account how deep poverty is in a country at a given income level, countries conditionally converge, reflecting a negative impact of poverty on growth. Although the estimated effect of poverty on growth may be biased, the more important conclusion is that conventional convergence models are also subject to an omitted variable bias because they do not take into account the detrimental effect poverty has on convergence in low-income countries. As initial income and poverty are negatively correlated and both have a negative impact on growth, not simultaneously controlling for them will blur estimated convergence effects. There is some evidence that the convergence effect itself is a function of (that is, depends on) the depth of poverty, while the evidence for the supplementary effect of volatility is more ambiguous.

Given its income level, LAC suffers from relatively deep poverty, which might have hindered the region from converging toward higher income levels. The results in this chapter suggest that if LAC had lowered its poverty gap to a level "appropriate" for its income, it would have (conditionally) converged 20–35 percent faster.

These findings suggest that the economic benefits from overcoming poverty-related lack of opportunity may potentially be large. However, this would require a deeper understanding of the country-specific links that affect poverty and the potential for aggregate growth. In a broader perspective, the results also suggest that mainly short-term and demand-focused policy measures (such as transfers like Brazil's Bolsa Familia or Mexico's PROGRESA program, or stabilization policies) may affect growth and income in the longer term by influencing aggregate supply, and that neglecting equity and volatility issues would lead to an incomplete macroeconomic policy agenda, as suggested by Birdsall, de la Torre, and Valencia Caicedo (2010) in their assessment of the "Washington Consensus."

Annex 7A

Rationale and Parameterization of Figure 7.2

Consider a household with the isoelastic utility function

$$u(c) = \frac{c^{1-\eta} - 1}{1 - \eta}, \tag{A7.1}$$

maximizing consumption (c) over two periods (where $1/\eta$ measures the intertemporal elasticity of substitution of consumption between time periods). The household can stay in its business/sector, in which case there will be no change in income: $Y = Y_1 = Y_2$. Or the household can invest a certain (discrete and predefined) amount $a > 0$ in period 1, which increases its income in period 2 by $a + [1/(aY)]$. This expression reflects diminishing marginal returns to investment (or income), which gives rise to convergence in the neoclassical growth model. The discrete and predefined size of a is motivated by assuming a lump-sum type of cost when switching business/sector. Suppose, however, that under this second option, the household faces a risk q^* to its income, which is given by:

$$q^* = \begin{cases} +q & \text{with probability } P \\ -q & \text{with probability } (1-P) \end{cases} \tag{A7.2}$$

This uncertainty reflects that the relative desirability of a sector (or business) can repeatedly rise and fall (which induces hysteresis effects; see Dixit and Rob 1994). Disregarding subjective intertemporal discounting or possibilities to transfer income across periods (that is, there is neither insurance nor lending, nor store of value, so individuals cannot achieve insurance indirectly by consumption smoothing over time), the household's utilities under these two options are then given by:

$$u(\text{option 1}): u(c_1) + u(c_2) = u(Y) + u(Y) = u(2Y) \tag{A7.3a}$$

$$u(\text{option 2}): u(c_1) + E[u(c_2)] = u(Y - a) + Pu\left(Y + a + \frac{1}{aY} + q\right)$$

$$+ (1-P)u\left(Y + a + \frac{1}{aY} - q\right), \tag{A7.3b}$$

where a is the amount invested in period 1. This example is parameterized by assuming $a = 0.5$, $q = 0.3$, $P = 0.5$, and a risk aversion $\eta = 1$, in which case the utility function becomes the limiting case $u(c) = \ln(c)$, so $u < 0$ for $c < 1$. That is, $c = 1$ can be interpreted as a poverty line below which utility is negative (for example, because of starvation [absolute] or social exclusion [relative]). The difference in utilities of these two options with respect to different incomes under the given parameters is depicted in figure 7.2, with a positive difference indicating that option 2 would be the optimal household choice.

Although the expected two-period consumption under option 2,

$$E(c_1 + c_2) = (Y - a) + Y + a + \frac{1}{aY} + E(q^*) = 2Y + \frac{1}{aY} > 2Y \;\; \forall a, Y > 0, \tag{A7.4}$$

would be higher than under option 1 (by a magnitude decreasing in Y as long as $Y > 0$), a certain income level is required for option 2 to provide a higher utility and become optimal. The intuition for this result is the aversion of the household of falling below a certain consumption level ("poverty line"), which weighs more than the potential benefits of an investment that would otherwise deliver the highest payoffs for poor households (which is also reflected by the utility difference in figure 7.2 falling again after reaching a peak at a certain income Y and approaching 0 as $Y \to \infty$ in the term $1/[aY]$ in equation A7.4). It is finally relevant to note that not only the uncertainty about consumption in period 2 detains the household from investing, but that with uncertainty (q) rising, the optimum of option 2 requires a higher income level.

Table 7A.1 Summary Statistics for Key Variables

Series	Mean	Standard deviation	Description and source
$\Delta\ln(Y)$	0.02538	0.02672	Annualized growth rate of GDP per capita in PPP from PWT 7.1
$\ln(GDP)_{t-1}$	7.8599	0.9541	GDP per capita in PPP from PWT 7.1 (series rgdpl)
$\ln(\text{poverty gap})_{t-1}$	2.0068	2.1620	Poverty gap at PPP US\$2 a day from WDI
$\sigma(\text{growth})$	0.03632	0.02954	Standard deviation of annual growth rate of GDP per capita in PPP over the last five years of the sample period, based on data from PWT 7.1

Note: Summary statistics are for the OLS sample of 102 low- and middle-income countries. GDP = gross domestic product; OLS = ordinary least squares; PPP = purchasing power parity; PWT = Penn World Table; WDI = World Development Indicators.

Data

Ravallion (2012) and CCKW (2013) use data from household surveys and focus on the poverty headcount ratio (as a percentage of the population). This chapter instead uses more aggregated macro data and looks at the poverty gap. The chapter takes gross domestic product (GDP) data from the Penn World Table (PWT) 7.1 as purchasing power parity (PPP) converted GDP per capita at constant 2005 prices (PWT series rgdpl). The standard deviation of growth (as opposed to the standard deviation of GDP in CCKW 2013) over the past five years is calculated for each year. Aggregate data for the poverty gap at PPP US\$2 a day are retrieved from the World Bank World Development Indicators. These data are not available for every country in every year, and are only available for low- and middle-income countries, so there are no high-income economies in the sample.

For each country where data are available, I take the earliest and last observations that have a poverty data point. The resulting timespan ranges from three years (Czech Republic and Montenegro) to 32 years (India), starts as early as 1978 (India) and as late as 2005 (Montenegro), and ends as late as 2010 (34 countries) and as early as 1992 (Trinidad and Tobago). Annual real PPP GDP per capita growth rates are calculated over these periods.

Notes

The source of the epigraph that opens this chapter is a press briefing for the World Economic Outlook, International Monetary Fund, Washington, DC, April 8, 2014.

1. On the role of poverty and inequality for growth, see, for example, Berg, Ostry, and Zettelmeyer (2012), Ostry, Berg, and Tsangarides (2014), Lopez and Servén (2009), and Ravallion (2012). Kraay and McKenzie (2014) provide a skeptical review of the literature on poverty gaps. The importance of volatility for growth is emphasized in the seminal paper by Ramey and Ramey (1995), and confirmed by various contributions since (Aghion et al. 2010; Berument, Dincer, and Mustafaoglu 2011, 2012; Hnatkovska and Loayza 2005; Kose, Prasad, and Terrones 2006). Similar to the effect of poverty on growth, however, the exact channel of volatility affecting growth remains opaque. Kose, Prasad, and Terrones (2006) thus stress the need for "further research … to provide a better understanding of the roles played by various shocks in driving the relationship between volatility and growth."

2. For the class of poverty measures $p = 1/N \sum [(z - yi))/z]^\alpha$, where z is the poverty threshold, N is the population, and the sum Σ runs over all poor households, the

poverty headcount index is defined as $\alpha = 0$, while for the poverty gap $\alpha = 1$. The latter is hence "closer" to a distributionally sensitive (convex) poverty measure of the so-called Atkinson class ($\alpha > 1$) for which risk/volatility will lead to an increase in expected poverty under less stringent assumptions than those for the headcount index (see Ravallion 1988).

3. $\dfrac{d[k(t)-k^*]}{dt} = -\big[1-\alpha(k^*)\big]\big(n+\delta+g\big)\big[k(t)-k^*\big]$, that is, the more negative $[k(t)-k^*]$ is, the higher the growth of $k(t)$ over time (because of the negative prefix).

4. Morduch (1994) formalizes a related rationale in a two-period model where a poor agricultural household has to choose the share of safe (but on average less profitable) activity under a borrowing constraint. Because of the borrowing constraint, less risk is taken and expected profits are sacrificed for greater self-protection against bad shocks for which financial market protection is unavailable.

5. Eden and Nguyen (chapter 3 in this volume) assess the relevance of technology adoption lags for LAC.

6. For example, see the contributions of Bliss and Stern (1982, chapter 8), Morduch (1995), Moser and Barrett (2006), Yesuf and Bluffstone (2009), and Dercon and Christiaensen (2011).

7. For the relevance of innovation for LAC's income gap, see Nguyen and Jaramillo (chapter 6) in this volume as well as Brown et al. (chapter 5) in this volume.

8. For the effect of sectoral structural change on income in LAC, see Schiffbauer, Sahnoun, and Araujo (chapter 4) (and Brown et al. [chapter 5]) in this volume.

9. For example, if a poor household moves to another location, its payoff might negatively (price competition) or positively (network and linkage effects) depend on other agents becoming active there as well. However, the latter is often difficult to anticipate. Similarly, the payoffs may depend on external political shocks (for example, whether a certain transportation project is implemented. See Murphy, Shleifer, and Vishny (1989) on these issues.

10. See Drèze and Sen (1995) and Ravallion (2009) for the case of China. This aspect is less studied for Vietnam but McCaig and Pavcnik (2013) provide an assessment of the importance of structural change for the country's impressive development performance.

11. A related literature focuses on firms' adjustment costs toward more productive/profitable activities under uncertainty/volatility and emphasizes that the latter might give rise to an ex post inefficiency (Bertola 1995; Dixit and Rob 1994; Ramey and Ramey 1991).

12. This differs from the results of Ravallion (2012) and CCKW (2013), who use the poverty *headcount ratio* instead of the poverty gap.

13. Statistically, the bias of the ordinary least squares (OLS) estimator for parameter β in equations 7.4 and 7.5, with $\beta < 0$, in the presence of an omitted variable (like poverty Z) that influences growth with $\delta < 0$, is given as: bias $\left(\hat{\beta}\right) = E\left[\left(X'X\right)^{-1}X'Z\delta\right]$. Poverty Z and income X are expected to be negatively related, $X'Z < 0$, which ends up as a *positive bias* after multiplying with $\delta < 0$. The estimated convergence $\hat{\beta}$ will thus be larger than the "true" (negative) β. Economically, the hypothesis implies a different aggregate production function because of poverty (and potentially its interaction with volatility) influencing aggregate investment, which in turn defines the capital stock K that enters the aggregate production function Y. In other words, if poverty (and its interaction with

volatility) is a serious impediment to convergence, it would be expected there would be *convergence conditional on poverty* (and volatility), that is, after controlling for the latter.

14. The poverty gap is the mean shortfall from the respective poverty line (counting the non-poor as having zero shortfall), expressed as a percentage of the poverty line. This measure thus not only reflects the incidence of poverty (as the headcount index), but also the depth of poverty.

15. If lower-income countries face higher volatility and the latter has a detrimental effect on growth, correcting for volatility should increase convergence. However, the correlation between volatility and initial log GDP is slightly positive (correlation coefficient 0.06 in the sample). In the unconditional model of Ramey and Ramey (1995), the effect of volatility is also not statistically significant (t-statistic 0.67), with a similar coefficient (−0.147) as in table 7.1, and only becomes significant after controlling for other factors. The unconditional effect in the sample of low- and middle-income countries of Kose, Prasad, and Terrones (2006) is weakly significant (p-value .094) and of similar size (−0.182).

16. The estimated interaction coefficient is not statistically significant at conventional levels, but the standard error is smaller than the estimated parameter and this interaction is significant in the IV regression reported in the next section.

17. The correlation coefficients of ln(povertygap) with ln(life expectancy) and ln(primary education) are −0.63 and −0.53, respectively. Multicollinearity will inflate the estimated standard errors (thus lead to lower statistical significance), while the coefficients are still consistently estimated.

18. The model including the poverty gap (column 1) is also preferred to the restricted model in column 2 by the Akaike and the Schwarz information criterion. Furthermore, a likelihood ratio test allows rejecting the null hypothesis that the model without poverty provides the same fit as the model including poverty (at the 5 percent level of statistical significance).

19. The effect of volatility in Ramey and Ramey (1995) requires controlling for the right variables.

20. The issue might be of special relevance for Caribbean countries that experienced a considerable slowdown in growth rates in the past decades against the background of particularly high poverty levels and historically high exposure to volatility and shocks.

21. To test for the possibility that the poverty gap has a different effect in LAC than in the rest of the sample ("parameter heterogeneity"), I also run the regression in column 2 in table 7.1 adding the LAC-specific poverty gap. The latter is slightly smaller but not statistically different from the overall poverty gap effect.

22. Previous research has further pointed out the nature of volatilities in LAC and its macroeconomic links (for example, Gavin et al. 1996; Gavin and Hausmann 1998) as well as its feedback loop on poverty (CCKW 2013; IDB 1995). Given the limited and non-robust evidence for this channel in the empirical investigation above, I refrain from taking into account this effect.

23. The average beginning year of covered periods for LAC is 1986 (the latest one 1993). The average period for LAC countries lasts until 2006 (and until 2010). When regressing ln(poverty gap) on ln(GDP) and a LAC dummy at the end of the period, the estimated parameter of the LAC dummy is 1.40, which is slightly higher (but not statistically different from) the 1.29 estimated for the beginning of the period. However, even this later assessment might not reflect the full extent of the region's recent progress in poverty reduction.

Bibliography

Aghion, P., G. M. Angeletos, A. Banerjee, and K. Manova. 2010. "Volatility and Growth: Credit Constraints and the Composition of Investment." *Journal of Monetary Economics* 57 (3): 246–65.

Araujo, Jorge Thompson, Markus Brueckner, Mateo Clavijo, Ekaterina Vostroknutova, and Konstantin M. Wacker. 2014. *Benchmarking the Determinants of Economic Growth in Latin America and the Caribbean*. Washington, DC: World Bank.

Berg, A., J. D. Ostry, and J. Zettelmeyer. 2012. "What Makes Growth Sustained?" *Journal of Development Economics* 98 (2): 149–66.

Bertola, G. 1995. "Uninsurable Shocks and International Income Convergence." *American Economic Review* 85 (2): 301–06.

Berument, H. Hakan, N. Nergiz Dincer, and Zafer Mustafaoglu. 2011. "Total Factor Productivity and Macroeconomic Instability." *Journal of International Trade and Economic Development* 20 (5): 605–29.

———. 2012. "Effects of Growth Volatility on Economic Performance—Empirical Evidence from Turkey." *European Journal of Operational Research* 217 (2): 351–56.

Birdsall, Nancy, Augusto de la Torre, and Felipe Valencia Caicedo. 2010. "The Washington Consensus: Assessing a Damaged Brand." CGD Working Paper 211, Center for Global Development, Washington, DC.

Bliss, Christopher, and Nicolas Stern. 1982. *Palanpur: The Economy of an Indian Village*. Oxford: Oxford University Press.

Crespo-Cuaresma, Jesús, Stephan Klasen, and Konstantin M. Wacker. 2013. "Why We Don't See Poverty Convergence: The Role of Macroeconomic Volatility." *Courant Research Centre Discussion Paper* 153, Göttingen, Germany.

de la Torre, A., J. Messina, and S. Pienknagura. 2012. "The Labor Market Story behind Latin America's Transformation." Semiannual Report, Regional Chief Economist Office, Latin America and the Caribbean, World Bank, Washington, DC.

Dercon, Stefan, and Luc Christiaensen. 2011. "Consumption Risk, Technology Adoption and Poverty Traps: Evidence from Ethiopia." *Journal of Development Economics* 96 (2): 159–73.

Dixit, Avinash, and Rafael Rob. 1994. "Switching Costs and Sectoral Adjustments in General Equilibrium with Uninsured Risk." *Journal of Economic Theory* 62 (1): 48–69.

Dollar, David, Tatjana Kleineberg, and Aart Kraay. 2013. "Growth Still Is Good for the Poor." Policy Research Working Paper 6568, World Bank, Washington, DC.

Drèze, Jean, and Amartya Sen. 1995. *India: Economic Development and Social Opportunity*. Delhi: Oxford University Press.

Gavin, Michael, and Ricardo Hausmann. 1998. "Macroeconomic Volatility and Economic Development." In *Proceedings of the IEA*, Conference Volume No. 119: 97–116.

Gavin, Michael, Ricardo Hausmann, Roberto Perotti, and Ernesto Talvi. 1996. "Managing Fiscal Policy in Latin America and the Caribbean: Volatility, Procyclicality, and Limited Creditworthiness." Working Paper 326, Inter-American Development Bank, Washington, DC.

Hnatkovska, Viktoria, and Norman Loayza. 2005. "Volatility and Growth." In *Managing Economic Volatility and Crises: A Practitioner's Guide*, edited by Joshua Aizenman and Brian Pinto, 65–100. Cambridge, UK: Cambridge University Press.

IDB (Inter-American Development Bank). 1995. "Overcoming Volatility in Latin America. Report on Economic and Social Progress in Latin America." IDB, Washington, DC.

Kose, Ayhan M., Eswar S. Prasad, and Marco E. Terrones. 2006. "How Do Trade and Financial Integration Affect the Relationship between Growth and Volatility?" *Journal of International Economics* 69 (1): 176–202.

Kraay, Aart, and David McKenzie. 2014. "Do Poverty Traps Exist?" Policy Research Working Paper 6835, World Bank, Washington, DC.

Lopez, Humberto, and Luis Servén. 2009. "Too Poor to Grow." Policy Research Working Paper 5012, World Bank, Washington, DC.

McCaig, Brian, and Nina Pavcnik. 2013. "Moving Out of Agriculture: Structural Change in Vietnam." NBER Working Paper No. 19616, National Bureau of Economic Research, Cambridge, MA.

Morduch, Jonathan. 1994. "Poverty and Vulnerability." *American Economic Review* 84 (2): 221–25.

———. 1995. "Income Smoothing and Consumption Smoothing." *Journal of Economic Perspectives* 9 (3): 103–14.

Moser, Christine M., and Christopher B. Barrett. 2006. "The Complex Dynamics of Smallholder Technology Adoption: The Case of SRI in Madagascar." *Agricultural Economics* 35 (3): 373–88.

Murphy, Kevin M., Andrei Shleifer, and Robert W. Vishny. 1989. "Industrialization and the Big Push." *Journal of Political Economy* 97 (5): 1003–26.

Ostry, J. D., A. Berg, and C. G. Tsangarides. 2014. "Redistribution, Inequality, and Growth." IMF Staff Discussion Note 14/02, International Monetary Fund, Washington, DC.

Ramey, Garey, and Valerie A. Ramey. 1991. "Technology Commitment and the Cost of Economic Fluctuations." NBER Working Paper No. 3755. National Bureau of Economic Research, Cambridge, MA.

———. 1995. "Cross-Country Evidence on the Link between Volatility and Growth." *American Economic Review* 85 (5): 1138–51.

Ravallion, Martin. 1988. "Expected Poverty under Risk-Induced Welfare Variability." *Economic Journal* 98 (393): 1171–82.

———. 2009. "A Comparative Perspective on Poverty Reduction in Brazil, China and India." Policy Research Working Paper 5080, World Bank, Washington, DC.

———. 2012. "Why Don't We See Poverty Convergence?" *American Economic Review* 102: 504–23.

Solow, Robert. 1956. "A Contribution to the Theory of Economic Growth." *Quarterly Journal of Economics* 70 (1): 56–94.

Swan, Trevor W. 1956. "Economic Growth and Capital Accumulation." *Economic Record* 32 (2): 334–61.

World Bank. 2014. *Social Gains in the Balance: A Fiscal Policy Challenge for Latin America and the Caribbean*. Washington, DC: World Bank.

Yesuf, Mahmud, and Randall A. Bluffstone. 2009. "Poverty, Risk Aversion, and Path Dependence in Low-Income Countries: Experimental Evidence from Ethiopia." *American Journal of Agricultural Economics* 91 (4): 1022–37.

Environmental Benefits Statement

The World Bank Group is committed to reducing its environmental footprint. In support of this commitment, the Publishing and Knowledge Division leverages electronic publishing options and print-on-demand technology, which is located in regional hubs worldwide. Together, these initiatives enable print runs to be lowered and shipping distances decreased, resulting in reduced paper consumption, chemical use, greenhouse gas emissions, and waste.

The Publishing and Knowledge Division follows the recommended standards for paper use set by the Green Press Initiative. The majority of our books are printed on Forest Stewardship Council (FSC)–certified paper, with nearly all containing 50–100 percent recycled content. The recycled fiber in our book paper is either unbleached or bleached using totally chlorine-free (TCF), processed chlorine-free (PCF), or enhanced elemental chlorine-free (EECF) processes.

More information about the Bank's environmental philosophy can be found at http://www.worldbank.org/corporateresponsibility.

green
press
INITIATIVE

www.ingramcontent.com/pod-product-compliance
Lightning Source LLC
Chambersburg PA
CBHW080526220326
41599CB00032B/6216